CRETE &
PRE-HELLENIC

DONALD A. MACKENZIE

SENATE

Crete & Pre-Hellenic – Myths & Legends

First published by The Gresham Publishing
Company, London

This edition published in 1995 by Senate, an imprint of
Studio Editions Ltd, Princess House, 50 Eastcastle
Street, London W1N 7AP, England

ISBN 1 85958 090 4

Printed and bound in Guernsey by
The Guernsey Press Co. Ltd

PREFACE

This volume deals with the myths and legends connected with the ancient civilization of Crete, and also with the rise and growth of the civilization itself, while consideration is given to various fascinating and important problems that arise in the course of investigating pre-Hellenic habits of thought and habits of life, which are found to have exercised a marked influence in the early history of Europe. In the first two chapters the story of European civilization is carried back to remote Palæolithic times, the view having been urged, notably by Mosso, that a connection existed between the civilization of the artistic cave-dwellers in France and Spain, and that of the Island of Minos. It is shown that these civilizations were not, however, contemporary, but separated by thousands of years, and that in accounting for close resemblances the modern dogma of independent evolution is put to a severe test. The data summarized in the Introduction emphasize the need for caution in attempting to solve a complex problem by the application of a hypothesis which may account for some resemblances but fails to explain away the marked differences that existed even between contemporary civilizations of the Neolithic, Copper and Bronze Ages.

To enable the reader to become familiar with the geological, ethnological, and archæological evidence regarding the earliest traces and progressive activities of man in Europe, who laid the foundations of subsequent civilizations, a popular narrative is given in the first chapter, the scientific data being cast in the form of a legend following the manner of Hesiod's account of the Mythical Ages of the World in the *Work and Days*, and of that of the Indian sage Markandeya's story of the "Yugas" in the *Máhabhárata*, and of Tuan MacCarell's narrative of his experiences in the various Irish Ages. Footnotes provide the necessary references.

Consideration is also given, in dealing with Cretan origins, to Schliemann's hypothesis regarding the "Lost Atlantis", and the connection he believed existed between the Mexican, early European, and Nilotic civilizations. It is brought out that the historical elements in Plato's legend are susceptible of a different explanation.

Cretan civilization has not yet been rendered articulate, for its script remains a mystery, but of late years a flood of light has been thrown upon it by the archæologists, among whom Sir Arthur Evans is pre-eminent. We can examine the remains of the palace of Minos; tread the footworn stones of the streets of little towns; examine pottery and frame a history of it; gaze on frescoes depicting scenes of everyday life in ancient Crete, on seal engravings which show us what manner of ships were built and navigated by mariners who ruled the Mediterranean Sea long before the Phœnician period, what deities were worshipped and what ceremonies were performed; we can study a painted sarcophagus which throws light on funerary customs and conceptions of the Otherworld, and stone vases which afford glimpses of boxers, bull-baiters, soldiers, and processions; and we can also examine the jewellery, weapons, and implements of the ancient folk. With the aid of these and other data we are enabled to reconstruct in outline the island civilization and study its growth over a period embraced by many centuries. It has even been found possible to arrange a system of Cretan chronology, approximate dates being fixed with the aid of artifacts, evidently imported from Egypt, and of Cretan artifacts found in the Nilotic area and elsewhere. The idea of the "Hellenic miracle" no longer obtains. It is undoubted that Crete was the forerunner of Greece, and that the Hellenes owed a debt to Cretan civilization the importance of which was not realized even by the native historians of ancient Greece.

Various problems arise in dealing with the growth of civilization in Crete and the influence exercised by it in Central and Western Europe. These include the race question, the migrations of peoples from the area in which the agricultural mode of life was first adopted, the question of cultural contact, of trade routes on sea and land, of homogeneity of beliefs of common origin, and of the influence of locality in the development of beliefs and material civilization. In the pages that follow, these problems are presented in their various aspects, and such representative evidence as is available has been utilized with purpose to throw light upon them.

Readers cannot fail to be impressed by the note of modernity which prevails in the story of Cretan life. It is emphasized to a remarkable degree in Minoan art. In this connection the coloured illustrations in the present volume, by Mr. John Duncan, A.R.S.A., are of peculiar interest. In preparing these designs Mr. Duncan has deliberately sought to follow the style of the Minoan artists themselves, as displayed in the relics of frescoes, and in pottery, seal engravings and impressions, &c., recently unearthed. The colours are confined to those used by the native craftsmen, while the decorative borders are essentially Cretan in character. In the Plate facing p. 248 a suggestive parallel is drawn between Celtic and Minoan patterns and symbols. It will be noted that the Celtic treatment of complicated patterns of common origin is more thorough and logical than the Minoan, as, for instance, when we compare No. 3, which has incomplete curves, with the finished and exact No. 4. The examples dealt with include a symbol of the Egypto-Libyan goddess Neith.

The note of modernity in Cretan art inclines us perhaps to be somewhat generous and enthusiastic in our praises of it. An eminent archæologist has declared that "it yields to none that was contemporary and hardly to any that came after it". This is a strong claim, especially when we give consideration to the extraordinarily full and varied art of Egypt. In Crete, for instance, we do not meet with the skilled technique and psychological insight of some of Egypt's notable portraiture in stone, nor with faces of such high intellectual and moral qualities; nor do we meet with the masculine energy, the disciplined ferocity and brilliant directness of appeal that characterize the finest products of Assyrian art; nor can we help noting the absence of the idealistic tendencies of Greek art, with its aim to visualize mental and spiritual impressions, its moral ascendancy, and its preoccupation with the idea of beauty of form and character. No doubt it is because Cretan art is infused with a lyrical carelessness and freedom, not only in subject, but also in execution, that it makes a very special appeal to modern eyes. There are certainly notable instances of excellency in delicate modelling, a love of colour—who can refrain, for instance, from admiring the golden afternoon effects of Vasiliki pottery?—a delight in natural objects, a marked absence of formalism in the best work, and an extreme and arresting grace, especially in the ivory work. Yet it is possible to overestimate the artistic value of such works as the "Harvester Vase" (p. 212), with its liveliness of movement and expression, and to commend even its defects, and forget that there are finer examples of low relief in Egypt, where the artists have left us in no doubt as to what they meant; it is possible also to infuse our art criticisms with archæological enthusiasm, as when, for instance, we gaze on the fresco of the Cup Bearer (p. 118), which is an impression of a very ordinary, good-looking, young man, with formal eyes, and hand and arm out of drawing. Yet while, as a whole, Cretan art is very unequal, there are a few masterpieces which set it on a high level. The ivory figurine of "The Leaper" is one of these (p. 48). Its Parisian elegance and Greek-like accuracy and beauty of modelling take the eye at once. It is much worn, but the unbroken parts exhibit fine craftsmanship. The bones and muscles of the arm and hand especially are expressed with the modesty and animation of nature; there is none of the gross exaggeration so often found in Assyrian art. Another outstanding masterpiece is the bull's head in steatite (p. 108). We are struck by its fine dignity, the noble poise of the head, the alert eye, the mobility of the pricked ears, and the

combination of naturalism with simplicity, grace, and
loftiness of treatment. A contrast is presented by the
other bull's head in plaster relief (p. 124), with the
magnificent blaze of the great eye and the exhausted gasp
of mouth and nostrils; the noble animal has evidently
fallen a victim in the ring; it is powerful and grand even
when death takes it. Special mention may also be made
of the goat suckling its kid, an admirable piece of realism
characterized by grace and insight (p. 152).

The spirit of naturalism pulsating in Cretan art is
also found in Palæolithic art, of which two notable
examples are given (p. 20) from the cave paintings.
These remarkable relics of the Pleistocene Age are typical
products of Palæolithic art, the advanced condition of
which suggests a long history, and even the existence,
in such remote times, not only of devoted personal study,
but also of an organized system of training. The civilization reflected by such an art must have been of no
mean order. Evidently it met with disaster during the
Fourth Glacial Period, but subsequent discoveries may
yet demonstrate that its influence was not wholly lost
to mankind.

D. A. MACKENZIE.

CONTENTS

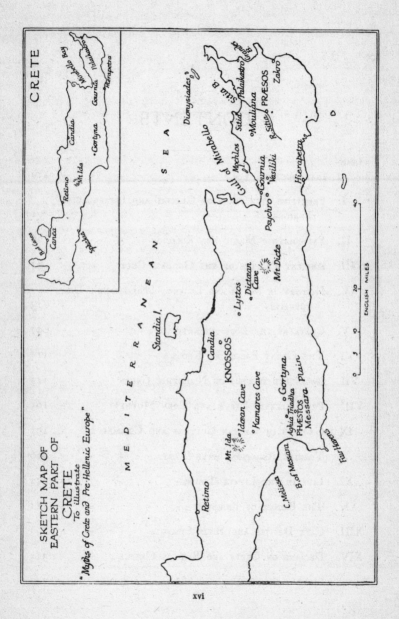

SKETCH MAP OF
EASTERN PART OF
CRETE
To illustrate
"Myths of Crete and Pre-Hellenic Europe"

CRETE

INTRODUCTION

In relating how Crete has risen into prominence as the seat of a great and ancient civilization, one is reminded of the fairy story of Cinderella. The archæological narrative begins with the discovery made by Schliemann of traces of a distinctive and high pre-Hellenic culture amidst the ruins of the Peloponnesian cities of Tiryns and Mycenæ, which he assigned to the Homeric Age. Evidence was soon forthcoming that this culture was not of indigenous character, but had been imported from some unknown area after it had reached its highest development and was beginning to show signs of decadence —a sure indication of its great antiquity. A dramatic search followed for the centre of origin and diffusion. The wonderful slipper had been found, but where was Cinderella? In the end, after several claims had been urged, the last comer was proved to be the missing princess of culture, and the last comer was Crete. Research on that island had been long postponed on account of the disturbed political conditions that prevailed under the Turkish regime.

A new first chapter has since been added to the history of European civilization. We no longer begin with Hellenic Greece, or believe that Hellenic culture sprang full-grown into being like the fabled deity who leapt from her parent's head. In this volume it is shown that the myths and legends preserved in the works of various classical writers regarding the sources of Grecian culture were well founded, and that the traditions of the "Heroic Age" did not have origin in the imaginations of poets and dramatists.   But, wise as we chance to be, after the event, we need not regard with scorn the historians of a past generation who hesitated to sift and utilize such elusive myths as the Cretan origins of Zeus and Demeter, and the semi-historical references to Crete, in the works of Homer, Thucydides, and others, to find a sure basis for a convincing narrative worthy of the name of history.

It is only within recent years that the necessary archæological data have been available which enables students of ancient civilization to draw with some degree of confidence upon the abundant but confused contents of the storehouse of folk memory.

The discovery that Crete was the birth-place of Ægean civilization, which radiated in the pre-Hellenic times throughout Europe—"the little leaven that leavened the whole lump"—does not, however, set a limit to the work of research, or solve all the problems which are involved. Although it has been demonstrated that the Cretan leaven was in existence and at work at the dawn of the Egyptian Dynastic Age, and when the Sumerians were achieving their earliest triumphs in the Tigro-Euphratean valley, we are still confronted with the problem of remote origin. The earliest settlers in Crete had, as their artifacts demonstrate, already obtained a comparatively high degree of Neolithic culture.   Houses were built of stone as well as of wattles daubed with clay, a sea trade was in existence, for obsidian was imported from Melos, and a section of the community had adopted the agricultural mode of life. Withal, beliefs were well developed and had assumed a fixity which remained until they were merged in the accumulated mass of Grecian inheritance, and suffered, as a result, for long ages, complete loss of identity. The earliest settlement of people at Knossos has been assigned to about 10,000 B.C., an approximate dating which is based on the evidence of the archæological strata.

But the earliest traces of an artistic culture in Europe belong to a still more remote age. Although during the vast periods of the Neolithic, or Late Stone Age, there existed savage communities, just as happens to be the case at the present day in various parts of the world, there were also, as in Crete, Egypt, and Babylonia, refined and progressive peoples who were already "heirs of all the Ages"—the Ages when ancient Europe passed through stages of climatic oscillations of such pronounced character that the remains of mankind are found in strata yielding alternately tropical, temperate, and Arctic flora and fauna. The period in question, the lengthiest in the history of civilization, is the archæological Palæolithic, or Early Stone Age. Towards its close, for which the minimum dating is 20,000 B.C., there existed in Europe at least two races, whose cultures are referred to as Aurignacian and Magdalenian. A stage called Azilian links the Palæolithic with the Neolithic Age, and the continuity of culture from the earliest times is now generally regarded as an established fact.

The story of Cretan civilization may constitute, as has been said, the first chapter of European history. But the "Introduction" is derived from the Palæolithic Age, before and during the Fourth Glacial Epoch of the geologists.

Our introductory data are obtained from the famous Palæolithic cave-dwellings of France and Spain, which are dealt with in Chapters I and II. No definite traces are yet obtainable, among the scanty human remains that have been discovered, of racial types resembling those of early Egypt or early Crete, but remarkable evidence has been forthcoming which not only establishes the great antiquity of certain artistic motifs of finished artistic skill and even of certain customs that afterwards appeared on the Island of Minos and in the Nilotic and Tigro-Euphratean areas.

The links with Crete are so close and suggestive that writers like Angelo Mosso have expressed the belief in the Neolithic and Cretan origin of Aurignacian and Magdalenian art. But the geologists have established beyond a shadow of doubt that the civilization of which this art is an eloquent expression must be assigned to the latter part of the Pleistocene period, when the reindeer roamed through the valleys of France.

Those ancient Palæolithic hunters were skilled artists and carvers of bone and ivory. They painted and engraved on cave roofs the figures of animals with a realism and freedom which were never surpassed in Greece; they also carved ivory female figurines in the round which are worthy of comparison with similar artistic products of Egypt, and not always to their disadvantage.

"The resemblances", writes Mosso, "between the most ancient female figures in France and the Neolithic figures of Crete and Egypt are very striking." Among the rock pictures of women he sees "the girdle and the Egyptian mode of hairdressing". Describing a Palæolithic painting, he writes: "The women's hair flows down upon their shoulders like that of the Minoan women; the bosom is uncovered and the breasts much developed. The triangular shape of the heads indicates a hood or a kind of mitre. Two of them wear a bracelet on the upper arm near the elbow, and all have a very slender waist, with the body shaped like an hour-glass." He

also comments in another instance on the skirts, which
were also characteristic of Crete.[1]   Comparisons between
the Cretan frescoes and the Palæolithic cave-paintings of
Spain and France have likewise been made by the Abbé
Breuil, Don Juan Cabre Aguila, and other Continental
archæologists.

One of the racial types which existed during the
Aurignacian and Magdalenian periods, or stages of culture, was the Cro Magnon.   It can still be traced in
Europe, especially in the French Dordogne valley, and
among the Berbers in North Africa, as Dr. Collignon has
shown.[2]   Evidence of Cro-Magnon migration in Late
Pleistocene times has also been forthcoming from Belgium,
while traces of their burial customs have been found in
Moravia and elsewhere.   How and by what route Aurignacian influence reached Crete, after the lapse of thousands
of years, we have as yet no means of knowing.   It seems
reasonable to assume that this civilization did not end
without leaving heirs somewhere.   The Greeks were heirs
of Crete, and yet it is but quite recently that this fact has
been fully demonstrated.

Not only has the antiquity of European art been
established ; the Palæolithic data which have been accumulated emphasize also the remote beginnings of certain
magical and religious beliefs and practices.   The suggestion is thus rendered plausible that some of the widespread myths and folk-tales may be as old as the French
and Spanish cave-paintings and ivory carvings.   Who
will venture, for instance, to date the origin of that far-
travelled tale about the lovers who escape from the giant's
den and throw down pebbles which become mountains
and twigs which create forests, to delay their angry pur-

---

[1] *Dawn of Mediterranean Civilization*, Angelo Masso, pp. 175 *et seq.*
[2] Quoted in Ripley's *The Races of Europe*, pp. 172 *et seq.*

suer? The late Mr. Andrew Lang has shown that it is found in Zulu, Gaelic, Norse, Malagasy, Russian, Italian, and Japanese folk-literatures. The author "will never", he wrote, "be known to fame", although, among story-tellers, he has achieved "the widest circulation in the world".[1]

A now popular hypothesis, first urged by Hugh Miller, is usually held to offer a conclusive explanation for the wonderful resemblances between certain legends collected in various parts of the world. "I have seen", Miller wrote about eighty years ago, "in the museum of the Northern Institution (Inverness) a very complete collection of stone battle-axes, some of which have been formed little earlier than the last age, by the rude natives of America and the South Sea Islands, while others, which have been dug out of the cairns and tumuli of our own country, bear witness to the unrecorded feuds and forgotten battle-fields of twenty centuries ago. I was a good deal struck by the resemblance which they bear to each other; a resemblance so complete, that the most practised eye can hardly distinguish between the weapons of the old Scot and the New Zealander. . . . Man in a savage state is the same animal everywhere, and his constructive powers, whether employed in the formation of a legendary story or of a battle-axe, seem to expatiate almost everywhere in the same ragged track of invention. For even the traditions of this first stage may be identified, like his weapons of war, all the world over."[2]

Since Miller's day experts have become so familiar with the stone implements and weapons of primitive men that they experience no difficulty, not only in distinguishing between the characteristic products of various

---

[1] *Custom and Myth*, pp. 87 *et seq.*   [2] *Scenes and Legends*, pp. 31–32 (1835).

countries, but also of the various ages, or stages of
culture, in one particular area. We find ourselves, however, on less sure ground when we deal with traditional
tales. Miller's hypothesis in regard to these must still
receive acceptance but with certain qualifications. It
certainly accounts for striking resemblances, although not
for equally striking differences. If it were to be urged
in every instance, the work of research would be stultified
and rendered somewhat barren. "There is a well-known
tendency", as Mr. Hogarth reminds us, "to find one
formula to explain all things, and an equally notorious
one to overwork the latest formula."[1]

The intensive study of the mythology of a particular
civilization, like that of Crete or Egypt, for instance,
reveals marked local divergencies which are not easily
accounted for. It is an extremely risky proceeding, therefore, when we find a fragment of a legend, or a clue to
some archaic religious custom, in a cultural centre like
Crete, to undertake the work of reconstruction by select-
ing something from Australia, adding a Chinese idea, and
completing the whole with contributions from Russia,
Greenland, or Mexico. We may find similar symbols
in different countries, but it does not follow that they
had originally all the same significance; similar alpha-
betical signs have not always the same phonetic values.
The human mind is not like a mould which produces
automatically the same shapes for the same purposes,
or the same ideas to account for the same problems, in
every part of the world.

Myths are products of beliefs, and beliefs are products of experiences. They are also pictorial records
of natural phenomena. Mankind have not had the same
experiences everywhere, nor have they found the world

[1] *Ionia and the East*, p. 107.

lacking in variety of contour and climate. Certain peoples, for instance, have achieved progress in civilizations based on the agricultural mode of life. Their beliefs have consequently been influenced by their agricultural experiences, and their myths have been given an agricultural significance. Before the Calendar was invented, the farmer who profited from the experiences of his ancestors, and handed on his knowledge to posterity, did not speak about "ploughing in spring" and "reaping in autumn", or explain the futility of sowing seed, say, in December and expecting crops in April. He framed instead a system of myths which guided the agricultural operations of his kin for long centuries. In India, which suffers at one season from great heat and drought, he conceived the Drought Demon which imprisoned the fertilizing waters in a mountain cave. Just when the world is about to perish, the god Indra comes to its rescue armed with his thunderbolt. He attacks and slays the demon, exclaiming:

> I am the hurler of the bolt of thunder;
> For man flow freely now the gleaming waters.

After this thunder-battle, rain descends in torrents, the withered grass sprouts luxuriantly, and the rice harvest follows.

In Babylonia the demon is the water-monster Tiamat, who enters the Euphrates and causes it to flood. She is slain and cut up by Merodach, who thus sets the world in order. Then the farmer sows his seeds. In Egypt the inundation of the Nile is brought about by Ra, who, having undertaken to destroy his human enemies, relents and withdraws the waters, so that seeds may be cast in the fertilized soil and the harvest gathered in season. Pious worshippers of the deities who controlled the forces

of nature were expected to perform ceremonies and offer
sacrifices to assist or propitiate them. Thus the local
forms of religion were shaped by local phenomena of
which the myths are reflections.

Peoples who lived among the mountains and followed
the pastoral mode of life had different experiences from
those who found their food-supply in river valleys. In
districts where the rainfall was regular and abundant
they knew nothing of India's droughts, or Egypt's floods.
On the other hand, they might have experiences of binding frost, fierce blizzards, and snow-blocked passes, which
forced them to migrate to districts where they could
winter their flocks and herds. Their myths were consequently based on experiences and natural phenomena
which contrasted sharply with those of the Nilotic and
Tigro-Euphratean peoples, with the result that their
systems of religious beliefs developed upon different
lines. Similarly, peoples who dwelt upon islands and
along sea-coasts and gathered the harvest of the deep,
and forest-dwellers who lived on fruits and trophies of
the chase, formulated and perpetuated modes of thought
which were products of their particular modes of life in
different environments. It is obvious, therefore, that the
mind of man did not everywhere follow "the same rugged
track of invention". In different districts and at different
periods sections of mankind achieved independent development on sharply differentiated lines, with the result
that religious conceptions, like outstanding racial types,
had their areas of characterization.

Consideration should next be given to cultural influence resulting from contact. The oscillations of climate
which followed the last glacial epoch caused widespread
migrations of peoples. Racial types which are still recognizable were already fixed; mankind at the dawn of

the Neolithic or Late Stone Age had attained full mental[1]
and physical development.   Races were distributed far
and wide, and settlers favoured those areas which were
suitable for their habits of life.   The barriers of ice and
snow which had separated peoples for thousands of years
vanished before the warm sun, and as the various races
prospered and increased they came into contact with one
another.   Let us picture a pastoral tribe issuing from a
region of steppe lands and entering a valley occupied by
agriculturists.   They come with a heritage of beliefs and
customs as alien as their language to those who rear
crops and dwell in villages.   The small farmers regard
them as demons, and go out to battle to conquer or be
conquered.   If the invaders prevail, they remain in the
district and in time fuse with the conquered.   Then the
beliefs of the mingled peoples are fused also.   The result
is a compromise between the distinctive religions.   In the
valley the earlier faith secures ascendancy because the
invaders have no agricultural religion and no words even
for "corn" and "furrow" and "plough".   But a portion
of the conquerors follow their old habits of life as pastoralists and hunters, and occupy the grazing-lands round
the valley and among the hills, where they find a new
Olympus for their gods.   In time a pantheon is formed
which embraces the deities of conquered and conquerors.

Trade springs up between various communities and
the influence of culture flows along the trade routes.
The knowledge of how to grow corn passes from tribe
to tribe.   But the isolated hunters in a northern valley
who become agriculturists do not simply import implements and seeds; those who instruct them how to till
the soil instruct them also regarding the ceremonies
which are necessary to ensure growth and the harvest.

[1] That is, so far as can be indicated by skull capacity.

So the agricultural religion of Egypt or Babylon passes through Europe and Asia, and is adopted by peoples who mix with it their own peculiar local practices inherited for untold generations from their remote ancestors.

In Denmark the northern huntsman and fisherman came into contact with the little farmers from the south, or tribes who had acquired the southern art of agriculture. They learned to sow the seed in sorrow and to beat their breasts when they cut the corn, and thus slew the corn spirit, and to return rejoicing carrying the sheaves. Magical ceremonies were considered to be as essential to agricultural success as ploughs and reaping-hooks. Consequently they adopted the magical ceremonies that had origin somewhere on the shores of the Mediterranean or in the Nile valley. So we find in Denmark the myth of Scef, the child god, who comes over the sea with the first sheaf of corn, which so closely resembles the Babylonian myth of Tammuz, who comes as a child from the Underworld and the Deep every new year.

The non-agricultural mountain-folk, who migrated hither and thither, knew naught of the corn-child. They conceived of a god who shaped the mountains with his hammer, the thunderbolt; each blow was a peal of thunder. He also hammered the sky into shape. Meteorites which fell from the sky were found to be of iron; it was consequently believed that the sky was formed of iron, which became known as "the metal of heaven". Iron was regarded as a protective charm. It was associated with the great deity who slew demons. A mortal had only to "touch iron" to drive demons away, for by doing so he established a magical connection between himself and the hammer deity.

Worshippers of the mountain-god went northward and called him Thor. In Asia Minor he was Tarku and

Teshub; in India, Indra, son of Dyaus; in Greece, Zeus. Those worshippers who reached Palestine called him Pathach (the Hebrew name), and those who settled in Egypt knew him as Ptah, and, although thunderstorms are rare in Egypt, the Memphites never forgot the hammer of Ptah and the heaven of iron which he had beaten into shape. In time Ptah acquired new attributes. As the artisan-god he was credited with the invention of the Egyptian potter's wheel, on which he shaped the sun and moon, and the first man and woman. He was thus localized. Yet he ever remained distinctive among the deities of Egypt.

Tradition dies hard. Once an idea became impressed on the human mind it remained there, and new ideas were superimposed upon it. The Egyptians achieved great progress as thinkers and artisans, yet they clung to beliefs and customs of savage origin. So did the Greeks, who never forgot Cronos, the bloodthirsty god who swallowed his children and had to be murdered by his heir. It does not follow, however, that this tendency to conserve ancient beliefs and modes of thought was opposed to the growth of culture, or that men and women who perpetuated them were as ignorant and bloodthirsty as their primitive ancestors. In our own day an individual with a university degree may dread to spill salt, regard a black cat as lucky, and refuse to occupy a hotel bedroom numbered 13. Motor-cars and flying-machines carry mascots, as did the galleys of ancient Egypt, Crete, and Phœnicia. The writer has seen a Girton girl perpetuating a religious custom of her remote ancestors by attaching a rag to a tree that overhangs a "wishing well", and wishing silently her wish quite as fervently as do less highly cultured members of her sex in places as far removed as the Scottish Highlands and the Island of Crete.

Superstitious practices which are familiar in our everyday lives have a long history. They have survived nearly two thousand years of Christian influence. Who will undertake to date their origins? They may go back to the Bronze Age, the Late Stone Age, and even to the interglacial periods of the Palæolithic Age. The following comparative notes will serve to illustrate the antiquity of at least one remarkable folk-belief.

In Upper Egypt discovery has been made of bodies which were buried in hot dry sands about sixty centuries ago. Not only have the bones, skin, hair, muscles, and eyes been preserved, but even the internal organs. The contents of stomachs and intestines have been examined by Dr. Netolitzky, the Russian scientist, who ascertained in this way what food the ancient people ate. "The occasional presence of the remains of mice in the alimentary canals of children, under circumstances which prove that the small rodent had been eaten after being skinned, is", writes Professor Elliot Smith, "a discovery of very great interest, for Dr. Netolitzky informs me that the body of a mouse was the last resort of medical practitioners in the East several millennia later as the remedy for children *in extremis*."[1] Until comparatively recently the liver of a mouse was in the Scottish Highlands the "old wife's cure" for children dangerously ill. The writer was informed regarding it in more than one locality, long before the Egyptian discovery was made, by women who professed to have had experience of the efficacy of the mouse cure.

The ashes of a mouse baked alive used to be a cure for rheumatism in Suffolk. In Lincolnshire fried mice were given to children suffering from whooping-cough and quinsy. According to Henderson[2] a whooping-cough

---

[1] *The Ancient Egyptians*, p. 43.   [2] *Folk-lore of Northern Counties*, p. 144.

patient in the northern counties had to be seated on a donkey, with face towards the tail, when the mouse was being eaten. The custom of entombing a live mouse in an ash-tree, to cure children or charm cattle against attack, prevailed in Leicestershire.[1] A similar custom obtained in Scotland, where the shrew-mouse was believed to paralyse a limb it chanced to creep over.[2] The traditional fear of mice among women is of interest in this connection. Roasted mouse was, in the north-eastern counties of Scotland, a cure for cold or sore throat.

In Egypt the mouse was associated with the lunar god Thoth, who cured Horus when he was bitten by the scorpion, restored the sight of his eye which was blinded by the black Set pig, and assisted in uniting the fragments of the body of Osiris. The mouse crouches at the base of his rod of destiny, on which he measured out the lives of men.[3] In Greece the mouse was associated with Apollo. This god was identified by the Romans with the sun, but Homer knew him as Smintheus Apollo, "Mouse Apollo", who struck down the Greeks with his arrows of pestilence.[4] According to Strabo, there were many places which bore the Apollo mouse name.[5] Mouse feasts were held at Rhodes, Gela, Lesbos, and Crete. According to a Trojan story, the settlement took place in Anatolia of Cretans who were advised by an oracle to select the first place where they were attacked by the children of the soil. At Hamaxitus, in the Troad, a swarm of mice ate their bow-strings and the leather of their armour, and they decided to make that place their home.[6] In India

---

[1] *Leicester County Folk-lore Series*, p. 29. In White's *Selborne* reference is made to the "shrew ash" in Hampshire.

[2] Dalzell's *Darker Superstitions of Scotland*, pp. 191–2.

[3] *Religion of the Ancient Egyptians*, A. Wiedemann, p. 226.

[4] *The Iliad*, I, 1 et seq.   [5] *Strabo*, XIII, 604.

[6] *Strabo*, XIII, 604, and also *Ælian, H. A.*, XII, 5.

the mouse was associated with Rudra, to whom the poet prayed:

> Give unto me of thy medicines, Rudra,
> So that my years may reach to a hundred.[1]

Rudra, like Apollo, sent diseases, and was therefore able to prevent and cure them.

The mouse feasts referred to by ancient writers may have been held to ensure long life among those who, like the Egyptians, connected the mouse with the moon, the source of fertility and growth and the measurer of the days of man. The Egyptian lunar god Khonsu was the divine physician and the love-god. All fertility deities, indeed, cured diseases. The King of Mitanni sent the image of Ishtar to Thebes when Pharaoh Amenhotep III was ill. Isaiah refers to the mouse-eating practice: "They that sanctify themselves and purify themselves in the gardens behind one tree in the midst, eating swine's flesh, and the abomination, and the mouse, shall be consumed together, saith the Lord."[2] When the Philistines, who came from Crete, were stricken by a pestilence, they placed five golden mice in the ark and sent it back to the Israelites.[3] Thus we find the Highland mouse-cure belief going back for 6000 years and reaching to the remotest areas settled by representatives of the Mediterranean race. Other superstitions may be as old, or older. The ancient Egyptians, like our own people, inherited beliefs from their savage ancestors.

The evidence summarized in this volume (Chapter II) regarding Palæolithic customs and beliefs tends to emphasize that, while mankind everywhere may arrive at similar conclusions under similar circumstances, some conceptions were handed down by tradition and distributed over wide

---

[1] *Rigveda*, II, 33. [2] *Isaiah*, lxvi, 17. [3] *Samuel*, i, 5–6.

areas by wandering peoples long before the dawn of the Neolithic period in Europe and Egypt. If the mouse cure can be traced back for sixty centuries it may well have been known for a further sixty centuries. In Palæolithic times, at least 20,000 years ago, the spine of a fish was laid on the corpse when it was entombed, just as the "ded" amulet, which was the symbol of the backbone of Osiris, was laid on the neck of the Egyptian mummy. Anthropologists have favoured the theory that the animal-headed deities of Egypt are links between animal and anthropomorphic deities. Animal-headed deities with arms uplifted in the Egyptian attitude of adoration figure in Palæolithic cave-drawings. The process of change, if such it was, must therefore have commenced thousands of years before the Dynastic Egyptians became supreme in the Nile valley. It used to be urged that the Phœnicians were the inventors of alphabetic script, but linearized signs "of curiously alphabetic aspect—at times even in groups—are seen engraved on reindeer horns or ivory, or on the surface of the rock itself", which were the work of Palæolithic folk in the Fourth Glacial Period. "Certain signs", says Sir Arthur Evans, from whom we quote, "carved on a fragment of reindeer horn, are specially interesting from the primitive anticipation that they present of the Phœnician *alef*. . . . It is interesting to observe that among the existing peoples of the extreme north of Europe, whose conditions most nearly represent those of the old Reindeer folk, the relics of pure pictography were preserved to modern times. . . . These Lapp pictographs themselves belong to a widely diffused primitive group—illustrated by the paintings and carvings on rocks and other materials—which extends across the whole Fenno-Tataric region from the White Sea to the Urals and throughout Siberia to the borders of China.

Terra-cotta Disk from Phæstos, with pictographic script which reads from the centre outwards, but has not been deciphered. It is believed to have come from Lycia, Asia Minor. Heads with feather head-dress similar to that worn by the Philistines appear on the disk.

INSCRIBED TABLETS FOUND IN CRETE

It was probably from an early offshot of this great family of pictorial signs that the elaborate characters of the Chinese writing were ultimately evolved." Similar pictographs are found in Scandinavia, Ireland, Brittany, Portugal, Spain, North-West Africa, the Canaries, in the Maritime Alps, the Vosges, Dalmatia, in Transylvania and on early Trojan artifacts.[1]

In addition to the pictographs there also passed from the Palæolithic into the Neolithic and Bronze Ages certain burial customs, decorative designs developed from animal drawings, the custom of shaping figurines of the mother goddess with female characteristics emphasized, and the bell-shaped skirt which found favour in Crete. Palæolithic pottery found in Belgium has Neolithic characteristics. It has also been demonstrated, as stated, that what is known as the Azilian stage of culture links the cultures of the Early and Late Stone Ages. After the close of the Fourth Glacial Period the early pioneers of the Mediterranean race came into contact in Europe with the remnants of the Palæoliths and mingled with them in localities. Among a large number of skulls taken recently from an old Glasgow graveyard, into which an Infirmary extension intruded, were a considerable sprinkling of Palæolithic types. The interments at this part were made during the 18th century and the early part of the 19th century. Apparently there were descendants of the Palæoliths among the makers of modern Glasgow.

Certain beliefs and customs and folk-tales appear also to have survived with the peoples of the Reindeer Period, among whom they were prevalent. And as the culture of that period (the Fourth Glacial Epoch) developed from the cultures of the earlier periods, it is possible that some surviving modes of thought may have obtained for

[1] *Scripta Minoa*, pp. 3, 4, 6.

40,000 years. The Chellean hand-axe of the Second Interglacial Period in France was distributed far and wide; it travelled across the Italian land-bridge to Africa and penetrated as far as Cape Colony; it was imitated in Asia and passed across the Behring Straits land-bridge to America, and reached the utmost southern limits of South America. It never reached Australia. Perhaps Mr. Lang's "far-travelled tale" was similarly given widespread distribution at a remote period in the history of the human races. The culture of a particular people reached remote corners of the globe to which descendants of its originators may never have penetrated. We are familiar with this phenomenon even at the present day. It should be borne in mind, therefore, that although the mind of man may have in primitive times conceived similar ideas and invented similar tales in various regions widely separated, the masses of humanity on the whole have also been more prone to conserve what they have acquired than to welcome something new. Nothing impresses the student of comparative mythology more than the barrenness of the primitive mind. New ideas are the exception rather than the rule. Changes in religious ideas were forced upon ancient peoples either by intruding aliens or by the influence exercised by physical phenomena in new areas of settlement. Even when a change occurred the past was not entirely cut off. Rather a fusion was effected of the new ideas with the old.

In dealing with a mythology like that of Crete, which has not yet been rendered articulate, for the script has still to be deciphered, we expect to find traces of more than one stage of development in religious ideas, and also of the ideas of settlers on the island of peoples from different cultural centres. Certain relics suggest Egyptian influence and others point to an intimate connection with archaic Grecian beliefs. No doubt Crete inherited much from Egypt; and certain Greek States in which Cretan colonists settled borrowed much from Crete. It remains to be proved, however, that the Cretans, after settling on their island, developed on the same lines as primitive peoples elsewhere, or even that they previously passed through the different stages of religious culture regarding which evidence has been gleaned from various parts of the world.

It is sometimes assumed that the religious history of the human race is marked by well-defined layers of thought—Naturalism or Naturism, Totemism, Animism, Demonology, Tribal Monotheism which with the fusion of tribes leads to Polytheism, and then ultimately sole Monotheism. All these stages may be traced in a particular area. But we must not expect to find them everywhere. Human thought has not accumulated strata of ideas in regular sequence, like geological or archæological strata. Some peoples, for instance, have never conceived of a personal god, or even of distinctive animistic spirit groups. Mr. Risley has shown that the jungle-dwellers of Chota Nagpur fear and attempt to propitiate " not a person at all in any sense of the word. If one must state the case in positive terms," he adds, " I should say that the idea which lies at the root of their religion is that of Power, or rather of many Powers. . . . Closer than this he does not seek to define the object to which he offers his victim, or whose symbol he daubs with vermilion at the appointed season. Some sort of Power is there, and that is enough for him. . . . All over Chota Nagpur we find sacred groves, the abode of equally indeterminate things, who are represented by no symbols and of whose form and function no one can give an intelligible account. They have not yet been clothed with individual attributes;

they linger on as survivals of the impersonal stage of religion."[1] The Australian natives, on the other hand, and even those who are more primitive than the Chota Nagpur jungle-dwellers, have a god whose voice is imitated by the "bull roarer". Palæolithic man of the Reindeer Age, as has been said, had animal-headed deities and shaped, in ivory, figurines of the mother goddess. In Egypt and Babylonia there were composite deities, half animal and half human, from the earliest times of which we have knowledge. The Chinese have deities also, but have specialized as ancestor-worshippers. Argue as we may regarding well-defined "mental processes", it must be recognized that religious phenomena all over the world cannot be explained by a single hypothesis, and that we are not justified in assuming that the same stages, or all the recognized stages, of development can be traced everywhere. There may have been Totemic beliefs in Crete and Greece and there may not. Until definite proof is forthcoming that there were, the problem must remain an open one. Similarly, we should hesitate to accept the hypothesis that patriarchal conditions were preceded by matriarchal and that goddesses preceded gods everywhere. In India the gods were prominent in the Vedic period; during the post-Vedic period goddesses ceased to be vague and became outstanding personalities as "Great Mothers".[2]

This brings us to an interesting phase of Cretan religious and social life. From the evidence afforded by idols, pictorial art, symbols, and traditions it would appear that the goddess cult was supreme on the island. Priestesses were as prominent as they were at Dodona. In fact, women appear to have taken a leading part in

---

[1] *Census of India* (1901), Vol. I, Part I, pp. 352 *et seq.*
[2] *Indian Myth and Legend*, pp. 148 *et seq.*

religious ceremonies, as Jeremiah found was the case in Jerusalem, where women baked cakes which were offered to the "Queen of Heaven", the Eastern mother-goddess. "Probably in Minoan Crete", writes Mr. Hall, "women played a greater part than they did even in Egypt, and it may eventually appear that religious matters, perhaps even the government of the State itself as well, were largely controlled by women. It is certain they must have lived on a footing of greater equality with the men than in any other ancient civilization, and we see in the frescoes of Knossos conclusive indications of an open and easy association of men and women, corresponding to our idea of 'Society', at the Minoan Court unparalleled till our own day."[1] Among the goddess worshippers of Sumeria women enjoyed a high social status also. But among the Semites of the god cult this was not the case. Women were not depicted in Assyria as in Crete. It was when Babylonian influences entered the Assyrian Court that Queen Sammu-ramat—the Semiramis of tradition—rose into prominence. Professor Sayce has drawn attention to the significant fact that when the Semites translated the Sumerian hymns they transposed "women and men" (equivalent to our "ladies and gentlemen") into "men and women". The law of descent by the female line which obtained in Egypt and elsewhere among peoples of the Mediterranean race was probably a relic of customs which had a religious significance.

The view has been strongly advocated that in all primitive communities matriarchal conditions preceded patriarchal conditions, and goddess worship the worship of gods. It is not now generally accepted, however: some peoples seem to have been worshippers of male

[1] *The Ancient History of the Near East*, p. 48.

deities and others of female deities from the earliest times. The fusion of the god and goddess cults in Egypt and Babylonia and elsewhere was probably one of the results of the fusion of peoples. In some countries, where patriarchal peoples formed military aristocracies, they may have ordered succession by the male line. But there is also evidence to show that they adopted the wiser method of marrying the heiresses of estates and thrones to win the allegiance of the masses. "Mother-right" prevailed in Egypt, for instance, until the end. The problem involved is too complex to be accounted for by a single hypothesis.

It would appear that the activities of the Cretan women were chiefly confined to indoor life. As in Egypt, they were depicted by painters with white skins, while the men were, with the exception of princes, given red skins. Women were also more elaborately attired and bejewelled than men.

In dealing with ancient civilizations it is of importance to take note of burial customs. There can be little doubt that these have been ever closely associated with religious beliefs. What are known to archæologists as "ceremonial burials" must have been performed, it is reasonable to suppose, with some degree of ceremony with purpose either to promote the welfare of the deceased or to secure the protection of the living. The Dynastic Egyptians, for instance, mummified their dead because they believed that the soul could not continue to exist in the Otherworld unless the body were preserved intact in the tomb. On the other hand, the Homeric Achæans burned their dead, so that the soul might be transferred by fire to Hades, from which it would never again return.[1] In pre-Dynastic Egypt the

[1] *Iliad*, XXIII, 75.

body was laid in a shallow grave in crouched position, with food-vessels, implements, and weapons beside it. A similar custom prevailed in Babylonia and throughout Europe in the Neolithic and Bronze Ages. Dwellers on the northern sea-coast of Europe set their dead adrift in boats, as was Balder in the Eddic legend and Sceaf in the Beowulf poem. Others buried their dead in caves, threw them to wild beasts, or ate them.

In some cases it would appear that the beliefs connected with burial were suggested by local phenomena. In Upper Egypt bodies are naturally mummified in the hot dry sands. It is possible, therefore, that the custom of embalming the dead may have grown up among that section of the Egyptian people whose religious beliefs were formulated in the area where the corpse was naturally preserved. They may have been horrified to find that bodies did not remain intact in new districts to which they migrated. But the custom of burning the dead cannot be explained in this way.

Burial customs may not always afford us definite clues regarding religious beliefs. It does not follow that the pre-Dynastic Egyptians, the Babylonian Sumerians, and the Neolithic Europeans who favoured crouched burials had all the same ideas regarding the destiny of men, or the same beliefs regarding the Otherworld. Different conceptions might be prevalent in a single country. It is found that in Wales, for instance, ideas about the future state varied considerably. Folk-lore and mediæval poetry have references to an Underworld in which the dead continue to live in organized communities and work and fight as they were accustomed to do upon earth, to happy islands situated far out to sea, to fairy dwellings below rivers and lakes where souls exist like fairies, and to the woods of Caledonia where shades wander about as did

the ancestors of the people who migrated from Caledonia
to Wales.   In one Welsh poem the Otherworld is referred to as "the cruel prison of the earth, the abode
of death, the loveless land".[1]   The Babylonian Hades
was similarly gloomy and was similarly dreaded.   Ishtar
descends to—

The house out of which there is no exit . . .
The house from whose entrance the light is taken,
The place where dust is their (the souls') nourishment and their
    food mud.
Its chiefs are like birds covered with feathers.

But in pre-Dynastic Egypt the worshippers of Osiris,
like a section of the Welsh folks, believed that the Otherworld was a land of plenty in which corn was sowed and
crops reaped in season.   A similar Paradise was believed in
as far north as Scotland.   It is referred to in a Perthshire
fairy story.   A midwife is taken to a fairy mound to
nurse a fairy child, and is given a green fluid with which
to anoint the eyes of the little one.   The fairy woman
moistens the right eye of the midwife with this fluid, and
bids her look.   "She looked", the narrative proceeds,
"and saw several of her friends and acquaintances at
work, reaping the corn and gathering the fruit. 'This',
said the fairy, 'is the punishment of evil deeds.'"[2]   In
ancient Egypt the fairy would have said it was "the
reward of good deeds".

Burial customs afford us no exact evidence regarding
these varying beliefs, which grew up in localities and
were imported from one country to another.   In Egypt
the adherents of the cults of Osiris and Ra who believed
in different Paradises mummified their dead, although, in
the one case, happiness in the after state was believed to

[1] *Celtic Religion*, E. Anwyl, pp. 60 *et seq.*
[2] Graham's *Picturesque Sketches of Perthshire.*

be the reward of good conduct in this life, and, in the
other, of those who by performing ceremonies obtained
knowledge of the formulæ which were the "Open
Sesames" required by departed souls to secure admission
to the boat of the sun.

Similarly, it does not follow that the cremation
custom had the same significance at all periods. In the
Iliad the ghost of Patroklos declares that he will never
again return from Hades when he has received his meed
of fire. Modern Hindus burn their dead,[1] but the soul
may either depart to Paradise or continue its round
through other existences on this earth. In Sanskrit
literature the fire-god, Agni, "the corpse devourer", conducts souls to the "land of the fathers". The Persian
fire-worshippers do not cremate their dead, although they
may have done so at one time, but expose them to be
devoured by wild birds. Of special interest is the practice of the Mongolian Buriats. The bodies of those who
die in autumn and winter are piled up in a log-house in
the midst of a forest. When the cuckoo begins to call,
in May, this house is set on fire and the accumulated
bodies are cremated together. Persons who die during
the summer are burned immediately.[2] That the Aryo-
Indians had knowledge at one time of the belief involved
is suggested by a reference in the *Mahabharata*. Describing the heaven of Yama, the sage Narada says that
he saw there "all sinners among human beings as also
(those) that have died during the winter solstice".[3] The
explanation may be that there were lucky and unlucky
hours, days, and months for death as for birth. The

---

[1] Except, as was the case in Rome (*Juvenal*, XV, 140), the bodies of infants. Those under eighteen months are in India buried head downwards in jars. Mothers who die in childbed are not cremated either, but buried.

[2] *A Journey in Southern Siberia*, Jeremiah Curtin, p. 101.

[3] *Sabha Parva*, Section VIII (Roy's translation, p. 27).

omens at birth which foretold an individual's fate were
supposed to give indication of his manner of death.   One
of the Scottish midwife prophecies runs:

> Full moon, full sea,
> Great man shalt thou be,
> But ill deith shalt thou dee.[1]

Omens at death threw light on his fate in the after life.
The Buriat custom has evidently a long history behind it.
Perhaps it was originally believed that those who died
in winter were doomed to exist ever afterwards in cold
and darkness.   Such a belief imported into India would
in time cease to have any significance.   The new country
had new terrors which supplanted the old, and influenced
the development of religious beliefs.

Among certain peoples who did not believe, like the
Achæans, the Aryo-Indians, and others, that the soul
was transferred to Paradise through the medium of fire,
burning was a punishment.   Erring wives in ancient
Egyptian and Scottish folk-tales are burned at the stake.[2]
Similarly, witches were burned alive.   Sir Arthur Evans
has brought together interesting evidence regarding "the
revival of cremation in Europe in mediæval and modern
times to get rid of vampires".[3]   Bodies of persons whose
ghosts had become vampires, which attacked sleepers and
sucked the life-blood from their veins, were taken from
tombs and publicly burned.   The vampires were thus
prevented from doing further harm.   Herodotus tells
that when Cambyses, the son of Cyrus, caused the mummy
of Pharaoh Amasis to be burned, he displeased both the
Persians and the Egyptians.   "The Persians", he says,
"hold fire to be a god, and never by any chance burn

---

[1] Lamont's *Chronicle of Fife*, p. 206.

[2] *Indian Myth and Legend*, p. xxxvii, and *Egyptian Myth and Legend*, p. 143.

[3] *Comptes Rendus du Congrès International d'Archéologie*, 1905, Athens, p. 166

their dead. Indeed, this practice is unlawful, both with them and with the Egyptians—with them for the reason above mentioned, since they deem it wrong to give the corpse of a man to a god; and with the Egyptians, because they believe fire to be a live animal, which eats whatever it can seize, and then, glutted with the food, dies with the matter which it feeds upon. Now, to give a man's body to be devoured by beasts is in no wise agreeable to their customs, and, indeed, this is the very reason why they embalm their dead, namely, to prevent them from being eaten in the grave by worms."[1]

The evidence afforded by the Cretan burial customs is of special significance. From the earliest times until the close of the Bronze Age the dead were buried. Then cremation was introduced by invaders, who are believed to have been identical with the Achæans of Homer. The new custom had, in this instance, not only a religious but an ethnic significance.

Like certain of the Palæolithic tribes in western Europe, the early Cretans buried their dead in caves and rock shelters. As caves were dwellings, this was a form of house-burial. House-tombs have been found in Cretan as in Babylonian towns. The custom is referred to in the Ethiopic version of the mythical life of Alexander the Great. That hero was reputed to have "asked one of the Brahmans, saying: 'Have ye no tombs wherein to bury any man among you who may die?' And an interpreter made answer to him, saying: 'Man and woman and child grow up, and arrive at maturity and become old, and when any one (of them) dieth we bury him in the place wherein he lived; thus our graves are our houses. And our God knoweth that we desire this more than the lust for food and meat which all men have; this

[1] *Herodotus,* III, 16

is our life and manner of dwelling in the darkness of our tombs.'"[1]   This conversation can never have taken place in India, but it is of interest in so far as it reflects a belief with which the author was familiar.

In Palæolithic times a cave was deserted after the head of the family was buried in it. There were also, however, burial-caves. The Cro-Magnon people, for instance, sometimes deposited whole families, or the members of tribes, in one of these. One cave has yielded no fewer than seventeen skeletons. Caves and rock-shelters were similarly utilized in Crete. It became customary, however, to construct chamber-tombs, which may have been imitations of caves. One at Aghia Triadha, near Phæstos, in south-central Crete, is some 30 feet in diameter. The remains of no fewer than 200 skeletons of men, women, and children were found in it. Other chambers adjoining added fifty to this number. Family tombs of this kind, which were entered by narrow passages, were sometimes circular, and developed into the beehive style of tomb found in Mycenæ and Tiryns. They date back to early Minoan times (c. 2800 B.C.). Others were of rectangular shape, like those found near Knossos. The Cretans also buried their dead in terracotta chests, in which the bodies lay in crouched position as in the pre-Dynastic graves of Egypt. These *larnakes* or sarcophagi were probably of Egyptian origin. They have also been found in Sicily and Italy. Sometimes the Cretan sarcophagi were profusely decorated. Like the tombs, they contained vessels, seals, daggers, amulets, &c.

The Cretans were worshippers of the Great Mother goddess who inhabited the abode of the buried dead. She was the Earth Mother. Caves were entrances to the Underworld over which she presided. In Crete,

---

[1] *The Life and Exploits of Alexander the Great*, E. Wallis Budge, pp. 133-4.

LIMESTONE SARCOPHAGUS, SHAPED LIKE A CHEST, FOUND AT AGHIA TRIADHA (See pages 289-290)

The thin plaster covering is painted with scenes connected with the cult of the dead.

where no temples were erected, votive offerings were deposited in caves, the most famous of which were those on Mount Dicte and Mount Ida. According to Greek legend, the mother-goddess Rhea gave birth to Zeus in a Cretan cave. The ferocious mother-goddesses of England and Scotland, as is shown (Chapter III), were cave-dwellers. Palæolithic artists drew and painted their magical figures of animals in the depths of great caves.

Demeter of the Grecian Phigalia—the Black Ceres—lived in a cave, which is still regarded as sacred. This deity, who is believed to be a form of the Cretan Great Mother, was also associated with stone circles. Pausanias, writing of the town of Hermione in the Peloponnese, says that near it "there is a circle of huge unhewn stones, and inside this circle they perform the sacred rites of Demeter".[1]

Stone circles, single standing-stones, and groups of stones like those at Karnak in Brittany were erected at burial-places. Offerings were made to the dead whose spirits had become associated with the Earth Mother. These spirits might be summoned from their tombs to make revelations. When Odin visited the Underworld to consult the Vala (witch or prophetess) regarding Balder's fate—

> Round he rode to a door on the eastward
> Where he knew was a witch's grave,
> He sang there spells of the dead to the Vala,
> Needs she must rise—a corpse—and answer.[2]

Folk-memories of the ancient custom of summoning the spirit of the dead still survive in rural districts. An archæologist who recently conducted investigations at a stone circle in northern Scotland asked a ploughman if

---

[1] *Pausanias*, II, 34.   [2] *The Elder Edda*, O. Bray, p. 241.

he knew anything regarding it. The answer was to this effect: "It is said that if you walk round it three times against the sun at midnight, you will raise the devil." Our demonology is the last stage of pagan mythology. The summoning of the devil, or the spirits of the Underworld, was a ceremony performed for purposes of divination, or to compel the aid of infernal beings. As only one grave is sometimes found in stone circles, it may be that a circle was erected when a great chief, or great priest or priestess, died, so that the ghost might be propitiated and called up to assist his or her kinsfolk in times of need. A patriarch or teacher would thus be worshipped after death like a god, and especially as a guide to the spirit world. The Babylonian Gilgamesh was a hero who first entered the cave which led to Paradise. So was the Indian Yama; he was the first man to "find the path for many", and he became god of the dead. Osiris, as Apuatu, was "opener of the ways", and similarly reigned in Hades. The Cretan Minos is in the *Odyssey* a lawgiver, like Osiris, of the Underworld. In Greek mythology the guide of travellers, who conducts the soul on his last journey, is Hermes. His name appears to be derived from *herma*, which signifies a cairn or a standing-stone. The Thracian "square Hermes" was a pillar surmounted by a human head—a form which is evidently a link between a standing-stone and the statue of an anthropomorphic deity. It may be that some of the anthropomorphic deities were simply deified ancestors, priests, or priestesses.

The Great Mother, who was worshipped by the Cretans and other pre-Hellenic peoples in south-eastern Europe, was the goddess of birth and death, of fertility and fate. As the ancestress of mankind she gathered to her abode in the Underworld the ghosts of her progeny.

She was the source of the food-supply, which she might withhold at will by raising storms, causing floods, or sending blight and disease. It was important that account should be taken of her varying moods—that her intentions should be ascertained by means of oracles, so that she might be propitiated, or controlled by the performance of magical ceremonies. She assumed various forms at different seasons and under different circumstances. Now she was the earth serpent, or the serpent of the deep—the Babylonian Tiamat—and anon the raven of death, or the dove of fertility; she might also appear as the mountain hag followed by savage beasts, or as a composite monster in a gloomy cavern, like the horse-headed Demeter of Phigalia. The beautiful northern goddess of the Greek sculptors was a poetic creation of post-Homeric times, when her benevolent character only was remembered. Still, Rhea ever retained her lion, which crouched beside her throne—a faint memory of her ancient savage character.

The Achæan conquerors who burned their dead were worshippers of the sky- and thunder-god, the Great Father. They believed that the souls of the dead ascended to a Paradise above the clouds. Hercules burned himself on a pyre and fled heavenwards as an eagle; the soul of the Roman Emperor ascended from the pyre on which his image was placed, on the back of an eagle. The eagle was the messenger of Zeus, and the god himself may have originally been an eagle. The Zu eagle of Babylonia and the Garuda eagle of India were ancient deities; indeed, Tammuz, in his Nin-girsu form at Lagash was depicted as a lion-headed eagle. Cyrus claimed to be an Achæmenian—that is, a descendant of the patriarchal Akhamanish, who was reputed to have been protected and fed during childhood by an eagle.

The double-headed eagle of the Hittites, which now figures in the royal arms of Russia, was a deity of great antiquity. In Egypt one Paradise was the Underworld of Osiris and the other the Paradise above the sky to which Horus ascended in the form of a falcon. Baby-lonian mythology makes references to the Paradises of Anu and Bel and Ishtar, to which the patriarch Etana ascends on the back of an eagle, as well as to the island Paradise discovered by Gilgamish and the gloomy Under-world where souls eat dust and drink muddy water. So do the beliefs of mingled peoples survive in complex mythologies.

The archæological evidence of Crete and Greece shows clearly that the cremation custom had an ethnic significance. Whence then came the Achæans of Homer who were the cremating people, or at any rate were identified with them in tradition? Professor Ridgeway[1] has summarized a mass of important archæological data regarding prehistoric burial customs, and writes: "From this rapid survey it is now clear to the reader that cre-mation was not developed in the countries lying around the Mediterranean, whilst on the other hand it was already practised in Central Europe, possibly even in the transition period from stone to bronze. But as the Achæans practised it at least 1000 B.C., there is a very high probability that they had come into Greece from Central Europe, where the fair-haired peoples were cer-tainly burning their dead before the end of the Bronze Age, or at least 1200 B.C." He regards with favour the view that the ancestors of the cremating Hindus—the Aryans and Indo-Europeans of the philologists—migrated from Europe into Asia before the Iron Age.

The theory that the Achæans were a Germanic people

[1] *Early Age of Greece*, Vol. I, pp. 481 *et seq.*

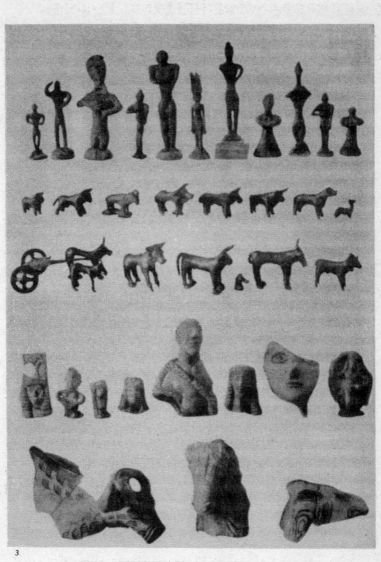

3

VOTIVE OFFERINGS FROM THE DICTEAN CAVE

The three upper rows are bronze objects: those in the two lower rows are made of terra-cotta.

(See page xlv; also Chap. XIII, pages 297–299)

and that the cremation custom originated in the forests of Germany has not received wide acceptance. Account must be taken of the archaic cremation custom of the Mongolian Buriats which has been referred to. No trace of seasonal burnings have been found in Europe. The Achæan dead might be cremated at any time of the year. Were the ancestors of the Buriats in touch at some remote period with a people among whom cremation was practised before it obtained in Central Europe?

The earliest evidence yet obtained of cremation comes from southern France. M. Verneau, who is the authority on the burial customs of the Palæolithic cave-dwellers of Grimaldi, has found that among the Cro-Magnon peoples of the Third Interglacial Period ceremonial interment by inhumation was the general rule. He found, however, a single instance of cremation. Offerings similar to those found with buried bodies were associated with the burned bones. Of course, we know nothing about the beliefs regarding the destiny of the soul which obtained among the Cro-Magnon peoples. The majority of these, it may be noted, were tall, averaging about 5 feet 10 inches in stature. M. Verneau, however, discovered two skeletons of alien type which he refers to as members of "a new race".

Next in chronological order, but separated by thousands of years, come the Early Neolithic cremating people of Palestine who dwelt in the Gezer caves. "One of the caves", writes Professor Macalister, "had evidently been used by this people as a place for the disposal of the dead. The body, placed at the sill of a chimney-aperture that provided a draught, was burnt, the remains becoming ultimately scattered and trampled over the whole surface of the floor. From one point of view this is unfortunate: the bones were too much destroyed by the action of the fire to make any very extensive examination of their ethnological character possible. All we can say is that we have to deal with a non-Semitic race, of low stature, with thick skulls, and showing evidence of the great muscular strength that is essential to savage life."[1] We have no knowledge of the beliefs connected with the Neolithic cremation custom in Palestine.

Among the Australian natives the body of the dead is sometimes cremated. The ashes are afterwards placed in a skin bag which is carried about. Various other funerary practices, including the eating of the corpse, have been recorded. The belief regarding the soul's destiny, among the Australian cremators, is neither Aryo-Indian nor Achæan in character.

The cremation custom of the Bronze Age had in Europe a precise significance as a ceremony. It was not a punishment, or a safeguard against attack by vampires, but a process whereby the souls of the dead were enabled to pass to another state of existence. The cremating invaders swept westward and north and south and formed military aristocracies. In Sweden only the wealthy people were cremated. The evidence of British archæology shows that cremation and inhumation were practised in some districts simultaneously, and that even one member —perhaps the chief—of a family might be cremated while the others were buried. Ultimately cremation died out altogether in Ancient Britain. The earlier faith prevailed. In southern Europe, however, it lingered on until early Christian times, as did mummification in Egypt. The fact that the Christians were opposed to these distinctive burial customs emphasizes that they had a religious significance.

[1] *A History of Civilization in Palestine*, pp. 15, 16.

Dr. Dörpfeld[1] has urged the hypothesis that the Achæans burned their dead only when engaged in distant wars, and practised inhumation in the homeland. He thinks that cremation arose from the custom of scorching bodies prior to burial for hygienic reasons.

No traces of partial burning have been found in the pre-Dynastic graves of Egypt, or in the vast majority of similar graves in Europe. Dr. Dörpfeld refers, however, to charred fragments found in tombs at Mycenæ and elsewhere in support of his theory. Here again the evidence of Crete is of special importance. In the tombs near Knossos have been found, in addition to food vessels, clay chafing-pans and a plaster tripod, filled with charcoal. These may have been portable hearths intended to warm and comfort the dead, or may, on the other hand, have been utilized in connection with magical rites. Deposits of charcoal are often found in Bronze Age graves throughout Europe, and it is suggested that the food intended for the nourishment of the dead was cooked in the grave. On the other hand, the grave fire may have been lit to charm the corpse against the attacks of evil spirits. As a rule, the charcoal deposits are not very considerable. That fires were associated with early burials is suggested by the folk-belief about "death lights" which are seen before a sudden death takes place travelling along a highway, entering a churchyard, and passing over the spot where a grave is to be opened. Early burials took place at night,[2] and the leader may have cast his torch into the open grave so that it might be used by the dead on the journey to the Otherworld. Hermes, the guide of souls, was at one time a god of night and dispensed sleep and dreams.

---

[1] *Melanges Nicole* (in honour of Jules Nicole), 1905, Geneva, pp. 95 *et seq.*

[2] For particulars of the custom of using torches and lights at funerals, see Brand's *Popular Antiquities*, Vol. II, pp. 276 *et seq.* (1899 ed.).

The Cretan portable fire-vessels were, perhaps, substitutes for torches. Lamps are also found in graves. The few partial burnings in the graves of Mycenæ and elsewhere may have been due to accidents at burials. Of course, it is also possible that the individuals met their deaths in house fires.

It will be seen from the evidence passed under review that the theory of the Germanic origin of the cremation custom is hardly conclusive. Evidence may yet be forthcoming that it persisted somewhere in Europe or Asia from Palæolithic times. The evidence afforded by the Gezer cremation cave is suggestive in this connection. As cremation had during the Bronze Age a distinct religious significance, the theory is possible that it was an essential tenet of a cult formed by some great teacher like Buddha, Zoroaster, or Mohammed, who welded together his followers by the strongest ties which bind humanity—the ties of a religious faith and organization. The cremating peoples were conquerors. They achieved ascendancy over the tribes of Indo-European speech who had been migrating into northern India for several centuries between 2000 B.C. and 1200 B.C.; they have left traces of their influence in northern Asia to the present day among the Mongolian Buriats, whose earth and air spirits are called *Burkans* or "masters". In Europe they appear to have subdued a considerable part of the Danubian cultural area, and formed there, as elsewhere, a military aristocracy. It is uncertain whether they owed their successes to superior organization or to the use of iron. The Aryo-Indians, in Rig-Vedic times, used a metal called *ayas*, a word which may have denoted bronze or iron, or both. In Brahmanic times iron was called *syama ayas*, "swarthy ayas", or simply *syama* and also *karsnayasa*, "black ayas", while copper or bronze was

known as *lohayasa*, "red ayas".[1]   The Homeric Achæans
used bronze and iron, but the earlier bands of Achæans
who drifted into southern Greece and reached Crete used
bronze only, and, it is of significance to note, did not
cremate their dead.   Possibly, therefore, the late Achæans
were led by the cremating intruders of Thrace and had
adopted their religious beliefs, which they fused with their
own.   Geometric pottery and iron weapons were introduced into southern Greece when cremation began to be
practised there.

The fusion of the various peoples who struggled for
supremacy in Greece before and during the early Hellenic
period culminated in the growth of its historic civilization.
But the influence of its earliest culture, that of Crete, ever
remained.   It first entered the Peloponnesian peninsula,
and although it was overshadowed there and elsewhere
during the long period of unrest which followed the
Dorian invasion, it continued to develop in contact with
alien cultures in the Anatolian colony of Ionia, which in
turn proved to be "the little leaven which leavened the
whole lump" once again.

So far, nothing has been said regarding the evidence
of language, of which so much was made by the scholars
of a past generation.   But can much really be said with
certainty in this connection?   The idea that the peoples
of Indo-European speech were of common racial origin
and inheritors of a common stock of religious beliefs no
longer obtains.   "Language is shown by experience", as
Mr. Hogarth says, "to be changed by conquest more easily
than type of civilization. . . . The Turkish conquering
minority (of Asia Minor) has imposed its tongue on the
aborigines of Ionia, Lydia, Phrygia, and Cappadocia alike.

[1] *Vedic Index of Names and Subjects*, Macdonald and Keith, Vol. I, pp. 31, 32, and
151.

Yet the type of civilization and the fundamental cult-beliefs of the people are not those of the true Turks." Referring to Greece, he says that "later Greek speech may have been fundamentally mid-European, largely contaminated with Ægean survivals; or it may have been fundamentally Ægean with mid-European intrusions, as our own language is fundamentally Anglo-Saxon largely contaminated by the speech of Norman conquerors".[1]

The chapters which follow begin with the Palæolithic Age in Pleistocene times, and the reader is afterwards presented with a popular account of the archæological discoveries in Crete and Greece which have thrown so much light on the growth of pre-Hellenic civilization. Classical traditions are also drawn upon, and comparisons made between Cretan and Greek deities. Comparative evidence is provided in dealing with the growth and significance of primitive beliefs, and various theories which have been advocated are either indicated or summarized. As environment has ever had a formative influence in the development of religious beliefs and in determining the habits of life of which these are an expression, descriptions of natural scenery in various parts of the Ægean area are given to enable the reader to visualize the conditions of life under which pre-Hellenic civilization grew and flourished. In the historical narrative the chief periods of the contemporary civilizations of Egypt, Babylonia, Assyria, and the land of the Hittites are noted, and there are frequent references to early Cretan connections along the trade routes, by land and sea, with the remote ancestors of the peoples of the present day in Central and Western Europe.

---

[1] *Ionia and the East*, pp. 105-7.

MYTHS OF CRETE AND PRE-HELLENIC EUROPE

CHAPTER I

Primitive Europeans of the Glacial and Inter-glacial Periods

Geological and Mythical Ages of the World—Myths as Products of Environment—The Deluge and Great Winter Legends—New World Cataclysms—Doctrines of Decadence and Evolution in World's Ages Myths—Sages of the "Wandering Jew" Type—The Monsters of Geology and Mythology—Story of the Pleistocene Age—First Glacial Period—Mauer (Heidelberg) Man—Second Glacial Period—The Age of Chellean Culture—The Piltdown Skull—Acheulian Culture Stage—Third Glacial Period and Mousterian Man—Cro-Magnon Race and Grimaldi "Bushmen"—Aurignacian Cave Pictures and Beliefs—Solutrean Culture—Fourth Glacial Period and Magdalenian Man—The Problem of Eoliths—Approximate Duration of Palæolithic Age.

THE system which obtains among modern scientists, of dividing the history of the earth into geological epochs and the pre-history of man into cultural periods, was anticipated by the priestly theorists of ancient civilizations, who established the doctrine of the mythical Ages of the World. These early teachers were, no doubt, as greatly concerned about justifying their own pretensions and the tenets of their cults as in gratifying the growing thirst for knowledge among the educated classes. When they

1

undertook to reveal the process of creation and throw light on the origin and purpose of mankind, they exalted local deities in opposition to those regarded supreme at rival centres of culture and political influence.   Many rival systems of a national religion were thus perpetuated. But the various city priesthoods of a particular country found it necessary to deal also with problems of common concern.   Among other things, they had to account for the various races of whom they had knowledge and to give divine sanction to existing social conditions; nor could they overlook the accidental discoveries which were occasionally made of the relics of elder and unknown peoples and the bones of extinct animals.

These mythology-makers, of course, possessed but meagre knowledge of their country's past, and were accordingly compelled to draw freely upon their imaginations; but they should not be regarded on that account as merely dreamers of dreams and inventors of miraculous stories.   Indications are forthcoming which show that they were not wholly devoid of the scientific spirit.   They were close observers of natural phenomena, and sometimes made deductions which, considering the narrowness of areas available to them for investigation, were not unworthy of thinking men.   It seemed perfectly reasonable to the Babylonian and Egyptian scientists, who saw land growing from accumulations of river-borne silt, and desert wastes rendered cultivable by irrigation, to conclude, for instance, that water was the primary element and the source of all that existed.

This doctrine, which holds that the Universe is derived from one particular form of matter, has been called " Materialistic Monism ".   Ultimately, when mind was exalted above matter, the belief obtained that the inanimate forces of nature were subject to the control of the supreme Mind, which was the First Cause. This later doctrine is known as "Idealistic Monism". It was embraced by various cults in Babylonia, India, and Egypt. In the latter country, for instance, the great god of Memphis was addressed:

Ptah, the great, is the mind and tongue of the gods. . . .
It (the mind) is the one which bringeth forth every successful
    issue. . . .
It was the fashioner of all gods. . . .
At a time when every divine word
Came into existence by the thought of the mind
And the command of the tongue.[1]

In Egypt and Babylonia, where inundations of river valleys were of periodic occurrence, and where, at rare intervals, floods of excessive volume caused great destruction and loss of life, and even brought about political changes, it was concluded that the old Ages were ended and new Ages inaugurated by world-devastating deluges.

The deductions of the early scientists in northern Europe were similarly drawn from the evidence afforded by environment, and similarly influenced by persistent modes of thought. They saw shoals formed and beaches overlaid by sand washed up by the sea from, as it appeared, some sand-creating source, and conceived that on the floor of ocean there stood a great "World Mill" propelled by giantesses, which ground the bodies of primeval world-giants into earth meal. "'Tis said", a saga author set forth, "that far out, off yonder ness, the Nine Maids of the Island mill stir amain the host-cruel skerry-quern—they who in ages past ground Hamlet's meal. The good chieftain furrows the hull's lair with his ship's beaked prow."[2]

---

[1] Breasted's *History of Egypt*, p. 357.
[2] Translation from *Amlodi Saga*, by F. York Powell.

In the *Elder Edda* the god of the mill, who appears to be identical with Frey and the original Hamlet, is called Mundlefore, "the handle-mover":

> The Mover of the Handle is father of Moon
> And the father eke of Sun.

This "World Mill" caused the heavens to revolve round a fixed point marked by the polar star, which was called *veraldar nagli*, the "world-spike".

Believing that sun and moon rose from the ocean, and that therefore light came from darkness, they concluded that winter preceded summer at the beginning.

> Untold winters ere Earth was fashioned
> Roaring Bergelm was born;
> His father was Thrudgelm of Mighty Voice,
> Loud-sounding Ymer his grandsire.[1]

In the north it was observed also that growth was promoted when the ice melted, and the teachers reasoned that the first being, Ymer, came into existence when sparks from the southland, or "poison drops from the sea", fell upon the primeval icebergs, and caused drops of trickling water to fertilize the clay.

> From Stormy-billow sprang poison drops
> Which waxed into Jotun form.

The Babylonians, on the other hand, who were familiar with the part played by reeds in accumulating mud and binding river-banks, taught that—

> Marduk (Merodach) laid a reed upon the face of the waters.
> He formed dust and poured it out beside the reed. . . .
> He formed mankind.[2]

---

[1] Bergelm and Thrudgelm, nature-giants, and Ymer, the primeval world-giant. *The Elder Edda*, O. Bray, pp. 47, 49; and *Teutonic Myth and Legend*, pp. 1 *et seq*.

[2] *The Seven Tablets of Creation*, L. W. King, p. 129.

It may be, too, that the ancient teachers, who framed creation myths and expounded local forms of the doctrine of the World's Ages, mingled at times with their pseudo-scientific deductions and brilliant imaginings dim and confused racial traditions of early migrations and varied experiences in different areas of settlement. Some of these traditions may have had origin before the dawn of the Neolithic or Late Stone Age. As will be shown, certain customs, which are familiar to students of ancient civilizations, were prevalent among primitive peoples in the vast Palæolithic or Early Stone Age. With these customs may have survived in localities legends associated with or based upon them. The possibility remains, therefore, that in Persian mythology there are memories not only of an area of settlement among the mountains where severe winters were as greatly dreaded as exceptional floods in river valleys, but even of one of the last recurring phases of the Ice Age. A poetic narrative relates that the patriarch Yima, who afterwards became Lord of the Dead, constructed a shelter to afford safe protection for mankind and their domesticated animals during the "evil winter", with its "hard, killing frost". He had been forwarned of this approaching world-disaster by the supreme god Ahura Mazda (Ormuzd). Perhaps the "shelter" was a southern valley to which the proto-Persians were compelled to migrate on account of the growing severity of successive winters and the lowering of the perpetual snow-line around mountain-fringed plateaus they were accustomed to inhabit. It is related in the *Avesta*, one of the Persian sacred books, that "before the winter the land had meadows. . . . The water was wont to flow over it and the snow to melt." A similar prolonged winter is foretold in Icelandic mythology. According to the *Prose Edda*, which is a

patchwork of fragmentary legends of uncertain origin
and antiquity, it will precede the destruction of the
universe by the giants of frost and fire (lightning). "In
the first place will come the winter, called Fimbul winter,
during which snow will fall from the four corners of the
world; the frosts will be very severe, the wind piercing,
the weather tempestuous, and the sun impart no
gladness."[1]

From the Voluspa poem of the *Elder Edda* we gather
details of—

> A Sword Age, Axe Age—shields are cloven,
> A Wind Age, Wolf Age, ere the world sinks.

Then, after describing a period of universal destruction,
the soothsayer proceeds:

> I see uprising a second time
> Earth from the ocean, green anew:
> The waters fall, on high the eagle
> Flies o'er the fell and catches fish.[2]

Various accounts of universal cataclysms come from
the New World. Representative of these are the legends
of the Arawaks of North Brazil regarding periods of flood,
storm, and darkness, and those of the Mexicans, which
deal with the destruction of early races by deluges caused
by several succeeding suns perishing from lack of sus-
tenance.

The most highly developed doctrinal systems of World
Ages which have survived from antiquity are found, however, in the Mythologies of India, Greece, and Ireland.
There is more than one account in Aryo-Indian literature of the periodic Ages called Yugas. These are embraced in longer Ages of sufficient duration to satisfy the

---

[1] Mallet's *Northern Antiquities*, p. 451.
[2] *The Elder Edda*, O. Bray, pp. 291, 295.

requirements of modern geologists. Four Yugas extend over a period of " divine years " equal to 4,320,000 years of mortals, and a thousand of the combined Yugas comprise a "Day of Brahma", the individualized "World Soul". The Yugas begin with the Krita or Perfect Age, which is White, and decline from that to the Treta, which is Red, and the Dwápara, which is Yellow, to Kali Yuga, "the Black or Iron Age".

Hesiod, in his *Work and Days*, begins the Greek system with the perfect Golden Age, which is followed by the Silver and Bronze Ages, and the two Ages of Heroes and Iron, which may have been local subdivisions of the fourth Age, represented in India by Kali Yuga.

Both in India and Greece, man, it will be noted, was believed to have relapsed from a primitive state of perfection. The system found in Ireland, which was probably imported from Gaul with the doctrine of transmigration of souls and the custom of widow-burning or slaying, follows, on the other hand, an evolutionary process. The first Irish Age, that of Partholon and his race, is an Age of folly. It is followed by Nemed's Age, which was distinguished for cruelty, and the Age of the Fir Bolgs, in which the power of evil was supreme. Then comes the Danann Age of benevolent deities and heroes, who are the reputed "ancestors of the men of learning in Erin". The last Age is the Milesian, and during it St. Patrick reached Ireland and preached Christianity.

This ancient doctrine of the World's Ages, which may be traced in Egypt and Babylonia, where certain gods lived for periods upon earth as human kings, was adapted to suit the needs of different cults in different areas of localization. In India the four great castes were each connected with a Yuga: the Brahmans had origin in the White Age, the Kshatriyas (military aristocrats) in the

Red Age, the Vaisyas (traders and agriculturists) in the Yellow Age, and the Sudras (Dravidians and pre-Dravidians) in the Black Age. In Greece an Age was devoted to the Trojan heroes, and in Ireland the Fir Bolgs, Dananns, and Milesians were identified with existing racial types whom St. Patrick found there.

One of the versions of the Indian legend of Mythical Ages is related by the deathless sage Markandeya, who lived through all the Yugas, and was protected during the Deluge by the child-god Narayana. The Irish account was put into the mouth of Tuan MacCarell. He had been a contemporary of Partholon, and afterwards existed for periods as a stag, a boar, a vulture or eagle, and a salmon. In the end his salmon form was devoured by the wife of King Carell, with the result that he was re-born as her son. Another sage of this class is the famous Mágus of the Icelandic *Bragda Mágus* saga, who renewed his youth periodically by casting his skin. He also figures in the Charlemagne romances.

If the ancient teachers, who professed to have received revelations from sages like the " Wandering Jew ", had been acquainted with the scientific data which is now available, their narratives of past Ages would have described greater changes than ever they conceived of. Nor would these be lacking either in picturesqueness or imaginative appeal. The priestly sages would have no cause to lament with the poet:

> Do not all charms fly
> At the mere touch of cold philosophy?
> There was an awful rainbow once in heaven:
> We know her woof and texture; she is given
> In the dull catalogue of common things.

Even greater and more ferocious monsters than were

dreamt of in their philosophy might have figured in their wonder-compelling and fearsome legends. Instead of the composite demons of Egypt and Babylonia, the Eur-Asian dragons, the flying serpents of the Nile valley, and the great snakes of ocean, they could have told of the gigantic reptiles of the Triassic and Jurassic systems, the great mammals of the Tertiary Period, and those contemporaries of man in the Pleistocene Age, the hairy mammoths, bulky with fat and fur, the fierce woolly rhinoceroses, the huge cave-bears, and the immense sabre-toothed tigers. No ancient legend of fabled monsters surpasses the modern scientist's account of extinct gigantic fauna. Nor can the creation-myths on Egyptian papyri, Babylonian bricks, or Indian palm-leaf books approach in grandness and charm the dramatic story of the four great geological Ages of the World.

The author of the Tuan MacCarell legend would in our day begin his narrative with the dawn of the Pleistocene Age, which endured for at least 620,000 years, and was yet much shorter than any of the four Tertiary Ages —the Eocene, Oligocene, Miocene, or Pliocene.

In the post-Pliocene, or early Pleistocene period, Tuan, let it be supposed, awakens from magic sleep in Europe. He gazes with wonder on forests of strange and mighty trees. Monstrous wild animals come and go. Several resemble elephants, and the greatest of these is the long-tusked mastodon of colossal bulk. Hippopotami snort in the rivers, on the banks of which crouch, basking in sunshine, ponderous Dinotheriums, resembling sea-cows, with downward-curving tusks and short trunks. Across verdurous plains gallop herds of little horses with divided hoofs. The dreaded sabre-toothed tiger crouches in the jungle ready to pounce upon its prey.

Tuan, who alternately sleeps for long centuries and

wanders about the earth like the legendary Jew, continues his narrative. "When next I awoke", he tells, "I found that Europe had been completely transformed. No great forests flourished on its central plains; bare stretches of frozen ground extended far and near. From northern Germany to the Pole, valleys and rivers were shrouded by ice and seas were frozen over. Great mountain-peaks towered grimly above curving glaciers like rocky islands in a foam-white ocean. Icebergs drifted down the Atlantic past the coast of Spain. This was the First Glacial Period.

"When next I awoke the ice was vanishing, the rivers surged from the melting glaciers, many valleys were flooded, and vegetation flourished. In the years that followed I saw the forests extending northward from the Mediterranean coast, and the ocean ebbing gradually farther and farther away, owing to the widespread elevation of land, until great islands became uplands in vast plains, and continents linked with continents around the world. I must describe Europe as it appeared to me before I next fell asleep. The Mediterranean Sea was divided into two great lakes when Italy became attached to a triangular plain which jutted out from the north African coast. The Strait of Gibraltar was closed, and a broad valley united Spain with Morocco. Corsica and Sardinia formed a promontory when the Gulf of Genoa vanished, and the Balearic Isles were mountains on a finger of land attached to western Spain. The Baltic Sea became a shrunken inland lake, the English Channel and the North Sea had disappeared. The British Isles were then joined to the Continent, and the plains which enclosed them extended far westward beyond Land's End, the western coast-line of Ireland and that of the Scottish Hebrides, and stretched north-eastward beyond the Shetland Isles to the coast of

Norway. A "land-bridge", which shrank to a narrow neck 100 miles north-west of Cape Wrath, united Scotland and Iceland, and narrowed again ere it met the extended coast of Greenland. The Rivers Elbe and Rhine drained the broad valley which had been the North Sea, and were united about 150 miles eastward from the Aberdeenshire coast after the Rhine had received the waters of the Forth and Tay. The Conon poured through the valley which had been the Moray Firth, and, sweeping eastward past the Orkney and Shetland Islands, entered the sea 20 miles westward from the mouth of the Elbe. The Seine cut through the valley of the English Channel, and the Severn united, 100 miles westward from Land's End, with a river flowing from a long narrow loch which divided Ireland from Scotland, and extended southward to Carnsore Point in Wexford.

"Over the Eur-African land-bridges came many of the great animals which I saw during the first period of the Pleistocene Age. Attracted by the genial temperature, even the rhinoceros came north, and with the sabre-toothed tiger prowled on the upland plains of England, where I saw also the giant sloth, the hippopotamus, the mastodon, the triple-toed horse, great tortoises, the giant fallow deer, the well-armoured glyptodon,[1] as big as an ox, and numerous great snakes and nimble apes.

"For a long period I searched in vain for traces of mankind, but at length I discovered a tribe of most primitive savages at Mauer, on the banks of the River Neckar, then very broad and deep, near where Heidelberg now stands. They hunted down the horse and the elk, and dreaded greatly the rhinoceros and the cave-lion. Their homes were among the branches of high trees. In aspect they were extremely repulsive: they had low, sharply-

---

[1] Resembling the armadillo.

(C 808)

retreating foreheads, squat noses, big bulging mouths, and chinless jaws.[1] I never saw these savages except in this First Interglacial Period.

"When next I awoke from the slumber of centuries I found that Europe had once more been transformed. The Mediterranean Sea had snapped the Italian land-bridge and flowed through the Dardanelles to the Black Sea; a blue strait separated Gibraltar from Morocco. The British Islands were entirely isolated. Roaring tides swept up and down the English Channel, and the broad North Sea, overswept by foam - churning tempest, was dotted over by innumerable icebergs. Each succeeding winter the ocean encroached farther and farther inland, burying in deep sand-banks the great trunks of forest trees, creeping up river valleys and forming stony beaches where wild flowers had bloomed and birds had carolled and built their nests. At length the advancing billows shaped out a rough shore-line round the island coasts over 40 feet above their present level. In time the land was re-elevated and the sea shrank back again.

"The snow - line of Scottish mountains crept down gradually lower and lower, and glaciers appeared once more. Ultimately vast fields of ice jutted across the North Sea, and the Baltic remained frozen during the months of summer. Icebergs were stranded on Dogger Bank and drifted down the English Channel in early summer through veils of white fog into the Bay of Biscay and round Cape Finisterre.

"Ere I went to sleep again the ice-fields had obliterated Holland and Belgium and crept up the Elbe valley almost to the plain of Bohemia, where the climate was sub-arctic

---

[1] The jaw-bone of the earliest European was found in a Mauer sand-pit, 78 feet from the surface. Sollas holds that this primitive German belonged to none of the existing races of mankind. The jaw-bone has Simian characteristics.

and tundra conditions prevailed as in northern Siberia at the present time. Scotland, Ireland, and Wales were ice-locked, and England was covered over as far south as Essex on the east and Gloucester on the west, except where the battling glaciers left bare patches in the middle districts and in the East Riding of Yorkshire. This was the Second Glacial Period. When it had reached its maximum, I wandered southward through France, then a dreary waste, and saw herds of musk-oxen and reindeer, lumbering woolly rhinoceroses, and fat mammoths with great recurving tusks and shaggy red manes.

" I had sought shelter from a blinding dust-storm in a cave on a bare hill-side, and slept there. When next I awoke and crept forth, I found myself in a deep shady forest. It was a fragrant morning of bright sunshine, and although it seemed to be midsummer, the sweet spring season had not yet spent itself. The rivers at this, the dawn of the Second Inter-glacial Period, ran broad and deep, swollen by the melting glaciers, but they shrank gradually as weeks of heat and dryness went past. Wide shallow lakes grew smaller each succeeding summer until they vanished entirely, and their dark beds grew verdant with long grasses. When I went northward I found that the British Isles were once again a part of the Continent. The African hippopotamus snorted in the Thames, the rhinoceros lumbered along the plains of the English Channel, and through the forests of the North Sea valley herds of elephants ranged as far north as the banks of the Forth. I saw many tribes of human beings. I first met them at Chelles, on the banks of the Seine, 8 miles eastward from the site of Paris. The Chellean men were of higher type than the grotesque tree-dwellers of Mauer. Their dark skins bespoke their southern origin, and they resembled certain tribes of Australian savages. They were entirely devoid of clothing. The men carried long staves, which were sharpened to points, with which they speared fish and hunted the little wild horse. I saw them chipping flint and shaping " hand-axes ",[1] which they used for a variety of purposes—cutting branches from trees, skinning and dividing animals, and weapons. They also made small flint scrapers and small flint daggers with rough curved hefts.

" I saw these men hunting in England and in Central and Western Europe. They crossed over to Africa by the Italian land-bridge, round the rock of Gibraltar, and along the Palestinian coast, and they were numerous in Persia and India. Ere I fell asleep I was transported round the world, and saw thousands of human beings following the edible animals over the northern land-bridge from Asia to Canada, and down the western sea-coast to South America. Then I slumbered again.

" Long centuries went past as I slept. When next I awoke I found that Europe had once again become changed. The sea was washing round the shores of the British Isles, and the Italian land-bridge to Africa had been severed. Crete was no longer a part of the mainland, and the green mountains which had towered on the well-watered valley connecting Greece with Asia Minor were islands in the Ægean Sea. The temperature had suffered decline. Summer was shorter and winter longer and of growing severity. During the warm weather the southern animals wandered through France, and, when the snow began to fall, the mammoth, the woolly rhinoceros, and the reindeer came down from the north in search of food. I saw new types of humanity which had

---

[1] The so-called *coup-de-poing* of the French archæologists; also named "bouchers", after M. Boucher de Perthes, who half a century ago identified them as primitive artifacts of human contemporaries of extinct wild animals.

arrived from Asia. They mingled with Chellean men in some localities, and in others fought with them for possession of hunting-grounds. Many tribes were isolated in Britain when the land was lowered and the sea advanced. There were Asiatics in Sussex, and I saw some camping on the banks of the Ouse at Piltdown, near Uckfield.[1] During the winter these people sought shelter in caves.

"The change of climate had intensified the struggle for existence, and sharpened the wits of men. At St. Acheul, at Amiens, in the Somme valley, I found the flint-workers displaying increased skill and producing several new implements which the altered conditions of life had made necessary. Acheulian man had achieved a considerable degree of progress in other directions. Those tribes which remained in western and central Europe, owing to the winter season found it necessary to provide themselves with skin clothing, but the great majority migrated to genial climes, and these continued their old habits of life. I fell asleep at the close of this the Second Interglacial Period, which was longer and more genial than any of the others.

"The Third Glacial Epoch was well advanced when next I set forth a wanderer through the valleys of Europe. It was less widespread than the second. Two-thirds of England and about a fourth of Ireland were clear of ice, nor was the Zuyder Zee frozen during summer. The site of Berlin, however, was well within the glacial area, as was also that of Warsaw. The Alpine snow-line had crept down over 3000 feet. Yet although Europe resembled in some parts Greenland and in others North Siberia in the present Age, I saw numerous tribes of human beings. They were of small stature but muscular and active. Their heads were narrow but of great

[1] The Piltdown skull of a broad-headed woman was discovered in 1913.

size, and their faces, although not devoid of intelligence, were exceedingly rugged; their big dark eyes were over-shadowed by enormous brow ridges, they had broad flattened noses, projecting mouths, and chinless jaws.[1] They made their homes in caves, and in these they lit fires, round which they sat to chip their flints and fashion their skin garments.

"I will describe what I saw when I sought shelter with a tribe of these people at Le Moustier, in the valley of Dordogne, in south-western France. The River Vézère then flowed 90 feet higher than in modern times. I entered a cave on a damp and chilly summer day. Haunches of venison were being roasted on a fire-place constructed of upright stones, and near it several work-men were busily engaged chipping flints. They con-structed a greater variety of implements than the men of the Chellean and Acheulean Periods, and showed greater skill in economizing their material: flakes were removed at a single blow and utilized for smaller arti-facts, and when an implement was given form it was carefully dressed with minute chipping until it became an artistic product, exceedingly pleasing to the eye. Men took delight in their work and rivalled one another to gain the praises of their fellows. The tailors cut the dried skins with their sharp hand-axes. Then they squatted with crossed legs to sew the pieces together into not unshapely garments. They made holes, through which to thrust their dried thongs, with little flint awls. In the evening a company of hunters returned from the chase, dragging on a skin sledge the carcass of a musk-ox; and when they had feasted heavily, I heard them tell of battles with the cave-bear, of escapes from the cave-lion and the dreaded woolly rhinoceros, of the slaying

[1] The Neanderthal-Spy type.

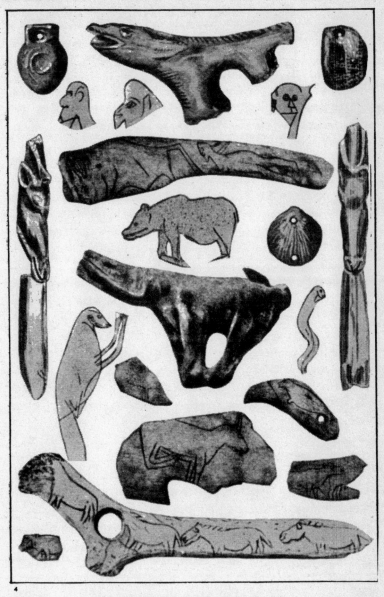

EXAMPLES OF PALÆOLITHIC ART

The objects include: handles of knives and daggers carved in ivory and bone, line drawings of wild animals, faces of men or demons, of animal-headed demon or deity with arms uplifted (compare Egyptian "Ka" attitude of adoration), of wild horses on perforated "arrow straightener", of men stalking a bison, of seal, cow, reindeer, cave bear, &c., and perforated amulets.

of a great mammoth, and of how they guarded their food-supplies against the ravages of prowling hyenas, gluttons, and arctic foxes. Meanwhile the women busily engaged themselves at the mouth of the cave cutting up the body of the musk-ox and cleaning the skin with flint scrapers. Ere night fell, the chief announced that on the morrow they would go eastward to hunt reindeer. I gathered that these people migrated northward during the summer, and returned again, on the approach of cold weather, to their southern caves. Not infrequently they had to fight with other tribes who took possession of their winter homes.

"I went to sleep during this period, and when next I awoke I found that the Third Inter-glacial Period had dawned. The glaciers melted and again there were great floods in the valleys, and the ice retreated from the lowlands of Scotland. The summers in Central Europe were exceedingly pleasant, but never so warm as during the Chellean Age, and dust-storms were of frequent occurrence. Forests were once again flourishing, and I saw in the midst of them many southern animals which were migrating farther and farther northward. During winter the mammoth and woolly rhinoceros came as far south as Prussia. Mousterian man was able to pursue the hunt high among the mountains, where he found caves in which to shelter himself from wild animals by night. He returned to the valleys when the blizzards of winter drove southward the fierce and numerous beasts of prey he dreaded most.

"I saw new types of mankind. In the Dordogne valley were tribes of slender-limbed human giants who were fearless warriors and mighty huntsmen. Some were 6 feet 6 inches in height. But it was not only in stature that they contrasted sharply with the vanishing

Mousterians, who were rarely higher than 5 feet 3 inches. They had big long heads and broad faces, high foreheads, deep-set brown eyes, prominent cheek-bones, sharply curved lips, and well-formed chins. They resembled modern Europeans more closely than any human beings I had yet met with. Their faces, tanned by wind and sun, were alert and keen, and, although rugged, were greatly softened when their ready smile laid bare their white gleaming teeth. I observed that the young men showed great respect for their elders. It was of common occurrence to see many gathered round a cave entrance listening to the counsel of some white-haired sage. An old man, who had achieved widespread renown as an explorer and leader of men, lived in a cave at Cro-Magnon, and was often approached to settle disputes and give advice regarding great undertakings; he was also skilled as a healer of wounds and a curer of disease. These men had greater regard for their dead than obtained among their Mousterian predecessors. I once saw them laying to rest a slain warrior in his family burial-grotto at Aurignac. He was clad in his skin robe. His head-dress was adorned with a string of sea-shells and round his neck was a collar of the perforated teeth of a reindeer, the skeleton of the salmon of wisdom was laid on his breast, and the whole body was sprinkled with magic pigment. A fire was lit, and the warriors danced round the grave with slow, measured steps, while a sage recited the mighty deeds performed by the dead man. Women knelt near at hand, wailing a chorus of sorrow. Beside the warrior they laid his weapons and implements as well as food which had been cooked for him and water for refreshment; then the grotto was closed up with a large slab of limestone. Aurignacian man of Cro-Magnon type was a lover of his kind.

" I saw other tribes which had entered southern France at this period from Africa. At a Grimaldi cave near Mentone I dwelt for a space with a family of dark-skinned people with broad noses and protruding mouths. They resembled somewhat the modern Bushmen of South Africa and were similarly of short stature, but their heads were larger and their faces more intelligent. Middle-aged women had enormous development of fatty tissue; their steatopygous figures were invariably exceedingly grotesque, but were yet greatly admired.[1]

" These Aurignacian peoples worshipped the mother-goddess, and there were among them clever artists who carved out of ivory and bone, limestone and steatite, female figures to represent their deity. Sometimes they depicted the slim-waisted, long-haired Cro-Magnon women, and sometimes the woolly-haired bulging forms of Grimaldi type. In those districts where the Bushmen-like people were the slaves of the tall huntsmen a steatopygous woman was sometimes selected at religious ceremonies to represent the mother-goddess.

" The Aurignacian artists were wont to decorate their caverns with figures of wild animals, which they sketched in outline with pointed flints, and often coloured with crayons of red ochre or painted with pigment which they carried in bone tubes. In the deep cave of Altamira, in Spain, I saw a great picture-gallery in which various artists had exhibited their skill. One part of the vaulted roof was covered with lifelike representations of edible animals, including wild horses, deer, and boars, and elsewhere I saw artistic productions of similarly high merit. In some caves, which were constantly inhabited, were impressions of human hands. These were intended to

[1] Two Grimaldi skulls which have been discovered have distinct negroid characteristics : the jaw protrudes sharply.

avert the influences of the evil eye and the attacks of
demons. Huntsmen left records of their experiences
in summer hunting districts by inscribing symbols on
cave walls, so that those who came nigh might know how
they were likely to fare there. They also depicted the
forms of monstrous demons that had to be propitiated.

"The hunters of the Aurignacian Age were the first
I saw using bows and arrows. In preparing the arrow-
shafts they utilized perforated bone straighteners.[1] Their
flint implements were worked with skill far surpassing
that of the Mousterian Age.

"How long I slept during this period I cannot tell.
When next I woke up I found that the temperature had
suffered sharp decline. Cro-Magnon man still inhabited
a great portion of southern France,[2] but I observed also
other types which were new to me. At Solutre, Saone-et-
Loire, where tall and short types gave evidence of race
intermixture, I fell in with highly-skilled artisans who
shaped flint lance-heads of laurel-leaf and willow-leaf
shape, and accomplished delicate secondary flaking by
pressure with bone implements. They also made comfortable skin clothing, which they sewed with bone needles
which had perforated eyes.[3] The winters grew gradually
longer and more severe, and the men of the Solutrean
Age achieved rapid progress in their conflict with the
elements. Huntsmen favoured the horse, but slew also
the reindeer.

"The Fourth Glacial Period followed, and it was suffering decline when I next went out to explore those districts
that had seen so many changes. I awoke at La Madelaine,
on the right bank of the Vézère, which then flowed higher

---

[1] This implement has also been called a "sceptre"; it was more probably an "arrow
straightener".   [2] And is still found there, as ethnologists have demonstrated.
[3] The bone needle with perforated eye is an invention of this period.

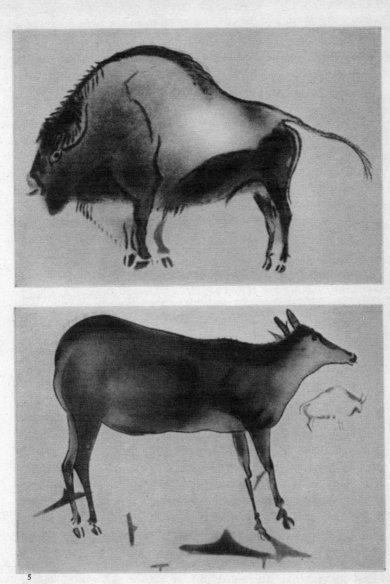

5

PALÆOLITHIC ART: REPRESENTATIVE PAINTINGS OF BISON AND
DEER, FROM THE CAVE OF ALTAMIRA, NEAR SANTANDER, SPAIN

The bison was evidently painted during summer, after it had rubbed its shaggy winter coat off the
greater part of its body.

From copies of the originals by L'Abbé Breuil

than at the present day. In this district the tall men of
Cro-Magnon type were less numerous than the stumpy
intruders of this Magdalenian Age, who had some resemblance to the present-day Esquimaux. Half-breeds, however, were not uncommon. The little men had much
more refined and intelligent faces than the Mousterians;
their foreheads were large and their chins prominent, and
they were clad in closely-fitting skin garments to resist
the sub-arctic climate. Like the cave-dwellers of the
Aurignacian Age, they were skilled artists and artisans.
The Grimaldi folks had migrated southward, and ivory
carvings of the mother goddess were modelled on the
slim-waisted female type. Artists continued to decorate
the caves with paintings of animals, and they also engraved
their implements and weapons, and even stones and
pieces of slate. The bison and the wild horse were often
depicted, but the most favoured models were the northern
animals of this cold European Age. Mammoths were
growing scarce, for men had acquired skill in trapping
them, and the artists engraved ivory charms with their
bulky forms, and numerous were their studies of reindeer
grazing on snowy plains, crouched up at bay, or panting
in rapid flight to escape the dogs and arrows of the huntsmen. The Magdalenian artists also drew the snarling
cave-bear, the double-horned and snouted head of the
woolly rhinoceros, the antelope and the chamois, and the
scampering wolf with gaping jaws. Among birds they
were familiar with the goose and the swan, and, as they
were accomplished fishermen, they could carve in many
characteristic attitudes the graceful salmon and the keen-
eyed seal. Many huntsmen had the handles of their
daggers fashioned to represent the animals they were wont
to stalk and slay.

"During this period flint-working declined somewhat,

for the fashion became prevalent of pointing lances and arrows with ivory and bone and reindeer horn. A great inventor equipped huntsmen with a new weapon—the barbed harpoon—and another provided for it a thrower made from reindeer horn, so that it could be thrown farther and directed with surer aim. A long cord was attached to the harpoon, which was utilized to catch salmon and seals. This wonderful invention was the means of increasing greatly the food-supply. It thus rendered the struggle for existence less arduous, especially when the tribes increased in number.

"Great changes took place when the Fourth Glacial Period began to decline, and more genial conditions became prevalent. The Magdalenian huntsmen migrated farther and farther northward as the ice area shrank in dimensions, because the reindeer deserted those districts which failed to yield them in sufficient abundance the lichens upon which they fed."

In the Gaelic legend of the Irish Ages it is stated that, when Tuan ended, "the auditors thanked him. . . . They remained a whole week talking with him." But his modern narrative deals with problems which are not likely to be solved in so brief a space of time. It touches the fringes of not a few controversies which have been waged vigorously for a number of years, and are likely to be continued indefinitely. In this volume, however, which deals mainly with the intellectual life of early peoples, it is unnecessary to state in detail the various conflicting views regarding the geological periods and the earliest traces of man in Europe; but a brief summary of the results of modern research may be given, so that the general reader may be familiarized with one particular phase of the subject which is pregnant with human interest.

In Tuan's references to early man in Europe, six stages of development, or levels of culture, have been referred to.

These are:

1. The Chellean, in the Second Inter-glacial Period.
2. The Acheulian, a late phase of the Chellean.
3. The Mousterian, in the Third Glacial Period and later.
4. The Aurignacian, in the Third Inter-glacial Period and later.
5. The Solutrean, in the late Third Inter-glacial Period and later.
6. The Magdalenian, in the Fourth Glacial Period.

Some archæologists place before the Chellean, Stage 1 the Mesvinian, and 2, the Strepyan, but others regard them as earlier phases of the Chellean. A still earlier stage, called the Mafflian, with which the Galley Hill (Kent) skeleton and implements were associated, has been taken down to the Strepyan Period of Chellean man. The various stages have been subdivided into Upper, Middle, and Lower Periods.

Of late years certain scientists have sought to establish a pre-Palæolithic Age called the Eolithic. They thus place the appearance of man in the geological Tertiary system, not only in the Pliocene Age, which preceded the Pleistocene, but also back through the Miocene and Oligocene Ages to the Eocene. The Tertiary stages of culture are called Reutelian, and are as follows:—

1. Eocene Age, Duan (Reutelian).
2. Oligocene Age, Fagnian (Reutelian).
3. Miocene Age, Cantalian (Reutelian).
4. Pliocene Age, Kentian (Reutelian).
5. Early Pleistocene, Thames basin (Reutelian).

Then follow the Mesvinian and Strepyan phases of early Chellean culture.

Professor James Geikie confesses he is "staggered" by the theory that man existed in the Tertiary system of Ages. "Since the Eocene Period, which must date back", he says, "several millions of years, the whole mammalian fauna has undergone modifications and changes, continuous evolution having resulted in the more or less complete transformation of numerous types, while many others have long been extinct. And yet, if we accept the eoliths as proofs of man's existence in Eocene and Oligocene times, we must admit that in this case—and in this case alone—evolution must have been at a standstill during a prodigiously extended period. For it must be understood that the eoliths of the older Tertiary formations cannot be distinguished from those met with in the Miocene, Pliocene, and even Pleistocene deposits.[1]

These "eoliths" are chipped flints which were either flaked by man or by natural causes—the movements of strata settling under pressure or the action of water. The problem is a difficult one. "The unprejudiced", says Professor Duckworth, "will maintain an open mind, pending the advent of more conclusive evidence than has been adduced hitherto."[2] Professor Sollas, on the other hand, is convinced that not a trace of unquestionable evidence of man's existence has been found in strata admittedly older than the Pleistocene.[3]

Estimates of the approximate duration of the Pleistocene Age vary considerably. Geikie, following Penck, gives 620,000 years as a minimum; Rutot confines it to 139,000 years, and thus reduces greatly the age of his "eoliths", while Sturge estimates that a single period of it lasted for 700,000 years. The majority of leading scientists, however, have of late inclined to favour Penck's

[1] *Antiquity of Man in Europe*, p. 5 (1914).
[2] *Prehistoric Man*, pp. 106–11 (1912).   [3] *Ancient Hunters*, pp. 67, 69 (1911).

system of dating, and to allow 400,000 years as a minimum for the Palæolithic or Early Stone Age, which begins with the first stages of Chellean culture. The dawn of the Neolithic, or Late Stone Age, is dated in southern Europe and Palestine at roughly 10,000 B.C.

In the next chapter consideration will be given to those traces which survive of the religious and magical beliefs of the Palæolithic peoples, and it will be shown that the evidence accumulated has an important bearing on the problems raised by Cretan and pre-Hellenic discoveries, as well as upon the study of the myths and legends of Babylonia and Egypt, and those of peoples less renowned but no less important from the point of view of the student of comparative mythology.

CHAPTER II

Palæolithic Magic and Religion

Intellectual Life of Palæolithic Man—Evidence from Present-day Savages
—Palæolithic Man progressive and big-brained—Bushmen and Cro-Magnon
Culture—Chronology of Aurignacian Period—The Inspiration of Primitive Art
—Steatopygous Figurines of Cave-dwellers, Babylonians, Maltese, and Egyptians—The Primitive Mother-goddess—Wasp-waisted Females in Fertility
Dance—Hand Impressions in Caves—Finger-mutilation—The Indian Evil-eye Charm—Foot-print Lore—Animal Pictures as Totems—Evidence of Australia—Magdalenian Art—Charmed Weapons—Palæolithic Ceremonial Burials
—Ornaments as Charms—Magic and Religion—Antiquity of Animal-headed
Deities—Origin of the Nude Goddess—The Aurignacian Claim.

It will be recognized at the outset, in dealing with the
intellectual life of the Palæolithic Europeans, that little or
no evidence can be derived from chinless jaws or skulls
with protruding brow ridges, and that the artifacts of the
Chellean and Acheulian phases of culture assist us only
in so far as they afford evidence regarding habits of life
and growing skill in craftsmanship. Not until we reach
the Mousterian stage, in the Third Glacial Epoch, and find
that the cave-dwelling hunters of reindeer and mammoths practised the ceremonial burial of the dead, is there
any sure indication that the Palæolithic mind was sufficiently concerned regarding the great problems of life and
death as to formulate definite beliefs regarding the destiny
of mankind. But it would be rash to draw far-reaching
conclusions from negative evidence. The results that
accrue from the comparative study of beliefs and customs

renders highly improbable the hypothesis that Chellean
and Acheulian men of the Second Inter-glacial Period
took no thought of the morrow because they were on
a plane of lower intellectual development than, for instance, the backward Australian savages who practise
elaborate ceremonials and perpetuate myths which were
anciently the products of speculative thought. Indeed,
there is no savage tribe on the globe at present which can
be said to be devoid of its intellectual life.

It is quite possible that the Chellean folks were even
more advanced than some of the existing types of primitive peoples. This view is supported by the evidence
obtained of their distinct progressive tendencies. Stages
of development can be detected in Chellean culture which
was raised to the Acheulian plane, and the increasing
number and excellence of the artifacts show clearly that a
further distinct advance was achieved when the Mousterian phase had fully developed. It is found, by the
examination of surviving Mousterian skulls, that despite
his rugged facial characteristics the Palæolithic European
was a big-brained man. Of course, skull capacity, especially in individual cases, cannot be regarded as proof of
intellectual power. Still, the fact remains that the really
progressive races in the world at present are those endowed with the most liberal cranial capacity. The early
inhabitants of Western Europe may, therefore, have surpassed as thinkers, as they certainly did as inventors,
those surviving remnants of ancient races to whom they
are usually compared. The Grimaldi skulls of the Aurignacian period may have Bushmen characteristics, but
they give indication of greater intellectual development
than can be credited to those ill-fated and interesting
African nomads who, prior to coming into contact with
the white races, at whose hands they have suffered so

shamefully, had not advanced much beyond the Aurignacian and Magdalenian stages of culture. The Bushmen
appear, in fact, to have remained through long ages in a
state of arrested development after breaking away from
the ancient progressive races from whom the elements of
their civilization were derived. Possibly they even degene-
rated in the interval.

It is probable that the Cro-Magnon peoples of the
Aurignacian stage of culture represented the race of unknown origin which exercised so marked an influence on
those of their contemporaries who were in touch with
them. They had the largest brains of any of the ancient
peoples. Indeed, according to the ethnologists, the skull
capacity of their women was greater than that of the
average male European in the present age.

This Aurignacian stage of culture, which some date
approximately at 20,000 B.C. and others at 30,000 B.C.,
affords ample indications not only of intellectual activity,
but also a marked degree of refinement of thought and
feeling. As has been shown in the "Tuan MacCarrell"
story of the Pleistocene Age, the Cro-Magnon cave-dwellers
of the Late Third Inter-glacial Epoch were accomplished
draughtsmen and ivory-carvers. They had an Art history
which must be regarded as a reflection of their social
history. Apparently they had solved the problem of
securing their food-supply with a minimum of effort and
had therefore leisure to cultivate the Arts; this triumph
they achieved by inventing new implements and improving those inherited from the Mousterian Epoch. Withal,
as one cave-picture shows, they possessed domesticated
cattle which the women engaged in herding. Consequently they had advanced from the hunting to the pastoral stage of civilization.

Their activities in the sphere of Art began with rude

childish efforts and culminated in the production of realistic drawings and carvings in the round, and even of decorative designs which stand comparison with those of later and more complex civilizations. It was considered incredible, when discovery was first made of their cave-pictures, that Palæolithic man could have been endowed with either such intense artistic insight and feeling or technical skill as these gave evidence of.

An interesting problem arises in connection with the artistic products of the Aurignacian and Magdalenian stages of culture. Were they connected with ceremonials, and therefore symbolic of religious and magical beliefs; or should they be considered simply as the expression of an Art movement which had been gradually developed for long ages by accomplished flint-knappers who, in producing exquisitely flaked artifacts of symmetrical proportions, displayed that infinite capacity for taking pains which amounts to genius?

There can be no doubt that the finest Aurignacian figurines wrought in stone and bone and ivory were conscious impressions of feminine beauty of form, and that the artists of the Cro-Magnon race were as devoted lovers of Art for Art's sake as those who at a later period shaped the exquisite Solutrean flint lances of laurel-leaf and willow-leaf design. The absence of male figurines, however, suggests that the art of this remote period was fostered as a cult product, and that we should regard these studies of nude women as religious symbols. This inference appears to be corroborated by the finds of grotesque steatopygous figurines, some of which display no inconsiderable degree of skilful craftsmanship. It is difficult to believe that when artists selected as models women with enormously developed hips and thighs the *motif* was purely an æsthetic one; their obvious desire was to exaggerate sexual characteristics for some special reason.

The evidence derived in this connection from other cultural areas is of undoubted value and interest. In Babylonia terra-cotta figurines, "with accentuation of the female parts", represented Ishtar in her character as the goddess of love and passion.[1] The steatopygous figurines which have been found in the prehistoric "sanctuaries" of Malta were associated with perforated axe amulets and other magical or religious ornaments. In some of the pre-Dynastic graves of Egypt occur figurines of two types: those of slim-waisted women and those of steato-pygous females with short beards.[2] It is not improbable that the Aurignacian, like the early Egyptian figurines, were tribal forms of the ancient love goddess and that the original " bearded Aphrodite " had a racial significance.

In addition to these figurines there are other evidences of the practice of religious ceremonials in the remote Aurignacian Age. In a cave at Cogul, near Lerida, in Spain, a quaint painting depicts several females, with " wasp waists " and bell-mouthed gowns reaching to their knees, dancing round a nude male figure. A phallus image of this culture stage has also been discovered.

Further light is thrown on Aurignacian beliefs by the imprints on cavern walls of human hands with mutilated fingers. Some hands had been first smeared with pig-ment and then impressed on the naked rock; others had been held against damped rock and dusted round with either red or black substances. Not a few of the fingers show that one or more joints had been removed either by accident or design.

---

[1] *Religious Belief in Babylonia and Assyria*, Morris Jastrow, pp. 136 *et seq.*

[2] The female beards suggest that this race's area of characterization was a cold country. On the other hand, it may be held that we have here the earliest evidence of belief in "intermediate types" among the ancient Egyptians.

GROUP OF FIGURINES, IN TERRA-COTTA, FROM PALAIKASTRO

The figurines represent priestesses dancing round the Snake Goddess, the birds are doves, while the separate figure shows a worshipper with right arm raised in prayer " salute ".

6

The practice of finger-mutilation obtained among Bushmen, certain Australian tribes, and communities of Canadian Indians. Independent investigators have ascertained that it was usually associated with burial customs and the ravages of disease. Bush women sacrificed a joint of the little finger when a near relation died, and Canadian natives acted similarly during times of pestilence "to cut off deaths". Finger mutilation in Australia was, among other things, occasionally a mark of caste.[1]

References are made to finger-mutilation in Gaelic stories. After or before great heroes performed deeds of valour, fighting against monsters or famous rivals, they fell into profound slumber. Heroines had to awaken them by cutting off a finger-joint, a part of an ear, or a portion of skin from the top of the head. In the story of Conall Gulban a "great man" came to carry off the lady called "Breast of Light", while Conall, her lover, lay asleep. "Fear would not let her cut off the little finger," it is stated, "and she could not awaken Conall."[2] This savage practice had evidently a magical significance. It may have been intended to renew strength and prolong life, and perhaps also to ward off threatened perils. In the latter case it may have been associated with the ceremony of purification. Among many primitive peoples those who dug graves or touched the dead were under taboo for varying periods, and not allowed to touch individuals or even handle their own food; in some instances they had to be fed by friends until the purification ceremony was completed.

Hand lore is as widespread as it is varied. Magical

---

[1] See *Travels in the Interior of Southern Africa*, W. J. Burchell, Vol. II., p. 61 (1824); *The Native Races of South Africa*, G. W. Stow, p. 129 (1905); *Report on the North-Western Tribes of Canada*, Representative of the British Association (1889), p. 837; and *Ancient Hunters*, W. J. Sollas, pp. 238 *et seq.* (1911).

[2] Campbell's *West Highland Tales*, Vol. III, p. 225.

signs were made by posturing certain fingers. "Children," says an old English writer, "to avoid approaching danger, are taught to double the thumb within the hand. This was much practised whilst the terrors of witchcraft remained. . . . It was the custom to fold the thumbs of dead persons within the hand, to prevent the power of evil spirits over the deceased."[1] In India the upper finger-joints are lucky, and the lower unlucky. Consequently the former only are used at prayer-counting. Throughout Europe much attention was paid to the fingers. The small finger was spat over for luck, and the forefinger of the right hand was supposed to be poisonous, and in the treatment of wounds was never utilized. It used to be considered unlucky to pare finger-nails on certain days. At any time finger-nail parings might be used by witches to work evil spells against individuals. Some mothers still hesitate to cut baby's finger-nails in the first year of life, and bite them off instead. The Scandinavian dead, who were buried with unpared nails, and therefore without ceremony, suffered torture in the Otherworld. The ship in which the demons sailed to wage war against the gods at Ragnarok was made of the nail-parings of wicked persons, and was called *Naglfar*, a name derived from *nagl*, a human nail. The fate of an individual was, and is still, believed by patrons of "palmists" to be indicated by the markings of the hand. Much attention used to be paid to dots on finger-nails; yellow spots foretold death, white spots gifts, and black spots bad luck. Hands were spat upon to seal bargains and bring luck, and kissed upon in connection with Pagan religious practices.

The Aurignacian custom of leaving imprints of hands on rocks is prevalent in modern times in Australia and elsewhere. In India it is part of a luck ceremony.

[1] Hutchinson's *History of Northumberland*, Vol. II, p. 4.

"During a marriage among the Madigas (Telugur Pariahs)", writes Mr. Edgar Thurston, a well-known investigator, "a sheep or goat is sacrificed to the marriage-pots. The sacrificer dips his hand in the blood of the animal, and impresses the blood on his palms on the wall near the door leading to the room in which the pots are kept. This is said to avert the evil eye. Among the Telugu Malas, a few days before a wedding, two marks are made, one on each side of the door, with oil and charcoal, for the same purpose. At Kadur, in the Mysore Province, I once saw impressions of the hand on the walls of Brahman houses. Impressions in red paint of a hand with outspread fingers may be seen on the walls of mosques and Mohammedan buildings."[1] In many Eur-Asian folk-tales the "Great Hand" is the only visible part of a destructive demon.

Those Indians who still charm their houses with hand imprints also trace wavy and interlacing lines in front of their doorsteps and on either side of the part approaching it. Similar lines are found on Bushman paintings of hunting-scenes and in Aurignacian cave-pictures in France and Spain. They may have been intended to snare demons as well as to cast a spell over wild animals. The hieroglyphics representing the name of a Pharaoh were surrounded by cartouches which were "name charms". On some of the sculptured stones of Brittany human footprints are depicted surrounded by meandering and serpentine lines. Perhaps these "luck lines", as they may be called, were inscribed with purpose to secure magical protection for individuals setting out on a journey. Primitive peoples rarely entered upon new undertakings without performing luck ceremonies. It

[1] *Omens and Superstitions of Southern India*, p. 119 (1912), and *Journal of Anthropological Institute*, XIX, p. 56 (1890).

is recorded in a minute of Dingwall Presbytery, dated 5th September, 1656, which refers to the prevalence of superstitious practices in a western parish of Ross-shire, "that future events in reference especiallie to lyfe and death, in takeing of Journeyis, was exspect to be manifested by a holl of a round stone quherein they tryed the entering of thair heade, which if they could doe, to witt, be able to put in thair heads, they expect thair returning to that place, and failing they considered it ominous". The writer in his boyhood took part with his contemporaries in performing various luck ceremonies which were evidently of remote origin.   Before dangerous cliffs were climbed an ash-tree, named the "rock tree", was visited, and each individual ascertained, by throwing a stone into a hollow in the trunk, whether he could safely undertake the proposed enterprise or not.   If a stone darted sideways, the boys shouted, "The danger goes past!" but if it returned to the feet of the thrower it was taken as a sign of ill luck for that day, and he turned homewards.   A large flat stone, called "the spitting-stone", was spat upon by those that remained.   The compact was thus formed; where one went everybody had to go. When a rocky chasm had to be leapt over, caps were first thrown to ensure that the owners would similarly cross lightly and land safely; those whose caps fell short refused to attempt to leap, and made a long and safe detour. When a rainbow appeared against a rain-cloud passing at a distance, the boys charmed away the threatened shower, which would render the rock slippery and more dangerous, by "breaking" the gleaming arch of colours. This they accomplished, as they believed, by laying on a boulder a withered sprig of grass, which they snapped with a single blow delivered by a small stone grasped tightly in the right hand, as Palæolithic man grasped his "hand-axe". It was noted that the upper part of the rainbow faded simultaneously. Hands were spat upon when a specially difficult portion of rock had to be negotiated, and it was believed that danger was averted from trickling water by wetting the tip of a finger and moistening the lips with it. A sacred well was invariably visited for an inspiring and strengthening draught of charmed water, and much reverence was shown for the wonderful skimming flies which were supposed to cleanse it of mud after it was disturbed. Luck-drinking was not uncommon in other days. Grose says: " There is a kind of beverage called 'foot ale' required from one entering on a new occupation ".[1] The "first-footing" ceremonies in Scotland and elsewhere on New Year's Day are the occasion for much eating and drinking. The familiar phrase, "putting one's foot in it", appears to have an interesting history.

"It is a world-wide superstition", says Professor Frazer, "that by injuring footprints you injure the feet that made them."[2] If, then, these line-surrounded footprints on the Brittany stones were not intended to protect individuals who visited them to perform magical ceremonies, they may have been inscribed to restrict the wanderings of the ghosts of heroes buried underneath. The primitive folks perhaps thought that when footprints were thus "snared" by "luck lines", ghosts were prevented from troubling the living.

A naked human footprint, which is not surrounded by these meandering and interlacing lines, survives on fine undisturbed sand on the floor of an Aurignacian cave (Altamira), near drawings of panting trout and a wounded bison.[3] In this case the Palæolithic cave-dweller may

---

[1] Brand's *Antiquities*, Vol. II, p. 333.

[2] *The Golden Bough* (The Magic Art), Vol. I., pp. 207 *et seq.* Professor Frazer gives numerous illustrations of this belief.

[3] *Ancient Hunters*, W. J. Sollas, p. 235.

have ensured his luck by connecting himself ceremonially with the animals he desired to obtain. "May luck follow in my footsteps," he may have exclaimed, as Highland boys, who, as they set out on bird-nesting expeditions were wont to say as they figured out eggs on a dusty highway: "May I get this and this and more."

Other signs, which appear to be magical also, are rows of dots. These figure in Australian and Bushman drawings and paintings. They figure likewise on or beside the artistic products of the Aurignacian Age, and sometimes are arranged in such a manner as to suggest constellations. More elaborate enigmatical signs, resembling birds in flight, fish, twigs, battle-axes, &c., appear to be primitive hieroglyphics.

Some anthropologists suggest that the animals depicted by the Palæolithic artists, in caves and elsewhere, were tribal or family totems. The following view is highly suggestive. "All the beasts thus represented (in caves)," says Professor Frazer, "appear to be edible, and none of them to be fierce carnivorous creatures.[1] Hence it has been ingeniously suggested by M. S. Reinach that the intention of these works of art may have been to multiply by magic the animals so represented. . . . He infers that the comparatively high development of prehistoric art in Europe . . . may have been due in large measure to the practice of sympathetic magic."

Professor Frazer, quoting from Messrs. Spencer and Gillen,[2] shows that the native Australians perform magical ceremonies "to multiply the kangaroos and emus". "The men of the emu totem in the Arunta tribe proceed as follows. They clear a small spot of level ground, and,

---

[1] Bears are depicted on stones, &c., but evidence has been forthcoming that these were eaten. It is possible that the primitive hunters feasted also on the flesh of the mammoth and woolly rhinoceros.

[2] *Native Tribes of Central Australia*, p. 176.

opening veins in their arms, they let the blood stream out until the surface of the ground, for a space of about three square yards, is soaked with it. When the blood has dried and caked, it forms a hard and fairly impermeable surface, on which they paint the sacred design of the emu totem, especially the parts of the bird which they like best to eat, namely, the fat and the eggs. Round this painting men sit and sing. . . ." The men of the kangaroo totem perform a similar ceremony. They inscribe figures of kangaroos on a rocky ledge, which they also decorate with "alternate vertical stripes of red and white to indicate the red fur and white bones of the kangaroo". The rock is reputed to be inhabited by kangaroo spirits which are waiting for mothers, and they are supposed to be driven out when human blood is poured over the ledge.[1]

M. S. Reinach's theory regarding the magical significance of Aurignacian art seems to be confirmed by a piece of chance evidence which has been recorded quite recently (1913). The Count Andreas Begouen, the French archæologist, has on his estate in the district of Montesquieu - Aventes a cavern known as the Tus Ditboubert. It had long been known to bear traces of occupation during Palæolithic times. Paintings could be distinguished on the walls, but few finds of importance were made in it until the count broke through a mass of stalactites that concealed an inner cavern. In this secluded part the Count discovered that Palæolithic man had begun to work clay at a remote period. At the base of one of the walls were curious little clay figurines of animals in a wonderful state of preservation. "One", says a French writer, "was a male bison and another a female. The first was 26 inches long and the second

[1] *The Golden Bough* ("The Magic Art"), Vol. I., pp. 85-8, third edition.

30 inches. They were almost intact, although cracked by the drying of the clay. Excavations on the floor of the cavern revealed a great number of bones of the bison, but no signs that the place had been used as a dwelling-place or as a kitchen by the cave-dwellers." In this eerie cave the Palæolithic folk had evidently conducted mysterious ceremonies. But for what purpose? the Count wondered. "It was an old peasant who gave him his clue. 'It is a charm,' said he, when his eyes fell on one of the relics. Questioned regarding his statement, this man went on to tell that the peasants of the neighbourhood have an ancient custom which they believe enables them to catch the foxes which raid their chicken-yards. They made, he said, a clay image of a fox which they rubbed with the blood of a fox, and then concealed among the rocks at certain places. Close to it they buried the carcass of a fox. Then they set traps near by, and towards these foxes were drawn by the magical influence of the modelled fox and were invariably caught." It is unnecessary to emphasize the importance of this evidence. Similar practices were widespread long centuries after the Palæolithic folk flourished in southern France. The Babylonians and Egyptians shaped waxen and clay images of demons and thrust them into a fire so as to injure or destroy the beings they thus depicted. Magical images were also made in Greece and Rome, and they are still being produced in various parts of the world. The Scottish Highland *corp chreadh* ("clay body") was an image of an individual whom the maker desired to afflict or slay magically.[1] Pins or nails were stuck into it so that the victim might suffer pain, and it was placed in running water so that he might "waste away". Images of fish, turtle, and dugong

---

[1] J. G. Campbell's *Witchcraft and Second Sight in the Highlands aud Islands of Scotland* (1902), pp. 46–8. The custom is not yet obsolete.

"were made by the islanders of Torres Straits and taken with them when they went fishing, with the idea that the image lured the real animal to its destruction; and men of the dugong clan, who were symbolically decorated, made mimetic movements with a dead dugong to constrain others to come and be caught."[1] The Palæolithic artists may have utilized the fragments of slate, stone, &c., on which animals were depicted for a similar purpose.

The Bushman cave-pictures closely resemble the Aurignacian in many details, and even retain certain mannerisms displayed by the ancient European artists. But no direct evidence has been forthcoming that they have, or had, a magical significance. It is possible, however, that those natives who were questioned in this connection may have been as reticent regarding their secrets as most superstitious peoples usually are. In Scotland, where there are many archaic survivals, it is believed that a charm may be broken if its purpose is revealed. Secrecy is necessary for its success; it conserves energy and prevents the working of counter-charms. Not unfrequently in the past Highlanders have misled investigators who, because of their inquisitiveness, were regarded with suspicion, and in consequence earned for themselves a reputation for evasiveness and duplicity.

During the Magdalenian phase of civilization, in the Fourth Glacial Epoch, there was a great art revival. Arctic and sub-arctic fauna were depicted in a variety of forms with artistic feeling and a degree of faithfulness which betokens close and even trained observation of animals. Decorative designs display overflowing artistic fancy. Everything the Magdalenian craftsmen touched he rendered beautiful. Handles of weapons were carved out of bone, horn, or ivory to represent wild animals, which

[1] *Magic and Fetishism*, A. C. Haddon, p. 19 (London, 1906).

were skilfully posed so as to combine utility with artistic excellence. Decoration was evidently, as M. Piette has insisted, generated primarily by the imitative instinct.[1]

Magdalenian art, like the Aurignacian, appears also to have derived inspiration from custom and belief. "Every weapon has its demon," runs an old Gaelic axiom. In the Indian epics, the *Máhabhárata* and the *Rámáyana*, the spirits of celestial weapons appear before the heroes, to whom they are gifted by deities, in attitudes signifying their willingness to render obedient and helpful service. When we find Magdalenian dagger-handles carved to represent charging mammoths or scampering deer, it may be inferred that their owners believed that these possessed the strength and prestige of the one animal and the swiftness and sureness of the other. Discovery has also been made of what appears to have been the Magdalenian "bull roarer". In Australia this implement is used to invoke spirits at initiation and other ceremonies, and elsewhere to raise the wind, that is to compel the attention of the wind-god. The Egyptian sistrum similarly summoned the god when it was tinkled in temples.

Ceremonial burials, which are sure indications of the existence of religious beliefs, took place, as has been indicated, as early as the Mousterian or Middle Palæolithic Period, and also in the later Aurignacian Period. Sometimes the dead were covered over with stones in their cave homes, which were then deserted. Sometimes artificial caves, or grottoes, were utilized as family or tribal burial-vaults. Certain of the skeletons appear to have been unfleshed and afterwards sprinkled over with ochre and ashes. Stone chambers were also constructed to protect the dead.

[1] *L'Art pendant l'Age du Renne.*

The corpse was usually laid on the right side, with the legs crouched up, the head resting on the right arm and the left arm extended. Occasionally, however, the arms appear to have been crossed. These postures suggest sleep, but it must have been believed that the dead would awake, for weapons and implements were left in the tomb, as well as cooked food. The deceased was also adorned with personal ornaments, which were evidently charms. Apparently he had need of protection, perhaps against demons. Strings of periwinkle shells were placed on the head of deceased, and were evidently worn also by the living. This custom in itself is sufficient to suggest that in these remote times belief in magic was well developed and exceedingly prevalent. Primitive peoples wear charms for a variety of reasons—to bring luck, to ward off disease, to cure, to give strength and inspire courage, to acquire the particular attributes they admire in the object, and so on. The periwinkle, which so greatly attracted the Palæolithic Europeans, was not necessarily regarded as "a thing of beauty and a joy for ever". It is only in modern times, when the significance of an immemorial custom has faded, that personal ornaments are selected on account of their purely decorative qualities, their rarity or cost. Our remote ancestors were intensely practical, and in adorning their bodies expected to derive some benefit from what they wore. The virtue of the periwinkles was supposed to pass to the warriors who charmed their heads with them, just as the virtue of the crawfish toe with which Cherokee women have been wont to scratch their babies' hands was supposed to pass to the child thus treated, and give him in after life a powerful grip.[1] It appears to have been believed that the

---

[1] *Nineteenth Annual Report of the Bureau of American Ethnology*, p. 308. (Washington, 1900.)

heads on which the periwinkle shell lay would be as difficult to injure and as quick to avoid attack as the heads of
these elusive sea-snails.   The Irish hero Cuchullin wore
pearls in his hair.   As frail pearls were protected by oyster
shells, they possessed protective virtue for those who
wore them.   In this manner the ancient believers in
magical charms were accustomed to reason.

Palæolithic hunters also wore necklaces of deer's teeth,
and these were fixed round the necks of the dead at
burials.   They were probably charms for swiftness of foot
and endurance.   African natives select for necklaces the
claws of leopards, which are supposed to impart to them
the fierceness and cunning of these dreaded animals, and
they believe that weariness is unknown to those who have
anklets of tortoise legs.   When certain South American
tribes go to battle they charm their bodies with the tusks
of the courageous and irresistible peccary.

Some anthropologists separate magic from religion,
and define the former as a process whereby the service of
the god is enforced, and the latter as a process to secure
by appeal and obedience the goodwill and favours of the
god.   Another theory is that magic was a means of leaguing
oneself with the evil powers as opposed to the religious
adoration of, and ceremonial connection with, the good
powers.   Among the most primitive peoples it is recognized that there is a right and a wrong way of obtaining
supernatural aid.   Individuals, like Faust, might form a
compact with the devil and obtain favours denied to pious
folk, who, however, secured full reward for their piety in
the after-life.

The believer in magic in primitive times had no well-
defined and systematized philosophy of life.   He appears
to have had a vague conception of world-pervading Power
which issued from a hidden and inexhaustible source, and

he endeavoured to "tap" the supply. This Power was manifested in many directions and in many forms. Here it specialized as the quality of strength or endurance, and there as cunning or keen-sightedness. It might also specialize as a curative influence, or be developed as a multiplying and exceedingly fertile agency. This hidden Power was also more potent at one season than another.

As man's mind developed, and he recognized his various deficiencies and needs in a world full of peril, he proceeded to increase his capabilities of acquiring a meed of this universal Power. He feasted on the body of a strong animal to increase his own strength, on a cunning animal to acquire more cunning, and, believing that life was in blood, sought to prolong his life by drinking blood. But he also believed that the virtues of an animal, for instance, were not only in its flesh and blood, but also in every part of its body. He picked up and stuck in his hair the feather of an eagle, believing that the feather would impart to him the keen-sightedness of that efficient bird of prey. His own clothing, his footprints, his saliva, his hair, his nail-parings, and so on, were so closely connected with himself that he could be injured or benefited if any of these things were brought into contact with magical energy. A man could be injured or hampered by injuring or hampering his footprints, by muttering spells over his nail-parings, by mixing his saliva with something infected with the energy of evil. There was another way of "tapping" the universal Power. It could be directed into certain channels by ceremonies, or by uttering potent words. Herein the belief is involved that a god or animal can be mesmerized by force of example and will-power. If it was desired to catch a deer, the hunter performed the part he wished the deer to play; he ran and then fell as he wished the deer to fall;

fishermen acted the part of fish by wriggling as if into a net, or towards baited hooks. Sailors whistled to raise the wind, and ceased whistling when it blew hard enough. Ceremonies were similarly performed to bring on rain in season, and so on.

It appears to have been recognized at an early period that there were two kinds of magic—the one kind brought good luck and the other bad luck. By effecting a ceremonial connection with the source of good-luck magic, mankind prospered. Wells were lucky, and those who visited them wished for what they desired and left some article to ensure the constant supply of desired energy; certain trees were sources of good luck, and certain trees were sources of bad luck. An individual might guard himself against the influence of bad luck by throwing a stone, as when, for instance, he threw one on a burial-cairn, or the spot where a disaster had occurred, or by spitting when an unlucky name was mentioned or an unlucky animal passed by.

Religious beliefs, it is argued, developed when mankind rose to a higher intellectual plane and recognized that the world is subject to intelligent control—that there is a Divinity "which shapes our ends, rough hew them how we will". It must be recognized, however, that when this hypothesis is given practical application it has to be subjected to qualifications. In civilized communities, like those of Babylonia and Egypt, the highest religious conceptions were associated with the crudest magical beliefs and practices. Deities were supposed to exercise control over the supply of "Power", but they might also be influenced by it themselves. In Babylonia the chief god of a pantheon attained his position by becoming possessed of the "Tablets of Fate"; he directed Power into certain channels, but another and older god usually generated

Power. Merodach, for instance, was king of the deities, but he had to co-operate with his father, Ea, the "Great Magician" of the gods. Ea generated Power by utilizing fire and water. There are also traces of the ancient belief that the moon was the supreme fountain-head of Power, creative, curative, fertilizing, and sustaining, and it was individualized as the bi-sexual deity Nannar (Sin), who was the Father and Mother in one. In Scotland and Ireland the moon was never individualized, and the moon remained simply as a magical crucible.

We may separate magic from religion, but this was not done by the early peoples who believed in both. They were fused in the common stock of inherited beliefs and ideas. The elements of religion can be detected in communities where magic is prominent, and the elements of magic can be traced in well-developed religious systems. It would appear that in the Palæolithic Age this confusion existed also. Primitive man was neither logical nor consistent. He embraced and perpetuated contradictory beliefs. Intensely conservative, he continued to cling to old ideas even after he embraced new ideas which were intended to supplant those which had become obsolete.

Religious ideas appear to have had origin when mankind were faced by crises. There came a time in every primitive community when it had to be recognized that magic failed them. A calamity visited charm-protected homes, charmed warriors fell in battle, starvation confronted a family or a tribe which had performed all the ceremonies required for procuring the food-supply. Mankind had to face disaster with faith and courage, and in doing so he faced the unknown. "Religion", says Mr. R. R. Marett, "is the facing of the unknown. It is the courage in it that brings comfort. . . . The courage involved in all live religion normally co-exists with a certain modesty or humility."[1]

This religious feeling necessitated the recognition of supernatural will. It brought to the stricken heart a dim conception of a divine individuality which acted voluntarily and in response to human appeals. The god, or chief of the gods, was not controlled by Power in the same way as mankind were. As this idea developed it was believed that good luck came from the god, the friend of man, and bad luck from the demon, the enemy of man. It was necessary to win the favour of the god and secure protection against the demon.

Magic, on the other hand, gave no recognition to a supreme controlling will. It was rooted in the belief that the world was governed by natural laws. Those who practised it attained some success, but they generally failed because of their ignorance of natural laws. Their ideas about Power were based on the science of their times. They endeavoured to "harness" it as their descendants have "harnessed" the Niagara Falls, and to attract it from a recognized source as a wireless telegraphic instrument attracts vibrating waves of electrical currents. In dealing with the elements they acted vainly, but often cunningly, for rain-making ceremonies, for instance, were never practised except when rain was expected. The wily magicians rarely attempted the impossible. They invariably achieved success, however, when they sought to influence individuals. The primitive folks lived in a world of terror. Many minds were unstable; there were few who had not deranged nervous systems. Magicians achieved far-reaching results by sheer "make-believe". It was no difficult task for them to secure the co-operation of those whom they undertook

---

[1] *The Birth of Humility and Anthropology*, p. 212.

to injure or cure, by hypnotic suggestion. At the present day many of the members of primitive communities are found to be exceedingly prone to hysteria, and these, of course, are excellent subjects for the magician. A savage who is prepared to face a lion or a Maxim gun, may shiver at the glance of a magician who works up excitement by performing a dance or some awesome and mysterious ceremony with purpose to influence the distribution of Power.

When, therefore, we find a particular community with individualized gods or demons, it may be recognized that they have conceived of supernatural Wills which exist apart from magical energy. All acts performed to influence these Wills in the interests of mankind are religious acts. A magical ceremony may thus be performed in a religious spirit. Some of the ancient peoples, however, performed religious acts in dealing with the gods, and practised magic when undertaking to baffle demons. "Those of the gods", said Isocrates, "who are the source to us of good things have the title of Olympians ; those whose department is that of calamities and punishments have harsher titles ; to the first class both private persons and states erect altars and temples; the second is not worshipped either with prayers or burnt sacrifices, but in their case we perform ceremonies of riddance."[1] In India the ritualistic Brahmans performed magical acts to prevent the demons intercepting sacrifices intended for the gods. Egyptian priests practised magic to influence the gods, although they also made offerings to them, and those of Babylonia did likewise. The fusion of religion and magic gave rise to many complex practices and systems of belief.

The Palæolithic folks had their gods or demons, or

[1] Isocrates, *Orations*, V, p. 117.

both, as well as their magical beliefs. Animal-headed supernatural beings were depicted in cave-drawings, with hands
and arms uplifted in the Egyptian attitude of adoration,
or dancing the "dance of fertility" like the "goat-men"
(satyrs) of Babylonia and the animal-headed deities of
the wandering Bushmen. The fertility dance was
"magical"; the dancer was a supernatural being, a religious conception.

In Babylonia the oldest deities are indistinguishable
from demons. Even the benevolent Ea, who instructed
his worshippers how to erect buildings, till the soil,
and frame humanitarian laws, had his demoniac form.
The Palæolithic gods were apparently half demons also,
"destroyers" as well as "preservers", "enemies of man"
as well as "friends of man", "bringers of calamity" as
well as "bestowers of blessings".

In shaping their gods the early people made them
ideals of what they sought most or feared most. The god
of the athlete was a giant big as a tree, who threw great
boulders farther than a human being could fling a pebble;
the goddess of love was a lawless wanton who revelled in
exaggerated love-matches, and her lovers were numerous
as those of Ishtar and her kind. She was worthily depicted as a steatopygous female, who was the ideal of
reproducing motherhood, or as the slim beauty who
charmed impressionable males. The god was a super-
man and the goddess a superwoman.

But the idea of gods was also affected by precon-
ceived beliefs. Worshippers of animals, who believed that
their ancestor was a particular animal, associated them
with their anthropomorphic deities. Ea, the culture-god
of Babylonia, was clad in the skin of the ancestral fish,
whose virtues he had acquired by performing a sacrifice.
The priest of a totemic cult similarly enclosed himself in

7

IVORY FIGURINE AND HEAD—"THE LEAPER"—FROM KNOSSOS

Reproduced from the "Annual of the British School at Athens", by kind permission of the
Committee and of Messrs. Macmillan & Co., Ltd.

the skin of the ancestral animal of his tribe or family, which provided the food-supply, or he wore a mask to represent the combination of the totem and the tribe in himself. Another theory which accounts for animal-headed deities is that they are a link between human gods and animal gods; man progressed from the worship of the "Great Beast" to the "Great Man" by degrees, the process being an evolutionary one. The problem is a difficult one, no doubt. But however we may attempt to solve it we have to deal with the fact that in the Aurignacian Age in southern and western Europe there were animal-headed gods. These therefore did not begin to be either in Egypt or Babylonia. The process, if there was a process, was well advanced ere the Tigro-Euphratean valley was rendered habitable for man, or the proto-Egyptians had begun to sow grain and reap harvests. A prolonged Age of culture had prepared for the builders of future civilization a tangled jungle of beliefs which they were to inherit and perpetuate, along with the decorative designs, &c., invented before and during the Fourth Glacial Epoch. Even the fashions of attire were fixed in the early period. The bell-mouthed skirts, hanging from wasp waists, which have been associated with Cretan civilization, are displayed in Aurignacian cave-paintings. Even the Assyrian goddess's postures are earlier than Assyrian civilization. An ivory carving of Ishtar as an Egyptian goddess has been discovered at Kuyunjik. "The Egyptian character of the figure", writes Mr. L. W. King,[1] "leaps to the eye. . . . In fact, everything about the figure is Egyptian with one exception—the position of the hands. The fact that the goddess holds her breasts at once betrays her Asiatic character. . . . The type, in fact, is characteristic of

[1] *The Journal of Egyptian Archæology*, Vol. I, Part II, pp. 107 *et seq* (1914).

western Asia and extends also into the Ægean." The
type and the pose are also characteristic of the Aurignacian Age; some steatopygous figures carved in ivory
similarly hold their breasts with their hands. "It is still
uncertain", adds Mr. King, "whether the nude goddess
is to be traced to a Babylonian, Anatolian, or Ægean
source." She may have survived from Aurignacian
times among the descendants of scattered Palæolithic
peoples who mingled with later immigrants into Europe
at the dawn of the Neolithic Age. In the next chapter
it will be shown that traces of an ancient goddess cult
survive in various areas, and that certain of these were
peopled by Palæolithic folks in post-glacial times, who met
and fused with the earliest settlers of the Mediterranean
Race.

CHAPTER III

Ancient Peoples of the Goddess Cult

Crete and Palæolithic Man—Traces in Malta, Egypt, Palestine, and Phœnicia—Links between Palæolithic and Neolithic Ages—Azilian Culture in
France, Denmark, and Britain—Evidence of Geology and Folk-tales—Palæolithic Types in Modern England—Coming of Neolithic Man of Mediterranean
Race—The Cretan Snake-goddess, Dove-goddess, and "Lady of Wild Crea-
tures"—The "Mother" of Crete—Identified with Rhea—Primitive Goddesses
as Destroyers—Black Annis of England and Black Kali of India—The Black,
Green, and Yellow Demeter (Ceres)—The Green Neith of Libya—Babylonian
Labartu and Black Scoto-Irish Hag—The "Terrible" Sekhet of Egypt—Tree
and Mountain Worship—Oak and Maypole and "Swain Motes"—Earth
Oaths in Greece and Scotland—The Greek Gæia—Cailleach and Artemis—
Wind Hags—Goddess Cult and Status of Women—Process of Myth-making.

No Palæolithic skulls have been yet discovered in Crete,
although traces have been forthcoming of an early stage
of culture not unlike the Azilian. As the island was at
one time connected with the mainland, it may be that the
bones of the early races and the animals associated with
them lie buried in the Ægean Sea, which, during the
Inter-glacial periods, was a broad plain watered by noble
rivers and covered by dense forests. The extensive land
depression along the North African coast has similarly
hidden from us the secrets of prehistoric Libya.

In Malta, where ancient sites favoured by man were
liable to less disturbance by builders than in Crete, skulls
of the middle Palæolithic periods have been discovered.
There are eleven specimens from Hal Saflieni in the
Valetta museum. Some are of mixed types, but two

have distinct Mousterian characteristics and especially the protruding brow ridges which distinguished the men of the Third Glacial Period.

One skull from Hagiar Kim has negroid traits and appears to link with those found in the Grimaldi cave near Mentone. As has been stated, steatopygous figures have been taken from Neolithic Maltese graves and sanctuaries, a sure indication that the Aurignacian proto-Bushmen were known to the early settlers of the Mediterranean race. Some of these figures are nude and others wear the flounced gown usually called "Cretan", and it is of interest to note here that they are associated among burial relics with perforated axe amulets of polished stone. No Cro-Magnon skulls have been discovered in Malta, but some race quite as tall must have mingled there with the early Neolithic folk. A male skeleton found at Santa Verna measures 5 feet 9 inches in length. "The man was of a noble type," writes an excavator; "he must have stood 6 feet high, his skull is massive and shapely, the jaws and teeth are even and regular, and the limbs powerful."[1] The Mediterranean Neolithic man was of slight build and medium stature.

The earliest Cretans were of the Mediterranean racial type, but among them were alien broad-heads. Ere the Neolithic folks settled on the island they came into contact, apparently, with mountaineers from the north, or descendants of Palæolithic races. Steatopygous figurines have been found in Cretan Neolithic strata.

In Egypt there was no hiatus between the Palæolithic and Neolithic Ages. Not only have steatopygous figurines been found in pre-Dynastic Egyptian and Nubian graves, but also flints which show that the artifacts of the later period were developed from those of the earlier. A

---

[1] *Malta and the Mediterranean Race*, R. N. Bradley, pp. 72 *et seq.*

reference to the "Smiting of the Troglodytes" on the Palermo stone of the First Dynasty may refer to descendants of the Palæolithic cave-dwellers.

Palestine, the high road from Egypt into eastern Europe, has yielded numerous relics of the early stages of culture. Chellean and Acheulian flints "have been picked up on the maritime plain, in yet greater numbers on the plateau south of Jerusalem, and in considerable quantities in the region to the south of Amman, east of Jordan. Some have also been discovered far to the south, in the region of Petra." Professor Macalister, from whom we quote, notes that "Palæolithic man in Palestine missed, however, the higher developments attained by his brother in France". Mousterian cave-settlements in Phœnicia have yielded characteristic flints and bone instruments, including needles. Dr. Max Blanckenhorn has assigned the date 10,000 B.C. to the earliest Neolithic settlement in this region. Sherds of pottery have been discovered in the Phœnician cave of Harajel "side by side with the bones of extinct fauna, especially the woolly rhinoceros". In the natural Gezer caves of a later age finds have been made of "rude pottery, ornamented with coarse moulding or roughly painted red lines; flint flakes, knives and scrapers; millstones; rounded stone pebbles, that could be used for a variety of purposes—hearth stones; heating stones; missiles; polishers, &c.", and "an amulet or two of bone or slate, perforated for suspension".[1]

In France the most remarkable link between the Palæolithic and later ages is formed by the Cro-Magnon racial type which first appeared in the Dordogne valley in the Aurignacian Period, before the Fourth Glacial Epoch. The "most curious and significant trait" of these people

[1] *A Histor of Civilization in Palestine*, pp. 9 *et seq.*

is that they have long heads and broad faces: that is, they have skulls with Mediterranean characteristics and faces which resemble those of the broad-headed Armenoids of the mountains. Summarizing the evidence of Dr. Collignon regarding the present-day inhabitants of the Dordogne valley, Professor Ripley says: "The people we have described above agree in physical characteristics with but one other type of men known to anthropologists. This is the celebrated Cro-Magnon race, long ago identified by archæologists as having inhabited the south-west of Europe in prehistoric times." Varieties of the type have occurred owing to the proximity of other races, but it is still common and easily detected. Individuals with the Cro-Magnon skull and "disharmonic face" are also found among present-day Berbers.[1] Skeletons of Cro-Magnon man of the Palæolithic Period have been found as far north as Belgium. Dr. Schliz finds traces at the present time of Cro-Magnon man throughout western Europe, and believes that even the Neanderthal-Spy (Mousterian) type has also left a slight but recognizable impress.[2] The high average stature and weight of the Scottish people, which has long puzzled ethnologists, may be due to a strong Palæolithic intermixture in early Neolithic times. The evidence obtained from the Glasgow graveyard, referred to in the Introduction, is suggestive in this connection.

Interesting evidence has been forthcoming at Mas d'Azil, in France, of the transition period between the late Palæolithic and early Neolithic culture. This stage of culture is called Azilian. It was of long continuance. Artifacts called "Azilian" found in Scotland may have been separated by a considerable period of time from those

---

[1] *The Races of Europe*, pp. 172 *et seq.*
[2] *Archiv für Anthropologie*, Band 35, Ss. 239 *et seq.*

discovered at Mas d'Azil. Cro-Magnon and Magdalenian men lived through and survived the Fourth Glacial Epoch. Then during the subsequent period of minor oscillations of climate the reindeer and other animals of the chase migrated northwards. These were followed, it would appear, by the huntsmen, a proportion of whom, however, remained behind and adopted new habits of life. As the Cro-Magnon folks of the Dordogne valley had domesticated animals, they no doubt found the struggle for existence in the homeland less arduous than their contemporaries, the small men of Magdalenian culture, who were hunters and fishermen and naught else.

Subsequent to the Fourth Glacial Period there was a re-elevation of land, and the Magdalenian wanderers were able to walk over the bed of the English Channel. The reindeer entered the British Isles also and survived in Scotland until the Middle Ages. A deer-horn implement, carved with a scene of the chase, which was picked up on the slopes of Ben Wyvis, was shown to the writer shortly after it was discovered. It lay for several years in the vestibule of a Dingwall hotel, but unfortunately has gone amissing. It appears to have been a relic of Palæolithic culture of the late period which must be assigned to it in northern Highlands. The carving had Magdalenian characteristics.

Professor James Geikie shows that after the Fourth Glacial Epoch genial conditions prevailed in Scotland. This is the period of the great forests, relics of which are embedded in peat mosses. He terms it " Lower Forestian ". A cold period followed and glaciers once again descended from the mountains, and some of these were not melted before they touched the sea. The forests decayed and the peat formed above the great trees which perished as each succeeding winter grew colder and each succeeding summer shorter and wetter. Meanwhile the land sunk and the sea washed round the 45 to 50 feet beaches. Another Inter-glacial Period followed, during which the forests again flourished. It constitutes Geikie's "Upper Forestian" Epoch. The last, or sixth, Glacial Period followed, with its small and local glaciers, during which the land sunk again, and the later peat beds covered great fallen trees. Thereafter the present Age was inaugurated by the raising of the land to more or less its present level with a gradual improvement of the climate.

Traces of man in the Azilian stage of culture have been found in Scotland.[1] The MacArthur cave, which overlooks Oban, was inhabited when the sea was 30 feet above its present level, and the Highland troglodytes —the earliest visitors—who were hunters and fishermen, left behind bone and horn implements, including the Azilian harpoon invented during the Magdalenian stage of culture of the Fourth Glacial Epoch in southern France. At Stirling harpoons of the same type were utilized at a period when whales spouted not far from the castle rock. Of late an interesting cave-dwelling, excavated at Rosemarkie in the Black Isle, has yielded a variety of bone and other implements, and human remains. A large fire-place, with upright smoke-blackened stones and surrounded by a cobbled floor, was laid bare. The cave is situated about 15 feet above the present sea-level.

Associated with these caves and other early settlements, chiefly on the ridges of the old coast-lines, are heaps of shells. These have been found as far north as Caithness.[2]

Those early settlers, of the "river-bed" race, are

[1] For earlier traces of Palæolithic man see *The Stone Ages in North Britain and Ireland*, by Rev. Frederick Smith (London & Glasgow, 1909). Dr. A. H. Keane calls the author the "Boucher de Perthes of Scotland".

[2] Huxley & Laing's *Prehistoric Remains in Caithness* (London, 1886).

believed to be of the same mixed stock, surviving from Palæolithic times, as the famous "beach-combers" of the Danish "kitchen middens". When the earliest Mediterranean racial pioneers of the Neolithic Age entered these islands, they met and mingled with the troglodytes who are referred to in Gaelic folk-tales.[1]

"It may quite well be", says Professor James Geikie, "that Neolithic man appeared in southern Europe before Palæolithic man had vanished from the Pyrenean region, and the two races may possibly have here come into contact." Most archæologists have abandoned the old hiatus theory. Dr. Robert Munro argues, after reviewing the latest evidence, that in Europe there was "no break in the continuity of human occupation from late Palæolithic to Neolithic times", and accepts Dr. Keith's view that "Palæolithic blood is as rife in the British people of to-day as in those of the European continent".[2] Dr. Keith finds everywhere in England numerous representatives of the "river-bed" Palæolithic folks.

The Neolithic folks, who came into contact with the remnants of the Palæolithic races in various parts of Europe, were representatives of the widespread Mediterranean or Brown Race. They were men of medium stature, with long heads and high but narrow foreheads, refined faces, dark eyes and hair, and slim bodies. Their brunette complexions suggest that their area of characterization was on the North African coast. Some ethnologists incline to the view that the homeland of this stock was Somaliland, the Punt of the Egyptian records, which, like Arabia, favoured the production of a larger population than it

---

[1] A cave-dweller in a Fingalian story is called Ciofach Mac a' Ghoill ("Ciofach, son of the stranger"). Another version refers to him as Ciuthach (pronounce "Kew'-ach"). Dealing with the legend of the Ciuthach, Professor W. J. Watson considers that he was a hero "of a different race from the Gael" (*Celtic Review*, January, 1914).

[2] *Prehistoric Britain*, p. 234. (London, 1914.)

was capable of sustaining permanently. In Egypt they adopted the agricultural mode of life long before the dawn of history. Periodic folk-waves, drifting westward and east, entered Europe across the Straits of Gibraltar and through Palestine and Asia Minor by the coast-line route. In the process of time they overspread southern, central, and western Europe, and entered the British Isles. Probably they crossed over to Ireland from Scotland. Their burial customs indicate that their religious beliefs were well developed prior to the period of "folk-wandering". The Neolithic graves in Europe and Africa are constructed on similar lines, and the great majority of the skeletons they contain are remarkable for their uniformity of type. "So striking", writes Professor Elliot Smith, "is the family likeness between the early Neolithic peoples of the British Isles and the Mediterranean and the bulk of the population, both ancient and modern, of Egypt and East Africa, that the description of the bones of an Early Briton of that remote epoch might apply in all essential details to an inhabitant of Somaliland."[1]

It is not necessary to assume that they waged a war of extermination against the Palæolithic huntsmen and fishermen of Europe, so as to account for their ultimate superiority of numbers. Their pastoral and agricultural mode of life made it possible for them to live in larger communities and prosper in smaller areas than the Palæolithic huntsman, whose activities had necessarily to extend over wide stretches of country. At any rate, they never overcame the Dordogne valley men of Cro-Magnon type. It is possible that in districts in western Europe, as well as in the British Isles, the Neolithic and late Palæolithic peoples formed mixed communities. Dr. Robert Munro

[1] *The Ancient Egyptians*, p. 58.

suggests that the latter became the servants and "clod-hoppers" of the agriculturists.

The Neolithic, like the late Palæolithic peoples, were goddess - worshippers. They believed that the "Great Mother" had given origin to the world, the gods, the demons, and the races of mankind. In the various countries in which early Neolithic civilization was developed traces still survive of this early belief, and it will be found that the conception of the "Great Mother" is as varied as were the degrees of culture attained by the separated communities of common stock. Primitive ideas appear to have persisted longer in isolated districts where ethnic disturbances were least frequent and habits of life less liable to undergo change.

In Crete there were three outstanding forms of the mother-goddess—the snake-goddess, the dove-goddess, and the "lady of wild creatures". These may have been different forms of an original deity, or representative of a group composed of mother and daughters. As in Egypt and Babylonia, it is found that the one goddess tends to absorb the attributes of the other. It is possible that the Mother was supposed to manifest herself in different forms, at different seasons, and in different districts, and that one of the results of local ritualistic development was to emphasize a particular form of the original deity. But there can be no doubt that the conception of the Mother was an essential part of the Cretan faith.

The great goddess was depicted wearing a flounced gown suspended from her slim waist, round which a girdle is clasped (Chapter VI). The upper part of the body is bare, and she has enormous breasts. Sometimes she stands on a mountain top, guarded by two great lions, and sometimes she is seated beside trees or plants. In addition

(c 808)

to the lions, her wild animals include the wild goat, the
horned sheep, the bull, the red deer, the snake, and the
dove; and among the symbols associated with her are
the horns of the bull, the double axe, the sacred pillar,
the moon crescent, and a staff or wand. She was apparently a goddess of death, battle, fertility, and the chase.
Offerings were made to her in a mountain-cave she was
supposed to inhabit.

It must be recognized at the outset that this ancient
deity, like others of her kind, was not necessarily an
attractive personality. Our conception of her must not
be based solely on Greek sculpture, for instance. She is
believed to be identical with Rhea, the mother of Vesta,
Demeter, Hera, Hades, Poseidon, and Zeus, and that
deity was depicted by Phidias as a benign mother of great
dignity and tenderness and beauty. The original mother
was worshipped and propitiated because she was feared.
She was the Fate who measured the lives of men, who
sent disasters as well as blessings, and was associated with
lions and snakes as well as doves and deer. Withal, she
was a voluptuous wanton. Like the Babylonian Ishtar,
who was the lover of Gilgamish in one hour and his
unrelenting enemy in the next, she was fickle and change-
able as the wind and the seasons. She gloried with
callous heart in her power to destroy, and was untouched
by tender emotions for mankind, when—

Looking over wasted lands,

Blight and famine, plague and earthquake, roaring deeps and fiery
    sands,
Clanging fights, and flaming towns, and sinking ships and praying
    hands.

Greek mythology, in which the beliefs of various ethnic
elements were fused, and savage traditions were ultimately
transformed by philosophic speculations, survives to us

mainly as the product of a cultured Age. But the poets and artists did not divest it wholly of its primitive traits. It is now generally recognized that the savagery of Cronus is not mere symbolism, or the wrath of Artemis, who required the sacrifice of a beautiful maiden, simply a myth based on natural phenomena and not a reflection of " old unhappy far-off things "—a reminiscence of primitive rites performed to propitiate a bloodthirsty deity.

In those parts of ancient Europe in which ancient rites were perpetuated till a comparatively late period the worship of pagan deities was a gloomy memory. The Irish Cromm Cruaich put prostrated hosts under " deadly disgrace " before his golden image—

> To him without glory
> They would kill their piteous, wretched offspring,
> With much wailing and peril,
> To pour their blood around Cromm Cruaich.

> Milk and corn
> They would ask from him speedily
> In return for one-third of their healthy issue:
> Great was the horror and the scare of him.[1]

The mother-goddess of ancient Europe was similarly remembered as a devourer of children. She survives in English folk-lore as a fierce demon. In Leicestershire she is Black Annis, who is associated with the Easter " hare hunt ", and has a " cat Anna " form. The earliest reference to her appears in the following extract from an eighteenth-century title-deed: " All that close or parcel of land commonly called or known by the name ' Black Anny's Bower Close '."

It must not be assumed, however, that Black Annis was a comparatively recent importation. She appears to

[1] *Celtic Myth and Legend*, p. 39.

be of as great antiquity as the customs associated with her name. It is impossible to limit the age of these and other customs and beliefs which survive to the present day, not only in rural districts, but even in cities and among the cultured classes, after so many centuries of Christian teaching. If they have persisted so long, in spite of the combined influences of Church, printing-press, and school, like rank weeds among flowers, for how long a period, it may be asked, did they flourish before they were condemned and shown to be unworthy of civilized communities? There can be little doubt that some have been inherited from the earliest settlers in these islands, who brought from the Continent in one of the Inter-glacial Epochs, and again in the Late Stone Age, the prototypes of the charms like the lucky pigs which now dangle from watch-chains and the mascots that figure on motor-cars and aeroplanes as they once figured on coracles, and boats hollowed from trunks of trees.

It is not to be marvelled at that the ancient goddess should be remembered in Leicester district. The city's name is fragrant with ancient memories. It was called after Llyr, the British sea-god,[1] who became the King Lear of the legend on which one of Shakespeare's great dramas was based. "He (King Lear) it was", wrote Geoffrey of Monmouth in the twelfth century, "that builded the city on the River Soar, that in the British is called Kaerleir, but in the Saxon Leicester (Leir-chester)."[2]

Black Annis Bower was a cave upon the Dane Hills,[3] which, during the past century, became filled up with

---

[1] *Celtic Myth and Legend*, pp. 252 *et seq.*

[2] "Kaer" and "Chester" signify cities. London was "Kaer-lud", called after the god Lud, whose name lingers also in "Ludgate".

[3] It is suggested that "Dane" is a corruption of the Celtic "Danann".

earth.   Over the cave grew an oak-tree, in the branches
of which the hag was wont to conceal herself so that she
might pounce out unawares and seize human victims,
especially children.   A local poet has immortalized the
hag and her cave:

> An oak, the pride of all the mossy dell,
> Spreads its broad arms above the stony cell;
> And many a bush, with hostile thorns arrayed,
> Forbids the secret cavern to invade.

Here Black Annis "held her solitary reign, the dread and
wonder of the neighbouring plain".   Shepherds attributed
to her the loss of lambs, and mothers their loss of children.
According to a local writer, the children of a past generation "who went to run on Dane Hills were assured that
Black Anna lay in wait there to snatch them away to her
'bower'."

> "Oft the gaunt maid the frantic mother cursed",

sang the poet, who has left the following interesting
description of the hag:—

> 'T is said the soul of mortal man recoiled
> To view Black Annis' eye, so fierce and wild.
> Vast talons, foul with human flesh, there grew
> In place of hands, and features livid blue
> Glar'd in her visage; whilst the obscene waist
> Warm skins of human victims close embraced.[1]

She appears to be identical with the "Yellow Muilearteach" of Gaelic legend:

> Her face was blue black of the lustre of coal,
> And her bone-tufted tooth was like red rust.
> In her head was one deep pool-like eye
> Swifter than a star in a winter sky.[2]

[1] *County Folk-lore* (Leicestershire and Rutland), by C. J. Billson, Vol. I., London,
1895 (Folk-lore Society's Publications).
[2] Campbell's *West Highland Tales*, Vol. III, p. 138.

Another description of her runs:

> The name of the dauntless spectre
> Was the bald-red, white-maned Muilearteach.
> Her face was dark-grey of the hue of coals,
> The teeth of her jaw were slanting red;
> There was one flabby eye in her head
> That quicker moved than lure pursuing mackerel.
> Her head bristled dark and grey,
> Like scrubwood before hoar-frost.

But the Scoto-Irish hag did not wear "warm skins of human victims".

> Oscar caught
> The embroidered skirt that was round her body;
> They took the apple from the wretch.

She had also a "girdle" like Aphrodite.[1] In India there is a ferocious goddess, who resembles Annis of Leicester. This is Black Kali. She is usually depicted dancing the "dance of fertility", like the Aurignacian and Bushman deities. Modern artists have given her normal eyes, but have retained also the primitive forehead eye. She wears a necklace of human or giant heads, and from her girdle dangle the hands and skins of victims. It would appear that Kali, whose body was smeared with the sacrificial blood, was a form of the earth-goddess; her harvest form was Jagadgauri, the yellow woman; while as the love and fertility deity she was the beautiful Lakshmi or Sri, she was Durga as the goddess of war.[2] The Greek goddess Demeter was black at Phigalia (Chapter VIII), but the ancient black statue of her was only a memory in the days of Pausanias. No doubt the rites associated with her worship were abandoned when "old times had gone and manners changed". Still the memory of Black Demeter

---

[1] *Waifs and Strays of Celtic Tradition*, Vol. IV, pp. 142 *et seq.* (London, 1891).
[2] *Indian Myth and Legend*, pp. xl. and 149–50.

survived as the mother of Persephone, the young corn-goddess. The "Green Demeter" was the green corn, and the "yellow Demeter" the ripened harvest grain. As the Roman Ceres her name is perpetuated in cereals—the gifts of the goddess.[1]

The Libyan goddess Neith was depicted with a green face. Her symbols included the "shuttle" or thunder-bolt, the bow and arrows of deities of fertility, lightning, rain, and war. In Babylonia, where the demoniac forms of gods and goddesses were perpetuated in metrical charms and incantations, the "Labartu" (Sumerian "Dimme") was a female demon. She resembled the English Annis and the Scoto-Irish Muilearteach. This primitive goddess haunted mountain and marsh, and devoured stray children who were not protected against her by wearing magical charms attached to neck-cords. The Egyptian Sekhet-Hathor was similarly a destroyer. In her primitive lion-headed Sekhet form, crowned with the solar disk and uræus serpent, she was sometimes depicted with a naked dagger grasped tightly in her right hand, and sometimes with a magic wand. Isis-Hathor, who personified all the goddesses of Egypt in late times, is referred to significantly in a Philae text as follows:—

> Kindly is she as Bast (the cat-goddess)
> Terrible is she as Sekhet.[2]

The association of the Cretan mother-goddess with trees and mountains will be dealt with more intimately in a later chapter. Here, however, it is of interest to note that the demoniac English deity, Black Annis, was a tree as well as a cave deity. Offerings of children were

---

[1] *Golden Bough* ("Spirits of the Corn and the Wild"), Vol. I, pp. 35 *et seq.* (third edition).

[2] *Religion of the Ancient Egyptians*, A. Wiedemann, p. 138 (London, 1897).

probably made to her in the archæological Hunting Period, as they were to the Irish Cromm Cruaich in the Agricultural Period in return for milk and corn. The oak in Leicestershire was reverenced as the habitation of the goddess. In Charnwood Forest the "copt oak" was a "trysting-place in olden time". It was long "a place of assembly. . . . Swain motes (courts for the common people) were held for regulation of rights and claims on the forest." In the Highlands Gaelic-speaking people who attend a court at the present day refer to it as a "mote". Trials were conducted at these assemblies, and it is not surprising to find that near the Leicestershire "swain's hill" is situated "Hangman's Stone". "Royal Oak Day" (May 29th) is the "May Day" for Leicestershire children.

In early times the maypole, usually made of oak, was the symbol of authority and justice, as well as of fertility. "The column of May", suggests one writer on the subject, "was the great standard of justice in the Ey Commons, or Fields of May. Here it was that the people, if they saw cause, deposed or punished their governors, their barons, or their kings." When the maypole was brought from the forest the youths and maidens joined in singing songs, of which the chorus was: "We have brought the Summer home".[1] Scrimmages took place between youths who were attired to represent winter and spring. A seventeenth-century writer says that "a company of yonkers, on May-day morning, before day, went into the country to fetch home a maypole with drumme and trumpet, whereat the neighbouring inhabitants were affrighted, supposing some enemies had landed to sack them. The pole being thus brought home and set up, they began to drink healths about it till they could not

[1] Quoted in *County Folk-lore*, Vol. I, pp. 29 *et seq*.

stand so steady as the pole did."[1] The maypole customs and the "motes" held under oak-trees are evidently relics of tree-worship. Probably the human representative of the Cretan goddess, seated below her tree, dispensed justice and ushered in the season of fertility and growth, like the May Queen.

In Scotland, where there are "motes" also, it is found that certain "church lands" were anciently associated with magical and religious ceremonies.[2] Twisting paths leading to wells and hillocks remain as "rights of way". It is of interest to find, too, that the habit of swearing by the earth was also prevalent. In a Gaelic story it is related that when the heroes formed a compact to avenge insults and injuries suffered by one of their number they "lifted a little piece of earth and shouted 'Vengeance'". They thus effected a ceremonial connection with the Earth Mother. In Greece "the most current formula of the public oath, when a treaty was to be ratified or an alliance cemented, was", writes Dr. Farnell, "the invocation of Zeus, Helios, and Ge (the Earth Mother). And doubtless", he adds, "one of the earliest forms of oath taken was some kind of primitive communion, whereby both parties place themselves in sacred contact with some divine force."[3]

Ge or Gaia was a vague and ancient deity who was sometimes identified with the "earth snake". She was the mother of Titans, Cyclopes, and Hecatoncheires. Similarly the Scoto-Irish hag known as "Cailleach" (old wife), "Grey Eyebrows", "Muilearteach", &c., was

---

[1] *Brand's Antiquities*, Vol. I, pp. 238 *et seq.*

[2] According to Cæsar, the Druids of Gaul held sessions at consecrated places of meeting which, from other sources, we learn were called *nemeta*. In old Irish the term appears as *nemed*, and in modern Scottish Gaelic it is *neimhidh*, which signifies "church land". The English rendering is *Navity* or *Nevity*.—Professor W. J. Watson in *Celtic Review* (1915), Vol. X, pp. 263 *et seq.*

[3] *Cults of the Greek States*, Vol. III, p. 5.

mother of the giants (Fomorians) who had monstrous forms, and against whom gods and mortals waged war. A black lamb was offered to Gaia. The Cailleach was apparently offered the "black boar", or the "green boar", slain by the heroes of folk-tales.

As the Earth Mother was sworn by, she must have been conceived of as an active force, capable of assuming concrete form. Rhea, Demeter, Artemis, and other deities were probably forms or manifestations of her at various seasons.

The Cailleach, with blue - black face and roaring mouth, appears to have been recognized in her Muil-earteach form as the spirit of tempest on sea and land. As the mountain-spirit of the Hunting Period she moved restlessly among the hills, followed by herds of wild animals, including deer, goats, and swine. In her right hand she grasped a "hammer", or "magic wand", like the gigantic Cretan goddess on her lion-supported mountain-peak. When standing-stones were struck with the "magic wand", they were immediately transformed into giant warriors, fully armed and ready for battle. After throwing away this, her symbol of fertility and authority, the Cailleach herself was transformed into a standing-stone "looking over the sea". She was also associated with rivers and lakes and overflowing wells.

This hag, who, according to one folk-tale, "existed from the long eternity of the world", was not only the mother of giants but also the ancestress of the various tribes of mankind. In Ireland she appears to have been the earlier Danu, the mother of the Danann gods and people, and Anu, the mountain-hag associated with "the Paps of Anu". As the "Old Woman of Beare" she had "seven periods of youth one after another", writes Professor Kuno Meyer, "so that every man who had lived with her came to die of old age, and her grandsons and great-grandsons were tribes and races".[1] In several stories she appears before a hero as a repulsive hag and suddenly transforms herself into a beautiful girl.

As the patroness of wild animals the Cailleach resembles Artemis, whom Browning, like certain of the Greek poets, idealized and consequently robbed of her primitive savage character.

> I shed in Hell o'er my pale people peace,
> On Earth, I, caring for the creatures, guard
> Each pregnant yellow wolf and foxbitch sleek
> And every feathered mother's callow brood,
> And all that love green haunts and loneliness.

Artemis occasionally appeared in the form of a hare, a hind, or a bear. As a goddess of the chase she might be depicted seated on the back of a stag or standing with bow in hand beside a hill surmounted by a boar's head. Human sacrifices appear to have been offered to her, and myths were formed in the process of time to justify the substitution of wild animals for girls and lads. Spartan boys were flogged and sprinkled with blood at rites connected with Artemis worship. As a wind-goddess she demanded the sacrifice of Agamemnon's daughter when the fleet assembled at Aulis in Bœotia ready to sail against Troy. The Scoto-Irish Cailleach had similarly control over the winds, as had also the hags who " brewed breezes" on Jochgrimm mountain in Tyrol. Artemis haunted the mountains Erymanthus and Taygetus and the banks of the River Eurotas in Laconia. It was in Crete that she was fabled to have slain the giant Orion because he loved her.

It will be seen that the idea of the mother-goddess

[1] *Ancient Irish Poetry*, p. 88.

prevailed in ancient times from India to Ireland and
throughout Egypt. Although she was closely associated
with the Mediterranean or Brown Race, which included
the Neolithic Europeans, the proto-Egyptians, the Sumerians, Southern Persians, and Aryo-Indians, she was
also a conspicuous figure in the Late Palæolithic Period.
Long before the ideal types of her had evolved in Greece,
she was a terror-inspiring conception among the common
people. In isolated areas, which were untouched by
Greek idealism, her memory was perpetuated as a repulsive and blood-thirsty hag who terrorized the people
and demanded annual dues of human and animal victims.
She was associated with the worship of stones, trees, wild
animals, wells and rivers, mountains and mounds. As
an earth-goddess she was a deity of death, destruction,
fertility, and growth; hunters preyed on her flocks and
had accordingly to propitiate her; pastoralists made
offerings to her to secure the supply of grass, and the
agricultural peoples recognized her as the mother of the
corn-spirits, male and female. She reflected the culture
of various stages of human development, and she assumed
the character of the various communities who developed
the ritual of her worship; she also mirrored the natural
phenomena of the different countries in which she received recognition. Yet she was never wholly divested
of her primitive traits. As in Aurignacian times, she
remained as the Mother who was the ancestress of all and
the source of good and evil, or luck and misfortune. In
Crete she was well developed before the earliest island
settlers began to carve her images on gems and seals or
depict them in frescoes. She symbolized the island and
its social life and organization. The Cretans, according
to Plutarch, spoke of Crete as their motherland and not
their fatherland.

As the mother-goddess in her various forms reflected the habits of life and the degree of civilization attained by her worshippers, it is possible also that the prominence given to the female principle in religious life caused women to be held in higher esteem than among the peoples of the god cult.   Mr. J. R. Hall, in his *Ancient History in the Far East*, referring to the social status of the women in Crete, says that "it is certain they must have lived on a footing of greater equality with men than in any other ancient civilization. . . . We see in the frescoes of Knossos conclusive indications of an open and free association of men and women, corresponding to our idea of 'Society', at the Minoan Court, unparalleled till our own day." Cæsar remarked on the matriarchal conditions which prevailed in certain parts of ancient Britain.   Among the Scottish Picts descent was reckoned by the female line, as in the royal families of Egypt and southern European states. It is possible that in Aurignacian times the women of the tribes similarly exercised considerable influence. They appear to have been prominent in the performance of magical and religious rites.   Indeed, it is the opinion of some anthropologists, like Bachofen, that women exercised a greater influence than men in developing primitive religious ideas.   "Wherever", he comments "gynæcocracy meets us, the mystery of religion is bound up with it, and lends to motherhood an incorporation of some divinity." [1]   The evidence gleaned from certain folktales suggests that women trained young huntsmen and warriors to perform feats of strength and skill.   When the Irish Cuchullin visited Alban, to complete his military education, he was tested by an Amazon.   Brynhild, of Iceland fame, like Brunhild of the *Nibelungenlied*, overcame many warrriors ere she was won.

[1] *Das Mutterrecht*, p. xv.

The comparative evidence dealt with in this chapter emphasizes the fact that in dealing with the Cretan and pre-Hellenic deities account must be taken of the primitive modes of thought which are traceable in the accumulated myths and legends attached to them. In the process of myth-making many influences were at work. Historical happenings had to be dealt with as well as the experiences of everyday life in a new environment. The growth of civilization changed the character of religious beliefs also. When old savage practices were abandoned, myths were framed to justify innovations, as when, for instance, the innocent girl Iphigenia was to be sacrificed to Artemis but was substituted by a stag. It was related that the goddess carried her off in a cloud and decided that she should become a priestess. The practice of offering up strangers in sacrifice obtained probably when a community began to abhor the idea of offering up one of its own members.

In the next chapter it will be shown how the study of ancient myths has led to the discovery of those traces of ancient civilization in Crete and the Ægean which has made it possible to reconstruct two thousand years of pre-Hellenic civilization.

CHAPTER IV

History in Myth and Legend— Schliemann's Discoveries

The Hellenes and Pelasgians—Evidence of Folk-legends—Thucydides on Cretan Origin of Ægean Civilization—Solar-myth Theories—Achilles and Odysseus as Sun-gods—The "Aryans" and the *Iliad*—Trojan War and Vedic Myths—Schliemann's Faith in Tradition—Story of his Life—Resolution in Boyhood to excavate Troy—How he became a Merchant Prince—Troy located at Hissarlik—Early Discoveries—First Treasure Hoard—Trouble with Turkish Officials—Excavations in Greece—Work at Tiryns—The Cyclopean Walls—Legends of Giant and Fairy Artisans—Hittite Method of Building—Excavations at Mycenæ—The Lion Gate—Ramsay's Finds in Phrygia—The Rich Mycenæan Graves—"Agamemnon's Tomb"—A Famous Telegram—Later Excavations—Schliemann's Scheme to explore in Crete—Death of the Famous Excavator.

THE knowledge possessed by European scholars a generation ago regarding pre-Hellenic civilization was of slight and doubtful character. Histories of Greece devoted small space to the Heroic Age. These usually began by stating that Greece was so called by the Romans, that it had been anciently known as Hellas and embraced several States—Attica, Arcadia, Achæa, Bœotia, &c.—and that the term Hellas had wider significance than was attached to it in modern times, having been used to denote the country of the Hellenes wherever they might happen to be settled, so that Cyrene in North Africa and Miletus in Asia Minor, for instance, were as essentially parts of Hellas as Arcadia or Bœotia. It was also recognized that the Hellenes were not the earliest inhabitants

73

of Greece proper. Before these invaders entered into possession of the country it had been divided between various "barbarous tribes", including the Pelasgi and their congeners the Caucones and Leleges. Thirlwall, among others, expressed the view "that the name Pelasgians was a general one, like that of Saxons, Franks, or Alemanni, and that each of the Pelasgian tribes had also one peculiar to itself". The Hellenes did not exterminate the aborigines, but constituted a military aristocracy. Aristotle was quoted to show that their original seat was near Dodona, in Epirus, and that they first appeared in Thessaly about 1384 B.C. It was believed that the Hellenic conquerors laid the foundation of Greek civilization.

Grote, on the other hand, declined to accept the theory that the Pelasgians constituted the sole indigenous element in Greece. "In going through historical Greece", he said, "we are compelled to accept the Hellenic aggregate with its constituent elements as a primary fact to start from. . . . By what circumstances, or out of what pre-existing elements, the aggregate was brought together and modified, we find no evidence entitled to credit. There are, indeed, various names affirmed to designate the ante-Hellenic inhabitants of many parts of Greece—the Pelasgi, the Leleges, the Kuretes, the Kaukones, the Aones, the Temmikes, the Hyantes, the Telchines, the Bœotian Thracians, the Teleboæ, the Ephyri, the Phlegyæ, &c. These are names belonging to legendary, not to historical Greece—extracted out of a variety of conflicting legends by the logographers and subsequent historians, who strung together out of them a supposed history of the past, at a time when the conditions of historical evidence were very little understood. That these names designated real nations may be true but here our know-

ledge ends.   We have no well-informed witness to tell
us of their times, their limits of residence, their acts, or
their character; nor do we know how far they are identical with or diverse from the historical Hellenes, whom
we are warranted in calling, not the first inhabitants of
the country, but the first known to us upon any tolerable
evidence."   The attitude assumed by this cautious his-
torian regarding the Pelasgians is still defensible in these
days when different archæologists apply the term in
different ways, one holding, for instance, that the Pelasgians were the Ægeans of Mediterranean race, and another
that they were a late "wave" of pre-Hellenic conquerors.
Grote insisted that all Herodotus knew about the Pelasgians was that they occupied a few scattered and inconsiderable townships in historical Greece and spoke a
barbarous language.[1]   He pointed out, however, that
our term "barbarian" does not express the same idea as
the Hellenic word, "which involved associations of re-
pugnance", although derived from it.   "The Greeks",
he explained, "spoke indiscriminately of the extra-Hel-
lenic world with all its inhabitants whatever might be the
gentleness of their character and whatever might be their
degree of civilization".   All non-Hellenes were, as the
Chinese put it, "foreign devils".

Historians who were more inclined than Grote to
attach weight to folk-traditions were yet unable to gather
much from those of the Hellenes regarding their origin,
except that they professed to have come from "the East"
and claimed to be descendants of an eponymous ancestor
called Hellen.   The story of this patriarch and his family
is given in the Hesiodic version of the World's Ages myth.
When Zeus resolved to destroy the wicked Bronze Race
by sending a great flood, he spared Deucalion and his wife

[1] *History of Greece*, Vol. II, pp. 350 *et seq.*

Pyrrha, who took refuge in an ark. According to one tradition, this couple, on praying to Zeus, were enabled to repeople the devastated world by throwing over their shoulders stones which were transformed into human beings. These were "the Stone Folk". Another tradition made Deucalion the ancestor of the whole Greek race, through his son Hellen, who had three children, named Dorus and Æolus, the ancestors of the Dorians and Æolians, and Xuthus, whose sons Achæus and Ion, were the progenitors of the Achæans and Ionians.

The period that elapsed between the early settlement of the Hellenes and the siege of Troy was called the Heroic Age, after the fourth Hesiodic Age of the World, or the Homeric Age, during which the civilization depicted in those great epics the *Iliad* and the *Odyssey* had full development.

Historians parted company when they came to deal with the prehistoric period. Thirlwall was inclined to sift historical matter from the legends. Grote, however, was frankly sceptical. "That which I note as Terra Incognita", he said, "is in his (Thirlwall's) view a land which may be known up to a certain point, but the map which he draws of it contains so few ascertained places as to differ very little from absolute vacuity."[1] Dealing with the Trojan war, he declared that, "though literally believed, reverentially cherished, and numbered among the gigantic phenomena of the past by the Grecian public, it is in the eyes of modern enquiry essentially a legend and nothing more". His answer to the question as to whether the war ever took place was: "As the possibility of it cannot be denied, so neither can the reality of it be affirmed".[2] We who are "wise after the event" may rail at Grote, but it must be remembered that he wrote at

---

[1] *History of Greece*, Vol. II, p. 358.   [2] *Ibid.*, Vol. I, pp. 434-5.

a time when little was known regarding ancient Egypt, Babylonia, and Assyria, except what could be derived from classical writers and Biblical references. He, however, recognized that the myths had a psychological if not a historical value when he wrote: " Two courses, and two only, are open: either to pass over the myths altogether, which is the way in which modern historians treat the old British fables, or else to give an account of them as myths; to recognize and respect their specific nature, and to abstain from confounding them with ordinary and certifiable history. There are good reasons for pursuing the second method in reference to the Grecian myths, and when so considered they constitute an important chapter in the history of the Grecian mind, and, indeed, in that of the human race generally." [1] He did not agree with those, however, who believed that the Homeric picture of life was wholly fictitious. Indeed, he drew, like others, upon the epics for evidence regarding customs and manners of life in early Greek times, although he held they contained " no historical facts ".

It was generally recognized that the petty states of Greece were ruled over by hereditary chiefs, whose power was limited by a military aristocracy. "Piracy was an honourable occupation," as one writer put it, "and war the delight of noble souls." Some historians added, on the authority of Thucydides,[2] that the commencement of Grecian civilization might be dated from the reign of King Minos of Crete, who had cleared the Ægean Sea of pirates. Grote could not, on the other hand, believe that the Minos legends had any historical value. "Here we have ", he wrote, "conjectures derived from the analogy of the Athenian maritime empire of historical times, sub-

---

[1] History of Greece, Vol. I, pp. 651–2.
[2] History of the Peloponnesian War, I, 3–4.

stituted in place of the fabulous incidents and attached to the name of Minos." [1]

It should not surprise us that the so-called " doubting Thomases" among the historians hesitated to make use of myths and legends. Grote held that if he were to proceed with a view to detect a historical base in the stories of Troy and Thebes, he would be compelled to deal similarly with the myths of " Zeus in Crete, of Apollo and Artemis in Delos, of Hermes and of Prometheus ". If Achilles was to be taken seriously, although he was of supernatural origin, what of Bellerophon, Perseus, Theseus, and Hercules ? These would also have to be " handled objectively ".

In time the exponents of the new science of Comparative Mythology, which at its inception was based chiefly on philological evidence, attracted much attention and impressed not a few serious students of classical history with their theory that classical legends were renderings of immemorial religious myths, the gods and goddesses having been transformed into human heroes and heroines. " In Greek mythology", it was contended, " each different aspect of nature had many different names, because a few simple elements crystallized into many different forms. This is why there are so many gods and goddesses." As much may be granted, although, as is now believed, the view is somewhat narrow. But when the theory was given practical application it led to rather too sweeping conclusions of rather fanciful character. " Zeus", wrote one authority, " is married to many different wives. The bright sky must look down on many lands. His visits to different countries are thus explained. . . . Achilles is child of the sea-goddess; so the sun often appears to rise out of the water. His bride is torn from him, and he

[1] *History of Greece*, Vol. I, p. 311.

sulks in his tent; so the sun must leave the dawn and be hidden by dark clouds.   He lends his armour to Patroclus except the spear; none other can wield the spear of Achilles: so no other can equal the power of the sun's rays."   And so on until the absurdity concluded with: "Achilles tramples on the dead body of Hector, but Hector is of dark powers, though noble in himself; so a blazing sunset tramples down the darkness.   Finally, Achilles is slain by an arrow from a Trojan.   He is vulnerable only in the heel, but the arrow finds him there. So the sun is conquered by the darkness in his turn, and disappears, a short-lived brilliant thing."

The hero of the *Odyssey* met a similar fate.   "Odysseus is the sun in another character, as a wanderer, and his adventures describe the general phenomena of daytime from the rising to the setting of the sun. . . . His journey is full of strange changes, of happiness and misery, success and reverses, like the lights and shadows of a gloomy day."

The *Iliad*, as a narrative, was regarded with contempt. "There is nothing noble or elevated in the gods or heroes", remarked one solar-symbolist, who referred to himself as "one of the advanced thinkers".   "Everyone knows", he went on, with unconscious humour, "that the *Iliad* is a poem which tells two stories: of a war between the Greeks and Trojans to recover a Grecian woman named Helen, who had run away from her lawful husband with a Trojan hero named Paris, and carried a great treasure with her; also of the anger of Achilles, a Grecian hero, and the dreadful consequences it brought upon the Grecian army encamped upon the plains around Troy."   A physical explanation of this "petty legend" had to be sought for.   Professor Max Müller declared: "The siege of Troy is a repetition of the daily siege of the East by the solar powers that are robbed of their brightest treasures in the West". One of his critics and followers, Mr. Cox, remarked with much justification that this was "not quite plain", but he only added to the confusion by urging a new hypothesis. "Few will venture to deny", he remarked, with the characteristic confidence of the theorist, "that the stealing of the bright clouds of sunset by the dark powers of night, the weary search for them through the long night, the battle with the robbers, as the darkness is driven away by the advancing chariot of the lord of light, are favourite subjects with the Vedic poets." So was Greece robbed of its heroes and Troy swept out of existence. "If such a war took place", Mr. Cox argued, "it must be carried back to a time preceding the dispersion of the Aryan tribes from their original home."

But while these and other examples of what Mr. Andrew Lang has characterized as "scholarly stupidity" impressed not a few prominent men, a small band of students strenuously declined to regard the Homeric legends as products of traditional myths "based on the various phenomena of the earth and heavens". One of these was the self-educated merchant, Henry Schliemann, whose faith in Homer led him to make discoveries which have thrown a flood of light on early Ægean civilization, and incidentally shattered forever the theories of the solar mythologists. "The Trojan War", he wrote in 1878, "has for a long time past been regarded by many eminent scholars as a myth, of which however they vainly endeavoured to find the origin in the Vedas. But in all antiquity the siege and conquest of Ilium by the Greek army under Agamemnon was considered as an undoubted historical fact, and as such it is accepted by the great authority of Thucydides.[1] The tradition has

[1] *Thucydides*, I, 8, 10.

even retained the memory of many details of that war which have been omitted by Homer. For my part, I have always firmly believed in the Trojan War; my full faith in Homer and in the tradition has never been shaken by modern criticism, and to this faith of mine I am indebted for the discovery of Troy and its treasure."[1]

The story of Heinrich Schliemann's life is a fitting prelude to an account of his epoch-making discoveries in Asia Minor and Greece which "led up", as Mr. Hawes says, "to the revelations in Crete from 1900 onwards". He was born on 6th January, 1822, in the little German town of Neu Buckow, in the duchy of Mecklenberg-Schwerin, and was scarcely twelve months old when his father, a Protestant clergyman, removed to Ankershagen, near Waren. At this village the future archæologist, who was a precocious child, received impressions before he was ten years old which influenced his whole life and prompted him to achieve renown as a pioneer in the domain of pre-Hellenic research. Ankershagen was enveloped in an old-world atmosphere; it was indeed an ideal "homeland", with its antiquities, legends, and superstitions, for one of Heinrich Schliemann's temperament and mental leanings. The summer-house in the manse garden was reputed to be haunted by the ghost of his father's predecessor, Pastor von Russdorf, and near at hand was a small pond out of which each night at the stroke of twelve a spirit maid was believed to rise up, grasping a silver cup in her hand. In the village a ditch-surrounded mound—one of the kind called a Hunengrab, or "Hun's grave"—had attached to it a story about a great robber who buried in it his favourite child in a golden cradle. Legends of similar character are told regarding "giants' graves" in these islands. Treasure was also said to lie concealed

[1] *Mycenæ*, p. 334.

under a round tower in the local land-proprietor's garden. "My faith in these treasures was so great", Schliemann wrote in after years, "that whenever I heard my father complain of his poverty, I expressed my astonishment that he did not dig up the silver bowl or the golden cradle and so become rich."[1]

An ancient castle also made a strong appeal to the boy's imagination. It was supposed to have the usual long underground passage leading to somewhere, and to be visited nightly by awesome spectres. At one time, the legend ran, it was the abode of a notorious robber knight, Henning Bradenkirl, who buried his treasure and committed suicide when, revelation having been made of his designs on the life of the Duke of Mecklenberg, his stronghold was besieged by that great nobleman. Henning found no rest in his grave, and it was whispered among the young folks that time and again he had thrust out one of his legs with purpose apparently to visit the spot where his hoard was concealed. "I often begged my father", Schliemann has told, "to excavate the tomb, in order to see why the foot no longer grew out." This belief that there was a kernel of truth in ancient legends caused him ultimately to search for traces of ancient Troy, and open the graves of heroes who, according to classic narratives, had been buried with their armour and rich ornaments. "My firm faith in the traditions", he wrote in 1877, "made me undertake my late excavations in the Acropolis (of Mycenæ) and led to the discovery of the five tombs, with their immense treasures."[2] So the boy was "father of the man".

The impecunious clergyman of Ankershagen cast over the mind of his son, Heinrich, the romantic glamour of classic myth and legend. The nursery stories he related

---

[1] *Ilios*, pp. 1 *et seq.*   [2] *Mycenæ*, p. 335.

were not of elves and giants, but of the last days of
Pompeii and Herculaneum, which were then being excavated and greatly talked about, and of the great deeds
of Homer's heroes on the windy plain of Troy.

It was a memorable day in Heinrich's life when he
received as a Christmas present, in his eighth year, an
illustrated child's history of the world—one of those
popular works which stimulate young minds with the
desire to acquire knowledge.   An engraving depicted the
last scene in the siege of Troy.   The "topless towers of
Ilium" were wrapped in flames, and amidst the smoke
and confusion the wounded warrior Æneas was seen
taking flight, carrying his father Anchises on his broad
back, and leading by the hand his son Ascanius.   From
that hour the spectacle of mighty Troy haunted the mind
of the little German boy, and the Trojan War became as
familiar to him as if it had been waged on the village
green and Ankershagen, instead of Troy, had been sacked.

Heinrich failed in his attempts to impress his boy
friends with glowing versions of Homer's narrative, but
he infected with his enthusiasm the minds of two girl
companions.   One of these, Minna Meincke, a farmer's
daughter, promised to marry him when she grew up, and
assist him to discover the Hun robber's golden cradle,
the silver cup of the pond nymph, the treasure concealed
by Henning, and to accompany him to the land of dreams
to explore the ruins of ancient Troy.   Strange to relate,
half a century afterwards, not Minna, but another who
became Mrs. Henry Schliemann, actually did help her
husband in his famous excavations, and one of the results
of their joint labours was the finding of the most valuable
treasure any archæologists have ever had the luck to
uncover.

Heinrich's father intended to give him a classical

education, but fell into financial difficulties, with the result that when the boy was fourteen he became apprenticed to a village grocer.   At nineteen he injured himself when lifting a heavy cask, and went to Hamburg, where he secured a situation as a cabin-boy on a brig bound for Venezuela.   The vessel, however, was wrecked on a sand-bank off the Island of Texel during stormy weather, but fortunately the crew escaped in a small boat. Heinrich afterwards secured a situation at a Hamburg warehouse.   Having a good deal of leisure time at his disposal, he studied languages with so much success that he acquired a wonderful knowledge of Dutch, English, Spanish, French, Italian, and Portuguese.

At twenty-four he was employed by the firm of B. H. Schroder & Co., and, having by this time obtained a knowledge of Russian, he was sent to St. Petersburg. He prospered there and began to trade on his own account, dealing chiefly in indigo.   At forty he found himself a millionaire.   Ere he retired, however, he studied modern and ancient Greek and Latin under Professor Ludgwig von Muralt.

Having wound up his affairs, he began to travel extensively.   For several months he resided in China and Japan, and wrote on his return his first book *La Chine et Le Japon*, which was published at Paris, where he settled down to study archæology.   The time was drawing nigh when he could visit the scenes of Homeric glory, and make search for traces of ancient Troy and the graves containing treasure.   He was resolved to realize the dream of his boyhood, which he had treasured during the years so full of business anxieties and cares.   "Father," he had once said, when his childish eyes were fascinated by the engraving of Troy, "if such walls once existed, they cannot possibly have been completely destroyed;

vast ruins of them must still remain, but they are hidden beneath the dust of ages." His father had shaken his head, but, to pleasure the lad, admitted that it was possible, and then agreed that when they were able to do so they would both search for and excavate the ruins of the famous city.

In 1868 Schliemann paid his first visit to the scenes of his future triumphs and wrote a book entitled *Ithaca, the Peloponnesus, and Troy*, in which he ran counter to the theories of those contemporary scholars who believed that Troy had existed, by locating its site, not on an inland summit near Bunarbashi, but farther north and near the seashore on the top of the hillock of Hissarlik. He also announced where he believed the graves of the Atreidæ at Mycenæ could be located. For this original treatise he received his doctor's degree at Rostock.

In the spring of 1870 Dr. Schliemann put his theories to the test by beginning to dig at Hissarlik. At the depth of 16 feet the first wall was laid bare, and he was then fully convinced that success would crown his efforts. Accordingly he made preparations for excavation work on an extensive scale. The Turkish authorities hampered him greatly, however, and it was not until late in the following year that he could proceed with the work. In the following year a great depth had been reached, but although a broad trench laid bare a series of walls and a fine piece of Greek sculpture, no definite conclusions could be reached from the results, promising and suggestive as these were. Work was resumed early in 1873, when the weather was so cold that "of an evening", wrote Dr. Schliemann, "we had nothing to keep us warm except an enthusiasm for discovering Troy". The weeks went past, and at length Fortune smiled and the dreams of boyhood began to find rich realization.   One day, during the dinner hour, when no workmen were near, Dr. Schliemann and his wife discovered a treasure hoard of gold and diadems and daggers, silver jars and copper vessels and weapons, which they hurriedly carried off and concealed.   Its mere monetary value was not far short of £1000.   During the winter Dr. Schliemann wrote an account of his discoveries which was published in book form under the title *Trojan Antiquities*.   He had cut through several successive towns on the hillock of Hissarlik.   The second city from the bottom was named by him "Homer's Troy"; he called its largest building "Priam's Palace", and the hoard he had discovered with his wife, "Priam's Treasure".   Most archæologists now believe, however, that the sixth city, which was much more extensive than the second, was the capital celebrated by Homer.

Schliemann's theories were ridiculed by the "authorities" in every country in Europe.   He was a "rank outsider" and regarded with suspicion by the theorists who were convinced that Troy could not possibly have been situated at Hissarlik.   Comic papers made fun of him as a dreamer of vain dreams, but a few open-minded scholars were profoundly impressed and anxious for more information.   Schliemann was not discouraged either by learned criticism or superficial ridicule.   What concerned him most was the attitude assumed by the Turkish Government, which was not entirely free from the suspicion or blackmailing propensities.   Operations at Hissarlik had to be suspended, but the undaunted pioneer did not waste his time.   He turned his back upon Troy and was led to Mycenæ, in Greek territory, by the ghost of Agamemnon.   There and at Tiryns his excavations resulted in the discovery of traces of a culture similar to that found in the sixth city at Hissarlik.   The results of this archæological "campaign", which was carried on during 1876–7, were published in *Mycenæ* in 1878. A preface contributed by the late Mr. W. E. Gladstone contains several passages which reflect the interest which was aroused throughout Europe at the time by Schliemann's work. "When the disclosures at Tiryns and Mycenæ were announced in England," wrote Mr. Gladstone, "my own first impression was that of a strangely bewildered admiration, combined with a preponderance of sceptical against believing tendencies, in regard to the capital and dominating subject of the Tombs in the Agora. I am bound to say that reflection and fuller knowledge have nearly turned the scales the other way. . . . I find, upon perusing the volume of Dr. Schliemann, that the items of evidence, which connect his discoveries generally with the Homeric poems, are more numerous than I had surmised from the brief outline with which he favoured us upon his visit to England in the spring." [1]

Tiryns, now called Palæocastron, was, according to Pausanius, named after Tiryns, a son of Argos. It was the reputed birthplace of Hercules, and famed for its Cyclopean walls. "The circuit wall," wrote Pausanias, "which is the only remaining ruin, was built by the Cyclopes. It is composed of unwrought stones, each of which is so large that a team of mules cannot even shake the smallest one: small stones have been interposed in order to consolidate the large blocks." [2]

Mycenæ was also reputed to have been built by these giant artisans, who numbered seven, and came from Lycia. It was probably on account of this legend that, as Schliemann suggested, the whole of the Argolis was referred to by Euripides as "Cyclopean land". Similarly, many ruins in Asia Minor and Mesopotamia were credited

[1] *Mycenæ*, Preface, p. vi.   [2] *Pausanias*, II, 25, 8, and *Mycenæ*, pp. 2–3.

by tradition to Semiramis, while the Egyptian Sesostris was supposed to have erected gigantic works in various localities. This habit of accounting for ancient remains as the handiwork of mythical and semi-mythical persons was of great antiquity and widespread character. Fairies and elves and giants were supposed to have erected dolmens and stone circles. Gaelic-speaking people in Lewis at the present day, for instance, refer to the standing stones at Callernish as *Tursachan*, a name which has been derived from the Norse word *Thurs*, a giant or goblin. In Cumberland another circle is associated with the memory of the mythical giantesses "Long Meg and her daughters". Several promontories in different localities have been credited likewise to fairy artisans who were endeavouring to bridge over an arm of the sea. Thor, according to the Teutonic wonder-tales, formed valleys by smiting a mountain range with his great hammer, while the "Flint Hills" were formed by the fragments he shattered from the great flint boulder flung towards him by a giant enemy. In Scotland numerous hillocks are referred to as spillings from the creel of the giantess (Cailleach) who erected mountain houses for her children. This custom of attributing not only hills, but also buildings, to supernatural agencies has survived even into Christian times. Not a few ruins of early chapels in these islands have still associated with them folk-tales about fairy builders, who accomplished their work in a single night.

Schliemann did not attach historical importance to the legends of Hercules, who was reputed to have held sway at Tiryns for a prolonged period. Indeed, like Max Müller, he was inclined to regard the famous folk-hero as a sun-god. But he was convinced that the Cyclopean walls were of great antiquity, and engaged in systematic

8

THE LION GATE, MYCENÆ

excavations with purpose to obtain evidence which would connect the civilization of Tiryns with that of his Homeric Troy. He found a number of terra-cotta female idols, with exaggerated breasts, and terra-cotta cows, which had evidently a religious significance. These he connected with the goddess Hera. Examples of primitive pottery were also brought to light, including hand-polished black vases and bulky jars. When he reached the prehistoric strata he collected obsidian knives, whorls of blue and green stone, &c. In some places he found the remains of walls built on the rock and of water conduits of rough unhewn stones. The stones of the ancient Cyclopean wall measured about 7 feet long and 3 feet thick in most cases, but some were of even greater dimensions.

At Mycenæ, "situated in the depth of the horsefeeding Argos", as Homer sang,[1] Schliemann's early researches were more productive. Here he set out to prove his theory that the graves of the Atreidæ were situated not outside but inside the citadel wall. He found that the wall revealed three different methods of construction, which he assigned to three separate periods. These are the Cyclopean, in which large boulders were secured by small blocks; the Polygonal, with accurately hewn joints; and the Rectangular, in which the blocks were "dovetailed".

In the north-west corner he cleared the famous "Lion's Gate". It measured 10 feet 8 inches in height, and was 9 feet 6 inches wide at the top, and 10 feet 3 inches at the bottom. The great lintel, which excited admiration, was found to be 15 feet long and 8 feet broad. At this point the wall, constructed on the Rectangular system, is composed of stones 6 and 7 feet in length, many of which

[1] *Odyssey*, III, 263.

are notched to fit into the corners, or jutting points, hewed in others. This system of rough "dovetailing" is characteristic of Hittite buildings. The Euphrates River wall at Carchemish, the oldest known engineering construction in the world, which has been utilized by the engineers in connection with a "Bagdad railway" bridge at this point, is a characteristic example of the Rectangular style of architecture.

Above the great lintel of the principal entrance to the Acropolis of Mycenæ lies the great limestone slab sculptured in relief, on which two lions rampant, heraldically opposed, rest their forepaws on the "altar" with its shapely pillar "crowned by a curious capital, composed of a fillet, moulding, roll, and abacus". Similar lion and pillar groups have been found by Professor Ramsay in Phrygia. In one instance the goddess Cybele takes the place of the pillar. "The idea of the lions as guardians of the gate arose", Professor Ramsay considers, "in a country where Cybele was worshipped, and where the dead chief was believed to be gathered to his mother, the goddess. . . . The Phrygians adapted an old heraldic type to represent the idea. . . . In the interchange of artistic forms and improvements in civilization which obtained between Phrygia and the Greeks, the lion type passed into Mycenæ during the ninth, or more probably the eighth century B.C."[1]

Schliemann's guide to Mycenæ was Pausanias, who wrote[2]: "Amongst other remains of the wall is the gate on which stand lions. They (the walls and the gate) are said to be the work of the Cyclopes, who built the wall for Proteus at Tiryns. In the ruins of Mycenæ is the fountain called Perseia, and the subterranean buildings of

Journal of the Hellenic Society, Vol. V, p. 242.
Pausanias, II, 16, 6, and Mycenæ, pp. 59, 60.

Atreus and his children, in which they stored their treasures. There is the sepulchre of Atreus, and the tombs of the companions of Agamemnon, who on their return from Ilium were killed at a banquet by Ægisthus. The identity of the tomb of Cassandra is called in question by the Lacedæmonians of Amyclæ. There is the tomb of Agamemnon and that of his charioteer Eurymedon, and of Electra. Teledamus and Pelops were buried in the same sepulchre, for it is said that Cassandra bore these twins, and that, while as yet infants, they were slaughtered by Ægisthus together with their parents. Hellanicus (495–411 B.C.) writes that Pylades, who was married to Electra with the consent of Orestes, had by her two sons, Medon and Strophius. Clytemnestra and Ægisthus were buried at a little distance from the wall, because they were thought unworthy to have their tombs inside of it, where Agamemnon reposed and those who were killed together with him."

This passage had been misinterpreted by certain writers, and Schliemann insisted, before he began to dig, that the wall referred to was not the city wall, as they believed, but the wall of the Acropolis. The city, besides, he argued, was in ruins in Pausanias's day (170 A.D.), and he might not have seen the remnants of the smaller city wall. Schliemann put his theory to proof by sinking a number of shafts, and then undertaking extensive excavations. When he had cleared away the debris from the Lion's Gate, some of which had been cast there when the Argives captured the Acropolis in the fifth century B.C., he found evidence that the city had been partially reoccupied after its fall, although Diodorus Siculus[1] and Strabo[2] had made statements to the contrary.

Schliemann penetrated to the lower and earlier city of

[1] XI, 65. [2] VIII, p. 372.

Mycenæ and there made discovery of great "beehive tombs", which were the "Treasuries" of Pausanias.

Schliemann excavated also five shaft tombs, and believed they were those of Agamemnon and his companions, who on their return from Troy were murdered by Clytemnestra and her paramour Ægisthus. They were of similar construction, and the burials appeared to him to have been simultaneous. "The five tombs of Mycenæ, or, at least, three of them," he wrote, "contained such enormous treasuries that they cannot but have belonged to members of the royal family." Thousands of pounds worth of antique valuables were discovered in these mysterious underground chambers.

An immense impression was made all over Europe on the publication of the following characteristic telegram which Schliemann dispatched to the King of Greece, announcing his great discovery.

"MYCENÆ, 16th (28th) November, 1876.

"With extreme joy I announce to Your Majesty that I have discovered the tombs which tradition, as echoed by Pausanias, designates as the sepulchre of Agamemnon, of Cassandra, of Eurymadon and their companions and their comrades, all slain during the repast by Clytemnestra and her lover Ægisthus. These tombs were surrounded by a double parallel circle of plaques, which can only have been erected in the honour of great personages. I have found in the sepulchres immense treasures in the way of archaic objects of pure gold. These treasures of themselves are enough to fill a large museum which shall be the most marvellous in the world, and which during centuries to come will draw to Greece thousands of visitors from every country. As I work purely for the love of science, I make naturally no claim to these treasures, which I give with the liveliest enthusiasm intact to Greece. May it be God's will that these treasures will become the corner stone of an immense national wealth.

"HEINRICH SCHLIEMANN."

It is not believed nowadays that Schliemann located the tombs of Agamemnon and his followers, but happened instead on those of royal personages who flourished in a different age. The authority of Pausanias is not sufficient to settle the problem. When that distinguished writer visited the ruins of Mycenæ over a thousand years had elapsed since Troy had fallen. Agamemnon bulked prominently in folk-imagination, and was identified with the memorials of forgotten rulers. The process involved is a familiar one. In our own country King Arthur has similarly had attached to his memory the deeds of mythical beings who dwelt in Fairyland or selected high hills as their seats, while in the Highlands as recent a hero as Prince Charlie has been associated with hiding-places, in districts he never visited, as far north as Caithness.

But Schliemann's confident statement regarding the "tomb of Agamemnon" need not detract from the value of the services he has rendered to archæology. In making search for traces of the heroes of his boyhood he achieved well-deserved renown as the pioneer who "opened to us the door into one of the sealed chambers of the past". He has caused early Greek history to be rewritten, and it is due to his example and triumphs that it is now possible to present a partial reconstruction of several thousand years of Ægean civilization.

It is indirectly to Schliemann, too, that we owe the late Mr. Andrew Lang's famous sonnet on Homeric Unity.

The sacred keep of Ilion is rent
By shaft and pit; foiled waters wander slow
Through plains where Simois and Scamander went
To war with gods and heroes long ago.
Not yet to tired Cassandra, lying low
In rich Mycenæ, do the Fates relent:
The bones of Agamemnon are a show,
And ruined is his royal monument.

The dust and awful treasures of the Dead,
Hath Learning scattered wide, but vainly thee,
Homer, she meteth with her tool of lead,
And strives to rend thy songs; too blind to see
The crown that burns on thine immortal head
Of indivisible supremacy.

Flushed with his Mycenæan successes, Schliemann was
ready to return to Troy in the summer of 1878. But his
difficulties with the Turkish officials delayed him. These,
however, were overcome on his behalf by another famous
explorer, Sir Austen Henry Layard, of Assyrian fame,
who happened to be at the time British Ambassador at
Constantinople. "I fulfil a most agreeable duty", Schliemann wrote in his *Ilios*, "in now thanking his Excellency
publicly and most cordially for all the services he has
rendered me, without which I could never have brought
my work to a close."

While waiting for his firman from the Turkish
Government, Schliemann began operations on the Island
of Ithaca, and discovered on Mount Ætos a king's palace
and nearly two hundred houses of Cyclopean construction.
Then he proceeded to Troy, where he was hampered for
a time by a Turkish commissioner. In the following
year Professor Virchow joined him, and he received visits
also from other scholars of repute. In 1880 he published
his great work *Ilios*. Dr. Dörpfeld joined him in 1882,

and together they operated chiefly in the city which has now been identified with Homer's Troy. In 1884 the results of later exploration were recorded in Schliemann's *Troja*, to which a preface was contributed by Professor Sayce. The tireless excavator then resumed operations at Tiryns, where an ancient palace was discovered. The work was continued here in the following year by Dr. Dörpfeld, who wrote several chapters in Schliemann's next book, to which a preface was contributed by Professor F. Adler.

Schliemann next turned attention to Egypt, where he excavated with Virchow with much success, and he desired also to operate in Crete, on Knossos Hill, but the political conditions on the island made systematic archæological work in that quarter an impossibility, while the Turkish Government showed no enthusiasm regarding his proposal. It was not considered desirable that the islanders should be reminded of the greatness of their ancestors. He had therefore to abandon his scheme to make search in Crete for " the original home of Mycenæan civilization ".

In 1890 Dr. C. Schuchardt, Director of the Kestner Museum, in Hanover, published his critical work on Schliemann's excavations, in which he wrote: " Dr. Schliemann is now in his sixty-ninth year, but his activity and love of enterprise show no signs of decay. We may still look to him for many additions to science, and we hope to thank him for disclosing the heroic age of Greece in the periods of its prime and of its decadence, which may perhaps be found in Crete, the land of Minos."[1]

On 26th December in the same year, however, Schliemann expired suddenly in Naples. His body was taken to Athens and buried in the Greek cemetery near the

[1] *Schliemann's Excavations*, translated by E. Sellers, p. 16.

Ilissos, a lofty monument being erected to his memory.
"He lies", writes Mr. Sellers, "in the land he loved so
well; but the example of noble ambition and patient
research which he set before the world will long abide
as a living spirit, not only among archæologists, but
among all who anywhere in the civilized world have
caught something of his devotion and enthusiasm for
classical learning and antiquity."

Among the honours conferred upon the great man
during the closing years of his life was the degree of
D.C.L. of Oxford and the fellowship of Queen's College.
The Royal Institute of British Architects awarded him
a gold medal, in which he took great pride. It is of
interest to note that he was a naturalized American
citizen.

CHAPTER V

Crete as the Lost Atlantis

Quest for Home of Pre-Hellenic Culture—The Legendary Clues—Myth of the Lost Atlantis—Schliemann's Remarkable Bequest—His Grandson's Researches—Supposed Connection of Egyptian with Central American Civilization—Views of Geologists regarding a Submerged Continent—Geikie versus Hull—Evidence of New and Old World Fauna—The Race Problem—Plato's Atlantis Narrative—Lost Island identified with Crete—Sea Trade, Palaces, and Bull Fights—Greek and Libyan Traditions—How the Lost Atlantis Myth Originated—Legend of Zeus and Europé—Water-bull and Water-horse Stories —The Legendary Minos and Osiris—The Minotaur—Story of Dædalus and Babylonian and Indian Parallels—Athens and Crete—The Theseus Legend— Value of Traditions.

ALTHOUGH Schliemann's theories regarding Priam's treasure and Agamemnon's tomb aroused a storm of criticism, it had to be recognized that he discovered traces of a brilliant pre-Hellenic civilization which had flourished in Greece and Asia Minor for many long centuries. The problem as to where it had originated, however, remained obscure, and towards its solution not a few skilled archæologists began to direct their energies. Indeed, the quest soon became hot and fast. The cumulative evidence of classical writers seemed to point to Crete. Homer, Hesiod, Strabo, Thucydides, and Herodotus had perpetuated traditions regarding King Minos, the great lawgiver, who had cleared the Ægean of pirates. He was reputed to have been a son of Zeus, and that deity, according to one legend, had been born in a Cretan cave.

Schliemann gave serious consideration to these clues, and had endeavoured, as has been stated, to make arrangements to excavate at Knossos. He also conducted researches with Virchow at Sais, in northern Egypt, but no discovery was made to indicate that pre-Hellenic civilization had emanated from the land of the Pharaohs in its fully-developed form. The larger problem appears to have engaged his mind: Where did Egyptian civilization originate?

Ere he died Schliemann formulated a bold theory to account not only for early northern European and North African civilization but also that of Central America as well. It was based on Plato's myth of the Lost Atlantis. He was convinced that this great island had had real existence, and that colonies of its inhabitants settled in Mexico, Egypt, and Greece at a remote period, introducing into these countries a full-blown culture.

Here, again, as will be shown, Schliemann had intuitive perception of a basis of fact embedded in the debris of tradition. Had he lived long enough he would no doubt have adjusted his view in the light of those discoveries which have been made during recent years, and accepted Crete as the mysterious island referred to by Plato.

The Atlantis theory appealed as strongly to the great pioneer's imagination during the last months of his life as did his Troy theory in the days of his boyhood. But the frailties of old age oppressed him, and he realized that he could never put it to proof. He desired, however, that the work should be undertaken by one of his kinsmen, and committed his secret to writing, enclosing his manuscript in a sealed envelope inscribed as follows:—

This can be opened only by a member of my family who solemnly vows to devote his life to the researches outlined therein.

Not long before he expired he asked for a pencil and piece of paper and wrote:

Confidential addition to the sealed envelope. Break the owl-headed vase. Pay attention to the contents. It concerns Atlantis. Investigate the east of the ruins of the temple of Sais and the cemetery in Chacuna valley. Important. It proves the system. Night approaches—Lebewohl.

This last document was enclosed, and afterwards deposited with the other in one of the banks of France by the party to whom both were entrusted. A large sum of money was set aside to defray the expenses of the mysterious undertaking.

In 1906 Dr. Paul Schliemann, a grandson of the great discoverer of pre-Hellenic civilization, vowed to devote his life to the researches referred to in the sealed envelopes, and made himself acquainted with their contents. A few years later he contributed to certain newspapers in New York and London a signed statement,[1] in which he made a revelation of his grandfather's last bequest.

The first paper said:

Whoever opens this must solemnly swear to carry out the work I have left unfinished. I have come to the conclusion that Atlantis was not only a great territory between America and the West Coast of Africa and Europe, but the cradle of all our civilization as well. There has been much dispute among scientists on this matter. According to one group the tradition of Atlantis is purely fictional, founded upon fragmentary accounts of a deluge some thousands of years before the Christian era. Others declare the tradition wholly historical, but not capable of absolute proof.

Dr. Schliemann's papers are of lengthy character. Briefly stated, they set forth that he found at Troy a

[1] It appeared in the *London Budget* (which has since ceased to exist) on 17th November, 1912.

bronze vase containing fragments of pottery, images, and coins of "a peculiar metal", and "objects made of fossilized bone". He added: "Some of these objects and the bronze vase were engraved with a sentence in Phœnician hieroglyphics. The sentence read, 'From the King Chronos of Atlantis'."

Ten years later, when in the Louvre, Paris, he examined a collection of objects taken from Tiahuanaco, in Central America, and "discovered pieces of pottery of exactly the same shape and material, and objects of fossilized bone which reproduced line for line those I had found", Schliemann wrote, "in the bronze vase of the 'Treasure of Priam'". Among these objects was an owl-headed vase. He also professed to have read, or to have had read to him, extracts from Egyptian papyri preserved in the Museum at St. Petersburg which made reference to the "Land of Atlantis", whence had come the ancestors of the Egyptians "3350 years ago" and the "sages of Atlantis" who flourished during a period of "13,900 years". Another inscription, discovered near the Lion's Gate at Mycenæ, set forth that Thoth was a son of a "priest of Atlantis" who "landed after many wanderings in Egypt. He built the first temple at Sais, and there taught the wisdom of his native land."

Dr. Paul Schliemann has broken open the "owl-headed vase" at Paris, referred to in his grandfather's last memorandum, and states that he found in it a coin or medal of "silver-like metal" inscribed in Phœnician as follows: "Issued in the Temple of Transparent Walls". He claims, also, to have made discoveries in Egypt, Mexico, and elsewhere which justify his grandfather's theory. "I have reasons", he has written, "for saying that the strange medals were used as money in Atlantis forty thousand years ago."

The first question which arises in connection with the late Dr. Schliemann's theory is: Did the "Lost Atlantis" ever have existence in fact? On this point Professor James Geikie has written as follows:—

"Geologists have often speculated as to a former connection between the Old World and the New. There can be little doubt, indeed, that such a land connection did obtain between Asia and Europe at a geologically recent date, and it is quite possible that there may have been a land bridge also between Europe and North America by way of the Farŏe Islands.[1] Others have suggested the former existence of a land bridge further south. They suppose that the North Atlantic may have been dry land—traversed from west to east by a Mediterranean Sea—of which the existing Mediterranean and the Gulf of Mexico are the remaining portions. But the facts which have suggested that speculation have been otherwise accounted for. All that is definite and certain is that there has been considerable loss of land so far as Europe is concerned. Our continent formerly extended further westward. But I know of no geological evidence that puts it beyond doubt that the Atlantic basin is the site of a drowned continent. On the contrary, such evidence as we have leads rather to the belief that the Atlantic basin, like that of the Pacific, is of primeval origin."[2]

That veteran geologist, Professor Edward Hull, takes a different view of the problem, and has written:

"The tradition of Atlantis 'beyond the Pillars of Hercules' can scarcely be supposed to have originated in the mind of man without a basis of reality. In the centre of the North Atlantic Ocean rise from the surface the Azores volcanic islands, the summits of a group of islands rising from a platform corresponding to the continental platform of Europe on one hand and of America on the other. The rise of the level of the ocean bed, amounting from 7000 to 10,000 feet, as shown by the soundings on the Admiralty

[1] See Chapter I.
[2] *London Budget*, 8th December, 1912. See also Geikie's *The Deeps of the Pacific Ocean and their Origin*, *The Great Sea Age*, *Prehistoric Europe*, and *The Antiquity of Man in Europe*.

charts, would have reduced the depth of the ocean by so much, and have extended the land areas to an extent which would have brought Atlantis within navigable distance of both continents for early inhabitants using canoes. We know from our investigations[1] that this elevation occurred during the post-tertiary period,[2] and at a presumed date 9000 or 10,000 B.C. If we add 1000 years of our era, the question arises: Would not this lapse of time have been sufficient to account for the subsidence which the region in question underwent in order to restore the land and sea to their present limits? Of course, this would depend on the rate of subsidence. But, at anyrate, the result, as regards Atlantis, would have been the submergence under the ocean, with the exception of its present islands. The glacial period, when much of Europe and the British Isles was covered by snow and ice, can scarcely have been farther back than 10,000 years, and this is presumably the age of Atlantis."

Dr. Scharff, Director of the Natural History Museum, Dublin, is also a believer in the "Lost Atlantis". He has been led to the conclusion, in his studies of the migrations of animals between the continents of America and Europe,[3] that a land bridge once crossed the Atlantic Ocean between Southern Europe and the West Indies. "It probably became disconnected", he says, "in Miocene times. Since then this land once more became united with our continent, and may not have been finally severed until the Pleistocene period. United with the West Indies and Central America in early Tertiary times, it probably subsided partly during the Oligocene period[4] and later, leaving only a few isolated peaks as islands in the midst of the vast ocean which has since replaced it."

It will be seen that scientific opinion is divided re-

---

[1] Professor Hull and Professor J. W. Spencer in *Sub-Oceanic Physiography of the North Atlantic Ocean* (London, 1912), and Professor Hull in *London Budget*, 1st December, 1912.

[2] During the Pleistocene Age.   [3] *Distribution and Origin of Life in America.*

[4] A vast interval—perhaps millions of years—separated the Oligocene period from even the earliest culture stages of Pleistocene times.

garding the existence of a mid-Atlantic continent. If, however, the views of Hull and Scharff are accepted, they cannot be held to prove that Plato's Atlantis was situated beyond the "Pillars of Hercules". Schliemann's hypothesis, as expounded by his grandson, renders it necessary to assume that this lost country, "which used the ancient medals as an equivalent of labour, had a more advanced currency system than we have at present". If such was the case, it appears strange that no traces of the high civilization have survived on those islands which are referred to as the "few isolated peaks" of the submerged continent.

The particular race which is supposed to have come from Atlantis has yet to be identified. Was it represented in Europe by Chellean man? The Chellean "hand axe" has been traced from France to South Africa, through Asia, across the "land bridge" to North America, and southward through South America. It never reached Australia or New Zealand. But Chellean man was a savage, not much more advanced, indeed, than were the Tasmanians. Cro-Magnon man, on the other hand, had achieved a high degree of culture, but no traces either of his physical type or of his cave drawings have been discovered in the New World. Besides, his culture developed from the Chellean through the Acheulian and Mousterian stages, as has been fully demonstrated. He cannot therefore be claimed for Atlantis. Nor can Mediterranean man, who had spread through Egypt and along the North African coast, and had settled in Southern and Western Europe, as well as in Mesopotamia, before the age of metal. There are no aboriginal representatives of his type in America.

Have the settlers from Atlantis vanished entirely in the New and Old Worlds? Did they perish like the mythical elder races of Mexico, India, Babylonia, Greece, and Ireland?

Another insurmountable difficulty is the fact that copper was not utilized in Egypt and Central America at the same early period. The Egyptians and Sumerians worked that metal at about 3000 B.C. In Crete the Bronze Age was inaugurated between 3000 B.C. and 2800 B.C., and in Great Britain before 1500 B.C. The American peoples did not begin to utilize metal until a considerable period after bronze had been supplanted by iron in Europe. "Most students of American archæology are agreed that the Mexican and Peruvian bronzes are not of any great antiquity, and that the Bronze Age must have been over in China long before it began in the New World."[1]

In Dr. Heinrich Schliemann's day the antiquity of Central American civilization was greatly exaggerated. We now know that the Maya did not develop their culture on the Mexican plateau much before the eighth century of the Christian era, and that the Aztecs arrived about 1200 A.D.; the later Mexican confederacy had flourished for only a century before it was shattered by Cortez.[2] Most of the resemblances which have been noted between the Egyptian and Central American civilizations are of a superficial character.

Plato's legend regarding the "Lost Atlantis" was of Egyptian origin. It is related in the *Timæus* and *Critias*. A certain Solon visited Sais, where he "was very honourably received" by the priests of the goddess Neith. One of the eldest of these spoke with contempt regarding the "puerile fables" of the Greeks, and said: "You are unacquainted with that most noble and excellent race of men who once inhabited your country, from whom your whole

[1] British Museum *Guide to the Antiquities of the Bronze Age*, pp. 110, 111.
[2] *Through Southern Mexico*, H. Gadow (1908), and *Bureau of American Ethnology*, E. Forstemann, Bull. 28 (1904),

present state are descended, though only a small remnant of this admirable people is now remaining". He went on to say that, according to Egyptian annals, Athens once overcame "a prodigious force", when "a mighty warlike power, rushing from the Atlantic sea, spread itself with hostile fury over all Europe and Asia". The narrative continues:

"That sea (the Atlantic) was then navigable, and had an island fronting that mouth which you in your tongue call the Pillars of Hercules; and this island was larger than Libya and Asia put together; and there was a passage hence for travellers of that day to the rest of the islands, as well as from those islands to the whole opposite continent that surrounds that the real sea. . . . In this Atlantic island, then, was formed a powerful league of Kings, who subdued the entire island, together with many others, and parts also of the Continent; besides which they subjected to their rule the inland parts of Libya, as far as Egypt, and Europe also, as far as Tyrrhenia. The whole of this force, then, being collected in a powerful league, undertook at one blow to enslave both your country and ours, and all the land besides that lies within the mouth. This was the period, Solon, when the power of your state (Athens) was universally celebrated for its virtue and strength; for surpassing all others in magnanimity and military skill, sometimes taking the lead of the Greek nation, at others left to itself by the defection of the rest, and brought into the most extreme danger, it still prevailed, raised the trophy over its assailants, kept from slavery those not as yet enslaved, insured likewise the most ample liberty for all of us without exception who dwell within the Pillars of Hercules.

Subsequently, however, through violent earthquakes and deluges which brought desolation in a single day and night, the whole of your warlike race was at once merged under the earth; and the Atlantic island itself was plunged beneath the sea and entirely disappeared; whence even now that sea is neither navigable nor to be traced out, being blocked up by the great depth of mud which the subsiding island produced."[1]

[1] The *Timæus*, Section VI.

An anonymous contributor to the *Times*[1] was the first to draw attention to the remarkable resemblance between Plato's Atlantis and the island of Crete. His theory that the Egyptian priest's legend was based on traditions regarding Cretan sea-power and the raids of piratical bands on the Egyptian coast during the Nineteenth and Twentieth Dynasties has found general favour among prominent archæologists.

Crete, one of the largest islands in the Mediterranean, is about 160 miles long, and varies in breadth from about 35 miles in the middle to 10 between Retimo and Sphakia, and only 6 miles in one place between the Gulf of Mirabello and the coast of Hierapetra. Deep gulfs indent its northern coast, and its southern shore is rugged and rock-bound. A ridge of hills extends from east to west, culminating about the centre in well-wooded Mount Psiloriti, the ancient Mount Ida, which rises to a height of about 8159 feet. Strabo called the hills in the western part of the island Leuca Oré, or "the white mountains". In the south-west the mountains almost fringe the shore. The ancient capital was situated at Knossos, near Candia, on the north. In ancient days the island was four days' sail from Egypt and two from Cyrenaica. It may well be said of Crete, as of Atlantis, that "there was a passage hence for travellers of that day to the rest of the islands, as well as from those islands to the whole opposite continent".

In the *Critias*[2] Plato says of Atlantis:

"The whole region was said to be exceedingly lofty and precipitous towards the sea, and the plain about the city (?Knossos), which encircles it, is itself surrounded by mountains sloping down to the sea, being level and smooth, all much extended, three thousand stadia in one direction, and the central part from the

---

[1] 19th February, 1909.   [2] Section XIII.

sea above two thousand. And this district of the whole island
was turned towards the south, and in an opposite direction from
the north. The mountains around it, too, were at that time
celebrated, as exceeding in number, size, and beauty all those of
the present time, having in them many hamlets enriched with
villages."

In Atlantis also, as in Crete, the prosperity of the
island kingdom depended on its sea trade. They (the
island kings) were "rulers", Solon was informed, "in the
sea of islands (? the Ægean), and, as we before said, yet
further extended their empire to all the country as far as
Egypt and Tyrrhenia".

During recent years archæologists have discovered
that a great civilization — the earliest in Europe —
flourished in Crete for many long centuries before the
rise of Mycenæ and Tiryns. It was already well developed ere the pyramids near Cairo were erected, and
before the dawn of the Twelfth Dynasty a palace had
been built at Knossos. Some time during the Eighteenth
Dynasty, and ere the famous Akhenaton was born, Crete
was overrun by raiders, who displaced the native rulers,
as the Egyptian Pharaohs had been displaced at an earlier
period by the Hyksos. This calamity was sudden and
overwhelming, and must have made a deep impression on
those states which had commercial relations with the
famous island kingdom. Its sea traders had intimate
relations with Egypt for many centuries. Evidence has
been forthcoming that they visited the Delta coast as
early as at least the Old Kingdom period. During the
time of Queen Hatshepsut and Thothmes III they were
depicted on the walls of Theban tombs, and were known
as the Kheftiu and "Princes of the Isles in the midst of
the Great Green Sea". But no reference was made to
them after the middle of the Eighteenth Dynasty. The

Cretan sea traders vanished entirely, and their place was taken ultimately by the Phœnicians.

In the Atlantis legend there are several pointed references to a civilization closely resembling that of Crete. We read of busy harbours and far-travelled merchants, of a king's palace, like the palace of Knossos, which was built of stone, and of private and public baths; "the king's baths", says Plato, "and those of private persons were apart", and there were "separate baths for women". Crete was famous for its sacrificial bull fights; so was Atlantis; and it is suggestive to find that on both islands the method obtained of capturing the animals without the aid of weapons. Plato says of Atlantis in this connection:

"As there were bulls grazing at liberty in the temple of Poseidon, ten men only of the whole number, after invoking the god to receive their sacrifice propitiously, went out to hunt swordless, with staves and chains, and whichever of the bulls they took, they brought it to the column and slaughtered it."[1]

Plato's legend used to be regarded by European scholars as "wholly mythical". It would now appear, however, that it had a genuine historical basis.

Solon visited Egypt over a thousand years after Crete had been divested of its ancient supremacy as a maritime power, and the aged priest of Sais evidently repeated to him traditions regarding it. Whether he was informed, or concluded from the Egyptian references, that Atlantis was situated beyond "the Pillars of Hercules" is quite uncertain. It was "the island farthest west", and this "would well describe Crete", Hawes suggests, "to a home-staying Egyptian of the Theban Empire".

When Crete was suddenly overwhelmed by invaders

[1] *The Critias*, Section XV.

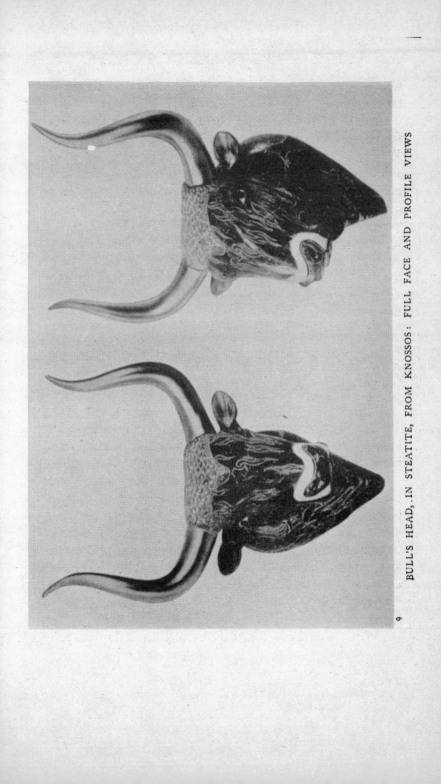

BULL'S HEAD, IN STEATITE, FROM KNOSSOS: FULL FACE AND PROFILE VIEWS

at the height of its power and prosperity, and its sailors and traders vanished from the Mediterranean, many wild rumours must have obtained currency. It need not surprise us to find that some believed the island itself "was plunged beneath the sea", and that in time the age during which flourished its kings and seafarers and bull-baiters, "won its way to the mythical", as Thucydides says in another connection.

Plato had no idea that Crete was so "old in story", and that its ancient inhabitants were the pioneers of civilization in Europe, although he may have believed, like Herodotus, that the island was at one time "wholly peopled with barbarians"[1] (non-Hellenic folk). He had even less knowledge of the Atlantic Ocean, otherwise he could not have believed that navigation beyond the Pillars of Hercules was hampered by the mud-banks which marked the site of the "lost Atlantis".

It is possible that the Egyptian legend was influenced by the ancient folk-tale, "The Shipwrecked Sailor". This hero sojourned on an island which afterwards vanished in the midst of the sea.[2] Or, perhaps, some Egyptian navigator, who set out on a voyage to Crete, at a period subsequent to the fall of Knossos, went off his course and got into trouble with sand-banks. On his return home he may have told as marvellous a story as the "shipwrecked sailor", believing that the island he sought had really been submerged.

The priest of Sais appears also to have mingled with his legend of Atlantis information derived from traditions and records regarding the settlement of Europeans on the North African coast, and the sea-raids during the reigns of Meneptah and Rameses III,[3] when, as one Egyptian

---

[1] *Herod.*, I, 173.   [2] *Egyptian Myth and Legend*, pp. 248-251.
[3] *Ibid.*, pp. 349, 350.

record sets forth, "the isles were restless, disturbed among themselves". Certain tribes from these isles, who had established themselves in Libya, actually provided mercenaries for the army and fleet of Rameses III to drive back the "late comers".[1] As Plato says of the conquerors from Atlantis, they had "subjected to their rule the inland parts of Libya, as far as Egypt".

It will thus be seen that Schliemann was not far astray when he identified Plato's Atlantis as the cradle of Ægean civilization. Had he been able, as he desired, to excavate in Crete, he might have changed his mind regarding the real significance of the Græco-Egyptian myth.

The poets and historians of ancient Greece had preserved several suggestive legends regarding Crete. They had much to say regarding its King Minos, who flourished before the Trojan war. According to Strabo[2] he resided at Knossos, and made just laws which were afterwards borrowed by the Greeks. Thucydides[3] states that he was the first to have a navy, and that he cleared the Ægean of pirates. The poet of the *Odyssey* says:

> There is a land amid the wine-dark sea
> Called Crete; rich, fruitful, girded by the waves;
> She boasts unnumbered men and ninety towns . . .
> One city in extent the rest exceeds,
> Knossos; the city in which Minos reigned—
> The King who 'gan to reign in his ninth year
> And converse held with Zeus.[4]

Minos was fabled to be the son of Zeus by a human mother, the beautiful Europé, daughter of Agenor, King of Phœnicia. The legend sets forth that one day Europé was bathing with her maids, when Zeus beheld and fell in love with her. He changed himself into a

---

[1] Between 1200 and 1190 B.C.   [2] *Strabo*, X.   [3] *Thucydides*, I, 4.
[4] *Odyssey*, XIX, 170 *et seq.*

bull, whose comely form and tameness attracted the attention of the princess. She advanced towards the animal, and was so fascinated by it that she mounted on its back. When she did so, the bull rushed into the water and swam to Crete. There she became the mother of Zeus's three sons, Minos, Rhadamanthus, and Sarpedon.

This story resembles the Scottish kelpie or "water-horse" stories. When a human being mounts on the back of one of these supernatural animals, he or she finds it impossible to dismount, and is carried away to a dark loch. Sometimes the "water-horse" makes love in human form.

Herodotus states that "certain Greeks, who would probably be Cretans, made a landing at Tyre, on the Phœnician coast, and bore off the King's daughter, Europé."[1] He suggested that Europe may have been so called after the Tyrian princess, and had been nameless before her time.[2]

Minos was supposed to have received his code of laws from his father Zeus, whom he visited in his cave on Mount Ida while the people were assembled round its base.[3] When he died he became, like the Egyptian Osiris, a judge in Hades. Ulysses related in the *Odyssey*, in the account of his visit to the land of shades:

There saw I Minos, offspring famed of Jove (Zeus);
His golden sceptre in his hand, he sat
Judge of the dead; they pleading, each in turn,
His cause, some stood, some sat, filling the house,
Whose spacious folding gates were never closed.[4]

It was related of Minos—the later king of that name—that his succession to the Cretan throne was disputed.

---

[1] *Herodotus*, I, 2.   [2] *Ibid.*, IV, 45.   [3] *Strabo*, 476.
[4] *Odyssey*, Cowper's trans., XI, 696-700.

To emphasize his divine right, he stated that the gods would grant him anything he desired. Accordingly he invoked Poseidon, god of the deep, to send him a bull from the ocean, which he promised to offer up in sacrifice. When, however, the animal appeared he was so greatly fascinated by its beauty that he substituted another. Poseidon was wroth, and caused Minos to be punished by causing his wife, Pasiphaë, to give birth to a monster, half bull and half man, called the Minotaur.

It was necessary to build a special residence for the Minotaur, to whom sacrificial offerings had to be made. Minos accordingly employed Dædalus,[1] a skilled Athenian artificer, on his return from Egypt, to construct a labyrinth at Knossos, similar to the one situated near Lake Mœris. When the work was accomplished Minos had Dædalus confined in the Labyrinth, but he was secretly liberated by Queen Pasiphaë. Then he procured wings for himself and his son Icarus. Together they flew over the Ægean, but Icarus soared so near the sun that the wax with which his wings were fastened to his body melted, and he fell into the Icarian Sea, to which his name was given. Dædalus alighted without mishap at Cumæ in Italy, where he erected a temple to Apollo, to whom he dedicated his wings.[2]

Icarus thus met a similar fate to Etana, of Babylonian fame, Nimrod in the Koran legend, and the son of the eagle giant Garuda, in the Indian epic *Ramayana*. Etana and Nimrod ascended on the backs of eagles, whose pinions were burnt by the sun. The Indian eagle was similarly punished for its presumption.[3]

Dædalus afterwards took refuge in Sicani (Sicily), where Cocalus was king. Minos fitted out a great

---

[1] *Thucydides*, I, 4.   [2] *Virgil*, Book VI.
[3] *Babylonian Myth and Legend*, pp. 165 *et seq.*

THE THRONE OF MINOS, KNOSSOS (See description, page 122)

10

expedition and visited Sicily in pursuit of Dædalus, whom he desired to put to death. There he was treacherously murdered by Cocalus or his daughters. A temple erected to his memory was dedicated to Aphrodite.

Minos had previously decreed that every year Athens should send to Crete seven youths and seven maidens to be devoured by the Minotaur.

This punishment was imposed upon the Athenians because they had jealously murdered Androgeos, son of Minos and Pasiphaë, who had surpassed all his opponents at the Panathenaic games.

For two years this tribute of human lives was paid by the subject city. But at length the hero, Theseus,

> vowed his life to sell
> For his dear Athens, which he loved so well,
> So that funereal ship might sail no more
> Freighted with living death to Creta's shore.[1]

In the third year he sailed with the sons and daughters of the noblest families in Athens. On his arrival in Crete he was informed that he must enter the Labyrinth naked and alone, and there be devoured by the Minotaur.[2] He invoked the goddess Aphrodite, who caused a beautiful Cretan maiden to fall in love with him. This was Ariadne, daughter of Minos. She secretly gave Theseus a magic sword to slay the Minotaur, and a clue of thread, with the aid of which the hero could be enabled to extricate himself from the Labyrinth. As he passed along the winding and intricate passages he unwound the clue. He slew the Minotaur, and thus delivered Athens from its tribute. On his return voyage he was accompanied by Ariadne, whom, however, he deserted at Naxos.

[1] *Catullus*, 64 (Martin's translation).
[2] *Classic Myth and Legend*, pp. 182 *et seq.*

It is believed that this legend is reminiscent of a period when Athens was subject to the rule of Crete, and it had to provide male and female toreadors for the bull-ring at Knossos. According to the exponents of the solar myth theories, Minos was the sun and Pasiphaë the moon, or the Minotaur was the sun, and the Labyrinth the sky by night, its windings being the course followed by the moon.

Hesiod, Homer, Thucydides, and Herodotus make reference to only one Minos, the son of Zeus, the great lawgiver. But Diodorus[1] and Plutarch[2] tell of a second Minos, who was the oppressor of the Athenians and the king who obtained the bull from Poseidon. Certain archæologists are of opinion that Minos was not a personal name, but a royal title which was used as is Pharaoh in the Bible, and that each Cretan ruler may have been a Minos, as each Egyptian king was an Osiris. Others hold that Minos became as popular a throne name as Rameses in Egypt and Cæsar at Rome.

It was chiefly because persistent Greek legends gave recognition to Crete as the source of pre-Hellenic culture and religion that archæologists desired to excavate on that island. In the next chapter it will be found that when opportunity came to test tradition in this regard the results obtained exceeded the most sanguine expectations.

---

[1] IV, 60.   [2] *Theseus*, 20.

CHAPTER VI

The Great Palace of Knossos

Early Discoveries in Crete—How "Tattered Legends" have been "re-clothed"—Dramatic Revelations at Knossos—Famous Fresco of the Cup-bearer—Pre-Hellenic Peoples not Barbarians—The Kheftiu of the Egyptian Texts—Phœnicians' Blue Dye came from Crete—Blue Robes of "Lost Atlantis" People—The Throne and Council Chamber of Minos—How Men were judged—Plaster Relief of Sacred Bull—Traces of Earlier Palace—A Visit to the Knossos—"Wooden Walls" of the Island Kingdom—Official, Religious, and Domestic Quarters—Frescoes in Queen's Megaron—Boxing and Dancing in the "Theatral Area"—Drainage Systems of Crete and Sumeria—Phæacians of Homer as the Cretans—Glimpses of Palace Life from the *Odyssey*—Votive Offerings in Shrines and Caves—How Queen Victoria honoured an Ancient Custom—Sacred Animals and Symbols—Snake Goddess and Priestess—How Cretan Ladies were dressed—Greek and Maltese Crosses—The Star Form of Isis.

"The ancient history of Crete", it used to be customary to write, "begins with the heroic or fabulous times. Historians and poets tell us of a king called Minos, who lived before the Trojan War. Then comes the well-known story of the Minotaur, Theseus, and Ariadne." The solar symbolists disposed of the various legends as poetic fictions.

The controversy aroused by the discoveries of Schliemann at Mycenæ and Tiryns was being waged with vigour and feeling when a native Cretan excavated at Knossos a few great jars and fragments of pottery of Mycenæan character. The spot was afterwards visited by several archæologists, including Dr. Schliemann and Dr. Dörpfeld, and a preliminary investigation brought to light undoubted indications that the remains of an ancient palace, partly built of gypsum, lay beneath the accumulated debris of ages. It was impossible, however, to make satisfactory arrangements with the local proprietors or the Turkish Government. The view expressed by Mr. W. J. Stillman, that the ruins were those of the famous Labyrinth, did not attract much attention.

In 1883 some peasants in the eastern part of the island happened upon ancient votive objects in the Dictæan cave, which they had been in the habit of utilizing as a shelter for their goats. These they put on the market, and as there was a great demand for them, a brisk trade in Cretan antiquities sprang up. Archæologists were again drawn to the island, and excavations which did not produce great results were conducted in front of the cave. This made the peasants redouble their efforts to supply a growing demand, and as they met with much success the archæologists became more and more impressed by the possibilities of the island as an area for conducting important research work. In 1894 Sir Arthur Evans and Mr. Hogarth paid a visit to Crete, and examined both the site of Knossos and the Dictæan cave. The times were inauspicious for their mission, for the island was seething with revolt against the Turkish authorities. Sir Arthur, however, was able to effect the purchase of part of the Knossos ground, having become convinced that great discoveries remained to be made. What interested him most at the time were the indications afforded by mysterious signs on blocks of gypsum of a system of hitherto unknown prehistoric writing. It was not, however, until 1900 that he was able to acquire by purchase the entire site of Knossos and conduct excavations on an extensive scale.

During the interval, further investigations were conducted by different archæologists at the Dictæan cave, which is double-chambered. Inscribed tablets and other finds came to light, but all research work had to be abandoned in 1897, when it was found that the upper cave was blocked with fallen rock. The political unrest on the island, besides, made it unsafe for foreigners to pursue even the peaceful occupation of digging for ancient pottery and figurines of bronze and lead.

In 1900, however, Sir Arthur Evans operating at Knossos, and Mr. Hogarth at the Dictæan cave, achieved results which more than fulfilled their most sanguine hopes. What they accomplished was to reveal traces of an ancient and high civilization, of which the Mycenæan appeared to be an offshoot. No such important discovery had been made since Schliemann, twenty - five years previously, unearthed the graves he so confidently believed to be those of Agamemnon and his companions. "Here again", as Mr. Asquith said at the annual meeting of the subscribers to the British School at Athens,[1] " scepticism received an ugly blow. Legends", he added, " which had become somewhat ragged and tattered have been decently reclothed. The mountain on which Zeus was supposed to have rested from his labours, and the palace in which Minos invented the science of jurisprudence, are being brought out of the region of myth into the domain of possible reality."

Sir Arthur Evans went to Crete as a trained and experienced archæologist, and was assisted from the beginning, in March, 1900, by Dr. Duncan Mackenzie, who had already distinguished himself by his excavations on the island of Melos, and Mr. Fyfe, the British School of Athens architect. A large staff of workers was employed, and by the time the season's work was concluded

[1] London, 30th October, 1900.

in June a considerable portion of the Knossos palace was laid bare.

Among the most remarkable finds were the wall paintings that decorated the plastered walls of the palace corridors and apartments. These did more to arouse public interest in pre-Hellenic civilization than even the burnt city of Troy or the gold masks of kings in the graves at Mycenæ. Here were wonderful pictures of ancient life vividly portrayed, of highly civilized Europeans who were contemporaries of the early Biblical Pharaohs, and lived in splendour and luxury long centuries before Solomon employed the skilled artisans of Phœnicia to decorate his temple and palace. And what manner of people were they? Not rude barbarians awaiting the dawn of Hellenic civilization, but men and women with refined faces and graceful forms, whose costumes resembled neither those of the Egyptians, Greeks, nor Romans. There was a note of modernity in this antique and realistic art and the manners of life it portrayed. The ladies with their puffed sleeves, narrow waists, and flounced skirts, might well have walked, not from a Cretan palace, but some Paris *salon* of the 'eighties and 'nineties.

In his first popular account of his excavations, Sir Arthur Evans gave a vivid description of his dramatic discovery of the fresco named the "cup-bearer".

"The colours", he wrote, "were almost as brilliant as when laid down over three thousand years before. For the first time the true portraiture of a man of this mysterious Mycenæan race rises before us. There was something very impressive in this vision of brilliant youth and of male beauty, recalled after so long an interval to our upper air from what had been till yesterday a forgotten world. Even our untutored Cretan workmen felt the spell and fascination.

THE CUP-BEARER, KNOSSOS

From a photograph kindly lent by Sir Arthur Evans

"They, indeed, regarded the discovery of such a painting in the bosom of the earth as nothing less than miraculous, and saw in it the 'icon' of a saint! The removal of the fresco required a delicate and laborious process of under-plastering, which necessitated its being watched at night, and old Manolis, one of the most trustworthy of our gang, was told off for the purpose. Somehow or other he fell asleep, but the wrathful saint appeared to him in a dream. Waking with a start, he was conscious of a mysterious presence; the animals round began to low and neigh, and there were visions about; 'φαντάζει', he said, in summing up his experiences next morning, 'The whole place spooks!'"[1]

This life-sized figure of a youth remains in a wonderful state of preservation from the thighs upwards, and is a feature of Candia museum. He carries in front a long pointed vessel, adorned with silver and gold, with "wine foam" at the brim, one raised hand grasping the handle and the other clutching it at the tapering end. His face is finely depicted in profile, the well-proportioned features are quite modern, and he is clean-shaved; the forehead is ample, the eyes dark, and the hair black and curly. Sir Arthur Evans thinks the skull is of "brachycephalic" (broad-headed) type; others regard it as "mesacephalic" (medium). Round the neck is a necklace of silver, and there is an ear-ring in the only ear shown, which appears to be mounted with a blue stone. There is an armlet on the upper part of the right arm, and a bracelet with what appears to be a seal round the left wrist, which looks just like the "wristlet-watch" worn at the present day. The body is well developed, and the waist tightened by a girdle. He wears a closely-fitting loin-cloth, which is richly embroidered.

[1] *Monthly Review*, March, 1901, p. 124.

Before the famous figure was reached, the excavators had laid bare a paved corridor nearly 4 yards wide. The left wall retained traces of plaster which had been decorated with a continuous fresco of a procession of male and female dignitaries. None of the faces, however, survived. It was noted that the figures resembled closely those of the "Keftiu" depicted in Egyptian tombs.

An interesting feature of these and other frescoes was the evidence they afforded of the use of a blue dye among the Cretans. Some male figures wore bright-blue robes, and others white robes bordered with blue. Apparently the Phœnicians were not the first to utilize the famous dyes which have long been so closely associated with them. Proofs were subsequently forthcoming to place this belief beyond doubt. Long before the Phœnicians supplanted the Cretans as sea-traders the islanders produced bright-blue garments, which were worn, it would appear, on special ceremonial occasions. It is of interest to note in this connection that the inhabitants of Plato's Atlantis had a similar custom. After the bull was sacrificed, and the sacred cup deposited in the temple of the gods, and "the fire round the sacrifice had been cooled, all of them dressed themselves in beautiful dark-blue robes . . . and then mutually judged one another as respects any accusations of transgressing the laws. After the acts of judgment were over, when day came, they inscribed their decisions on a golden tablet, and deposited them as memorials, together with their dresses."[1]

A hoard of inscribed clay tablets was discovered by Evans in a bath-shaped terra-cotta receptacle within a small chamber. These were embedded in charcoal, indicating that they had been placed in a wooden box which at some period was destroyed by fire.

[1] *The Critias*, Sec. XV

As the work of excavation made progress, many remarkable discoveries were made in that first season which appealed to the imaginations of scientists and workers alike. The glimpses of life afforded by fragmentary frescoes set the ghosts of vanished Cretans walking once again; the wind rustling through the disinterred ruins by night seemed "like light footfalls of spirits" passing up and down the stately corridors; the past "out of her deep heart spoke". By day

> There streamed a sunlight vapour, like the standard
> > Of some aetherial host;
> > Whilst from all the coast
> Louder and louder, gathering round, there wandered
> Over the oracular woods and divine sea
> Prophesyings which grew articulate.

The prophesyings of the excavators were no vain dreams; with dramatic swiftness they were revealed almost as soon as they were conceived. Confidently search was made for tangible evidence that this palace had been occupied by the legendary Minos, or one of the kings who bore that name or title, when his very council chamber was unearthed, and the most ancient throne in Europe brought to light.

In the heart of the palace this priceless relic of an antique civilization had lain buried in debris all through the ages that saw the coming and going of Homer's heroes, the rise and fall of Assyria, the fading beauty of Babylon, the flickering loveliness of Egypt, Persian splendour, the glory of Greece and the grandeur of Rome. The kings that sat in it had long faded into the region of myth and fancy; it was believed by wise scholars that they never existed at all. And here was the royal throne to tell another story!

The "Throne Room" was situated between the upper part of the spacious central court of the palace and the "long gallery" of the western wing. It was entered, however, from the court alone. Those who sought the presence of the king had first to pass through a small ante-room about seven yards square, the rubble walls of which, the excavators found, had been plastered with clay and faced with stucco made beautiful by artists who were skilled draughtsmen and brilliant colourists.

Stone benches were ranged round the walls of the council chamber, and between two of these on the north side stood the gypsum throne of the king on a raised slab. Here sat the Minos surrounded by his high officers of state. There is seating accommodation for about twenty on the benches.

The throne, which was found intact, is of graceful form. It presents an interesting contrast to that on which the statue of the Egyptian King Kafra of Pyramid fame is seated. Its back, which is higher and less severe, has an undulating outline, and resembles somewhat an oak leaf. The base broadens downward from the seat, which is hollowed to fit the body comfortably, and the sides are gracefully carved, the "double moulded arch" in front resembling "late Gothic" designs.

To this chamber may have been led such a wanderer as brave Ulysses, who desired to accelerate his return to his native home. He would have found the grave Minos enthroned amidst his councillors, who sat "side by side on polished stones", and perhaps heard him speak like the Phæacian king in the *Odyssey*:—

Chiefs and Senators! I speak
The dictates of my mind, therefore attend.
This guest, unknown to me, hath, wand'ring found
My palace, either from the East arrived.

Or from some nation on our western side.
Safe conduct home he asks, and our consent
Here wishes ratified, whose quick return
Be it our part, as usual, to promote;
For at no time the stranger, from what coast
Soe'er, who hath resorted to our doors,
Hath long complained of his detention here.
Haste—draw ye down into the sacred Deep
A vessel of prime speed, and, from among
The people, fifty and two youths select,
Approved the best; then, lashing fast the oars,
Leave her, that at my palace ye may make
Short feast, for which myself will all provide.
Thus I enjoin the crew, but as for these
Of sceptred rank, I bid them all alike
To my own board, that here we may regale
The stranger nobly, and let none refuse.
Call, too, Demodocus, the bard divine,
To share my banquet, whom the gods have blest
With pow'rs of song delectable, unmatch'd
By any, when his genius once is fired.[1]

Opposite the "high seat" of Minos in the "Throne Room" was a shallow tank with stone breastwork. Its use is uncertain. The theory that ambassadors and others washed here while awaiting the king is not convincing; there were bath-rooms elsewhere in the vast palace in which travel-wearied men could refresh and cleanse themselves. Perhaps it was simply part of the decorative scheme. Fish may have been kept here to give a touch of realism to the scenes painted on the stucco-plastered walls. Traces survive of a riverside fresco, with reeds and grasses and budding flowers beside flowing waters, which must have imparted to the chamber an air of repose. On either side of the door were two gleaming griffins, crested with peacock's plumes, "showing", says Sir Arthur Evans,

---

[1] Cowper's *Odyssey*, VIII, 30–54.

"that this Indian fowl was known to the East Mediterranean world long before the days of Solomon". A flowery landscape formed a strangely-contrasting background, with ferns and palm-trees fringing the soft blue stream.

Before this chamber was swept by the fire which destroyed the palace, it must have been at once stately and beautiful. No doubt the benches were strewn with richly-embroidered rugs and cushions to complete the brilliant colour scheme of which fragmentary traces survive. The throne appears to have been richly decorated. "The whole face of the gypsum", writes Sir Arthur Evans, "had been coated with a fine white plaster wash, and this again coloured in various ways. The seat showed distinct remains of a brilliant red colour. A minute examination of the back disclosed the fact that fine lines had been traced on it such as are also visible on the wall frescoes, a technical device, borrowed from Egyptian practice, for guiding the artist's hands. It would appear, therefore, that the back of the throne had been once decorated with an elaborate colour design."[1] The paved floor was also, apparently, set in a border of gypsum covered with plaster and richly adorned.

Another interesting early find was the "wine cellar" of the palace—or rather the "cellars". In the lengthy corridors were found intact rows of great jars from which wine was drawn by the "cup-bearers" for the feast, and oil was likewise stored. Worthy of special mention is also the painted plaster relief of a bull which dignified the wall of one of the chambers. "It is life-sized, or somewhat over", its discoverer wrote at the time. "The eye has an extraordinary prominence, its pupil is yellow and the iris a bright-red, of which narrower bands again

[1] *The Annual of the British School at Athens*, Vol. VI, p. 38.

PAINTED PLASTER RELIEF—BULL'S HEAD—KNOSSOS

From a photograph kindly lent by Sir Arthur Evans

appear encircling the white towards the lower circumference of the ball. The horn is of greyish hue. . . . Such as it is, this painted relief is the most magnificent monument of Mycenæan plastic art that has come down to our time. The rendering of the bull, for which the artists of this period showed so great a predilection, is full of life and spirit. It combines in a high degree naturalism with grandeur, and it is no exaggeration to say that no figure of a bull at once so powerful and so true was produced by later classical art."[1]

The first season's discoveries made it evident that the palace had been of great dimensions and splendour. Nothing was found to indicate that it flourished after the Mycenæan period. It had evidently been destroyed by fire in pre-Hellenic times, before the thirteenth century B.C. Traces were also found of a still earlier palace, below which were the layers of the Neolithic (Late Stone Age) period. Regretfully Sir Arthur Evans had to suspend operations in June 1900 on such a promising site, owing to the malarious conditions and distressing dust-clouds raised by the south wind from Libya. Nine brief weeks, however, had revealed enough to satisfy even so fortunate an archæologist as Sir Arthur, who had the luck of Schliemann combined happily with richer experience and technical skill. No doubt could any longer remain that a great pre-Homeric civilization had flourished in Crete, and that Minos had been rescued from the fairyland of the solar symbolists to take his place once again among the mighty monarchs of the great days of old.

Were it possible for us, by waving the wand of a magician, to conjure before our eyes this wonderful palace, as it existed when Queen Hatshepsut reigned over Egypt and Thothmes III was fretting to seize the reins of

---

[1] *Annual of the British School at Athens*, Vol. VI, pp. 51-3.

power, we should be first of all impressed by the modernity of its aspect.

We are guided from the sea-shore, like the hero of the *Odyssey*, who visited the dwelling of Alcinous, the Phæacian king, by a goddess in human guise. At a favourable point of vantage on the poplar-fringed highway, we are afforded the first glimpse of the palace of Knossos. It is situated beside a river[1] on a low hill in the midst of a fertile valley, about $3\frac{1}{2}$ miles from Candia. The dominating feature of the landscape is sacred Mount Juktas, with its notched peak. It seems as if the "hammer god" had intended to shape the mountain like an Egyptian pyramid, and, having finished one side, abandoned the task soon after beginning to splinter out the other.

The palace, which is approached by paved roadways, has a flat roof and forms a rough square, each side being about 130 yards long. No walls surround it. Crete, like "old England", is protected by its navy—its "wooden walls". The Minos kings have suppressed the island pirates who were wont to fall upon unprotected towns and plunder them, and hold command of the sea.[2]

We enter the palace by the north gate, passing groups of soldiers on sentry duty. A comparatively small force could defend the narrow way between the massive walls which lead us to the great Central Court. Note these little towers and guard-houses, from which they could discharge their arrows against raiders. There are dark dungeons beneath us, over 20 feet deep, in which prisoners are fretting their lives away, thinking of "Fatherland, of child, and wife, and slave", and "the wandering fields of barren foam" on which they had ventured to defy the might of Minos.

[1] The river used to flow nearer the palace site than it does at present.
[2] *Thucydides*, I, 2–4.

The Central Court in the middle of the palace is over 60 yards long and about 30 yards wide. On the eastern side are the private apartments of the royal family, but these are not entered from the Court, but along mazy corridors which are elsewhere approached. The first door on the western side leads us through an ante-room to the Throne Room. Farther down, and near the centre of the Court, is the shrine of the Snake goddess. Behind it are the west and east Pillar Rooms and the room containing temple repositories; these apartments appear to have a religious significance. Farther south is the large "Court of the Altar". We pass out of the Court at the northern end, and penetrate the western wing of the palace. We find it is divided about the middle by the "Long Gallery". Walking southward, we pass, on the right, numerous store rooms, until we reach an entrance leading to the sacred apartments behind the shrine of the Snake goddess. It has already dawned upon us that we are in a labyrinthine building, if not the real Labyrinth with its intricate and tortuous passages through which the famous Theseus was able to wander freely and extricate himself from with the aid of the clue given to him by the princess Ariadne. One apartment leads to another, and when our progress is arrested by blind alleys we turn back and find it difficult, without the help of a guide, to return to the Long Gallery that opens on the zigzag route back to the Central Court. The eastern wing is similarly of mazy character. In the southern part of it are reception rooms, living-rooms, bedrooms, and bath-rooms. These include the "Hall of the Colonnades", the "Hall of the Double Axes", the "Queen's Megaron", and the "Room of the Plaster Couch".[1] Stairways lead to the upper stories.

The rooms assigned to the ladies are approached

---

[1] These and other names were given to the apartments by Sir Arthur Evans.

through a dark "dog's-leg corridor". We enter the "Queen's Megaron" and are silenced by its wonderful beauty. The paved floor is overlaid with embroidered rugs, and has a richly-coloured "surround" of painted plaster. Frescoes adorn the walls. Here is a woodland scene with a brilliantly-plumaged bird in flight. On the north side is the whirling figure of a bright-eyed dancing girl, her long hair floating out on either side in rippling bird-wing curves, her arms responding to the rise and fall of the music. She leans slightly forward, poised on one foot. She wears a yellow jacket with short arms, with a zigzag border of red and blue. Other dancers are tripping near her. Beyond these are the musicians.[1] We are reminded of one of the scenes on the famous shield of Achilles:—

> There, too, the skilful artist's hand had wrought,
> With curious workmanship, a mazy dance,
> Like that which Daedalus in Knossos erst
> At fair-hair'd[2] Ariadne's bidding framed.
> There, laying on each other's wrist their hand,
> Bright youths and many suitor'd maidens danced:
> In fair white linen these; in tunics those
> Well woven, shining soft with fragrant oils . . .
> Now whirl'd they round with nimble practised feet,
> Easy, as when a potter, seated, turns
> A wheel, new fashioned by his skilful hand,
> And spins it round, to prove if true it run:
> Now featly mov'd in well-beseeming ranks.
> A numerous crowd, around, the lovely dance
> Survey'd, delighted.[3]

Another fresco is a picturesque study of sub-marine life. Fish dart to and fro above the ocean floor about

---

[1] Only one dancing figure has survived of this fresco.
[2] Or "Ariadne of the lovely tresses".
[3] *Iliad*, XVIII, 590 *et seq.* (Derby's translation).

two great snouted dolphins, the air bubbles darting from
their fins and tails to indicate that they are in motion.[1]

In the Queen's Megaron the Cretan ladies are wont
to chatter over their needlework during the heat of the
day. They admire the works of art on the walls, and
discuss the merits of the various draughtsmen who reside
elsewhere in the palace. Note how little furniture they
require. They won't have anything that is not absolutely
necessary in their rooms, and what they have is beautiful.
The charm of wide spaces appeals to them. A broad
fresco must not be interrupted by ornaments that might
distract attention from such a masterpiece. It is sufficient
in itself to fill a large part of the room.

Visitors who arrive dusty and weary are conducted
to the bath-room, which is entered through a door at the
north-west corner. Its walls are plainly painted, but
relieved from the commonplace by a broad dado of
flowing spirals with rosette centres. Portable tubs are
provided, and attendants spray water over those who use
them.

We pass from this, the south-eastern, to the north-
eastern wing, and find it is occupied by artistic craftsmen
who are continually employed in beautifying the palace.
Art is under royal patronage. Here, too, are the rooms
of musicians. Farther on are the butlers; these provide
the stores for the cooks, who occupy the domestic quarters
south of the Queen's Megaron and beneath it.

Once again the guards permit us to walk along the
corridor of the north entrance, and we turn from their
guard-houses and sentinel-boxes to visit the "Theatral
Area" at the north-western corner of the palace. On

---

[1] These dolphins resemble closely the so-called "swimming elephants" on Scottish
sculptured stones. Like the doves they had evidently a religious significance. Pausanias
tells of a Demeter which held in one hand a dolphin and in another a dove.

two sides are tiers of stone steps on which spectators seat
themselves.   One is the royal "grand stand", and it has
accommodation for about 200 people; the other is reserved
for young people.   The crowds stand round about in a
circle behind the wooden barriers.   Sometimes the attrac-
tion is an athletic display.   Boxers and wrestlers are
popular.   Here, too, the dancers display their skill when
the king calls upon them to "tread the circus with
harmonious steps".   Their dances have a religious
significance.

Turning southward from the Theatral Area we walk
along the broad west court outside the palace.   It is
paved and terraced.   Almost the whole of this outer
portion of the western wing is occupied by stores, and
the court is the market-place.   Here come the traders
who sell their fruit and vegetables and wares; and here
too those who pay their taxes in kind.   Officials and
merchants pass to and fro; here is a great consignment of
goods from Egypt which is being unpacked.   The scribes
are busy checking invoices, and issuing orders for its disposal.   A group of young people gather round a sailor,
who is accompanied by a native Egyptian, and fills their
ears with wonderful stories regarding the river Nile and
the great cities on its banks.

Our steps are directed to the southern side of the
palace.   Here is the door leading to the "Court of the
Altar" and other sacred rooms.   Farther on is the
"Court of the Sanctuary" in the southern part of the
east wing.   Workmen are busy near us extending the
palace beyond the royal apartments.

We have now taken a rapid survey of the great square
palace of Knossos.   There are many details, however, that
have escaped our notice.   The Cretans were not only
great builders, but also experienced sanitary engineers.

A GLIMPSE OF THE EXCAVATED REMAINS OF THE PALACE OF KNOSSOS

13

An excellent drainage system was one of the remarkable features of the palace. Terra-cotta drain-pipes, which might have been made yesterday, connect water-flushed closets "of almost modern type", and bath-rooms with a great square drain which workmen could enter to effect repairs through "manholes". Rain water was introduced into the palace, and its flow automatically controlled.

Crete, however, was not alone in anticipating modern sanitary methods. Long before the Late Minoan period, which began about 1700 B.C., the Sumero-Babylonians had a drainage system. Drains and culverts have been excavated at Nippur in stratum which dates before the reign of Sargon I (c. 2650 B.C.), as well as at Surghul, near Lagash, Fara, the site of Shuruppak, and elsewhere. It is uncertain, however, whether the Cretans derived their elaborate drainage system from Sumeria. What remains clear, however, is that on the island kingdom, and in cities of the Tigro-Euphratean valley, the problem of how to prevent the spread of water-borne diseases had been dealt with on scientific lines.

A glimpse of such a palace as that of Knossos, if not of this palace itself, is obtained in the *Odyssey*, and in that part from which quotation has been made in dealing with the "Throne Room".

Ulysses (Odysseus), the wanderer, is cast ashore on the island of Scheria, the seat of the Phæacians, "who of old, upon a time, dwelt in spacious Hypereia". Dr. Drerup[1] and Professor Burrows[2] have independently arrived at the conclusion that Scheria is Crete, Hypereia being Sicily, "and that the origin of the Odyssey is to be sought for in Crete". Burrows adds: "It can be at once granted that attention has been unduly concentrated on Ithaca, Leukias, and Corcyra, while the numerous refer-

---

[1] *Homer* (1903), pp. 130 *et seq.*   [2] *The Discoveries in Crete* (1907), pp. 207 *et seq.*

ences in the *Odyssey*[1] to the topography of Crete have been neglected ". Dr. Drerup draws attention to a most suggestive passage in the seventh book, in which the secret is "let out". The Phæacian King, Alcinous, promises that his seamen will convey the shipwrecked stranger to his home, "even though it be much farther than Euboea, which ", he explains, "certain of our men say is the farthest of lands, they who saw it, when they carried Rhadamanthus of the fair hair, to visit Tityos, son of Gaia ".[2] Now Rhadamanthus was the brother of the Cretan King Minos. "What was he doing in Corcyra?" asks Professor Burrows. "The Phæacians," adds the same writer, "themselves mariners, artists, feasters, dancers, are surely the Minoans of Crete."

Ulysses (Odysseus) is found on the sea-coast by the princess Nausicaa. She provides him with clothing and food, and says—

> Up stranger! seek the city. I will lead
> Thy steps towards my royal father's house
> Where all Phæacia's nobles thou shalt see.

Her proposal is to lead him to her father's farm, where he will gaze on the safe harbour in which

> Our gallant barks
> Line all the road, each stationed in her place,
> And where, adjoining close the splendid fane
> Of Neptune,[3] stands the forum with huge stones
> From quarries hither drawn, constructed strong,
> In which the rigging of their barks they keep
> Sail cloth and cordage, and make smooth their oars.

She intends to leave him at this point, fearing that the sailors might ask, "Who is this that goes with Nausicaa?"

---

[1] III, 291–300; XIX, 172–9, 188–9, 200, 338.
[2] Butcher and Lang's *Odyssey*, p. 113.   [3] Poseidon in the original.

and cast imputations on her character. Apparently the
gossips were as troublesome in those times as in our own.
She adds naively:

> I should blame
> A virgin guilty of such conduct much,
> Myself, who reckless of her parent's will
> Should so familiar with a man consort,
> Ere celebration of her spousal rites.

The princess then advises the wanderer to make his
way from the royal home farm to the palace:—

> Ask where Alcinous dwells, my valiant sire.
> Well known is his abode, so that with ease
> A child might lead thee to it.

When he is received within the court he should at once
seek the queen, her mother.

> She beside a column sits
> In the hearth's blaze, twirling her fleecy threads
> Tinged with sea purple, bright, magnificent!
> With all her maidens orderly behind.

If he makes direct appeal to this royal lady he will be sure
to "win a glad return to his island home".

The wanderer is much impressed by the gorgeous
palace of the Phæacian king, towards which he is led by
the grey-eyed goddess Athene, who assumed the guise of
a girl carrying a pitcher. He pauses on the threshold,
gazing with wonder on the inner walls covered with brass
and surrounded by a blue dado. Doors are of gold and
the door-posts of silver. He has a glimpse of a feasting
chamber; the seats against the wall are covered with
mantles of "subtlest warp", the "work of many a female
hand". There the Phæacians are wont to sit eating and
drinking in the flare of the torches held in the hands of
golden figures of young men.

Fifty handmaidens attend on the King and Queen. Some grind the golden corn in millstones. Others sit spinning and weaving with fingers

> Restless as leaves
> Of lofty poplars fluttering in the breeze.

So closely do they weave linen that oil will fall off it. Just as the Phæacian men are skilled beyond others as mariners, so are the women the most accomplished at the loom. The goddess Athene has given them much wisdom as workers, and richest fancy.

Outside the courtyard of the palace is a large garden surrounded by a hedge. There grows many a luxuriant and lofty tree.

> Pomegranate, pear, the apple blushing bright,
> The honied fig, and unctuous olive smooth.
> Those fruits, nor winter's cold nor summer's heat
> Fear ever, fail not, wither not, but hang
> Perennial . . .
> Pears after pears to full dimensions swell,
> Figs follow figs, grapes clust'ring grow again.
> Where clusters grew, and (every apple stript)
> The boughs soon tempt the gath'rer as before.
> There too, well-rooted, and of fruit profuse,
> His vineyard grows . . .
>   On the garden's verge extreme
> Flow'rs of all hues smile all the year, arranged
> With neatest art judicious, and amid
> The lovely scene two fountains welling forth,
> One visits, into every part diffus'd
> The garden ground, the other soft beneath
> The threshold steals into the palace court,
> Whence ev'ry citizen his vase supplies.

The wanderer, having gazed with wonder about him, enters the palace. He sees men pouring out wine to keen-eyed Hermes, the slayer of Argos, before retiring for the night. Athene again comes to his aid, and wraps him in a mist so that he passes, unseen by anyone, until he reaches the queen. He tells her of his plight, and asks for safe conduct to his native land, and the great lady takes pity on him. The wanderer is given food and wine. Before he retires to rest he relates to King Alcinous how he was cast on the island shore and conducted to the farm by the princess. Recognizing that the girl has compromised herself, his majesty offers her in marriage to the stranger, promising

> House would I give thee and possessions too
> Were such thy choice.

He adds, however, that if he prefers to return home no man in Phæacia "shall by force detain thee". The wanderer's decision is, "Grant to me to visit my native shores again". So the matter ends. Odysseus is conducted to

> a fleecy couch
> Under the portico, with purple rugs
> Resplendent, and with arras spread beneath
> And over all with cloaks of shaggy pile.

The king and queen retire to an "inner chamber".

Next morning the king and his counsellors assemble as indicated in the description of the Throne Room of Knossos palace, and arrangements are completed to give Odysseus a safe conduct home. Before he goes a feast is held, at which "the beloved minstrel", Demodocus, sings of the Trojan war. Then a visit is paid to the "Theatral Area", where athletes display feats of strength. A young man challenges the stranger boastfully. Roused to wrath by his speech, Odysseus says:

> I am not, as thou sayest,
> A novice in these sports but took the lead

> In all, while youth and strength were on my side.
> But I am now in bands of sorrow held,
> And of misfortune, having much endured
> In war, and buffeting the boist'rous waves.

He, however, flung a quoit and broke all records.   Then he challenged the young man who taunted him

> To box, to wrestle with me, or to run . . .
> There is no game athletic in the use
> Of all mankind, too difficult for me.

The challenge is not accepted, however.   Then the king says:

> We boast not much the boxer's skill, nor yet
> The wrestler's; but light-footed in the race
> Are we, and navigators well informed.
> Our pleasures are the feast, the harp, the dance;
> Garments for change, the tepid bath, the bed.
> Come, ye Phæacians, beyond others skilled
> To tread the circus with harmonious steps,
> Come play before us; that our guest arrived
> In his own country, may inform his friends
> How far in seamanship we all excel,
> In running, in the dance, and in the song.[1]

In these passages we probably have, as some authorities think, real Cretan memories.   It is uncertain whether or not actual Cretan poems were utilized in the *Odyssey*. Professor Burrows suggests that the glories of the palace of Alcinous " were sung by men who had heard of them as living realities, even if they had not themselves seen them; men who had walked the palaces (Knossos and Phæstos) perhaps, if not as their masters, at least as mercenaries or freebooters ".[2]

It will be noted that Alcinous says the Phæacians do

---

[1] Extracts from the *Odyssey*, Books VII and VIII (Cowper's translation).
[2] *The Discoveries in Crete*, p. 209.

not boast much of the skill of their boxers. Yet the Cretan pugilists are found depicted in seal impressions, on vases, &c., suggesting that they were regarded with pride as peerless exponents of the " manly sport ". It may be, however, that in the last period (Late Minoan III) the island boxers were surpassed by those among the more muscular northerners, who were settled in Crete in increasing numbers. "Late Minoan III", writes Professor Burrows, " is a long period, and marks the successive stages of a gradually decaying culture." The " Cretan memories" in the Homeric poems " refer to Late Minoan III".[1] Apparently the islanders were still famous as skilled mariners, while their dancing was much admired; but as athletes and warriors they had to acknowledge the superiority of the less cultured invaders who had descended on their shores.

Reference has been made to the sacred rooms in the great palace of Knossos. Unlike the Egyptians, the Cretans erected no temples. Their religious ceremonies were conducted in their homes, on their fields, and beside sacred mountain caves. Sir Arthur Evans discovered in the south-eastern part of the palace, near the ladies' rooms, a little shrine which could not have accommodated more than a few persons.

Another shrine was entered from the Central Court to the south of the Throne Room in the western wing. It would appear that this part of the palace was invested with special sanctity. In one of the apartments were found superficial cists in the pavement. The first two had been rifled. Then an undisturbed one was located and opened. It contained a large number of what appeared to be deposits of religious character—vessels containing burnt corn which had been offered to a deity or

---

[1] *The Discoveries in Crete*, pp. 209-10.

to deities, tablets, libation tables, and so on.   Fragments
of faience (native porcelain) had figures of goddesses, cows
and calves, goats and kids, and floral and other designs.
A number of cockles and other sea-shells artificially tinted
in various colours also came to light.   Apparently these
cists answered the same purpose as sacred caves in which
religious offerings were placed.

This custom of effecting a ceremonial connection with
a holy place still survives in our own country.   Portions
of clothing are attached to trees overhanging wishing and
curative wells, and coins and pins are also dropped into
them.   "Pin wells", sometimes called "Penny wells",
are not uncommon.   In some cases nails are driven into
the tree.   Special mention may be made of the well and
tree of Isle Maree, on Loch Maree, in the Scottish county
of Ross and Cromarty.   It was visited on a Sunday in
September, 1877, by the late Queen Victoria.   Her
Majesty read a short sermon to her gillies, and afterwards, with a smile, attached an offering to the wishing
tree.   Such offerings are never removed, for it is believed
that a terrible misfortune would befall the individual who
committed such an act of desecration.   In ancient Egypt
offerings were made at tombs, and in Babylonia votive
figures of deities mounted on nails were driven into
sacred shrines.

Seal impressions, which have been found in the Cretan
palace cists, are of special interest.   Among the designs
were figures of owls, doves, ducks, goats, dogs, lions
seizing prey, horned sheep, gods and goddesses.   Flowers,
sea-shells, houses, &c., were also depicted.   One clay
impression of a boxer suggests that it was deposited by
the pugilist himself to ensure his good luck at a great
competition in the Theatral Area.   The shells suggest
that sailors desired protection.   One seal of undoubted

A CRETAN SHRINE: RESTORED BY SIR ARTHUR EVANS

Snake goddesses, or goddess and priestess, "fetish cross", shells, libation jugs, stones hollowed for holding offerings, &c.

14

maritime significance shows a man in a boat attacking a dog-headed sea-monster.   The floral seals were probably offerings to the earth mother in Spring.   No doubt the cow suckling its calf and the goat its kid were fertility symbols.

The faience relief of the wild goat and its young is one of the triumphs of Cretan art.   It is of pale-green colour, with dark sepia markings.   The animals are as lifelike as those depicted in the Palæolithic cave-drawings. One of the kids is sucking in crouched posture, and the other bleats impatiently in front.   The nimble-footed mother has passed with erect head and widely-opened eyes.   She is the watchful protector and constant nourisher of her young—a symbol of maternity.   The cow and calf is also a fine composition.   Commenting on these, Sir Arthur Evans says that "in beauty of modelling and in living interest, Egyptian, Phœnician, and, it must be added, classical Greek . . . are far surpassed by the Minoan artist".

Among the marine subjects in faience is one showing two flying fish (the "sea swallows" of the modern Greeks) swimming between rocks and over sea-shells lying on the sand.

Nothing, however, among these votive deposits can surpass in living interest the faience figures of the Snake goddess and her priestess.   The former is a semi-anthropomorphic figure with the ears of a cow or some other animal.   The exaggerated ear suggests "Broad Ear", one of the members of the family of the Sumerian sea-god Ea. She may have been thus depicted to remind her worshippers that she was ever ready to hear their petitions. On the other hand, it is not improbable that she had at one time the head of a cow or sow.   Demeter at Phigalia was horse-headed, and there were serpents in her hair.

This goddess of Crete has a high head-dress of spiral pattern, round which a serpent has enfolded itself, and apparently its head, which is missing, protruded in front like the uræus on the Egyptian "helmets" of royalty. Another snake is grasped by the head in her right hand and by the tail in the left, and its body lies wriggling along her outstretched arms, and over her shoulders, forming a loop behind, which narrows at her waist and widens out below it. Other two snakes are twined round her hips below the waist. These reptiles are of green colour with purple-brown spots. Evidently they are symbols of fertility and growth of vegetation. The goddess is attired in a bell-shaped skirt suspended from her "wasp waist", and a short-sleeved, tight-fitting jacket bodice, with short sleeves, open in front to display her ample breasts. Her skin is white, her eyes dark: she wears a necklace round her neck, and her hair falls down behind but only to her shoulders, being gathered up in a fringed arrangement at the back of the head.

The priestess, or votary, has her arms lifted in the Egyptian attitude of adoration. In each hand she grasps a small wriggling snake. A stiff girdle entwines her narrow waist. Unfortunately the head is missing. The jacket bodice is similar to that of the goddess, and the breasts are also ample and bare. "The skirt", writes Lady Evans, "consists of seven flounces fastened apparently on a 'foundation', so that the hem of each flounce falls just over the head of the one below it. . . . Over this skirt is worn a double apron or 'polonaise' similar to that of the goddess, but not falling so deeply, and not so richly ornamented. The main surface is covered with a reticulated pattern, each reticulation being filled with horizontal lines in its upper half. The general effect is that of a check or small plaid. . . . The whole costume of both figures seems to consist of garments carefully sewn and fitted to the shape without any trace of flowing draperies.[1]

Among the symbols, which had evidently a religious significance, are the "horns of consecration", the sacred pillars and trees, the double axe, the "swastika" (crux gammata), a square cross with staff handles, and the plain equal-limbed cross. These are represented on seals, in faience, and on stones. Sir Arthur Evans suggests that a small marble cross he discovered—he calls it a "fetish cross"—occupied a central position in the Cretan shrine of the mother goddess. "A cross of orthodox Greek shape", he says, "was not only a religious symbol of Minoan cult, but seems to be traceable in later offshoots of the Minoan religion from Gaza to Eryx". He adds: "It must, moreover, be borne in mind that the equal-limbed eastern cross retains the symbolic form of the primitive star sign, as we see it attached to the service of the Minoan divinities. . . . The cross as a symbol or amulet was also known among the Babylonians and Assyrians. It appears on cylinders (according to Professor Sayce, of the Kassite period), apparently as a sign of divinity. As an amulet on Assyrian necklaces it is seen associated, as on the Palaikastro (Crete) mould, with a rayed (solar) and a semi-lunar emblem—in other words it once more represents a star." The Maltese cross first appears on Elamite pottery of the Neolithic Age: it was introduced into Babylonia at a later period. In Egypt it figures prominently in the famous floret coronet of a Middle Kingdom princess which was found at Dashur, and is believed by some authorities to be of Hittite origin.

If the Cretan cross was an astral symbol, it would appear that the snake or dove goddess was associated, like

[1] *The Annual of the British School at Athens*, Vol. IX, pp. 74 *et seq.*

the Egyptian Isis and the Babylonian Ishtar, with Sirius
or some other star which was connected with the food
supply.   The rising of Sirius in Egypt coincides with the
beginning of the Nile flood.   It appears on the "night of
the drop".   The star form of the bereaved Isis lets fall
the first tear for Osiris, and as the body moisture of deities
has fertilizing and creative properties, it causes the river
to increase in volume so that the land may be rendered
capable of bearing abundant crops.   Osiris springs up in
season as the rejuvenated corn spirit.

Other sites in Crete will be dealt with in the chapters
which follow.   But before dealing with these in detail,
it will be of interest to glean evidence from the general
finds regarding the early stages of civilization on the
island and the first peoples who settled there, and also
to compare the beliefs that obtained among the various
peoples of the ancient race who, having adopted the
agricultural mode of life, laid the foundations of great
civilizations, among which that of Crete was so brilliant
an example.

CHAPTER VII

Races and Myths of Neolithic Crete

The Cave-dwellers of Crete—Azilian Stage of Culture—The Neolithic Folk—Obsidian obtained from Melos—Neolithic Finds at Knossos and Phæstos —Island inhabited at 10,000 B.C.—Settlers of the Mediterranean Race—The Evidence of Early Egyptian Graves—Migrations from North Africa into Europe—Appearance of Anatolians in Crete—The Agriculturists and Bearded Pastoralists—Racial Religious Beliefs in Scotland and Greece—The Various Cults of Zeus—Political Significance of Zeus Worship—Legend of the Cretan Zeus—The Tomb of the God—Traditional Holy Places appropriated by Early Christians—Cretan Zeus like Osiris, Adonis, Tammuz, Attis, and other Young Gods—Kings as Incarnations of Deities—Egyptian and Greek Mysticism— Demeter and Dionysus—Totemic Animals Tabooed—Pig Sacred in Egypt and Crete—The Sacred Goat—Bull Cult of Knossos—Links between Libya and Crete—The Double-axe Symbol—Maltese Story of "Axe Land"—Etymology and Labyrinth—Neolithic Houses in Crete—Survival of Palæolithic Traditions and Customs and Types—Religious Borrowing.

WHO were the earliest inhabitants of Crete and whence came they? The problem is involved in obscurity, but certain suggestive facts may be stated which throw some light upon it. As already indicated (Chapter III) no bones of Palæolithic man have been discovered on the island. Signor Taramelli, an Italian excavator, recently explored, however, the interesting grotto of Miamu, which was inhabited by early settlers who appear to have been either in the Late Magdelenian or the Azilian stage of culture. The deposit of the partly artificial cave yielded on examination a number of bone heads of weapons and bone spatulas, somewhat like the "spoon-shaped celts" of the Swiss lake-dwellings and the Rhone valley, which were probably utilized by huntsmen for scooping out marrow from the bones of roasted animals. Evidently, therefore, Crete had been occupied at a remote period by cave-dwellers. The lower grotto deposit was overlaid by Bronze Age remains.

During the long interval which followed the last glacial epoch, there was a gradual and general subsidence of land round the Mediterranean as elsewhere. But after Crete had become detached from Greece, it still remained for a period of uncertain duration connected with Asia Minor, where there were, no doubt, communities of cave-dwellers as in Phœnicia and Palestine. These ancient folks of the Cretan grotto of Miamu may have been isolated from their congeners on the mainland like the "beachcombers" of the "kitchen middens" in England and Scotland. We cannot say whether they became extinct or not. It is possible that the seafaring pioneers of the Neolithic Age found inhabitants on the island.

The earliest traces of the Neolithic folk have been discovered in the vicinity of the mountain village of Magasa. Among the relics were polished stone axes, numerous bone awls, and fragments of coarse pottery belonging to a similar stage of culture to that which obtained among the Neolithic cave-dwellers of Gezer, Palestine, who, as has been indicated, made pottery also. Apparently the Magasa settlers came from the north in their many-oared galleys, resembling those depicted on the painted pre-Dynastic pottery of Egypt. As much is indicated by the finds of obsidian flakes. Neolithic man, it may be explained, not only constructed knives, saws, arrow-heads, and other small implements from flint found in chalk deposits, and chert nodules embedded in limestone, but also from obsidian, which is the "glassy" variety of volcanic rock—hardened lava—known as liparite,[1] the "frothy" variety being "pumice-stone". Now, there is no obsidian in Crete. The only source of it in the Ægean is the Island of Melos (now Milos, or Milo), where the famous statue of Venus de Milo was discovered. Evidently an early Neolithic civilization had local development in the Cyclades, amidst

> the sprinkled isles,
> Lily on lily, that o'erlace the sea,
> And laugh their pride when the light wave lisps "Greece".[2]

Obsidian artifacts have been found in various islands of the Ægean, as well as on the mainland at Mycenæ and elsewhere, on the island of Cyprus, and as far westward as Malta, where it was imported, apparently from Melos, to be worked, for flakes as well as knives have been found, and also in Sicily. Schliemann discovered knives and flakes of obsidian in "the four lowest prehistoric cities at Hissarlik". He remarked regarding them at the time: "All are two-edged, and some are so sharp that one might shave with them".[3] The Jews still use flint and obsidian knives in religious ceremonies. Obsidian implements have also been taken from Neolithic strata near Nineveh. In Egypt, during the Old Kingdom Period, the beaten-copper statues of Pepi I and his son were given eyes of obsidian.

When Knossos and Phæstos were first selected as settlements, the Cretans had advanced into the later stage of Neolithic culture. Their obsidian knives were finely wrought, and have been found associated with serpentine maces, axes of diorite and other hard stone, and, as it is of special interest to note, clay and stone spindle whorls, indicating that the art of spinning was well known.

---

[1] So called after the semi-crystalline rock emitted as lava from the chief volcano of the Lipari Islands. [2] Browning's "Cleon". [3] *Ilios*, p. 247.

It has been stated that the beginning of the Neolithic Age has been dated approximately 10,000 B.C. The calculation has been arrived at by the comparative study of the stratified deposit at Knossos. The layers of the historic period are about 18 feet deep. Below these are the Neolithic layers, through which a depth of about 20 feet has been reached. Roughly about 3 feet was accumulated every thousand years. Allowing for variation in the deposits, the minimum date 10,000 B.C. appears to be safe; even 12,000 B.C. or 13,000 B.C. is possible. There is no trace in the first layer of a culture so low as that of Magasa. The earliest "folk-wave" which reached Knossos came with a form of culture which had been developed elsewhere.

Unfortunately no human remains have been unearthed in the Neolithic deposit to afford evidence regarding the racial affinities of these pioneers of civilization. Ethnologists are of opinion that they were representations of the Mediterranean race, and arrive at their conclusion on the following grounds: The large majority of the skulls found in Bronze Age graves are long, and are similar to those taken from Neolithic graves in Greece and elsewhere throughout Europe, especially in the south and west, as well as those from the pre-Dynastic graves of Egypt. The average stature of the Minoan Cretans was about 5 feet 4 inches. In the early Bronze Age there was a broad-headed minority.

It has been found that, as Dr. Collignon says, "when a race is well seated in a region, fixed to the soil by agriculture, acclimatized by natural selection, and sufficiently dense, it opposes an enormous resistance to absorption by the new-comers, whoever they may be". This view finds conspicuous support in the permanence of the Cro-Magnon type of mankind in the Dordogne valley. An interval of at least 20,000 years has not altered particular skull and face forms there. In Egypt at the present day the fellaheen resemble to a marked degree their Neolithic ancestors. Ethnologists explain in this connection that physical characteristics are controlled by the females of a community. Intrusions of males as traders, settlers, or conquerors may have been productive of variations, but the tendency to revert to the original type has operated to a marked degree, the "unfits" being eliminated by local diseases from generation to generation. In those districts, however, where settlers of alien type were accompanied by their wives and families, ethnic changes have been more pronounced. It is not surprising to find, in this connection, that in a country like Great Britain primitive types should be found to be still persistent. The majority of the invaders who crossed the seas were evidently males.

Since Sergi first roused a storm of criticism by advancing his theory of the North African origin of the Mediterranean race, a considerable mass of data has been accumulated which tends to confirm his conclusions. Egypt has provided evidence which sets beyond dispute the fact that once a racial type had been fixed it persisted for many thousands of years with little or no change. The problem as to why some heads are long and some are broad still remains obscure. All that can be said is that certain peoples developed in isolation during untold ages their peculiar physical characteristics, which changes of food and location have failed to alter.

Numerous graves were found during recent years in Upper Egypt in which the bodies have been preserved for a space of at least sixty centuries—"not the mere bones only", says Professor Elliot Smith, "but also the skin and hair, the muscles and organs of the body; and even such delicate tissues as the nerves and brain, and, most marvellous of all, the lens of the eye. Thus", he adds, "we are able to form a very precise idea of the structure of the proto-Egyptian." This distinguished ethnologist's description of the early inhabitant of the Nile valley is of special interest: "The proto-Egyptian was a man of small stature, his mean height" was "a little under 5 feet 5 inches in the flesh for men, and almost 5 feet in the case of women. . . . He was of very slender build, for his bones are singularly slight and free from pronounced roughness and projecting bosses that indicate great muscular development. In fact, there is a suggestion of effeminate grace and frailty about his bones. . . . Like all his kinsmen of the Mediterranean group of peoples, the proto-Egyptian, when free from alien admixture, had a very scanty endowment of beard and almost no moustache. On neither lip were there ever more than a few sparsely scattered hairs, and in most cases also the cheeks were equally scantily equipped. But there was always a short tuft of beard under the chin." The burial customs and the ceramic and other remains of the Mediterranean peoples were of similar character everywhere.[1]

In some pre-Dynastic Egyptian graves the dead were wrapped in "flaxen cloth of considerable fineness". It is probable, therefore, that the spindle whorls found in Crete were invented in Egypt. The brunette complexion of the Mediterranean Neolithic folk was probably acquired on the North African coast whence they spread into Europe. As ships were depicted on Egyptian pre-Dynastic pottery, it is possible that companies of them crossed the Mediterranean Sea. The great majority entered Europe, however, across the Straits of Gibraltar, and by the Palestine

[1] *The Ancient Egyptians*, pp. 41 *et seq.*

and Asia Minor route, along the ancient "way of the Philistines".

The stomachs of some of the naturally mummified bodies have been taken out, and when their undigested contents were submitted to examination, discovery was made, among other things, of fish bone and scales, fragments of mammalian bones, remains of plants used as drugs, and husks of barley and millet. The Mediterranean folks who remained in Egypt were evidently agriculturists, stock-breeders and fishermen, and non-vegetarians.

A people who had adopted the agricultural mode of life were able to occupy more limited areas than huntsmen or pastoralists. Europe must have been thinly populated at the dawn of the Neolithic Age, when the Mediterranean peoples began to "peg out claims" in its valleys, round its shores, and on green inviting islands. The Cretan pioneers were undoubtedly agriculturists. They grew peas and barley, and ground their meal in stone mortars and querns; they fenced their land, and must therefore have had land laws; and they kept herds of sheep, cattle, pigs, and goats. The fig- and olive-trees were also cultivated. In short, they had imported to Crete the agricultural and horticultural civilization which the Egyptians credited to Osiris and Isis, before they had begun to carry on a sea trade with the home country. Evidence has also been forthcoming that the Neolithic peoples of western Europe and the British Isles were similarly agriculturists. Sometimes the teeth taken from graves are found to be in a ground-down condition. This was partly due to the deposit of grit in limestone and sandstone mortars and querns, which mixed with the meal.[1] The Neolithic folk who utilized soft stones for milling must have been as

---

[1] The writer and a friend once tested a limestone quern and ascertained that it deposited as much grit as covered a threepenny piece in about fifteen minutes.

familiar as some of their modern descendants with the agonies of toothache and indigestion.

The minority of broad-heads in the early Minoan period in Crete may have been survivals from Palæolithic times, or the descendants of slaves. It is more probable, however, that they represented an infusion of traders and artisans from Asia Minor. Professor Elliot Smith, who believes that the Egyptians were the first to work copper, suggests that "the broad-headed, long-bearded Asiatics", of Alpine or Armenoid type, "learned of its usefulness by contact with the Egyptians in Syria", and passed on their acquired knowledge to other peoples. Referring to Crete in particular he says: "We can have no doubt these people (the Armenoids) began to make their way into Crete, from Anatolia perhaps, at the time when the diffusion of the knowledge of copper was beginning".[1] At a much later period the artisans of North Syria and Anatolia were famous as metal-workers. One of the results of the wars waged by Egypt, after the expulsion of the Hyksos, was the introduction to the Nile valley of coats of mail, gilded chariots, gold and silver vases, and other articles which were greatly prized. "At this period", writes Professor Flinders Petrie, "the civilization of Syria was equal or superior to that of Egypt. . . . Here was luxury far beyond that of the Egyptians, and technical work which could teach them, rather than be taught."[2] Many thousands of prisoners were also taken, and, when tribute was arranged for, the Pharaoh made it a condition that his vassals should send "the foreign workmen" with it. Kings and noblemen also received wives from Syria and Anatolia. During the Eighteenth Dynasty the typical Egyptian face, as a result, underwent a change. The upper and artisan classes became half foreigners. As at

---

[1] *The Early Egyptians*, pp. 172, 173.   [2] *A History of Egypt*, Vol. II, pp. 146, 147.

the present day, however, the peasants were unaffected by the alien infusion, and they constituted the large majority of the inhabitants.

The broad-heads represent an ancient stock which had an area of characterization somewhere in Central Asia. They were apparently separated, during the Late Glacial and Inter-glacial Periods, for many thousands of years from the fair northerners and the brunette Mediterraneans —long enough, at any rate, to develop distinctive physical characteristics, and also, it would appear, distinctive modes of thought. They were mainly a pastoral people, and clung to an upland habitat along the grassy steppes. In contrast to the lithe and slight agriculturists from North Africa, they were heavily bearded and muscular; they also included short and tall stocks. During the Neolithic Period these broad-heads were filtering into Europe, but it was not until the early Copper Age that their western migrations assumed greatest volume.

Evidence as to the source of early Cretan culture and the homeland of the pioneer settlers may be obtained, not only by studying physical characteristics, but also early religious beliefs. There is nothing so persistent as "immemorial modes of thought". At the present day it is possible to find, even in these islands, small communities descended from alien settlers, who have for long centuries lived beside and never mixed with the descendants of the aborigines. Round the east coast of Scotland, for instance, the fisher-folks in not a few of the small towns are endogamous—they rarely marry outside their own kindred; and they not only speak a different dialect from their neighbours, but have different superstitions. So distinctive, too, are their physical traits that they are easily distinguished in certain localities.

In ancient times peoples of different origin lived more

strictly apart than is the case nowadays. Herodotus and other Greek writers sought for clues as to tribal origins by making reference to burial customs and religious beliefs.

The Carians maintain they are the aboriginal inhabitants of the part of the mainland where they now dwell, and never had any other name than that which they still bear; and in proof of this they show an ancient temple of the Carian Jove in the country of the Mylasians.[1]

There is a third temple, that of the Carian Zeus, common to all Carians, in the use of which also the Lydians and Mysians participate, on the ground that they are brethren.[2]

One of the interesting phases of Cretan religion was the worship of the local Zeus. The deity must not be confused, however, with the so-called Aryan or Indo-European Zeus of the philologists of a past generation. The name Zeus is less ancient than the deities to whom it was applied. It is derived from the root *div*, meaning "bright" or "shining". In Sanskrit it is Dyaus, in Latin Diespiter, Divus, Diovis, and Jove, in Anglo-Saxon Tiw, and in Norse Tyr; an old Germanic name of Odin was Divus or Tivi, and his descendants were the Tivar. The Greeks had not a few varieties of Zeus. These included: "Zeus, god of vintage", "Zeus, god of sailors," "Bald Zeus", "Dark Zeus" (god of death and the underworld), "Zeus-Trophonios" (earth-god), "Zeus of thunder and rain", "Zeus, lord of flies", "Zeus, god of boundaries", "Zeus Soter", as well as the "Carian Zeus" and the "Cretan Zeus". The chief gods of alien peoples were also called Zeus or Jupiter. Merodach of Babylon was "Jupiter Belus" and Amon of Thebes "Jupiter Amon", and so on.

The worship of Zeus, the father-god, had a political significance. He was imposed as the chief deity on

---

[1] *Herodotus*, I, 171.　　　　[2] *Strabo*, 659.

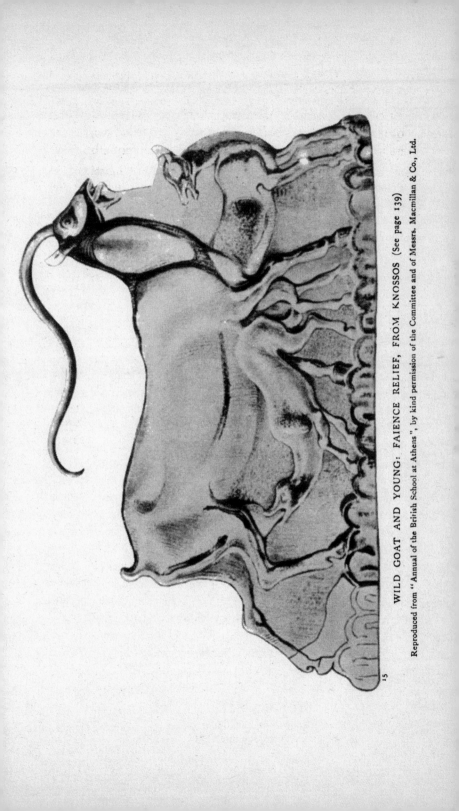

15

WILD GOAT AND YOUNG: FAIENCE RELIEF, FROM KNOSSOS (See page 139)

Reproduced from "Annual of the British School at Athens", by kind permission of the Committee and of Messrs. Macmillan & Co., Ltd.

various Pantheons by the Hellenic conquerors of prehistoric Greece, but local deities suffered little or no change except in name.   Dionysus might be called Zeus, but he still continued to be Dionysus, the son of the Great Mother, and did not become Zeus the self-created father-god.

The legend of the Cretan Zeus is as follows: It had been prophesied by Uranus and Gaia that Cronos would be displaced by one of his own children.   He endeavoured to avert this calamity by swallowing each babe that was born to his wife, Rhea.   After he had thus disposed of five of his family, Rhea went to Crete, and in a mountain cave there gave birth to Zeus.   She then returned to her husband and presented him with a stone dressed up as a babe, which he swallowed.

Rhea was assisted by her priests, the Curetes, who danced a war or fertility dance, and her child was fostered by nymphs (the Cretan "mothers"), who gave him honey, so that Cronos would not hear his cries.   Milk for nourishment was provided by the goat Amalthea.   So strong was the child that soon after birth he broke off one of the goat's horns, which he presented to the nymphs: it afterwards became known as Cornucopia, the "horn of plenty", because it became filled with whatever its owner desired.

When Zeus grew up he rescued his brothers and sisters from the stomach of Cronos, and also took forth the stone which had been substituted for himself: this stone became sacred to his worshippers.   Afterwards he deposed his father and sat on the throne as chief deity. Like other ancient gods, he reigned for a time and then died.   His grave was pointed out in Crete, as several classical authors have testified.[1]   Perhaps it was on

---

[1] *Diodorus Siculus*, III, 61; Cicero, *De natura deorum*, III, 21, 53; Lucian, *Philopseudes*, 3, &c.

account of their habit of repeating this and other ancient legends that the Cretans became so notorious among orthodox Greeks.   Paul wrote of them: "There are many unruly and vain talkers and deceivers . . . whose mouths must be stopped; who subvert whole houses, teaching things which they ought not. . . . One of themselves, even a prophet of their own, said, The Cretans are always liars."[1]

"Later Cretan tradition", writes Sir Arthur Evans, "has persistently connected the tomb of Zeus with Mount Juktas, which rises as the most prominent height on the land side above the site of Knossos. Personal experiences obtained during two recent explorations of this peak go far to confirm this tradition.   All that is not precipitous of the highest point of the ridge of Juktas is enclosed by a 'Cyclopean' wall of large roughly oblong blocks, and within this enclosure, especially towards the summit, the ground is strewn with pottery, dating from Mycenæan to Roman times, and including a large number of small cups of pale clay exactly resembling those which occur in votive deposits of Mycenæan date in the caves of Dikta and of Ida, also intimately connected with the cult of the Cretan Zeus."

In the vicinity is "the small church of Aphendi Kristos, or the Lord Christ, a name which in Crete clings in an especial way to the ancient sanctuaries of Zeus, and marks here in a conspicuous manner the diverted but abiding sanctity of the spot. Popular tradition, the existing cult, and the archæological traces point alike to the fact that there was here 'a holy sepulchre' of remote antiquity."[2]

Early Christian missionaries similarly appropriated elsewhere the "holy places" of the Pagan cults.   St. Paul's

[1] *Titus*, i, 10–12.   [2] *Journal of Hellenic Studies*, Vol. XXI, pp. 121, 122.

Cathedral in London probably marks the site of the ancient sanctuary of the god Lud, which was approached by Ludgate (the way of Lud). Ancient sculptured stones are often found built into the walls of old chapels. Sometimes the local saint was worshipped after death as if he had acquired the attributes of the Pagan deity he displaced. Bulls were offered up in Applecross, Ross-shire, in 1656, "upon the 25th August", runs a minute of Dingwall Presbytery, "which day is dedicate, as they conceive, to Sn. Mourie as they call him".[1]

The Cretan Zeus was a deity who each year died a violent death and came to life again. He thus resembled closely the Egyptian Osiris, the culture king, who introduced agriculture, was slain by Set (one of whose forms was the black pig), and afterwards became Judge of the Dead. We do not know what name was borne by this Cretan deity. It may have been "Velchanos", the youthful warrior of Cretan tradition. A Knossian cult may have called him Minos. As we have seen, this culture king, who during life was famed as a lawgiver, became one of the judges of the dead in the Homeric Hades. Apparently he was deified and regarded as a form of the Cretan Dionysus, who differed somewhat from the Thracian Dionysus.

At what period Zeus-Dionysus was introduced into Crete it is impossible to say with certainty. His close association with agriculture and the underworld suggests that he was known at an early period, but, as will be shown in the next chapter, not necessarily the earliest.

To the agriculturists the myths and customs associated with the sowing and reaping of grain were of as much importance as the implements they used. Every people who

---

[1] St. Maelrubha, the early Christian missionary, who gave his name to Loch Maree (formerly Loch Ewe). He flourished in the seventh century.

in early times adopted the agricultural mode of life adopted
also the religious practices associated with it.   Persistent
folk-legends in Greece pointed to Egypt as the fountain-
head of agricultural religion.   Diodorus Siculus says that
the mysteries of Dionysus are identical with those of
Osiris, and that the Isis and Demeter mysteries are the
same also, the only difference being in the names applied
to the deities.[1]   "Osiris", says Herodotus, "is named
Dionysus (Bacchus) by the Greeks."[2]

The Cretan Zeus-Dionysus links not only with Osiris,
but also with Tammuz of Babylon, Ashur of Assyria, Attis
of Phrygia, Adonis of Greece, Agni of India and his twin-
brother Indra, the Germanic Scef and Frey and Heimdal,
and the Scoto-Irish Diarmid.   Each of these deities was
apparently a developed form of a primitive culture-god,
who was a deity of love, fertility, and vegetation; he
symbolized the grass required by pastoralists, the fruit of
wild and cultivated trees, the spring flowers, and the
corn; in short, he was the provider of the food-supply,
and he was the life-principle in the food.

In pre-historic times, when the migrating peoples had
a vague conception of the mysterious Power which controlled the Universe and the lives of men, they did not
give concrete and permanent form to the deities they
worshipped and propitiated and controlled by the performance of magical ceremonies.   They believed that the
Power was manifested in various forms at different periods,
and existed in all forms at one and the same time.   Osiris
appeared among men as a wise king who introduced agriculture and inaugurated just laws; he was at the same
time the moon and the young bull, goat, or boar, who was
given origin by a "ray of light" issuing from the moon.
He was the ancestor of men and edible animals; he was

---

[1] *Diodorus Siculus*, I, 96.   [2] *Herodotus*, II, 144.

the "vital spark" or life-essence in all that grew; he was the Nile which fertilized the sun-parched desert. Each Pharaoh was an Osiris, and each pious individual who died became one with Osiris in the agricultural heaven which he attained by obeying the laws of Osiris. Thus Proclus says, in reference to the Greek mysteries: "The gods assume many forms and change from one to another; now they are manifested in the emission of shapeless light, now they are of human shape, and anon appear in other and different forms".[1]

The Cretan god was the son of the Great Mother who has been identified with Rhea. Apparently he also became her husband. Osiris was the son of Isis, or of Isis and Nepthys—"the bull begotten of the two cows Isis and Nepthys", and he was also at once the husband and father of Isis. Tammuz was the son and spouse of Ishtar, and the later Adonis the lover and son of Aphrodite.

The goddess Demeter and the god Dionysus, her son, were said to be of Cretan origin. According to Firmicus Maternus, Dionysus was the illegitimate son of King Jupiter of Crete, and was hated by Queen Juno. On one occasion, when Jupiter prepared to leave the island, he appointed Dionysus to reign in his place. Juno plotted, during her husband's absence, with the Titans, who lured the young prince away and devoured him. Minerva, his sister, however, rescued his heart and gave it to Jupiter on his return, and that high god enclosed the heart in a case and placed it in a temple which he erected, so that it might be worshipped. Other myths of similar character are told regarding the young god who was mangled like the Egyptian Osiris. One variation states that Jupiter had the heart pounded in a mortar and given to Semele, who, after eating it, gave birth once more to Dionysus.

[1] *Ennead*, I, 6, 9.

In the Egyptian Anpu-Bata story, Bata, who is evidently a primitive god resembling Osiris, exists in various forms at different periods. His soul enters a blossom, and when the blossom is destroyed the soul enters a sacred bull; the bull is slain and the soul is enclosed in two trees: the trees are cut down, and a chip having entered the mouth of the Pharaoh's wife, that lady gives birth to a child who is no other than the original Bata.

The identification of the god with an animal suggests totemism. In one of the early culture stages it was believed that the spirit of the eponymous tribal ancestor existed in a bull, a bear, a pig, or a deer, as the case might be. Invariably the animal was an edible one—the source of the food-supply, or the guardian of it. Osiris, in one part of Egypt, was a bull and in another a goat. He appears also to have had a boar form. Set went out to hunt a wild boar when he found the body of Osiris and tore it in pieces.

The sacred animal was tabooed for a certain period of the year, or altogether. In Egypt the pig was never eaten except sacrificially. Herodotus says: "The pig is regarded among them (the Egyptians) as an unclean animal, so much so that if a man in passing accidentally touch a pig, he instantly hurries to the river and plunges in with all his clothes on. Hence, too, the swineherds, notwithstanding that they are of pure Egyptian blood, are forbidden to enter into any of the temples, which are open to all other Egyptians; and further, no one will give his daughter in marriage to a swineherd, or take a wife from among them, so that the swineherds are forced to inter-marry among themselves. They do not offer swine in sacrifice to any of their gods, excepting Bacchus (Osiris) and the moon, whom they honour in this way at the same time, sacrificing pigs to both of them at the same full moon, and afterwards eating of the flesh. . . . At any other time they would not so much as taste it."[1]

According to one of the Cretan legends regarding Zeus-Dionysus, as related by Athenæus,[2] the animal which nourished with its milk the young god of the cave was a sow. "Wherefore all the Cretans consider this animal sacred, and will not taste of its flesh; and the men of Præsos perform sacred rites with the sow, making her the first offering at the sacrifice."[3] The pig taboo extended as far as Wales, Scotland, and Ireland, and is still remembered.[4]

Dionysus was also associated with the goat, as we have seen. A clay impression of a gem from Knossos shows an infant sitting beside a horned sheep.[5] Possibly we have here another form of the legend. The various animals may have been totemic. Different tribes claimed descent from different animals which were associated with the culture-god whom they adopted.

It would appear that the bull tribe achieved ascendancy in Crete, for the horns of that animal, a piece of "ritual furniture", which Sir Arthur Evans refers to "by anticipation" as "the horns of consecration", is the commonest cult objective on pottery, frescoes, gems, steles, and altars. The horns were evidently a symbol of the god of fertility. It would appear that before Zeus-Dionysus was depicted in human shape he was worshipped through his symbols or attributes.

Another symbol of the god was the 8-form shield. In North Africa it is found associated with the Libyan

---

[1] *Herodotus*, II, 47.   [2] *Pausanias*, VII, 17, 5.
[3] *Cults of the Greek States*, L. R. Farnell, Vol. I, p. 37.
[4] *Myths of Babylonia and Assyria*, pp. 293-4, and *Egyptian Myth and Legend*, pp. vi, vii.
[5] *Journal of Hellenic Studies*, Vol. XXI, p. 129.

goddess Neith, who was a Great Mother with a fatherless son.   On Mycenæan and Cretan signets and seals this shield is sometimes shown with human head and arms. It was used by one of the Hittite tribes, and may be identical with the Bœotian shield.   A similar pattern also "appears as an ornamental motive on a bronze belt of the latest Bronze or earliest Hallstatt period in Hungary".[1] The so-called "spectacle marking" on the Scottish sculptured stones, which sometimes appears upright and sometimes longwise, may have been an 8-form shield of symbolic significance—an attribute of the god or goddess of fertility.

The double axe was another distinctive symbol of the Cretan god.   In Malta certain folk-tales make reference to "Bufies", which is believed to signify "Axe-land", situated somewhere beyond the Sahara.   "Axe-land", says Mr. R. N. Bradley, "must be one of the original homes of the axe, and therefore possibly of Neolithic culture."[2] Votive stone axes, perforated for suspension, are common in Malta, Cyprus, and other Mediterranean islands.   On the sculptured stones of Brittany the double axe appears as a symbol or hieroglyph, and it is sometimes grasped by an outstretched hand.[3]   In Crete the double axe with long handle was depicted between the "horns of consecration" in outline on stones of pillars of palaces and the Dictæan inner cave, and inside houses, apparently as a charm.   It figures on a gold signet from Mycenæ in elaborate form, beside a goddess, seated beneath a vine.   On the upper part of the signet the sun and crescent moon are enclosed by "water rays".   Hovering high on the left is the 8-form shield with human head, an uplifted arm with a

---

[1] British Museum *Early Iron Age Guide*, p. 7.

[2] *Malta and the Mediterranean Race*, p. 126 (1912).

[3] See *The Mediterranean Race*, G. Sergi, p. 313, for illustration of axes on one of the sculptured stones.

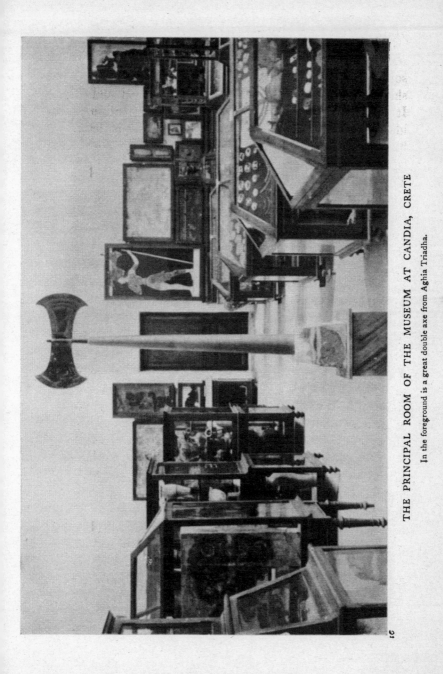

THE PRINCIPAL ROOM OF THE MUSEUM AT CANDIA, CRETE

In the foreground is a great double axe from Aghia Triadha.

staff or spear in the hand, and a single leg below. The goddess is approached by votaries, who make offerings of flowers including the iris and hyacinth. On a gem from Knossos the goddess grasps the double axe in her hand, as she does also on a mould from Palaikastro, and other objects found elsewhere. Sir Arthur Evans is of opinion that "labyrinth" is derived from *labrys*, the Lydian (or Carian) name for the Greek double-edged axe.[1] "The suffix in -nth has been conclusively shown", says Professor Burrows, "to belong to that interesting group of pre-Hellenic words that survives both in place-names like Corinth (Corinthos) and Zakynthos . . . and in common words that would naturally be borrowed by the invaders from the old population." Some of these are the words for "barley-cake", "basket", "hedge-sparrow", and "worm". "The similarly formed word for 'mouse'," he adds, "which remains as the ordinary Greek word, . . . is quoted by the Greek grammarians as a Cretan word."[2]

Words like "absinth" and "hyacinth" are similarly survivals that have been borrowed. Professor Burrows thinks, however, that *laura*, *lavra*, or *labra*, signified "passage". Laburinthos would thus mean "place of passages". He notes that "the early Eastern Church called its monasteries Laurai, or Labri as they were sometimes spelt. The name must have been originally given, either from the cloisters round them, or because of the long passages, with the monks' cells leading off them; but this does not seem to have been consciously felt, and the word was used for the monastery as a whole. The name indeed is still seen in The Lavra, a monastery at Mount Athos."[3]

The Cretan Zeus was, as a deity of vegetation, asso-

---

[1] *Journal of Hellenic Studies*, Vol. XXI, pp. 106 *et seq.*
[2] *The Discoveries in Crete*, p. 120.   [3] *The Discoveries in Crete*, pp. 118, 119.

ciated with tree- and water-worship.   In the myth about
Cronos swallowing the stone there is evidently a memory
of stone-worship also.

It would appear that more than one folk-wave entered
Crete during the thousands of years which were covered
by the Neolithic Period.   At Knossos the earliest settlers
constructed wattle huts, plastered with mud, and were
well advanced in civilization.   The Magasa folks, on the
other hand, who produced fewer and cruder artifacts, had
more substantial houses.   They built low walls of stone,
and erected a timber framework, which they enclosed in
brick.   A similar architectural method appears to have
obtained among the Anatolian Hittites in historic times.
Inside the Magasa house walls were plastered, and the flat
roofs were made of plastered reeds.   Both these sections
of Cretans, as has been shown, obtained obsidian from
Melos, and worked it beside their dwellings, as the finds
of flake testify.   Whether, however, either or both of
them were contemporaries of the dwellers in the artificial
cave at Miamu is uncertain.   It is suggestive, however,
to find that the historic Cretans had sacred caves like the
Hittites, the prehistoric people of Phœnicia, and the
French and Spanish Palæolithic folk of the Aurignacian
and Magdalenian stages of culture.   Did they adopt certain
of the religious customs of the descendants of the Palæolithic folks who survived on the island?   Or was there
among the earliest settlers a community of Libyans of
mingled stock?   The Cro-Magnon type survives till the
present day on the North African coast, where it has been
identified by Collignon and Bertholon among the Berbers.[1]
It may be that there were tall men among the Cretans,
who were distinguished as warriors, as was Goliath among
the Philistines.   The Philistines were of Cretan origin.

[1] Ripley's *Races of Europe*, p. 177.

Some of the athletes depicted on vases and frescoes appear to have been above the average stature. It is of interest to recall, too, in this connection, that the slim waists that distinguished the Cretans were characteristic also of the Aurignacian cave-dwellers. This custom of waist-tightening may have survived from the archæological Hunting Period. In Gaelic stories there are references to the " hunger belt". It is possible, too, that the Cretan girdle had a religious significance, like the " prayer belt" of Russia. Sir Arthur Evans found at Knossos snake girdles which had been deposited as votive offerings in a sacred place. Two snakes enfolded the hips of the snake-goddess. Aphrodite's girdle compelled love. The Germanic Brunhild's great strength lay in her girdle. The dwarf Laurin was subdued when his girdle was wrenched off by the heroic Dietrich.[1] Ishtar wore a girdle.

As has been indicated also (Chapter II), the bell-mouthed skirt worn by the Minoan women was similar to that of the Cro-Magnon women depicted in the Aurignacian caves 10,000 years ere the Neolithic folk settled in Crete. The gowns of the Egyptian women were of the " hobble" pattern.

Crete, of course, could not have maintained a large population of hunters. There can be little doubt that its inhabitants were not numerous at any period prior to the introduction of agriculture. As the great bulk of its historic population were of Mediterranean type, it would appear that North Africa was the source of the high civilization which obtained at Knossos during the Late Neolithic Period. The religion of the Cretan agriculturists resembled in essential details that of the Egyptians. Their chief deity was the Great Mother, whose son died, like Osiris, a violent death. No doubt religious borrowing

[2] *Teutonic Myth and Legend*, pp. 380 and 428.

took place when the Cretans traded with Egypt, and that the traditions preserved by Herodotus and other writers in this connection were not without some foundation. But, as there existed so close a resemblance between the fundamental beliefs of the separated peoples, it is impossible to discover to what extent Cretan religion was influenced by Nilotic. The Sumerian Tammuz myth, which also resembles the Osirian, was fully developed at the dawn of history, and Merodach, a fusion of Tammuz and Ramman, had for one of his names Asari, which has been identified with Asar (Osiris).

A conclusion which may be suggested is that the various sections of the Mediterranean race had, prior to their migrations to suitable areas of settlement from the North African homeland, adopted a system of religious beliefs which was closely associated with their agricultural mode of life, and passed it on afterwards to the peoples, who learned from them how to till and sow the soil and reap the harvest in season. The myths of the Phrygian Attis and the Germanic Scef are probably relics of cultural contact in bygone ages.

CHAPTER VIII

Pre-Hellenic Earth and Corn Mothers

Mythology and Floating Folk-beliefs—Legends of Egyptian Influence in Crete—Primitive Spirit Groups as "Holy Mothers"—Evidence from Modern Greece—Goddesses as Fairy Queens—The Great Mother of Gods, Demons, and Mankind—Twin Deities and Bisexual Deities—Cult of Self-created Great Father—Stages of Civilization reflected in Religious Beliefs—Female Demons of Modern Greece—The Pre-Hellenic and Hellenic Forms of Rhea, "Mother of the Gods"—The Egyptian "Mothers" Neith and Nut—Earth Mother as a Serpent—Demeter as the "Barley Mother"—Rhea and the Cretan Snake-goddess—The Eleusinian Mysteries—The Mysteries of Crete and Egypt—Isis and Demeter—The Corn and Earth Goddesses of India—Demeter-Persephone Myth—Its Antiquity and Significance—The Later Tammuz-Adonis Myth—The Demeter of Phigalia—Pre-Hellenic Cult of the Earth Mother—Fusion of Myths of the Hunting Pastoral and Agricultural Periods—Osiris and Minos—Osiris and the Minotaur—Eponymus Ancestor as a Son of Earth—Minos and Pelasgus—First Man of "Lost Atlantis"—Tribal Forms of Animal-headed Gods.

In a previous chapter[1] it has been shown that, during the Late Palæolithic and Neolithic Periods, the worship of a goddess of maternity, who was at once a destroyer and preserver, obtained among tribes of Eurafrican and Eurasian peoples, and that memories of her primitive savage character have been perpetuated in these islands in folk-tales and place-names until the present Age. The past similarly lives in the present in Crete and Greece, where it is still possible to find traces of the floating material from which Homeric and Thesiodic Mythology

[1] Chapter III.

165

was framed.   Herodotus pondered over this aspect of the problem and wrote:[1]

> Whence the gods severally sprang, whether or no they had existed from eternity, what forms they bore—these are questions of which the Greeks knew nothing until the other day, so to speak, for Homer and Hesiod were the first to compose Theogonies, and give their gods their epithets, to allot them their several offices and occupations, and describe their forms; and they lived but four hundred years before my time as I believe.[2]

Herodotus received his information regarding the literary conception of the deities from three priestesses of the Dodonæans, who also said:

> Two black doves flew away from Egyptian Thebes, and while one directed its flight to Libya, the other came to them. She alighted on an oak, and sitting there began to speak with a human voice, and told them that on the spot where she was, there should thenceforth be an oracle of Jove (Zeus). They understood the announcement to be from Heaven, so they set to work at once and erected a shrine. The dove which flew to Libya bade the Libyans to establish there the oracle of Ammon (Amon).

In Egypt Herodotus was given a different version of the legend.   The priests of Jupiter (Amon) at Thebes said:

> Two of the sacred women were once carried off from Thebes by the Phœnicians. The story went that one of them was sold into Libya, and the other into Greece, and these women were the first founders of the oracles in the two countries.

Herodotus also held that the names of some of the deities came from Egypt.

> In early times the Pelasgi, as I know by information which I got at Dodona, offered sacrifices of all kinds, and prayed to the gods, but had no distinct names or appellations for them, since they had never heard of any. They called them gods (θεοὶ,

---

[1] *Herodotus*, II, 53–5.   [2] That is during the ninth century B.C.

disposers), because they had disposed and arranged all things in such a beautiful order. After a long lapse of time the names of the gods came to Greece from Egypt, and the Pelasgi learnt them, only as yet they knew nothing of Bacchus, of whom they first heard at a much later date. Not long after the arrival of the names, they sent to consult the oracle at Dodona about them. This is the most ancient oracle in Greece, and at that time there was no other. To their question, "whether they should adopt the names that had been imported from the foreigners?" the oracle replied by recommending the use of the names of the gods, and from them the names passed afterwards to the Greeks.[1]

These statements seem to bear out what the results of modern research tend to emphasize: that the systematized mythology was a creation of priests and poets, and had a political as well as a religious significance. The most ancient conceptions and beliefs were perpetuated, however, by the masses of the people, and may still be winnowed from existing folk-beliefs and stories.

In Crete the dove and serpent goddesses appear to have evolved from primitive spirit groups. These were first conceived of as mothers. "The prominence of the idea of maternity in the Cretan religion", says Mr. Farnell, "is illustrated by the Cretan cult of 'Meteres', the 'Holy Mothers' who were transplanted at an early time from Crete to Engyon in Sicily."[2]

In modern Greece the memory of the spirit groups still survives. Nymphs and Nereids haunt mountains and valleys, oceans and streams, and are ruled over by the "Queen of the mountains", the "Queen of the shore", or primitive forms of the owl-headed Athene or the beautiful and blood-thirsty Artemis. They are, in short, exceedingly like our fairies, who obey the commands of Queen Mab. Some of the Celtic goddesses exist in

[1] *Herodotus*, II, 52.   [2] *Cults of the Greek States*, Vol. III, p. 295.

groups: " Proximæ (the kinswomen); Dervonæ (the oak spirits); Niskai (the water spirits); Mairæ, Matronæ, Matres or Matræ (the mothers); Quadriviæ (the goddesses of cross-roads). The Matræs, Matræ, and Matronæ are often qualified by some local name. Deities of this type appear to have been popular in Britain, in the neighbourhood of Cologne, and in Province. . . . In some parts of Wales 'Y Mamau' (the mothers) is the name for the fairies." [1] The " seven Hathors " of Egypt who presided at birth were similarly " mothers " and " fates ". The " Golden Aphrodite " of Greece was chief of the " deathless fates ". Demeter's priestesses, the earthly representatives of her nymphs, conducted a religious ceremony at weddings, as a Cos inscription shows. [2] Fairies in our folk-tales are so fond of pretty children that they endeavour to steal them, and, when they are successful, substitute changelings. The Greek Nereids have, according to modern folk-belief, similar propensities. [3]

Ancient and modern evidence tends to emphasize the widespread prevalence among the peoples of the Mediterranean race of the belief in the female origin and control of life. The primitive " queens " appear to have developed into goddesses, who were differentiated in localities to accord with human experiences and habits of life. Among the goddesses one was regarded as the Great Mother, who gave birth to the chief deities, male and female, the demons and the ancestors of mankind. " One is the race of men ", sang Pindar, " with the race of gods; for one is the mother that gave to both one breath of life; yet sundered are they by powers wholly

---

[1] *Celtic Religion*, Prof. Anwyl, pp. 41, 48.
[2] Rouse's *Greek Votive Offerings*, p. 246.
[3] *Modern Greek Folk-lore and Ancient Greek Religion*, J. C. Lawson, p. 141.

diverse, in that mankind is as naught, but heaven is builded of brass that abideth ever unshaken."[1]

Sometimes the Great Mother is of dual personality. The Egyptian sisters Isis and Nepthys were both mothers of Osiris, as has been indicated—"the progeny of the two cows Isis and Nepthys". In the Indian epic the *Máhab-hárata*, the monarch Jarasandha was similarly reputed to be the joint son of the two queens. The two parts of his body were united by Jara, the household genius, after birth, and his name signifies "united by Jara".[2] Two goddesses were associated with the Sumerian god Tammuz. These were Ishtar and Belit-sheri. Ishtar was his "mother", and he became her lover; Belit-sheri was his "sister". Isis was at once the "mother", "sister", "wife", and "daughter" of Osiris. Demeter and Kore, and Demeter and Persephone were Greek pairs who had similar functions. The model of a Mycenæan shrine discovered by Schliemann is surmounted by two doves which were, no doubt, sister goddesses. Images of goddesses holding a dove in either hand have also been found.

Another mystic conception was that the Great Mother was bi-sexual. The Libyan Neith was occasionally depicted as androgyne. Isis was the Egyptian "bearded Aphrodite", "the woman who was made a male", as one of the religious chants states, "by her father, Osiris".[3] The Babylonian Ishtar and the Germanic Freya were likewise double-sexed. This idea that deities were abnormal and super-human applied not only to goddesses. One of the Orphic hymns sets forth:

Zeus was the first of all, Zeus last, the lord of lightning;
Zeus was the head, the middle, from him all things were created;
Zeus was Man and again Zeus was the Virgin Eternal.

[1] Pindar, Nem. VI, 1, quoted by Lawson in *Modern Greek Folk-lore*, p. 65.
[2] *Indian Myth and Legend*, p. 229.
[3] *The Burden of Isis*, Dennis, p. 49. ("Wisdom of the East" Series.)

Adonis similarly was "both maiden and youth". The Babylonian Nannar (Sin), the moon-god, was "father" and "mother" of gods and men. So was the Syrian Baal. In India Shiva is sometimes depicted with the right side female and the left male. The Persian Mithra was a god and goddess combined. Herodotus, in fact, appears not to have known that he was other than a female deity. He says the Persians worshipped Urania, "which they borrowed from the Arabians and Assyrians. Mylitta is the name by which the Assyrians know this goddess, whom the Arabians call Alitta, and the Persians Mithra".[1]

At what remote period this conception became prevalent it is impossible to ascertain. It may have had origin in the Palæolithic Age, when bearded steatopygous female figurines were carved from ivory similar to those found in the pre-Dynastic graves of Egypt. Traces of the doctrine involved are found among the Esquimaux, whose artifacts so closely resemble those of the Magdalenian stage of culture, and among certain North American tribes. Another view is that the conception resulted from the early fusion of god and goddess cults, and of the rival fundamental ideas connected with them. Babylonia may have been the region from which the mystical doctrine was transferred to India on the one hand and Syria on the other. According to Richard Burton,[2] "the Phœnicians spread their androgynic worship over Greece".

In contrast to the conception of the peoples of the goddess cult, that life and the world was of female origin, was that of the peoples of the god cult, who believed that the first Being was the Great Father. The Scandinavians, or a section of them, believed that Ymer was the earth father, and that the underworld deities had origin from

---

[1] *Herodotus*, I, 131.   [2] *The Thousand Nights and a Night*, Vol. X, p. 231 (1886).

the perspiration of his armpits, while the demons sprang from his feet. One of the several creation myths in India sets forth that the world-giant Purusha was, like Ymer, the source of all life. The highest caste, the Brahman, sprang from his mouth, the second, the Kshatriya, from his arms, the third, the Vaisya, from his thighs, and the fourth, the Sudra, from his feet.[1] In Anatolia the Armenoid Hatti were father-worshippers. During the period of their political supremacy their "Lord of Heaven", a sky and atmospheric deity with solar attributes, was all powerful. "With the Hittites", says Professor Garstang, "fell their chief god from his predominant place. . . . But the Great Mother lived on, being the goddess of the land. Her cult, modified in some cases profoundly, by time and changed political circumstances, was found surviving at the dawn of Greek history in several places in the interior."[2] Zeus of the Hellenic Greeks was similarly a father god and was imposed, as has been indicated, on the pre-Hellenic inhabitants of Greece after conquest. In Egypt Ptah, the god of Memphis, who wielded a hammer like the Hittite father god, and was, therefore, a thunderer also, was a "perfect god". At the beginning he built up his body and shaped his limbs ere the sky was fashioned and the world set in order. "No father begot thee", a priestly poet declared, "and no mother gave thee birth. Thou didst fashion thyself without the aid of any other being."[3]

There is no trace of beliefs of the father cult in Crete. The Hellenic Zeus, as has been shown, was little more than a name on the island. It was applied to the young god who was the son of the Great Mother.

The various representations of the Cretan goddess

[1] *Indian Myth and Legend*, p. 89.   [2] *The Syrian Goddess*, pp. 17, 18.
[3] *Egyptian Myth and Legend*, p. 156.

suggest that, if they had no totemic significance, she was supposed to assume various aspects at different seasons and under different circumstances. As the Lady of Serpents she may have been the goddess of the Underworld, and as the Lady of Trees and Doves, the goddess of birth and fertility. She was also a mountain-goddess who wielded an axe or wand. It is possible that she was never sharply defined, and was closely associated with the vague spirit group of mothers—the "meteres", over whom she may have presided as "queen".

All the ancient deities reflected the habits of life of their worshippers, and retained traces of savage conceptions after they assumed benevolent attributes among cultured peoples. The Cretan Great Mother was evidently the goddess of the Neolithic folk who adopted the agricultural mode of life and kept domesticated animals. She was the earth mother and the corn mother, and the protector and multiplier of flocks and herds. As the Neolithic folk were also huntsmen, their goddess was associated with wild animals. She had evidently existence before Osiris taught his people how to sow grain and cultivate fruit-trees. When we find her guarded by lions it becomes evident that she was the dreaded being who had to be propitiated, like Black Annis of Leicester. This savage aspect of her character must not be lost sight of. It still survives in Greek folk-belief. The mother who gave origin to demons as well as gods was evidently, like the Babylonian Tiamat and the blood-thirsty Ishtar, possessed of primitive demoniac traits. The peasants of Greece at the present day remember Lamia, the "Queen of Libya" who was loved by Zeus. Her children were robbed by Hera, and she "took up her abode in a grim and lonely cavern, and there changed into a malicious and greedy monster, who in envy and despair stole and killed the

children of more fortunate mothers ".   Another kind of
Lamia, the Gello, transforms herself into a fish, a serpent,
a kite, or a skylark, and devours babes also.   When one
of these demons is slain, no grass grows where her blood
falls.[1]   In Gaelic folk-tales no grass grows under whin-
bushes or holly-trees, because the Cailleach has touched
the ground there with her hammer.

The Cretan mother-goddess appears to have possessed
the attributes of the various goddesses who were differentiated in classic mythology.   The pre-Hellenic Mother,
one of whose names appears to have been Rhea, was taken
over by the Greeks and given a place in the Olympian
group.   Her original character became vague.   She was
seated on a throne beside which her lion crouched in
repose, and her ancient functions were performed by her
children: Hestia, who resembled the Roman Vesta;
Demeter, who resembled the Roman Ceres; Hera, who
resembled the Roman Juno; and the gods Zeus and
Poseidon, her sons, who link with the Roman Jupiter
and Neptune.   Her husband was the savage Cronos, who
devoured his children like so many other primitive deities
in various lands.

But the Hellenic Rhea, although called the "Mother
of the Gods ", was not a self-created being, but the
daughter of Gaia, the earth mother, and Uranus, the
sky father, who equate with the Aryo-Indian Dyaus, and
Prithivi, the sky father and earth mother of Indra.   In
Egypt, on the other hand, the mother goddess was Nut
of the sky, and the father the earth-god Seb.   The Libyan
Neith, however, who appears to have been a form of Nut,
was an earth, sky, and atmospheric goddess.   Her worshippers made her declare:

I am what has been, what is, and what shall be,

[1] Lawson's *Modern Greek Folk-lore*, pp. 173 *et seq.*

and those of Nut said of that Great Mother:

> She hath built up life from her own body.

It would appear that the pre-Hellenic and Cretan Rhea was at once Gaia, Demeter, Artemis, and the earlier Aphrodite, and that she was originally identical with the pre-Hellenic Athene and Artemis, and the Phrygian Cybele.

Gaia was vaguely defined, yet belief in her was widespread. She was a divine prophetess, a fate, a power behind the gods. Like all primitive deities, including the Sumerian Tiamat, she had to be propitiated or fought against. Apparently one of her incarnations was the Delphian snake, others being snakes of different cults which were oracles. The priestesses who drank the blood of bulls and entered sacred caves to prophesy were believed to hold commune with the earth mother, the divine revealer. The wisdom with which serpents were supposed to be endowed was of great antiquity. They were also protectors of tribes and households, and symbols of fertility. In Egypt Isis and Nepthys had serpent forms. The tutelary goddess of the Delta was Uazit, the winged serpent, and oracles were ascribed to her. She was the guardian of the child Horus when Set sought for him with murderous intent. Snakes, "dragons", and "worms" were protectors of hidden treasure. Sacrifices were offered to these blood-thirsty monsters, so that they might be propitiated, either as protectors of households or givers of crops and edible animals. The ancient custom of slaying a human being or animal when foundation-stones were laid or seeds were sown appears to have been connected with the belief that the earth genius must be sacrificed to so that her goodwill and co-operation might be secured. In the snake-goddess of Crete we should recognize, it would appear, the anthropomorphic form of the primitive Gaia.

The earth mother who possessed stores of hidden treasure was, as Anesidora, "she who sends up gifts". One of her gifts was the food-supply. She provided grass for flocks and herds, caused trees to blossom and bear fruit, and to her agricultural worshippers gave rich harvests.

The specialized form of the goddess most closely associated with crops was Demeter. *Meter* signified "mother", but the meaning of the prefix is uncertain. According to W. Mannhardt *deai* was the Cretan word for "barley", and the goddess was the "Barley Mother".[1] Others hold that the prefix is a dialectic variant of the word for "earth".

But although the etymology of her name may remain doubtful, her real character is otherwise revealed. Melanippides and Euripides identified her with Rhea when they called her "mother of the gods", and the fact that the "earth snake" was invariably associated with her shows that she shared the attributes of Gaia, the elder "mother", and resembled closely the snake-goddess of Crete. She was associated with tree-worship, and the story was told that she punished Erysichthon by causing him to suffer dreadful hunger for cutting down trees in her sacred grove. In one of the hymns she is petitioned to gift the apple crop. As tree-goddesses were also water-goddesses, it is interesting to find that springs were dedicated to her in Attica and elsewhere, and that Euripides referred to her wanderings over rivers and the ocean. This poet also associated her with mountains, so that she must have been a guardian of animals like the primitive Scoto-Irish Cailleach, and a mountain-goddess like the Cretan "lady" who was depicted on the summit of a high peak.

[1] *Mythologische Forschungen*, pp. 292 et seq.

It was chiefly, however, as a provider of the food-supply that Demeter was addressed.   She was asked for gifts of cattle and corn and fruit, and bulls and cows were sacrificed to her.   Consequently she was a deity of fertility and a love-goddess.   The pig was also sacrificed to her as to other earth spirits.   As has been stated, pork was tabooed in Crete, and appears to have been eaten sacrificially only.   Demeter's connection with the underworld emphasizes her character as a Fate—a goddess of birth and death, who controlled and measured the lives of mankind.

Demeter's great festival was called the Eleusina, the legendary explanation being that it was first celebrated at Eleusis, in Attica.   One of its features was the mystic ceremony of initiation.   Little is known regarding the Eleusinian mysteries.   It would appear, however, from stray literary references to, and sculptured scenes of, the ceremony performed, that it was of elaborate character. The candidate fasted, and bathed in the sea with a young pig which was to be sacrificed.   Having thus been purified, he entered the sacred place, where he drank of a posset prepared from the "first fruits"—barley or grapes.   For a time his head and shoulders were covered by a cloth, so that he could not see what was happening about him. Probably he was terrorized.   A priest instructed him, and he performed symbolic acts, and took vows.

The ceremony appears to have had a religious significance.   "Whoever goes uninitiated to Hades", says Plato, "will lie in mud, but he who has been purified and is fully initiate, when he comes thither will dwell with the gods".[1]

According to Diodorus Siculus,[2] the Cretans professed that they gave the mysteries to Greece, and that they

[1] *Phædo*, 69 c.   [2] V, 77.

were performed openly on their island and communicated to everyone in ancient times. The same writer says that the Cretans received the mysteries from Egypt, the mysteries of Isis being the same as those of Demeter and the mysteries of Osiris the same as those of Dionysus.[1] Plutarch expresses a similar view.[2] Herodotus, referring to the festival at Busiris, in the Delta, says that " it is in honour of Isis, who is called in the Greek tongue Demeter".[3] Apparently there were strong resemblances between the mysteries of Isis and those of Demeter.

It does not follow, however, that the Cretans had no anthropomorphic goddess, and knew naught of the mysteries until they began to trade with Egypt across the Mediterranean Sea. The resemblance between Isis and Demeter may have been due to both Egyptians and Cretans having inherited similar beliefs from their common ancestors in the area where the Mediterranean race was characterized. As much is suggested by the fact that there existed apparently in Crete, and undoubtedly in pre-Hellenic Greece, an ancient myth in which Demeter is associated, not with the young god Dionysus, who links with Osiris, Attis, and Tammuz, but with a young goddess. This myth did not survive in Egypt; that, however, it existed there at one time is suggested by the close association of Isis and Nepthys, the joint mothers of Osiris. In India the story of Sita, who was an incarnation of Lakshmi, is suggestive in this connection. This heroine of the *Rámáyana*, having served her purpose on earth, departs to the Underworld.

The earth was rent and parted, and a golden throne arose,
Held aloft by jewelled Nagas[4] as the leaves enfold the rose,
And the Mother[5] in embraces held her spotless, sinless child.

---

[1] *Phædo*, 1–96. [2] *Isis et Osiris*, 35. [3] II, 59.
[4] Serpents. [5] Bashudha, the earth mother.

Then they vanished together. "In the ancient hymns of the *Rig Veda*", says Romesh C. Dutt, "Sita is simply the goddess of the field furrow which bears crops for men. We find how that simple conception is concealed in the *Rámáyana*, where Sita, the heroine of the epic, is still born of the field furrow, and after all her adventures returns to the earth." [1]

The daughter of Demeter was Kore - Persephone. The ancient legend regarding the abduction of the young goddess is as follows.

It chanced that one day Persephone, daughter of Demeter, was wandering in a flowery meadow gathering lilies and violets, roses and crocuses, and hyacinths and narcissuses. Suddenly the earth opened, and Pluto, god of Hades, appeared, seated in a golden car. Seizing the maiden, he carried her off. Her cries were heard by the golden-haired Demeter, who assumed a dark mantle and wandered over mountains, rivers, and oceans, searching in vain for her daughter. On the tenth day she met Hecate, who conducted her to the sun-god. This all-seeing deity informed Demeter that Pluto had carried off Persephone with the consent of Zeus. On hearing this, Demeter withdrew from Olympus, and she vowed never to return until her daughter was restored to her. She also cast a blight upon the earth, and men ploughed and sowed in vain; no barley grew, nor did trees yield fruit. The goddess retired to Eleusia, and the king's daughters found her sitting at the Maiden's Well below an olive-tree. Celeus, the king, received her hospitably, and she became the nurse of his sons Triptolemus and Demophon. She desired to make Demophon an immortal, and put him one night in a fire; but his mother screamed aloud, with the result that the spell was broken, and he perished.

[1] The *Rámáyana* condensed into English verse (Temple Classics, 1898).

Similarly, Isis thrust into the fire the infant son of the King of Byblus, whom she had been engaged to nurse, when searching for Osiris.[1] Demeter compensated the parents for their loss (or sacrifice) by giving Triptolemus seeds and instructing him in the art of agriculture. She also conferred upon him a chariot which was drawn by winged dragons. Pausanias says that she instructed Triptolemus and his father in the performance of her rites and mysteries.[2]

Many stories were related regarding Demeter's wanderings. One was that she fled from Poseidon as a mare, and that he assumed the form of a stallion. She afterwards became the mother of the horse Areion, which had the gift of speech. Hesiod, however, makes Medusa the spouse of Poseidon in his horse form and the mother of the winged Pegasus.

In Phigalia Pausanias[3] saw the cave "sacred to Black Demeter". Here she was fabled to have dwelt for a time sorrowing for her daughter. Meanwhile the blight remained upon the earth, and mankind were perishing from famine. The gods searched for, and Pan discovered, her hiding-place. Then Zeus sent the Fates to her, and when he was informed that she would not remove the blight until Persephone was restored to her, he commanded that she should be released by Pluto. The god of Hades accordingly restored Persephone to her mother. She was brought from Hades by Hermes, and was received with glad heart by her mother, who at once restored fertility to the earth.

Zeus, however, had made it a condition of Persephone's release that she had not eaten aught in Hades. To secure her return, Pluto gave her a pomegranate seed before her departure, and when this fact was revealed the young

[1] *Egyptian Myth and Legend.*   [2] II, 14.   [3] VIII, 42.

goddess had to return again to the gloomy Underworld. Once more Demeter sorrowed, and cursed the earth in her wrath. A compromise had, therefore, to be effected, and Zeus decreed that Persephone should spend one-third of each year on earth with her mother, and the remaining two-thirds with Pluto in Hades.

In this Demeter-Persephone myth the young goddess plays the same part as Tammuz and Adonis, who spent part of the year on earth with one goddess, and part of the year in the Underworld with the other. She is not slain and dismembered like these gods and the Egyptian Osiris. The part of Osiris is taken by Triptolemus, who received the grain seeds from Demeter, as Osiris, the deified king, received them from Isis. It is evident, therefore, that if the Cretans and pre-Hellenic Greeks borrowed the mysteries from Egypt, they did so before the Osirian myth was fully developed—that is, before the migration from North Africa of the tribes of the Mediterranean race. It is unnecessary to assume that the earliest agricultural settlers in Greece and Crete had no knowledge of the Mysteries. Even the Australian savages have their initiation and other rites.

It is evident that the primitive form of Demeter in Arcadia bore a close resemblance to the repulsive hags of England and Scotland. Like the snake-goddess of Crete, she retained in her symbols her early demoniac traits. Pausanias[1] tells that in the cave of Phigalia the ancient figure of the Black Demeter was of wood; it was seated on a rock and had a mare's head,[2] which had above it the figures of snakes and other monsters. She held a dolphin in one hand and a dove in the other. When this statue

[1] VIII, 42.
[2] The result, apparently, of the local fusion of the old earth-goddess cult and the horse cult of invaders.

was accidentally burnt, the Phigalians neglected the festivals and ceased to offer up sacrifices. Then a terrible famine afflicted the land. An oracle was consulted, and the people were informed that they were being punished for forgetting that Demeter had introduced among them the cultivation of corn.

Professor Frazer,[1] dealing with the form of the myth as it is given in the Homeric *Hymn to Demeter*, regards Demeter and Persephone as personifications of the corn —the former as the old corn of last year and the latter as the seed corn in autumn and sprouting in spring. Persephone's period in Hades was the period in which the sprouting seed remained under the earth.[2] The Black Demeter appears to have been the personification of the barren earth in winter, the Green Demeter the goddess of growing corn, and the Yellow Demeter the harvest deity. In their seasonal festivals the ancient agriculturists rejoiced and sorrowed alternately in sympathy with the goddess.

It would appear that the various names of the ancient earth mother were in turn individualized as separate deities. "As pre-Homeric offshoots of Gaia", says Dr. Farnell, "we must recognize Demeter, Persephone, and Themis."[3] Themis was the Titan who became the second wife of Zeus. Kore appears, too, to have been originally identical with Demeter. "From the two distinct names", Dr. Farnell considers, "two distinct personalities arose. . . . Then as these two personalities were distinct, and yet in function and idea identical, early Greek theology must have been called upon to define their relations. They might have been explained as sisters, but as there

---

[1] *Golden Bough* ("Spirits of the Corn and Wild"), Vol. II, pp. 37 *et seq.*
[2] The length of the period is differently estimated by various writers.
[3] *Cults of the Greek States*, Vol. V, pp. 119 *et seq.*

was a male deity in the background, and Demeter's name spoke of maternity, it was more natural to regard them as mother and daughter.   And apart from any myth about Demeter's motherhood, Persephone-Kore might well have been a very early cult title, meaning simply the girl-Persephone, just as Hera, the stately bride mother, was called, 'Hera the girl' at Stymphalos . . . or the facts could be brought into accord with another supposition. 'Kore' may have been detached from such a ritual name as Demeter-Kore, 'the girl-Demeter'."[1]

In Crete, therefore, the snake-, dove-, and mountain-goddesses may have been seasonal forms of the Mother Earth.   Until the inscriptions are read, however, it cannot be said with certainty whether or not they developed into separate personalities.   All that can be said is that the legends which associate Rhea and Demeter with Crete are highly suggestive in this connection.   Athene, a pre-Hellenic goddess, who was associated with the ubiquitous earth-snake, may have been a specialized form of Gaia also.   Like the Libyan Neith, she developed as a war- and fertility-goddess, and was identified with that deity by Herodotus and other writers.   The animals sacrificed to her were the bull, cow, sheep, and pig, and, once a year, the tabooed goat.

What appears to be certain is that in pre-Hellenic Greece and Crete, and elsewhere throughout Europe, the Earth Mother was worshipped and propitiated from an early pre-historic period.   Her mysteries were performed in caves, as were also the Palæolithic mysteries.   In the caves there were sacred serpents, and it may be that the prophetic priestesses who entered them were serpent-charmers.

Cave worship was of immense antiquity.   The cave

[1] *Cults of the Greek States*, Vol. V, pp. 119–24.

was evidently regarded as the door of the Underworld, in which dwelt the snake form of Mother Earth. Swine were sacrificed to her, a custom which appears to have had origin in the Archæological "Hunting Period". In the Scoto-Irish Fian (Fingalian) stories the love hero, Diarmid, the Adonis of the pre-Agricultural peoples, is slain by the boar leader of the swine-herd of Mala Lith, "Gray Eyebrows", the dark-visaged Cailleach (Old Wife), who was the mother of men and demons and wild animals. This legend may be a reminiscence of human sacrifice. Demeter's pig, like Athene's goat, was perhaps of totemic origin. The boar clan and the goat clan would have made blood offerings to their totems, as do the Australian Kangaroo and Witchetty-grub tribes to theirs, to secure the food-supply.

In the "Pastoral Period" sacrifices of bulls and cows must have become prevalent. The goddess was then the cow mother, who caused the herds to multiply, and provided them with grass. Hathor, the Egyptian goddess, had the body of a woman and the head of a cow. In one of the archaic versions of the Osirian myth Horus cuts off the head of his mother Isis, and the moon-god Thoth replaces it with a cow's head. Isis had also a serpent form, being evidently an earth-mother in origin.

When agriculture was introduced, the various tribes recognized their earth-black and grass-green mother-goddess in a new form—the harvest-haired corn spirit. But she still retained all her immemorial attributes: she did not cease to be the earth-snake, the hag huntress among the mountains and in valleys, the cow goddess of grassy steppes and green oases, and the spirit of fig-tree and olive and vine. Around her, too, hovered the animistic groups who were remembered in after time as nymphs and fairies. She also retained her association with the animal forms she assumed in season as the deity of fertility. There were serpents in her hair, a dove in one hand and a dolphin in the other, like the Demeter of the cave of Phigalia Withal, she was the standing-stone which was visited at certain phases of the moon by women who prayed for offspring. In the Scoto-Irish legend, the Cailleach, after the period of spring storms, transforms herself into "a gray stone looking over the sea". In India goats are sacrificed to the stone of the goddess Durga, which stands below a sacred tree. The legend of the birth of the Cretan Zeus is of special interest in this connection. Cronos swallowed a stone, believing it was Rhea's son, and it was afterwards set up as a sacred object at Delphi. The original Zeus was evidently worshipped as a stone pillar—the pillar which enclosed his spirit, or the spirit of his earthly representative, the priest-king.

The earliest form of the agricultural myth, judging from the Demeter-Persephone legend, appears to have been one in which goddesses only were concerned. All the ceremonies performed were based on the experiences of the sorrowing and wandering mother, the dark woman who concealed herself in a cave, and the abducted daughter condemned to pass part of the year in the Underworld.

It is possible that the Osirian legend, in which the daughter is displaced by the slain young god, came to Crete from Egypt by an indirect route—perhaps with a community of late invaders from Syria or Anatolia. After Osiris taught the Egyptians the art of agriculture he went abroad on a mission of civilization, and when he was slain, and set adrift in a chest, Isis voyaged to Byblus to recover his body. This may be a memory of the missionary enterprise of the Osirian cult. Minos, the Cretan king who resembles Osiris as an earthly king and lawgiver, became, like his prototype, a judge of the dead.

His mother, Europé, a princess of Phœnicia, who was abducted by the Zeus bull, may have been a form of the cow Isis.

The Minotaur may have been a still more primitive form of Osiris. That god, as Apuatu, his earliest known form, was " the opener ". He was therefore identical with the animal-headed Anubis. The mother of the Minotaur was Pasiphae, the queen. Like the Egyptian Queen Isis, she appears to have had originally a cow form, which gave rise to the legend that Dædalus constructed for her the image of a cow, which she entered. The legend that the Minotaur was slain by Theseus may have displaced an earlier myth about the slaying of the corn-god in his bull form. In the Anpu-Bata Egyptian story the sacred bull is slain so that its spirit may enter its tree incarnation. The Apis bull was periodically sacrificed in early times.

Although human sacrifices were offered to the Minotaur—the victims, no doubt, of the bull-ring—that fact need not be urged against the identification of the blood-thirsty monster with Osiris. It is not improbable that the primitive Osiris was a bull-headed man like the Minotaur, which in one of the Cretan seal impressions is depicted seated on a throne below a tree conversing with a priest; its close resemblance to Anubis and Sebek is highly suggestive of Egyptian origin.[1] Professor Breasted has proved, from the evidence of the early Pyramid texts, that Osiris had at one time as unsavoury a reputation as the Cretan Minotaur. He calls him " a dangerous god ", and adds: " The tradition of his [Osiris's] unfavourable character survived in vague reminiscences long centuries after he had gained wide popularity. At that time [the prehistoric period] the

[1] *The British School at Athens*, Vol. VII, p. 18.

dark and forbidding realm which he ruled had been feared and dreaded. In the beginning, too, he had been local to the Delta, where he had his home in the city of Dedu, later called Busiris by the Greeks. His transformation into a friend of man and kindly ruler of the dead took place here in prehistoric ages."[1]

Osiris in his later form was a deified ruler, who received knowledge of the art of agriculture from the earth-goddess, like the Greek Triptolemus. His violent death, with dismemberment, is suggestive of the sacrifice of the old king so that his spirit might pass to his successor. There can be little doubt that human sacrifices were at one time prevalent among the peoples of the Mediterranean race, although they were forbidden ultimately in Osirian texts. Isis and Demeter, as has been shown, burned children before they revealed to mankind the art of agriculture. Dr. Farnell favours the view that the ancient custom of human sacrifice has survived as a memory in the legend which relates that the daughters of Cecrops, having been driven mad by the goddess Athena, flung themselves down from the rock of the Acropolis of Athens. Of similar character is the tradition that the first lot of maidens who were sent from Locris to be priestesses and handmaidens in Athena's temple were slain and burnt, their ashes having been afterwards cast from a mountain into the sea. "It is clear", Dr. Farnell comments, "this is no mere story of murder, but a reminiscence of peculiar rites."[2]

Europé, as bride of Zeus, was probably, like Pasiphae, wife of Minos, a developed form of the Earth Mother. Minos and the Minotaur may similarly be regarded as forms of Osiris, the former an eponymous patriarch whose

---

[1] *Development of Religion and Thought in Ancient Egypt*, p. 38 (1912).
[2] *Cults of the Greek States*, Vol. I, pp. 260 *et seq.*

spirit passed from king to son, and the latter as a link between the animal and anthropomorphic forms of the tribal deity, who was also the eponymous ancestor. According to Pausanias[1] the Arcadians believed that the first settler in their land was Pelasgus, the eponymous ancestor, apparently, of the Pelasgians. Asius, he says, referred to him as follows:—

> Divine Pelasgus on the tree-clad hills
> Black earth brought forth, to be of mortal race.

"And Pelasgus", he proceeds, "when he became king contrived huts that men should be free from cold and rain, and not be exposed to the fierce sun, and also garments made of the hides of pigs, such as the poor now use in Euboea and Phocis. He was the inventor of these comforts. He, too, taught people to abstain from green leaves and grass and roots that were not good to eat, some even deadly to those who eat them. He discovered also that the fruit of some trees was good, especially acorns."[2]

A similar legend is related by Plato regarding the patriarch of his Lost Atlantis. He states that on the hill above the palace (Knossos) lived " one of those men who in primitive times sprang from the earth, by name Evenor. His wife was Leucippe. They had only one daughter, named Clito". Clito became the wife of Poseidon, and the ancestress of all the tribes.[3]

Minos, like Pelasgus, was evidently a semi-divine patriarch. Sir Arthur Evans shows that the "tomb of Zeus" was at one time called the "tomb of Minos". This "seems to record a true religious process", he says, "by which the cult of Minos passed into that of Zeus".[4]

Probably the legend of the birth of Minos was appro-

---

[1] VIII, 1.   [2] *Pausanias*, trans. by A. R. Shilleto, Vol. II, pp. 61–2.
[3] *The Critias*, Section VIII.   [4] *Journal of Hellenic Studies*, Vol. XXI, p. 121.

priated by the Zeus cult. The child was suckled, according to one legend, by a sow, and to another by a goat—totemic animals, perhaps, from whom the food-supply was received. A Knossos seal impression depicts a child suckled by a horned sheep. Sir Arthur Evans refers, in this connection, to the legends of the son of Akakallis, daughter of Minos, being suckled by a bitch; of Miletos, "the mythical founder of the Cretan city of that name", being nursed by wolves; and of the fabled suckling of the Roman twins by a she-wolf. "There is", he says, "some interesting evidence of a cumulative nature, which shows that Rome itself was indebted to prehistoric Greece for some of the oldest elements in her religion."[1] The Indian heroine, Shakuntala, was guarded at birth by vultures, as Semiramis was by doves, while the eagle protected Gilgamesh and the Persian patriarch Akhamanish. In Egypt Horus was nourished and concealed by the serpent-goddess Uazit.

All the eponymous heroes had probably animal forms at the earliest period. Serpents figure prominently in the winged disk of Horus, suggesting the fusion of the falcon and serpent clans of Egypt. The young god was usually depicted with a falcon's head and a human body, and he was an eponymous ancestor. In the bull-headed Minotaur, therefore, it would appear that we have a survival of an early form of a Cretan Osiris or Horus, the link between the bestial deity and human beings.

The Minotaur, however, was not the only man monster who received recognition in Crete. At Zagros Mr. Hogarth discovered a large number of clay sealings depicting man-stags, man-lions, man-goats, eagle-women, goat-women, and so on. One of the forms of the Sumerian Tammuz-Ningirsu was a lion-headed eagle.

[1] *Journal of Hellenic Studies*, Vol. XXI, pp. 128, 129.

It may be that, before the legendary Minos established his empire, Crete was divided into petty states, each of which had its separate animal-headed god or goddess. These deities may have been originally totems. When the totem was slain the priest-king was wrapped in its skin, as was the Sumerian Ea in the skin of the fish. The priest-king was an incarnation of the totem. If the custom of depicting deities partly in bestial and partly in human form arose in this way, it was of exceedingly remote origin, for, as we have seen (Chapter II), there were animal-headed deities in the Late Palæolithic Period.

Greek legends regarding Crete take no account of the stag- and eagle-headed monsters. The Minotaur with bull's head and forelegs and human body and legs overshadowed them all. This fact is highly suggestive. Possibly the explanation is that the bull clan of Minos, which was established at Knossos, attained political supremacy over the whole island, with the result that its Minotaur became the chief deity. This would account also for the myths regarding the sea-bull forms of Poseidon and Zeus, and the notorious ceremonies associated with the bull-ring at Knossos. The Minos clan may have invaded and conquered the island. Some authorities are inclined to regard Minos as a conqueror. Plato says of Atlantis that it was governed by a warrior class which lived separately in the more elevated parts, and had " common rooms of entertainment ".[1]

The same writer goes on to say that after a bull was captured at the annual festival, the people gathered round the fire in which it was sacrificed, to judge transgressors of the laws inscribed on a certain column.[2] The laws were probably those which were credited to Minos.

The conclusions which may be drawn from the evi-

[1] *The Critias*, Section VI.   [2] *Ibid.*, Section XV.

dence available are as follows: Traces survived in Cretan religion of various stages of culture. New settlements were effected on the island from time to time by peoples of common origin, who introduced advanced systems of religion which were grafted on to the old. The worship of the Earth Mother was ever pre-eminent. At first she was the culture deity who instructed mankind. Then the tribal hero whom she favoured was elevated to the Pantheon, the living king being his incarnation on earth, while the dead king was his incarnation in the Underworld as the judge of the dead. As this deified hero displaced an earlier man-monster, who was the son of the mother goddess, and her earthly representative, the legend arose that the hero had actually slain him.[1]   Minos, who hated the Minotaur, may have been the original of the legendary Theseus. That is, Theseus may have been a real king who released Athens from the sway of the Minoan kings and absorbed the Minos-Heracles myth of Crete. The Minos clan came, perhaps, like the legendary Europé, from the Syrian coast, where it had adopted the later Osirian faith. After Crete traded directly with Egypt cultural influences filtered across the Mediterranean. It is unlikely, however, that the religion of the Cretan people as a whole was so profoundly affected by the imported beliefs of the rival cults of Egypt and Libya as they were by those of kindred peoples who settled on the island and exercised direct political influence there. In pre-Hellenic times the Minoan kings colonized parts of Greece, and traditions of Crete's cultural influence survived long after the Homeric Age, although the splendour of its ancient civilization became a blurred and faded memory which in time was associated with the Lost Atlantis.

[1] The sacrificial slaying of the sacred animal may have also survived in the legend.

CHAPTER IX

Growth of Cretan Culture and Commerce

Cretan Origin of Ægean Civilization—The Historic Periods—Cretan and Egyptian Chronologies—Egyptian Evidence of Early Shipping—Pottery as Evidence of Racial Drifts—Asiatic Invasions—The Libyans and Early Cretans—Evidence of Imported Sea-shells—Physical Features of Crete—Prevailing Air-currents—Why Ægean Mariners sailed by Night—Homeric References to Night Voyages—Fertility of Crete—Its Natural Beauties—Life on Sea-coast and among the Mountains—Corn and Wine Harvests—Surplus Products for Early Commerce—Glimpses of Early Minoan Times—Relations with Egypt in Pyramid Period—Story of the Stone Jars—Invention of Potter's Wheel—Borrowings from Egypt—Cretan Ceramic Development—Problem of Sea Routes—Cretans as Ha-nebu and Keftiu.

THE discoveries in Crete have proved conclusively that its pre-Hellenic culture was of great antiquity and local growth. It had developed with unbroken continuity from Neolithic times, and so pronounced was its individual character that it could borrow from contemporary civilizations without suffering loss of identity.

Cretan civilization was immensely older than Mycenæan. Indeed it had reached its "Golden Age" before Mycenæ assumed any degree of importance as a cultural centre. This fact has compelled archæologists to select a new name which could be appropriately applied to it. Professor Reisch favours "Ægean", and, all things considered, this generic term appears to be the most appropriate. It takes into account the obscure influences which were at work during the lengthy Neolithic Period, when independent communities were settled on various islands and on points on the mainland and had begun to trade one with another. The Island of Melos, for instance, as we have seen, was exporting obsidian and importing in exchange apparently the products of other localities. The influence of environment was directing into new lines the common form of culture derived from the North African homeland by the predominant race.

Mycenæan civilization is placed in its proper perspective by referring to it as a late stage of Ægean. On the other hand, Cretan was an early and local form of it. "In Crete", says Mr. H. R. Hall, "it first developed, then spreading northwards it absorbed the kindred culture of the islands, and perhaps the Peloponnese; then it won Central Greece north of the Isthmus from its probably alien aborigines, becoming there 'Mycenæan', and finally, when its own end was near, forced its way into Thessaly, having already reached the Troad in one direction, Cyprus (and Philistia later) in another, Sicily and Messapia in another." [1]

Sir Arthur Evans has divided the history of Ægean civilization in Crete into three main periods, named after the legendary king, or Dynasties of kings, called Minos. These are:

> Early Minoan.
> Middle Minoan.
> Late Minoan.

Each of these periods has also been divided into three stages: Early Minoan I, Early Minoan II, Early Minoan III, and so on to Late Minoan III.

The Minoan Age begins with the introduction of bronze, which occurred, however, long after Ægean civilization had assumed distinctive form. Crete was then

---

[1] *The Journal of Egyptian Archæology*, Vol. I, p. 111 (April, 1914).

able to borrow and adapt to its own use the inventions of other countries, and yet maintain the individuality of its local institutions and art products. The introduction of bronze stimulated its industries, but caused no more change in its national characteristics than has been effected in China by the introduction of electric lighting in our own day.

Cretan archæologists as a whole are agreed as to the order and relative duration of the various historic periods, and most of them have adopted the system of Sir Arthur Evans. Nor do they differ greatly regarding the approximate dating of these. It has even been found possible, although the local script cannot yet be read, to frame a provisional chronological system based on the Berlin system of minimum dating, so as to fit the story of Crete into the history of the ancient world. Important clues have been forthcoming in this connection. From an early period trading relations existed between the island kingdom and the Delta coast, and various manufactured articles were consequently exchanged, as well as wheat and barley, oil and skins, and other perishable goods. The discovery in the deposits assigned to different and well-marked historic phases, of Egyptian products in Crete and Cretan products in Egypt, has made it possible for archæologists to ascertain which periods in either country were contemporaneous.

"With the help of Egyptian synchronisms", writes Mr. H. R. Hall, "we know that the Minoan civilization was nearly, if not quite, as old as the Egyptian. . . . If we date the beginnings of Egyptian history about 3500 B.C., we have not long to wait before we find indisputable traces of connection between Egypt and Crete." [1]

Early Minoan I begins, therefore, some time after the

---

[1] *The Journal of Egyptian Archæology*, Vol. I, pp. 111, 112 (April, 1914).

legendary Pharaoh Mena united by conquest Upper and Lower Egypt and founded the First Dynasty, and before the great pyramids near Cairo were erected. About the same period the Sumerian civilization of Babylonia was beginning to flourish, and the Hatti tribe of the Hittite confederacy had established itself in Anatolia.

Early Minoan II extended from about the period of the Fourth to that of the Sixth Egyptian Dynasty: that is from the Pyramid Age till the close of the Old Kingdom Period.

Early Minoan III covers the dark age of early Egyptian history extending from the Seventh till the Eleventh Dynasties.

Middle Minoan I commenced early in the Eleventh Dynasty Period. Middle Minoan II flourished during the part of the Twelfth and part of the Thirteenth Dynasties; and Middle Minoan III came to an end during the early period of the Hyksos occupation of Egypt.

The Late Minoan Period was the "Golden Age" of Crete. It began before the Hyksos were expelled from Egypt, and attained its highest splendour during the Eighteenth Egyptian Dynasty. During Late Minoan II, Thothmes III of Egypt received gifts from the island kingdom as well as from the Hittites. Late Minoan III was an age of decline. Foreigners were in occupation of Crete, and the mainland towns of Tiryns and Mycenæ were flourishing and influential. Ægean civilization had thus reached the Mycenæan stage. Iron was coming into use; the sixth city of Troy had been built. It was the Age of Homer's heroes. At the close of the Mycenæan period of the Ægean Age the northern conquerors of Greece were inaugurating the Hellenic era. "The so-called miracle of the rise of Hellenism, early in the first millennium B.C., is to be explained", writes Mr. D. G.

Hogarth, "by the re-invigoration of aboriginal societies settled for long previous ages in the Ægean area, and possessed of an ancient tradition and instinct of culture. . . . This process was chiefly due to the blood and influence of an immigrant population of less impaired vigour, which had long been cognizant of and participant in the mid-European culture, and was itself, both in origin and development, related to the elder society of the Ægean area."[1]

At what period Crete began to trade with Egypt it is as yet impossible to ascertain with certainty. Professor Flinders Petrie[2] found, in the lowest levels of the temple at Abydos, black pottery which he concluded came from Crete on account of its close resemblance to fragments discovered by Sir Arthur Evans in the Late Neolithic deposits of Knossos. He also characterized as Ægean several vases and pieces of painted pottery discovered in tombs of the First Dynasty. He maintained further that the Cretan and other foreign imports were brought to Egypt in the galleys depicted on pre-Dynastic vases.

This view has not found general acceptance. It has been urged that the galleys were ordinary Nile boats. "They have deck shelters", writes Mr. Hall, "just like the model funerary boats of the Middle Kingdom tombs, and they carry women on board. On one vase a woman is depicted waiting, with her hands above her head; it may well be that they actually represent the ferry boats of the dead. They carry purely Egyptian emblems. Now, we know of the Egyptians that they were never seafarers; they disliked the sea, and they held the seafaring inhabitants of the Delta coast in abomination: it was never the Egyptians who went to Crete in the early days or later. . . . Finally, the boats are represented amid ostriches,

---

[1] *Ionia and the East*, p. 99 (1909). [2] *Abydos*, Vol. II, p. 38.

oryxes, mountains, and palm-trees: that is to say, they are sailing on the Nile with the desert hills and their denizens on either hand."[1]

All that seems certain in this connection is that shipping was already well advanced in pre-Dynastic times. There is no evidence to show whether the seafarers on the Delta coast, or in Crete, possessed superior galleys to those used by the navigators of the Nile. No doubt they did. The Cretans who went to Melos for obsidian must have found it necessary to build galleys capable of withstanding the buffetings of wind and wave in the Ægean Sea. In fact, the early settlers could not have reached Crete unless they had superior craft to the prehistoric dahabeeyahs and feluccas of the Nile. It is possible, therefore, as Professor Flinders Petrie thinks, that oil and skins were carried across the Mediterranean from Crete in pre-Dynastic times, and exchanged for the corn and beans of Egypt. But on this point the evidence afforded by the pottery cannot be held to be conclusive.

The dark pottery with geometric designs belongs to a class of widespread distribution. Specimens with similar decorations, but of different texture, have been found as far apart as Anau by the Pumpelly expeditions, which conducted important researches in Russian and Chinese Turkestan, at Susa, the ancient capital of Elam, in Persia, at Hittite sites at Sakje Geuzi in North Syria, in Cappadocia and Boghaz'köi, and at points in the Balkan Peninsula. The black pottery of pre-Dynastic Egypt and Neolithic Crete may, therefore, have come from Anatolia. Some hold, indeed, that it has an ethnic significance. Mr. Pumpelly's view is that the Central Asian oases were the sources of Western Asiatic culture, but the evidence he brings forward in this connection is of somewhat slight

---

[1] *Journal of Hellenic Studies*, Vol. XXV., pp. 321 *et seq.*

MAGAZINE OF JARS AND KASELLES, KNOSSOS

The jars ("pithoi") are made of decorated earthenware and are of huge size. The "kaselles" are the small square openings in the floor of the
magazine, evidently used at one time for storage purposes.

character and hardly justifies his theory that Egypt and Babylonia derived their knowledge how to grow barley and wheat, and actually received certain breeds of domesticated animals, from this part of the world. As we have seen, cattle were domesticated in southern France in the Aurignacian period of the Palæolithic Age, before the Fourth Glacial Epoch.

Mr. Pumpelly[1] has, however, demonstrated that climatic changes which took place in the Transcaspian oasis caused the early civilization, of which he discovered important traces, to vanish entirely. The "Kurgans" were buried by drifting sand, and the agriculturists and pastoralists had therefore to migrate in search of "fresh woods and pastures new". It may be that their movements are indicated by the various finds of black pottery. Communities of the wanderers may have settled in Elam and Anatolia, and drifted into Egypt through Syria, and towards Crete through the Balkans. Professor Elliot Smith says that "a definitely alien strain made its appearance in the people of Egypt during the Early Dynastic period, and left its indelible impress in their physical traits for all time. The heterogeneous features appear in a form so pronounced as to justify the positive assertion that the alien element in the mixture was neither Egyptian nor did it belong to any of the kindred peoples. It was something quite foreign and certainly Asiatic in origin— that variety which Von Luschan has called Armenoid."[2] If the Anatolian "broad-heads" were the distributors of the black pottery obtained from the east, representatives of their stock may have reached Crete as well as Egypt before the introduction of metal-working. The evidence obtained from graves shows that they were pressing west-

---

[1] See also *The Pulse of Asia*, by Professor Huntington, a member of the staff of the Pumpelly Expedition in Turkestan.　　[2] *The Ancient Egyptians*, pp. 95, 96.

ward into Europe long before the close of the Neolithic Period, although not in such great numbers as in the Copper and Bronze Ages.

Another view of the problem has been urged by Dr. Duncan Mackenzie. He considers it probable that while the Libyans were developing the black-topped style of pottery "the allied Neolithic people of the Ægean, in a wider European context, were creating the peculiar style of black hand-polished ware typical, for that early period, of the Ægean. Well on in this Neolithic epoch", he says, "must come the Egyptian-looking black-topped ware found in the Copper Age tombs of Cyprus, whose significance in this connection was first pointed out by Furtwangler as being a new indication of race connection between the Egyptian and East Mediterranean of that period, and of a northward movement of the Libyan race consequent upon, and caused by, the first appearance of the Egyptians proper in the Nile land. If, as is likely, this northward movement began before the Ægean civilization had attained to such consistency in itself and such influence outwards as could have had any definite echo in Egypt, then we should have sufficient explanation of the fact that of imported remains in Egypt none from the Ægean region go back to this early period."[1] The pottery with geometric designs found by Professor Flinders Petrie at Abydos may therefore have come from North Africa.

It will thus be seen that the problem as to whether Crete traded with Egypt in Late Neolithic and the earliest Minoan times must be left in the realm of conjecture. What seems certain, however, is that the island kingdom received cultural influences directly or indirectly either from North Africa or Anatolia at an early period in its

[1] *Journal of Hellenic Studies*, Vol. XXIII, pp. 155 *et seq.*

history. This could not have occurred without navigation being well advanced. But, although such a conclusion seems highly probable, it would be rash to build upon it in absence of direct evidence regarding the existence of the regular and constant exchange of commodities, and the influence which would consequently be exercised in the development of art. "We can hardly as yet", writes Mr. H. R. Hall, "speak of relations between Egyptian and Ægean Art in Neolithic days, though it is by no means certain that such relations did not then exist, especially since there is a probability that the Ægean civilization was ultimately derived, in far-away Neolithic times, from that of Egypt, or rather from one of the primitive elements that went to form Egyptian culture."[1] It should be mentioned, however, that a piece of ivory was found in Neolithic strata at Phæstos, in Crete. It may have come from Egypt. Shells have also been discovered by Italian archæologists in the caves of Liguria, which do not belong to the north Mediterranean coast, but are common along the Libyan coast. These are wave-worn and were probably carried to Italy by early navigators, but whether these were Neolithic or Early Minoan Cretans is uncertain.

The makers of pottery with geometric designs must have regarded sea-washed Crete as a veritable Paradise, whether they came from Libyan grasslands fringing yellow desert, or the Delta region with its seasonal plagues, or from the uplands of Anatolia where in winter the passes are often snow-blocked. Quite a variety of climates is offered by the picturesque island, with its great mountain spine fretted by peaks which rise from 5000 to 8000 feet above the sea-level, its sloping forests of pine and oak and chestnut, and its sheltered valleys where grow the

---

[1] *Journal of Egyptian Archæology*, Vol. I, p. 110, and *Journal of Hellenic Studies*, Vol. XXV, p. 337.

olive and fig and vine.   A sharp contrast is afforded by
even its northern and southern shores, especially in winter,
when the former is chilled by bleak winds from the mainland, and the latter is as balmy as the North African coast.
During the greater part of the year the prevailing winds
blow alternately from the north-east and north-west, and
from the south-west and the south.   The northern winds,
ever welcomed through the ages in Egypt, attain greatest
velocity in late winter and whiten the mountains of
Crete with the snows they retain until July, while the
currents from the south come chiefly during the months
of autumn and early winter.   Easterly and westerly
breezes are invariably light and of short duration.   "The
cold current rushing over the easy north slope of the
Balkan, and through the Rumelian gap, gathers force",
writes Mr. D. G. Hogarth,[1] "as it nears the African
vacuum.   Local relief shelters the Adriatic coasts, and to
some extent western Macedonia, Thessaly, and Bœotia;
but Attica receives a full draught through the depression
between its low hills, Pentelicus and Hymettus; and the
isles, especially Crete, are scourged to such purpose that
the higher vegetation in many districts will only grow in
triangular patches to southward of sheltering rocks.   The
counter-current blows off the Sahara with terrific energy
for almost as many days annually as the steppe wind; but
the high relief of Crete breaks its force from the Ægean,
and it is on the slopes of the White Mountains, Kedros,
Psiloriti and Lasithi, and the western coasts and isles of
Greece that it expends the most of its storms and rains."
The north wind, however, brings more moisture to the
peninsula.   But the rainfall diminishes towards the south,
"till little is left to Attica or the Cyclad isles but a hard
cold current of more bracing and stimulating sort for the

---

[1] *The Nearer East*, pp. 99 *et seq.*

healthy human frame than is found anywhere else in the area of the Nearer East ".

Between July and September the north-east or north-west wind falls in the late afternoon, and then " the over-heated land begins to suck a current off the cooler sea— that familiar *inbat* breeze which, after a short interval of stillness following midday, sets the caiques dancing in every Levantine harbour ". At midnight the land breeze commences to blow seaward.

Early navigators among the isles must have soon learned to take advantage of morning and evening breezes as they passed from harbour to harbour with their com-modities. In the *Odyssey*[1] the wanderer Odysseus spends his last day among the Phæacians on the isle of Scheria longing for the sun to set.   He

to the radiant sun
Turned wistful eyes, anxious for his decline.

After supper he was escorted to the vessel which was to convey him to Ithaca.   Ere the port was cleared he " silent laid him down ", and when the rowers

With lusty strokes upturned the flashing waves,
His eyelids, soon, sleep, falling as a dew,
Closed fast.

All night long the vessel sped like a falcon, " swiftest of the fowls of heaven ".

The brightest star of heaven, precursor chief
Of day-spring, now arose, when at the isle
(Her voyage soon performed) the bark arrived.[2]

Telemachus also sails at midnight, when

blue-eyed Pallas from the west
Called forth propitious breezes; fresh they curled
The sable deep, and, sounding, swept the waves . . .

[1] Book XIII.   [2] Cowper's translation.

> A land breeze filled the canvas . . .
> Thus all night long the galley, and till dawn,
> Had brightened into day, cleared swift the flood.[1]

In early spring navigation is perilous in the Ægean, and even in summer winds may veer suddenly without warning. It was a *meltem* or summer gale that caused the ship on which St. Paul was being carried to Italy to meet with disaster. The "south wind blew softly", and "they sailed close by Crete".[2] Then arose "a tempestuous wind called Euroclydon", a hard north-eastern which comes in violent gusts and covers the heaving bays with sheets of foam. "And when the ship was caught," says the Biblical narrative, "and could not bear up into the wind, we let her drive." The *meltem* was encountered by the captain of the vessel, who paid so little heed to St. Paul's warning, in late autumn, when, as was wonted to be said, "sailing was now dangerous because the fast was now already past".[3]

Classic legends of heroes who were shipwrecked like Odysseus, and of sea monsters and syrens, are eloquent of the perils which the sea rovers of the Ægean confronted with unflinching courage and increasing skill wrung from hard experience. But as man has ever achieved greatest progress when confronted by difficulties, the islanders became the first traders on the Mediterranean. They were lauded for their seamanship in song and story—those self-confident men so proud and cold, of whom the goddess Athene spoke to Odysseus, the wanderer, when on the Island of Scheria:

> Mark no man; question no man; for the sight
> Of strangers is unusual here, and cold

---

[1] *Odyssey*, Book II (Cowper's translation), 530–53.   [2] *Acts*, xxvii.
[3] *Ibid.*, xxvii, 9.   The fast was the great day of atonement in the month of September.

The welcome by this people shown to such.
They, trusting in swift ships, by the free grant
Of Neptune traverse his wide waters, borne
As if on wings, or with the speed of thought.[1]

In early Minoan times Crete must have proved as attractive to settlers as it did to traveller Lithgow in 1609, when, describing the plain of Khania, in the north-west, he wrote: "Trust me, I told along these rocks at one time, and within my sight, some sixty-seven villages; but when I entered the valley, I could not find a foote of ground unmanured, save a narrow passage way wherein I was, the olives, pomegranates, dates, figges, oranges, lemmons, and pomi del Adamo, growing all through other, and at the rootes of which trees grew wheate, malvasie, muscadine, leaticke wines, grenadiers, carnobiers, mellones, and all other sortes of fruites, and hearbes the earth can yeld to man, that for beauty, pleasure and profit it may easily be surnamed the garden of the whole universe, being the goodliest plot, the diamond sparke, and the honey-spot of all Candy (Crete). There is no land more temperate for ayre, for it hath a double spring tyde; no soyle more fertile, and therefore it is called the combat of Bacchus and Ceres; no region or valley more hospitable, in regard of the sea having such a noble haven cut through its bosome, being as it were the very resting-place of Neptune."

The year is divided into three seasons. After the gales and rainstorms of Winter comes in March a luxuriant and balmy Spring, when fragrant and many-coloured wild flowers, anciently sacred to the Earth Mother, bloom everywhere in great profusion. Flocks and herds that were "wintered" in the valleys are driven once again to the uplands, where rich fresh herbage springs up in abun-

---

[1] *Odyssey*, Book VII (Cowper's translation), 39-44.

dance. Rivers and streams flash in the sunshine; torrents leap gladly among the rocks, and the sound of falling waters mingles with the constant hum of insects and the songs of melodious birds. In April turtle doves are numerous in passage; in Crete as in Egypt and Babylonia they were associated in other days with the goddess of love.

When the grey dusk blots out the splendour of sunset, and the olive warblers are silenced in the olive groves, the nightingale's sweet "jug-jug" and clear pensive carol ripples through the shadowy woodlands. The shepherd who has ascended the mountain slopes to his summer shelter does not hear the songster of night, but at dawn he is awakened by the wise thrush which "sings its song twice over", and ere long in the growing brightness his heart rejoices to hear once again the full-throated chorus of blackbirds and linnets and woodlarks in leafy woods, where silent lizards come out to listen to the pipes of Pan, where rough satyrs dance merrily, and wide-eyed nymphs peer shyly through congregated trees and whispering water reeds at the human intruders of their solitudes. Higher up the slopes are scented pine-woods that murmur in the breeze like the everlasting sea. Spring comes slowly up this way. Beyond the forest zone the snow retreats grudgingly, and is replaced by the bright foliage of Alpine plants in sheltered nooks, and especially on the southern mountain face. When the glistening diadem of snow is robbed from Mount Ida, and no storm-cloud comes nigh, its bald crest looms greyly across the blue Mediterranean.

There are villages on bracing upland valleys, and in these the present-day descendants of the ancient Cretans lead simple and secluded lives, like the earliest pastoralists. Herding their flocks, they climb shelves of rasping rock, wearing the quaint skin boots with protruding heel and toe pieces that were invented by their remote ancestors. Hither may have come by preference many of the booted Anatolians who were attracted to the island in Minoan times. In midsummer, when the valleys beneath are parched with heat, and their fields and gardens must needs be irrigated, a temperate climate prevails on the plateaus. The nights are cool and refreshing, and amidst the hushed silence of the mountains the voices of men who guard their flocks can be heard calling from great distances through the rarefied air, when the Sphakiots, who claim to be descendants of the Dorians, come to raid the sheepfolds.

It is on these uplands, where Artemis still cares for her nimble-footed herds, that the greatest activity is displayed in Spring-time and early Summer. In the rich alluvial valleys the small farmers have not much else to do than to survey their growing crops. Their fields were ploughed and sown before the "storm season" came on, and they secured ample nourishment from the drenching rains. The harvest falls in May on these lower grounds, but on the uplands it cannot be gathered in before July. After crops are threshed and stored, the fruit is ripe for plucking; then grape juice flows crimson from the wine press, and sweet oil from golden olives.

In ancient times Crete yielded a rich surplus of its products which was available for purposes of trade. Ships were loaded with skins and wine and oil, dried fish and sponges, dried fruits and sacks of barley, which were bartered for the commodities of other lands. The seamen visited island after island in the Ægean sea, and they ventured westward to Sicily; the mainland of Greece was but a day's journey; eastward lay the shores of Anatolia, where the second city of Troy had rich gifts to offer in

exchange for heavy cargoes. In time Egypt attracted the
fearless mariners. It lay towards the south-east, and
when favourable winds were blowing could be reached in
the space of two or three days. They may have heard of
this rich and wonderful land on the Syrian coast, or perhaps there were Cretan traditions regarding it. Birds that
flew thither may have guided them. In the story of
Uenuamen, the Egyptian emissary who was forced to
remain in Cyprus, that melancholy man laments, gazing
across the sea, " Seest thou not the birds which fly, which
fly back unto Egypt? Look at them; they go unto the
cool canal. And how long do I remain abandoned here!"[1]
Let us follow the island mariners to the homeland of their
ancestors, voyaging in the track of migrating birds.

In the Cretan period, Early Minoan I, is embraced
the Third Egyptian Dynasty (*c.* 2980–2900 B.C.). A
change had taken place in the administration of Egypt,
Pharaoh Zoser having transferred his court from the
south to Memphis, the London of the Nile Valley. He
was the builder of the first pyramid—the step pyramid of
Sakkara; and his activities extended to Sinai, whither he
sent annual expeditions to work the copper mines. Early
Cretan traders must have returned home with wonderful
stories of his great achievements. But they were doubtless more greatly impressed by the tireless Pharaoh Sneferu,
who did so much to strengthen and consolidate united
Egypt. He battled against Asian hordes which invaded
the Delta region, constructed roads there, and fortified
strategic points on the eastern frontier. This monarch
built great river vessels for purposes of trade and defence,
some of which were over a hundred and seventy feet
long. As he also dispatched on one occasion, as he duly
recorded, a fleet of forty ships to the Syrian coast to

---

[1] King and Hall's *Egyptian and Western Asia in the Light of Recent Discoveries*, p. 430.

obtain cedars from Lebanon, it is evident that Mediterranean navigation had been well advanced ere his time. He may have been not only familiar with the achievements of Cretan mariners, but perhaps even employed them.

Sneferu was the last king of his line. The Fourth Dynasty (c. 2900–2750 B.C.) produced the stern and masterful Pharaohs—Khufu, Khafra, and Menkaura—who erected the immense pyramids near Cairo. In this Age imposing royal statues were carved from material as hard as diorite, that of Khafra being one of the triumphs of Egyptian art.

Direct evidence of Crete's connection with Egypt during this, the Old Kingdom, period is of scanty character. It is not to be wondered, however, that such should be the case. The marvel is that any traces at all should survive of trading relations conducted at such a remote period.

To emphasize the importance of the few significant finds that have enabled the Sherlock Holmeses of Archæology to prove that such relations did exist, it should be explained that after copper came into use in Egypt, fine stone working became possible, and developed rapidly. The invention of the copper drill enabled workmen to construct shapely bowls, vases, jars, platters, and other vessels of porphyry, diorite, alabaster, and other suitable stones. Craftsmen took evident delight in their handiwork. In one of the tomb scenes, two of them are depicted squatting on the ground drilling out stone vessels. The artist imparted to their faces an expression of self-conscious reserve which suggests that they were accustomed to hear their praises sounded and took pride in their skill. Hieroglyphics placed between the figures record a characteristic conversation. "This is a very beautiful vessel," says one, and his comrade replies, "It is, indeed."[1]

These stone vessels were in great demand, and displaced in the market the rough hand-made pottery, which consequently deteriorated in quality; evidently it was manufactured chiefly for sale to the poorer classes, and, as burial rites have ever been of conservative character, to be placed in graves. The same thing happened in Crete after the introduction of metal. There, too, stone vessels caused much unemployment among the potters, and less skill was displayed by those who supplied cheap vessels of baked clay to a declining market.

It is of special interest to find in this connection that the Cretan stone vases among Early Minoan relics show points of resemblance to those of Egypt. The most important evidence, however, is derived from strata of Middle Minoan I. Some fragments of carinated bowls belonging to this period resemble closely characteristic Egyptian carinated bowls of the Third and Fourth Dynasties. The Cretan vessels were made of Liparite imported from the Lipari islands, which are situated to the north of Sicily, and were apparently visited by the adventurous mariners of Crete in Early Minoan times. No doubt can remain that these Cretan bowls were copies of Egyptian models, and these were probably carried direct from the land of the Pharaohs.

The copper drill, which filled the hearts of Egyptian potters with despair, was in time surpassed by a more wonderful mechanical contrivance, which ultimately restored the prestige and popularity of their ancient craft. Sometime during the Fourth Dynasty, when the industries were being stimulated by the Pyramid-building activities of the Pharaohs, and inventive minds were con-

[1] Breasted's translation, *A History of Egypt*, p. 96.

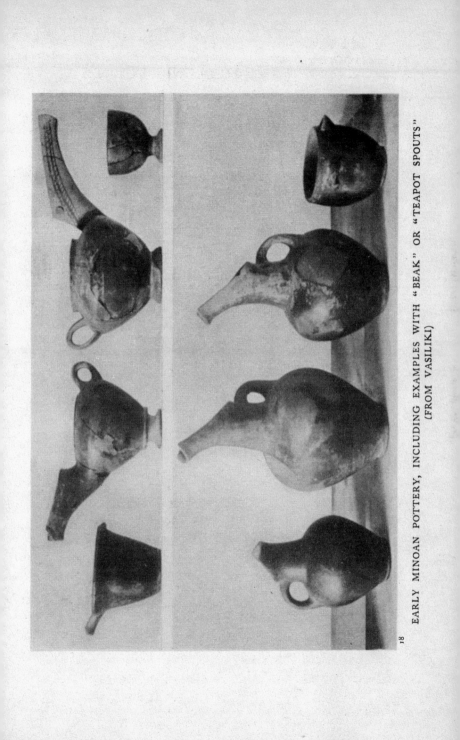

EARLY MINOAN POTTERY, INCLUDING EXAMPLES WITH "BEAK" OR "TEAPOT SPOUTS"
(FROM VASILIKI)

18

stantly directed towards the solution of difficult problems with purpose to simplify and expedite the work of construction, an ingenious craftsman produced the potter's wheel. He was probably a citizen of busy Memphis. As much is suggested by the fact that the new invention was afterwards associated with Ptah, the god of that city, and his southern form, Khnumu, of the First cataract colony of artisans. These deities were depicted shaping the sun and moon and the first man and woman on the potter's wheel. The discoveries and inventions of pious worshippers were always attributed to the culture deity.

As the shapely products of the potter's wheel had to be burned with more care than the old hand-made articles, the problem of firing was solved by the introduction of the enclosed furnace. Results were then obtained which placed the workmanship of the stone-vessel workers in the shade. One can imagine the proud inventor carrying his wonderful jars and vases to the royal palace to receive the congratulations of the Pharaoh, and perhaps a decoration of which he was richly deserving.

The new pottery attained speedy and widespread popularity. Both in Egypt and Crete the potters first imitated the vessels of stone and metal. Indeed the Early Minoan workers, when they decorated their productions, painted imitation rivets on the handles. The Cretan *Schnabelkannen* (vase form), with " beak spout ", " bridge spout ", or " teapot spout ", had been evidently modelled on similar copper and stone vases of the Egyptian Old Kingdom Period. Trading relations between the Cretans and the Nilotic peoples must therefore have been of a direct and intimate character.

But although Crete thus borrowed from Egypt, just as any modern country may borrow an invention from another, its civilization maintained its strictly local character. It was because the island craftsmen had attained a high degree of skill that they were able to adopt new methods, and contribute to the general growth of culture. They were not mere imitators who slavishly copied the methods of their neighbours. Their own inventions were in turn borrowed by others.

The study of Cretan pottery shows that its culture was of local growth and that development was not due merely to outside influence, although outside influences may have at periods provided the stimulus which caused craftsmen to produce something new and improve upon what was being done elsewhere. The spirit of rivalry involved has ever made for progress.

Dr. Duncan Mackenzie, who has acted as Sir Arthur Evans's "lieutenant" in Crete, and is "the chief authority on Early Cretan pottery", as Professor Burrows says,[1] was the first to deal with the development of ceramic art of the island in a manner which has thrown much light on the growth of its civilization. The American and Italian archæologists acknowledge freely his influence and example as an accurate observer, and constantly refer to his "masterly analysis" of Knossian ceramic art. He has woven a wonderful narrative from the collection of fragments dug out of the soil, setting in order what had for so long been confused and obscure.[2]

Trial pits were sunk at various points on the hill of Knossos and inside the palace, with purpose to ascertain the contents and depth of the Neolithic stratum. It was found that the average thickness from the virgin soil upwards was about six metres, the greatest being eight. In the lowest layer, fragments were obtained of a " sooty grey " pottery which had been hand-polished outside and

---

[1] *The Discoveries in Crete*, p. 48.
[2] *Journal of Hellenic Studies*, **XXIII** and subsequent volumes.

inside. The primitive potters made vessels of rough shape from poorly sifted clay, which had neither necks nor differentiated bases : there was no decoration. The second metre yielded a similar ware, but a few fragments were found to be ornamented with geometrical designs, the V-shaped zigzag being either filled in with or surrounded by dots. Some authorities believe that this geometric motive is of northern origin. It appears on Late Neolithic and Bronze Age pottery in our own country and throughout the continent.

In the third and fourth metres a small percentage of the fragments are incised. Then in the fifth metre appears a new development. The incised geometric designs are found to be filled with gypsum or chalk. Here begins the "light on dark" ornamentation of Cretan pottery. This style of pottery has been found in the first stratum of Troy and also in Egypt. Whether it was imported into the Nile Valley from Crete or Asia Minor is, however, uncertain. The evidence afforded indicates either a racial drift from some cultural centre, or the existence of commercial connections between widely separated districts at a remote period in the Neolithic Age. The interval represented by this stratum was of a lengthy duration.

Another new development occurs in the fifth metre. The commonest primitive ware, which shows gradually improving workmanship, is no longer wholly plain. After the vessels were polished, some of the potters began to decorate them with waved rills which gave a rippling aspect to the surface. This style of ornamentation increased in popularity during the period represented by the sixth metre, and was not only effected on the outsides of vessels, but also inside the jutting rims.

We now approach the close of the Neolithic Period.

The pottery increases in quantity, and among the new forms which appear are cups which are evidently the prototypes of the Kamares vessels of a later age.

In the seventh metre we are in the period of transition between the Stone and Bronze Ages. It comes up to the level of the floor of the first Knossian palace, and as the ground was levelled before this building was erected, the eighth metre of the Early Minoan Period appears to have been swept away. Fragments of it may have become mixed with those in the seventh stratum.

The seventh metre is of special interest because it contains the earliest specimens of painted ware. The potters who ornamented their vessels with white-filled geometric incised designs, began to paint them instead. This departure opened up endless possibilities of development. At first the early zigzags were imitated, but in time new decorative motives evolved, and then came a free use of various colours, with variations of "light on dark" and "dark on light" designs. Varnish was also used to give a more lustrous surface than was obtained by hand-polishing. This early painted and varnished ware was hand-made. In the Latest Neolithic Period, however, the clay was finely sifted and well baked. Instead of being dark, like the earlier productions, it was of a bright brick-red colour. Apparently the enclosed furnace had come into use in Crete before the introduction of the potter's wheel. It was when the potters succeeded in baking this red ware that the "dark on light" designs came into use.

At Phæstos similar results were forthcoming from a pit sunk below the palace floor. The hill had been levelled prior to the erection of the palace, and only 5½ metres of the strata remained. "I was able", writes Mosso, who conducted this excavation, "to confirm the result of Dr.

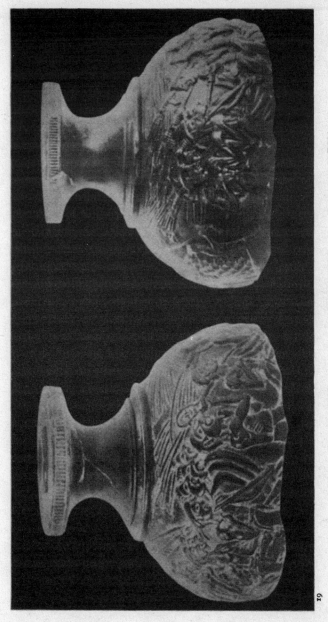

THE "HARVESTER VASE" (STONE) FOUND AT AGHIA TRIADHA

(See full description in Chapter XII, pages 287–289)

Mackenzie's investigation of the black pottery upon the virgin soil being plain. A little higher appears pottery with decoration of punctured dots and lines. In a later period the decoration of the pottery becomes more complex; imitation of basket-work is found, and the deeply incised lines are filled with white chalk. The vases become more elegant, and have decoration in white on a black ground. This pottery is identical with that found in the Troad and in Sicily."[1]

When Cretan pottery attained its highest development in the Middle Minoan Period, it found a ready market in Egypt, which never produced ware so richly coloured or elaborately ornamented. In another direction the Cretans also surpassed their teachers. This was in the carving of vessels of stone. The island craftsmen began by imitating Nilotic forms, but used a softer material which allowed their artists freer play. The greatest surviving triumph of Cretan decoration on stone is the so-called Harvester vase from Aghia Triadha, near Phæstos. With consummate skill the artist depicted upon it a procession of men marching four deep, who are evidently taking part in some ceremony. One of the figures holds in his right hand an Egyptian sistrum, and is followed by a number of lusty singers. The drawing is entirely devoid of Egyptian conventionalism, and possesses a degree of naturalism which is typically Cretan. It is a spirited impression of an emotional group of human beings, and strikes quite a modern note. These stone vases were manufactured in Crete long after the new pottery had displaced stone and metal vessels as articles of everyday use. It is believed they were covered with thin layers of gold, and could have been purchased only by wealthy persons.

Another direct connection between Egypt and Crete

[1] *Palaces of Crete*, p. 25.

is the button seal. It came into use in Crete during the Early Minoan II and III Periods. Mr. H. R. Hall thinks it passed from the island to the Nile valley, where the cylinder seal had long been the popular form. Sir Arthur Evans, on the other hand, is inclined to regard it as being of Delta origin. Be that as it may, there can be no doubt it is a relic of direct trade oversea between the two peoples.

The interesting problem here arises: By what route did the Cretans navigate their vessels to the Egyptian coast? One view is that they sailed across the open sea to the Libyan coast and the Delta, and another that their route was along the Asiatic coast by Cyprus. Mr. H. R. Hall has pointed out in this connection that the Mediterranean tribes "who attacked Egypt in the reign of Rameses III actually did take the longer route". He grants that single ships might have directly crossed the sea, but says that "the probability remains that the longer and safer route was the original one by which connection was first established, and that it was not until the approximate position of either Egypt or Sicily was well known that the direct route could be first dared".[1]

It is probable that the Cretan mariners first came into touch with the coast population of Egypt, who were known as the *Haau*, that is, "fen men" or "swamp men". They were a seafaring folk, and were regarded by the Dynastic Egyptians as aliens. The magical spells of the "Book of the Dead" were forbidden to them. About the time of the Sixth Dynasty references are made to the *Ha-nebu*, which meant "all the northerners". In the Eighteenth Dynasty it was applied to signify the Anatolians and the inhabitants of Greece. The early Cretans may have been called the *Ha-nebu* also. A more direct and later term

[1] *The Annual of the British School at Athens*, VIII, pp. 157-8.

applied to them was the *Keftiu*. Maspero has suggested that *Keftiu* signified the people and *Kefti* the land. According to Hall, *Keftiu* is the same expression as *Kefti*, "signifying 'at the back of', or 'behind'; i.e. the land Keftiu was the 'hinterland', the 'Back of Beyond' to the Egyptians".[1] In the Bible Crete is referred to as Caphtor.

Figures of the Keftiu in Egyptian tombs of the Empire Period are typically Cretan, with wasp waists and girdle and Minoan kilt, and hair falling over the shoulders in pleated tails. They carry vessels of Cretan shape with characteristic decorations. Towards the end of the Eighteenth Dynasty the racial designation Keftiu drops out of use, and names of tribes are given. By that time the island had been overrun by conquerors from the mainland who sacked and destroyed the palaces and overthrew the Knossian Dynasty.

[1] *The Annual of the British School at Athens,* VIII, pp. 159–60.

CHAPTER X

Trading Relations with Troy

Obsidian Finds in Troy—Early Shipping Traffic—Copper Age in Cyprus
——Doubt about Crete—Transition from Stone to Bronze in Troy—Was
Copper first worked in Egypt?—The Oldest Bronze Articles—Bronze manu-
factured in Crete—Probable Sources of Tin Supply—A Visit to Troy—Homeric
Memories—The Nine Cities at Hissarlik—The First and Second Citadels of
Troy—Hand-made and Wheel-made Pottery—Symbolic Decorations—Trojan
Eye Symbol on Yorkshire Relic—The Mother-goddess—Treasure of Priam
and a Cretan Hoard—Engravings of Ships with Sails—Cretan and Egyptian
Jewellery—Silver Cup and Silver Bowls—Homeric References—Ægean Influ-
ence on Anatolian Coast—The Inland Hittite Power—Ethnics of Anatolia—
Danubian Cultural Area—Troy's Connections with Thrace—Ancient Conflicts
on Plain of Troy—Problem of the Jade Traffic—European Jade Objects not
all imported—Crete and the European Trade Routes—Distribution of the
Developed Spiral.

THE influence of Ægean culture, which assumed its specific character in Crete, extended as far distant as Troad,
that strip of north-western Anatolian coastland which
came under the sway of the Trojans. "In the Early
Minoan period 'Crete'", writes Mr. and Mrs. Hawes,[1]
"was in contact with Egypt on the one hand and with
Hissarlik (Troy) and the Cyclades on the other—pupil of
the former, teacher of the latter." It is possible that
Troy's earliest connection with Crete goes back to the
Neolithic Period, for finds have been made in the stratum
of the first city of flakes and small artifacts of obsidian.
This highly-prized stone was probably carried over the
sea from Melos rather than along an overland trade route
from Sinai.

[1] *Crete, the Forerunner of Greece*, p. 19.

It would appear that there was a certain amount of regular shipping traffic on the Ægean Sea in Neolithic times. Crete, as we have seen, imported obsidian from Melos long before the introduction of metal working. The beginnings of the trade can be traced at Magasa, where the flakes were found to be associated with an extremely crude pottery of great antiquity, and it was well developed apparently during the later stage of Neolithic culture, to which the obsidian knives from Knossos are assigned. It is unlikely that Melos was uninhabited when obsidian was first worked there. Ultimately its people exchanged it for marble from Paros, which was utilized to shape rough amulets or figurines of the mother goddess. But, so far, except for the evidence afforded by these finds of obsidian, no other indications that the Cycladic islands were occupied during the Neolithic Age have been forthcoming. Stone weapons have, however, been found in southern Greece and on the large island of Eubœa. Some of these are so small that they seem to have been charms, or votive objects, rather than real weapons. The Ægean Neolithic folk were evidently a peaceful people, and it may be that island communities utilized wood freely for implements of daily use. Wooden hand ploughs and wooden bowls were used in the Scottish Hebrides until a comparatively recent date, and the Egyptian peasants carried staves to drive their herds, and found them sufficient for purposes of defence.

The early peoples who reached Crete probably came by way of the Cyclades, either from the Anatolian or Grecian coasts. Before they accomplished this feat, the art of navigation must have advanced considerably. If it is held, on the other hand, that they passed direct oversea from Cyprus or Libya, we must conclude that they were skilled mariners who possessed well-equipped vessels and were quite capable of conducting a sea traffic from the very beginning. Perhaps when the Cretan inscriptions can be read some light will be thrown on this aspect of the problem.

Among the isles, Crete, with its long record of human activity, was ever prominent in promoting commercial intercourse, and as mercantile enterprise was the principal factor in its development, Troy was probably reached by its wind-bronzed and adventurous mariners, who, having familiarized themselves with the "swan ways" of the Cyclades, undertook the exploration of the eastern and western shores of the Ægean Sea, gaining knowledge of prominent landmarks like Mount Athos and the massive mountain ridge of Samothrace.

Traffic by the sea, as well as by the land routes, must have been greatly stimulated after the knowledge of how to work metals became widespread. Ships could then be constructed more stoutly and with greater celerity, and must consequently have increased in number. Pharaoh Sneferu's order for a new fleet of forty odd vessels to convey timber from Phœnicia is an interesting example of the manner in which ambitious monarchs might strive for mercantile supremacy. No doubt it was in consequence of the growing competition that experienced seafarers made voyages of exploration and opened up new routes in all directions. Malta, as we have seen, received obsidian from Melos; it also imported jade, which probably came from Anatolia. Jade was carried as well to Sicily, and as the Cretans imported liparite from the Lipari islands, after they had established a connection with Egypt, it was probably by them that jade objects were distributed westward.

It is uncertain when Cyprus was first visited by the Cretan mariners. The Neolithic relics of that island are

notably scanty, and some think it was not occupied prior
to the age of metals, as it is devoid of Neolithic strata.
No doubt the earliest Cypriotes, who settled in the eastern
river valleys, came from the Syrian coast.   Their pottery
was hand-made, and ornamented with incised designs, and
compares more closely to Anatolian than pre-Dynastic
Egyptian or Cretan varieties.   The island had its Copper
Age, and towards the close of it wheel-made pottery was
manufactured.

It is held by some authorities, including Myers and
Hall, that copper was first worked in Cyprus.   If such
was the case, it is remarkable that the island has not
yielded traces of early commercial connections with Crete
and Egypt.   "Up to the present," says Mosso, "there
is no evidence that copper was worked in the Isle of
Cyprus before it was used in Egypt and Crete. . . . The
word Cyprus comes from the name of the plant κύπρος,
which is the henna (*Lawsonia inermis*), used for dyeing
the nails red."[1]   Cypriote copper blades are of later date
than those found in Crete, and the earliest flat axe of
copper is of Egyptian Neolithic form.[2]

There can be no doubt that Cyprus had a Copper
Age before the Age of Bronze.   The same cannot be
said with certainty, however, regarding Crete.   Copper
weapons have been found in tombs, but they are small
and of votive character, and the larger ones, of which they
were copies, were perhaps of bronze.   The few copper
dagger blades that have been unearthed are difficult to
place, and the view has been urged that bronze is as old
in Crete as copper.   The island of Minos "shows",

---

[1] *Dawn of Mediterranean Civilization*, pp. 299 *et seq.*
[2] Those who favour the Cypriote origin of copper-working urge that the earliest
Egyptian copper artifacts are copies of those of Cyprus.   It can be shown, on the other
hand, that some of the Egyptian copper artifacts are copies of Neolithic forms.

Mrs. Hawes says, "the same phenomenon as Hissarlik,[1] the sudden appearance of bronze at a date not later than 2500 B.C. On the evidence at present available no Copper Age can be predicated for the island. . . . The natural conclusion is that Crete knew nothing of copper until it knew tin also and the superiority of the alloy. This knowledge must have come through the extension of trade relations, not by conquest, for no country shows more independence in its metal series than Crete."[2]

Whence was the bronze obtained by the Cretans? Was it from Egypt or Anatolia? Both Crete and Troy were able soon after the dawn of their Bronze Ages to import silver, which during the Old Kingdom Period was rarer than gold in Egypt. The silver may have come from the same region as tin. One possible source of supplies of silver was Cilicia, where silver mines are still worked; the other was Spain, in which country evidence has been forthcoming of early commercial relations with Crete.

Once the secret of how to work metals passed from centre to centre of Neolithic culture, the ingenuity expended for long Ages in the shaping of artifacts of flint, obsidian, and jade was directed into new and inspiring channels. Cretans, Trojans, Cilicians, and Cappadocians alike may have been stimulated to inaugurate a new era by foreign influences, but they did not remain as slavish imitators. The pupil not only strove to excel the teacher, but even to surpass him. As in our own day a new invention may be improved by a people who have borrowed it, so at the dawn of the Metal Age the bor-

---

[1] Schliemann was wrong in asserting that Hissarlik (Troy) had a Copper Age.

[2] *Gournia*, Mrs. Hawes and Others, p. 33. (American Exploration Society, Philadelphia, 1908.)

rowers appear to have contributed towards the development of a discovery which was to revolutionize the ancient world. Ægean Bronze Age culture has distinctive features which establish its independent character. It was not of sporadic development. The indigenous influences which were manifested during the lengthy Neolithic Age were not cut off by the importation of metal, but were rather given opportunity to achieve freer and more brilliant growth in every sphere of human activity. That being so, we are confronted by an exceedingly difficult problem when we seek to discover whence either Crete or Troy imported bronze, or the copper and tin with which to manufacture it. The influences exercised by local cultures tend to conceal the sources from which borrowings were made.

Copper was known in Egypt in pre-Dynastic times. Indeed, some authorities hold that it first came into use in that country. "It was the custom of the proto-Egyptian women, and possibly at times of the men also," says Professor Elliot Smith, "to use the crude copper ore, malachite, as the ingredient of a face paint; and for long ages before the metal copper was known, this cosmetic had been an article of daily use. It is quite certain that such circumstances as these were the predisposing factors in the accidental discovery of the metal. For on some occasion a fragment of malachite, or the cosmetic paste prepared from it, dropped by chance into a charcoal fire, would have provided the bead of metallic copper and the germ of the idea that began to transform the world more than sixty centuries ago." At first copper was used for small ornaments and then to make needles, one end of a copper wire being bent down to form an "eye". In time, chisels and axes and other implements were manufactured in imitation of those of stone which were in use. "Every stage in the history and evolution of the working of copper", he holds, "is represented in Egypt, and is preserved under circumstances that enable us to appreciate in some measure the motives which led the Egyptians on, step by step, to the full realization of the immensity of the power they had thus acquired."[1]   Professor Elliot Smith follows Dr. Reisner in this connection.[2]

Others hold that copper was first worked in Asia. Professor Myers, as we have indicated, favours Cyprus.[3] Mr. Hall, who supports the view that the knowledge of corn passed from Palestine to Egypt and Babylonia, thinks that the knowledge of metal may have come from the same quarter, Sinai, Syria and Cyprus being "the original focus of the distribution of copper over Europe and the Near East. Copper came gradually into use among the prehistoric Southern Egyptians towards the end of the predynastic age. And they must have obtained this knowledge of it from the Northerners." Mr. Hall adds: "Dr. Reisner considers the Egyptian evidence alone, and not in connection with that from the rest of the Levant".[4]

It is also contended that the manufacture of bronze was not an Egyptian invention, and that Troy and Crete were probably in touch with the centre where copper was first hardened by tin and antimony. Mr. Hall suggests that this art "came from the Middle East, where tin is found, to Greece, as well as Babylonia and, eventually, to Egypt".[5] Babylonia, like Cyprus, had a long Copper Age.

No direct proof has yet been forthcoming, however, that Egypt imported its first bronze implements. The fact cannot be overlooked that the oldest bronze relics yet

---

[1] *The Ancient Egyptians*, pp. 3 et seq.
[2] *Prehistoric Cemeteries of Naga-ed-Der*, Vol. I, p. 134.
[3] *Science Progress*, 1896, p. 347.
[4] *The Ancient History of the Near East*, pp. 89 et seq. (1913.)   [5] *Ibid.*, p. 33.

found come from the Nile valley. No discovery has yet
been made that bronze was manufactured elsewhere prior
to 3000 B.C. A few objects of bronze have been found
in First Dynasty tombs. Maspero gave Angelo Mosso
a piece of metal plate from an Abydos tomb to analyse.
The test showed "copper 96.00 and tin 3.75 per cent".[1]
Another important relic is the famous "bronze rod of
Medum", which belongs to the Third Dynasty period.
It was found embedded in the fillings of a mastaba associated with the pyramid of King Sneferu. Pure copper was
also used extensively throughout Egypt for the manufacture of weapons and implements from pre-Dynastic times
till the Twelfth Dynasty. Iron was known at an early
period, and is referred to in the Pyramid texts. It probably had a religious significance.

The Egyptians may have received their earliest supplies of copper from Sinai, which they visited to obtain
turquoise in the Neolithic Age.[2] We know that expeditions were sent to work in the copper mines in that region
at a later period (Third Dynasty). Whence was the tin
obtained to harden the copper? A possible source of
supply is North-western Arabia. That it could be found
there is suggested by the Biblical reference to the spoils
taken by Moses from the Midianites, which included
"the gold and the silver, the brass, the iron, the tin and
the lead".[3] Another possible source is Anatolia, where
tin is said to exist. The raiders against whom Pharaoh
Sneferu of the Third Dynasty waged war on the Delta
frontier may have come down an ancient trade route,
having ascertained that rich plunder could be obtained in
Egypt. There is also tin in Italy as well as copper, but
the earliest copper weapons found in that country are of

---

[1] *Dawn of Mediterranean Civilization*, p. 57.   [2] *Ibid.*, p. 59.
[3] *Numbers*, xxxi, 22.

advanced Cretan type (Middle Minoan). Local forms which have been found are not of earlier date.

It may be that Egypt's scanty supplies of tin during the Old Kingdom Age came from more than one source. Mr. W. M. Muller sees on a Sixth Dynasty relief "Ægeans bearing tin into Egypt". If the figures referred to are Ægeans, they were certainly Cretans. It is of special interest to find in dealing with Egypt's early imports of metal that a socketed bronze hoe of the Sixth Dynasty resembles examples from Cyprus and South Russia which are preserved in the British Museum. This artifact may have come down the sea trade route by which sporadic supplies of tin and bronze were carried. The manufacture of bronze in Egypt never assumed great dimensions, on account of the difficulty experienced in obtaining tin, prior to the Twelfth Dynasty. Its early Metal Age was mainly a Copper one.

After the mariners of Crete began to bring home supplies of bronze, its traders no doubt did their utmost to acquire the secret of how to manufacture it. It may be that, like Solomon, who sent Hiram of Tyre annual supplies of wheat and oil in return for timber from Lebanon and skilled workers in metal,[1] a Cretan monarch made arrangements with an Egyptian or Anatolian Hiram to send him artisans who were skilled in the manufacture of bronze.

One of the places in Crete where bronze was cast was a headland on the Gulf of Mirabello about three miles east of Gournia. An ancient copper mine there is called by the peasants "Chrysocamino", which signifies "the oven of gold" or "the golden furnace". Describing it, Dr. Hazzidaki writes: "The seashore rises for above 100 metres, and here is the cave with so small an

---

[1] *I Kings*, v, 1–12, and vii, 14 *et seq.*

entrance that one has to go down and creep in on hands
and knees. The cave is 52 metres long, the roof is
irregular in height, about 2 metres near the entrance, that
is, 2 metres from it, and in the middle it reaches a height
of 20 metres, and at the far end it is 12 metres high.
The walls and roof are covered with stalactites, and the
rock is calcareous. Great blocks of stone have fallen from
above, especially at the far end of the cave." Small
fragments of primitive pottery of uncertain date were
found in the cave, and also pieces of Middle Minoan
times.

Smelting operations were carried on near the entrance
of the cave, as is indicated by a piece of crucible found by
Dr. Hazzidaki. Inside, pieces of scoria were picked up.
The copper appears to have been entirely worked out.[1]
Specimens of rock taken from a cliff in the vicinity have
yielded a small percentage of copper.

Bronze was also cast in Gournia. This is proved
"by the finding of scraps of bronze and slag, pure copper
adhering to smelting vessels, a crucible pot for carrying
a charge of metal, and by numerous stone moulds, into
which the molten metal was run for making knives, nails,
awls and chisels". Copper was used for the manufacture
of bowls, jars, and other utensils, but "weapons were of
bronze, containing as much as ten per cent alloy with
copper ".[2] Copper daggers with an extremely small percentage of tin have also been found.

But although copper could be found in Crete, the tin,
as has been indicated, had to be imported. "By the
beginning of the Bronze Age ",[3] writes Dr. Mackenzie in
this connection, "the valley of the Rhone must have
played a dominant role of communication between the

---

[1] *The Dawn of Mediterranean Civilization*, pp. 289-91.
[2] *Crete the Forerunner of Greece*, pp. 289-91.   [3] C. 2800 B.C.

great world of the Mediterranean and the north; by that
time it was probably already the high continental trade
route towards the tin mines of Britain." Angelo Mosso
also favours the hypothesis that Crete's early supplies
came from England. "We know the road", he says,
"followed by the caravans bringing English tin through
France to the mouth of the Rhone at the end of the
Neolithic period, while no trace of any trade in tin has so
far been discovered in the East." [1] Mosso's reference to
the "East" applies to "the mountains of China where
tin is found".

Mrs. Hawes, who favours a Nearer Eastern source,
writes as follows: "When the Pumpelly expedition
returned from Turkestan in 1904, one of the members
brought potsherds indistinguishable at first sight from the
brilliantly mottled ware found at Vasiliki during the same
season. . . . The strong likeness between the two fabrics,
of which the writer has personal knowledge from having
handled them together, is more reasonably explained by
intercourse than by accident. Moreover, Dr. Hubert
Schmidt, who accompanied the expedition, reports that a
neighbouring tumulus (near the large one in which the
pottery was found) gave him a three-sided seal-stone of
Middle Minoan type, engraved with Minoan designs—
man, lion, steer, and griffin. How shall we explain those
evidences of Ægean influence in Southern Turkestan?
They must be brought in line with other proofs of
contact."

This distinguished lady archæologist refutes Dr.
Muller's view that the Ægeans who carried tin into Egypt
obtained their supplies from a trade route that connected
Central Germany with the sea coast. "The backwardness
of Europe in learning to employ metal", she says, "is

[1] *The Dawn of Mediterranean Civilization*, pp. 62–3.

undeniable." Hungary, like Cyprus, had a Copper Age before bronze became known. "We see", she writes, "that at *c.* 2500 B.C. Asia Minor shared with the Ægean the knowledge of bronze, whereas three centuries later Europe was still in the Stone Age. . . . As further explanation of the priority of bronze in Asia Minor, we may now suggest the probability that, long before tin was discovered in Europe, it was being brought overland through Asia Minor, and also by way of Transcaucasia and the Black Sea from distant Khorassan, Strabo's Drangiana, where its presence has been confirmed. Excavations at Elizabethpol in Transcaucasia have revealed a culture in early contact with the Ægean." [1] She thinks that carriers " not unlike the swift Scythians of Herodotus, frequented both the tin-producing region south-east of the Caspian and the copper region of the Danube at an early date".[2]

Troy was a probable "clearing house" of the early tin and bronze trade. We should therefore visit it before dealing with Ægean commercial connections with Western Europe.

Our course is a north-eastern one across the island-strewn Ægean Sea. This way went the Homeric Achæans who fought for the possession of Helen, the heiress of the Spartan throne, and no doubt with desire also to expand their area of political influence in the interests of commerce. We cast anchor as we draw near the southern shore at the mouth of the Hellespont. Since the dawn of history myriads of vessels have passed beyond this point to navigate the narrow strait, the modern Dardanelles, that leads towards the Sea of Marmora and the great Black Sea beyond it.

[1] Mrs. Hawes refers in this connection to E. Rössler, *Zeits. f. Ethnol.*, XXXVII, 1905, pp. 114 *et seq.*   [2] *Gournia*, p. 33.

The famous Troad lies before us. It is a country which does not make much appeal nowadays, but must have offered many attractions to early settlers. The valleys are suitable for agriculture; there is excellent herbage on the hillsides for flocks and herds, and an abundance of game among the mountains. During winter the south winds from the Mediterranean impart to it a milder climate than prevails in the Balkans, or the uplands of Phrygia, and the summer heat is tempered by the cool Etesian winds. Water is plentiful; there are numerous springs and generous rivers flowing from the mountains. Withal there is an abundance of timber, much good clay for brick-making, and an endless supply of limestone with which to erect dwellings and strong, high walls to protect citizens and their domesticated animals against the attacks of bears and lions and cunning wolves that prowl through the forests and up and down the green valleys, not to speak of human enemies.

We land at the mouth of the famous river Scamander, turning our backs on the unpicturesque tongue of European land known to the ancients as Chersonesus, and in our day as the peninsula of Gallipoli; we also take our eyes from the shouldering hills of the island of Imbros, behind which towers sublime Mount Saoce, the loftiest peak of Samothrace, on which the god Poseidon aforetime sat to watch the Homeric heroes performing mighty feats of arms.

Our steps are directed inland, and we proceed to cross the long and windy Plain of Troy, remembering

> Old unhappy far-off things
> And battles long ago.

Yonder towards the south-east, blue above the ridges of woody hills, is the Anatolian range of Mount Ida, which forms a noble frontier of the Troad; there Paris was once a shepherd; thither, too, fled Æneas after Troy fell. To the west is the high coastland of the Ægean Sea, and eastward and north-eastward are broken groups of featureless mountains divided by pleasant valleys. Less than 4 miles in front of us we can distinguish a boat-shaped hillock, on the spur of a sloping hill, rising abruptly from the plain: that is famous Hissarlik, the site of the ruins of the various citadels of Troy.

The memoried plain is bordered on either side by the Rivers Simœis and Scamander. There are marshes to avoid, as in Homer's time, but these are easily detected at their utmost limits by the clumps of long grasses and weeds, and of whispering tamarisks which also fringe the steep and crumbling river banks.

The Simœis has shrunk to a few inches in depth, for it is now late summer; puffs of wind blow clay dust from its clay-caked and stone-strewn bed. Down a beautiful valley it flows westward, as if to cross the plain towards the Ægean Sea, until it curves round a ridge of hills and directs its course to the shore of the Hellespont. The more famous Scamander is about 2 feet deep and about 20 feet in breadth. When, however, the snows are melting on the Ida range it is exceedingly turbulent, and of such great volume that it carries down trees and boulders, and occasionally overflows its reedy banks to submerge the plain. The Simœis similarly rages furiously at this period.

There is an interesting reference in the *Iliad* to the sudden rise of the rivers after a "cloud burst". When Achilles drove one part of the Trojan army into the city and another into the Scamander,

> the plain he found
> All flooded o'er, and, floating, armour fair,
> And many a corpse of men in battle slain.

The Scamander was supposed to be increasing for the express purpose of resisting his advance. The roar of its spring flood resounds in the sonorous hexameters of Homer, but sinks to a spray-like hiss in an English translation.

> Rearing high
> His crested wave, to Simœis thus he[1] cried:
> " Dear brother, aid me with united force
> This mortal's course to check; he, unrestrained,
> Will royal Priam's city soon destroy.
> Nor will the Trojans his assault endure.
> Haste to the rescue then, and from their source
> Fill all thy stream, and all thy channels swell;
> Rouse thy big waves, and roll a torrent down
> Of logs and stones, to whelm this man of might." [2]

We reach Hissarlik and ascend it to survey a maze of ruins. The fields around us were tilled and irrigated aforetime, when there were watchmen on the " topless towers " to give warning of the approach of raiders. These keen-eyed men could see far up the valleys; nor could vessels cross the Hellespont without their knowledge; and they had glimpses to the west, across the Scamander, of the Ægean Sea, which is but $3\frac{1}{4}$ miles distant, and were thus able to herald the approach of the galleys of Crete.

Before Schliemann began to excavate on this wonderful hillock, by cutting a deep broad trench through the various strata, it towered about 160 feet above the level of the plain; but when the earliest Neolithic people first chose it as a settlement, it was not much more than 50 feet high. Distinct traces survive of nine cities in all, the latest being the Troy of the Roman Age. Each city, after the first, had been erected on the levelled debris of

---

[1] *Scamander.*   [2] *Iliad,* Book XXI (Derby's translation), 340 *et seq.*

the previous one. So the hill, like a stooping giant, gathered from age to age an increasing burden for its great unwearied back.

Troy I was built in the Neolithic Age. Its deposit of from 12 to 14 feet indicates that it endured for many long centuries. Portions of its walls constructed of small stones, here and there in herring-bone pattern, were laid bare by Schliemann. As the foundations, in some parts, do not reach the bedrock, it is evident that the hillock was occupied for a considerable period before stone was utilized for building purposes. The earliest defensive works may have been ramparts of earth.

Hissarlik was apparently from the earliest period the citadel of the city which lay round it on the plain. Here dwelt, in a palace, the king and his family, and here also were stored the treasure and winter food-supply of the tribe. When enemies poured down the mountain passes, or across the Hellespont from Europe, the citadel became a shelter for women and children, and for flocks and herds. Inside its walls, too, the warriors found safe retreat when attacked by overwhelming numbers. The hill forts and brochs of Scotland appear to have served a similar purpose.

Within the area of Troy's Neolithic citadel traces survive of the stone foundations of houses and of certain erections usually referred to as "sheep-folds". Of special interest are the remains of pottery which have come to light. The fragments unearthed by Schliemann were of the hand-made variety, and these are numerous and varied enough to show that the Trojan ceramic art was developed locally and attained a comparatively high degree of excellence. Invariably the pottery is dark and decorated with geometric designs, the incisions being filled in with white chalk as in Crete and Egypt. A fine surface finish was effected by the use of the smoothing-stone.

Doubt has been expressed as to whether all the bronze implements which Schliemann associated with this early stratum really belong to it. Some of these may have fallen down the sides of his trench, and got mixed up with the relics of a deposit with which they had originally no connection. It appears certain, however, that the Neolithic city was in existence at the dawn of the Metal Age in Crete, for some of the bronze implements in question are unlike those found in later strata.

The second city was erected before 2500 B.C. Whether or not there was a fresh racial infusion we have, as yet, no means of knowing. It is significant to find in this connection that there are distinct traces of development from the Neolithic period, especially in the ceramic relics, a sure indication that a considerable portion of the old stock remained. For the first time the hillock was levelled, a process which no doubt obliterated much valuable evidence, and it then stood about 100 feet above the sea-level. Retaining stone walls, which sloped inward, were also erected, and those round the south-western and western sides of the eminence can still be traced.

This was the city which Schliemann believed to be Homer's Troy, because it contained a great amount of burnt debris. But in this he was mistaken. Shortly before he died, however, he found some Mycenæan potsherds which afforded a clue to the mystery and enabled Dr. Dörpfeld, the distinguished German archæologist, who conducted subsequent excavations, to locate Homer's city in the sixth stratum.

Dr. Dörpfeld has divided the history of the second stratum into three periods. These may be referred to as Troy II A, B, C. The citadel of Troy II A, was little more than a tribal fortress about 100 yards in diameter. There were two main entrance gates, one on the south-

western side and the other on the southern. The pottery
which was manufactured resembled the hand-made variety
of the Neolithic settlement, but the workmanship displayed was on the whole inferior. Apparently we meet
here with the decadent period during which vessels of
stone were being constructed with the use of copper drills.

In the Stratum II B the new pottery makes its appearance. The Egyptian potter's wheel had evidently reached
Troy as well as Crete, while the enclosed baking-furnace
also came into use. There can be no doubt, therefore,
that a brisk trade was being conducted along the trade
routes both by land and sea. Considerable progress was
effected also in architectural work, brick as well as stone
being largely used.

The evidence of Stratum II c shows that the citizens
of Troy were progressing by leaps and bounds. Traces
of destruction by fire of earlier buildings suggest that
frequent conflicts were waged round the fortress, and it is
possible, therefore, that the extensions and alterations which
were effected from time to time were rendered necessary
to maintain the prestige of the city in stirring and difficult
times, when hordes of nomads were enabled by the acquisition of metal weapons to overrun large portions of territory.

It was during the period covered by the deposits of
the second city of Troy that the great masses of Asiatic
pastoral nomads pressed into Europe and conquered the
more passive and more highly-cultured agriculturists of
the Mediterranean race. As much is indicated by the
burial remains of the Early Bronze Age in Europe, which
show that a broad-headed people pressed westward, first
along the uplands and then across the valleys, in increasing
numbers, here adopting the funerary customs of their
predecessors, and there introducing their own.

Troy continued to develop its own civilization, resisting, it would appear, for a long period the raids of plundering barbarians. That its wheel-made pottery·was not imported is made evident by its distinctly local characteristics. The hand-made jars, with side projections, pierced for suspension, which were characteristic of Stratum II A, assumed more artistic character in Stratum II B, when the wheel came into use. Another link between earlier and later times is the "face urn". These interesting Trojan products indicate that the decoration of pottery may have had a mythological significance. Zigzag, St. Andrew's Cross, herring-bone, and V-shaped designs, as well as rippling lines, "trickle ornaments", and dots, may therefore have meant much to the people who believed that their food-supply was the gift of a deity, or group of deities, whose favours they constantly invoked by performing ceremonies and offering sacrifices. In the *Odyssey* the Phæacians toasted the deity when they drank together. King Alcinous, addressing his guests after Odysseus had partaken of his meal, spoke as follows:—

> Pontonoüs! mingling wine, bear it around
> To ev'ry guest in turn, that we may pour
> To thunder-bearer Jove (Zeus) . . .
> > When, at length,
> All had libation made, and were sufficed,
> Departing to his house, each sought repose.[1]

Food and drinking vessels may have been dedicated to deities as well as the potter's wheel, which, as has been indicated, was credited to the god Ptah in Egypt. The spirit of the god, or of one of his emissaries, may have been in the cup. It is of interest, therefore, to find that the lips of some of the Troy vessels are ornamented with

[1] Book VII (Cowper's translation).

20

GENERAL VIEW OF "THE TREASURE OF PRIAM"

(From the photograph by Schliemann in "Atlas Trojanischer Alterthümer")

The topmost row shows the Golden Diadems, Fillet, Ear-rings, and small Jewels. Second row—Silver "Talents" and Vessels of Silver and Gold. Third row—Silver Vases and curious Plate of Copper. Fourth row—Weapons and Helmet-crests of Copper or Bronze. On floor—Vessel, Caldron, and Shield (all copper).

circles enclosing dots. One characteristic fragment shows two circles with a straight line drawn down between them. It is obvious that the potter desired to represent a face with staring eyes. Schliemann believed that the face was intended for that of an owl, and constantly made reference to "owl-headed" vases. Another fragment, however, shows clearly that the crude artistic efforts were directed towards the representation of the human face. No attempt was made to indicate the nose line, but the eyes were fairly well shaped, and above these the eyebrows were drawn also. In other examples the eyebrows and nose were shaped like a bird in flight, the eyes being represented by perforated circles, while a straight line represented the mouth.

This tendency towards realism is found to be less pronounced, however, as the vessels become of more complicated and finer construction. The arched eyebrow, the eyes and ears, yield to purely decorative tendencies, and become symbols, as do also the dots, rings, and cones representing female breasts; the swastika on the lower part of the body is evidently a fertility symbol. This process of developing symbols from natural objects can be traced even in the Palæolithic Age. It does not follow, however, that the change robbed the ornaments entirely of their religious and magical character, difficult as it may be to discover where a symbol is divested of significance and a purely artistic motive begins.

The Trojan method of representing the human face, with the bird-wing-shaped nose and eyebrows and the eye dots, is paralleled by similar designs on objects from the Greek islands. Interesting examples of the same artistic motive have been found in the East Riding of Yorkshire. In a trench surrounding a burial cairn on Folkton Wold were discovered chalk drums associated with unburnt burials. These are ornamented with spirals, St. Andrew's Cross, and other characteristic Ægean designs, and also with the eyebrows and eye symbols. As the latter appear on standing-stones of the Marne and Gard valleys in France, and on early Bronze Age vessels in Spain, it may be that the chalk drums are interesting survivals of racial or cultural influence which reached these islands across the English Channel by way of Spain.[1]

The second stratum of Troy is remarkable for its treasure hoards. Schliemann found no fewer than seventeen of these. The most famous is the "royal treasure", or, as he called it, "the treasure of Priam", which, with the assistance of his wife, he concealed during the workmen's dinner-hour. The objects were of rich and varied character. In a silver jar had been stored two great diadems of elaborate construction, which were worn by females of high rank. One is composed of four rows of small heart-shaped leaves of gold connected with fine wire, and is fringed with a row of larger pendants suggesting the human form. On either side are tails, terminating with larger pendants in a bunch. This diadem is about the breadth of the forehead, and when clasped round the head the hair was bunched above it, while the tails fell downwards and lay on the shoulders. Elaborate ear-rings were also worn, as well as rich necklaces made of small gold rings strung together, and bracelets of twisted gold. Some of the ear-rings are of spiral design. The spiral is also associated with the rosette to ornament elaborate gold hairpins and broad bracelets. A small gold eagle-shaped ornament is of special interest, as it indicates the sanctity with which that bird was invested in this region.

Included in the hoard are several bars of silver, which

[1] *British Museum Bronze Age Guide*, pp. 89-91.

may, as Schliemann suggested, have been used for money. A silver dagger was no doubt a royal weapon used on occasions of great ceremony. Like the bronze daggers it was pierced so as to hold the rivet with which it was attached to the handle. One dagger handle is carved in ivory and is reminiscent of Palæolithic Magdalenian Art, for it is shaped to represent a crouched animal. A bronze handle of similar design has been discovered in Etruria, and is now in the Kestner Museum at Hanover.

Among the objects in lead, special reference should be made to a figurine of the mother-goddess. It is of somewhat conventional design, like the terra-cotta figurines found in Cyprus, Mesopotamia, and Greece, and those of marble and other stone in the Cycladic islands. The face is stern, with a hard drooping mouth, and the eyes stare cold and angrily. Long curls dangle down from the ears; the neck is exaggerated and crossed with symbolic markings, and the hands are clasped across the breast. The female characteristics are pronounced, and on the lower part of the body the swastika, or hooked cross, is depicted on a V-shaped projection surrounded by round bosses. The legs are merely suggested, and may have been used as a handle, or as a spike to be thrust into the soil of a holy mound. Votive figurines found at Anau in Turkestan, and those also from Sumeria, were attached to nails, or terminated like nails, so as apparently to be driven into sacred shrines, for the same reason as the visitors to sacred wells drop pins into them, or attach rags to overhanging trees. Prayer-nailing still obtains in the East.

It may be remarked here that the third, fourth, and fifth citadels of Troy, which cover a period between about 2000 B.C. and 1500 B.C., are of no great account. The city shrank in importance after the occurrence of a great disaster which is indicated by the fire-swept remains of

Stratum II c.   The sixth, or Homeric Troy, will be referred to in a subsequent chapter.

Since Schliemann's day, attempts have been made to relegate the "treasure of Priam" to a comparatively late period, one nearer Troy VI than Troy II A.   Indeed, it has been asserted that this rich hoard fell down the trench from the sixth city stratum.   But although Schliemann sometimes nodded, like Homer, his location of the treasure can no longer be disputed.   In 1908, Mr. Seager, the American archæologist, discovered a similar hoard on the island of Mochlos, which lies about two hundred yards off the north-eastern coast of Crete in the picturesque Gulf of Mirabello.   For some 4500 years the treasure had reposed in a necropolis of the Early Minoan Period, happily secure from the attentions of generations of tomb robbers.   The island is barren and without a water supply, and was consequently never suspected of containing anything of value.   At one time it may have been part of a peninsula which sheltered a natural harbour much frequented by the earliest mariners.

The hoard included gold diadems, rings, pendants, hairpins, and fine chains, "as beautifully wrought", Sir Arthur Evans has remarked, "as the best Alexandrian fabrics of the beginning of our era".[1]   There were no spiral designs as at Troy, but wonderful artificial leaves and flowers.   Of special interest are the gold bands "with engraved repoussé eyes for the protective blind-folding of the dead".   These, Sir Arthur suggests, were "the distant anticipations of the gold masks of the Mycenæ graves".   Bead necklaces were probably charms.   Associated with these articles were miniature stone vases of local material.   Some were of Early Egyptian form, and all were of exquisite workmanship.

[1] *Times*, 27th August, 1908.

21

GROUP OF JEWELS FROM THE HOARD DISCOVERED IN THE
ISLAND OF MOCHLOS

(See page 238)

An engraving on a ring in this hoard depicts a ship with a sail and a full equipment of oars. Troy may have been visited by the men who crossed the seas in vessels of this kind. Traces of Cretan commerce have been forthcoming at Hissarlik, and Trojan artifacts have been found in Crete. In 1909 discovery was made at Phaestos of a fragment of pottery which resembles fragments of the same date (Early Minoan II) found in the second city of Troy. Relics of Cretan connections with Troy have also been found at Vasiliki and other eastern sites.

Crete's reputation for metal-working was widespread among the ancients, but no one dreamed, before Mr. Seager made his important discovery, it was of such great antiquity. The remarkable technique displayed shows that the craft had a long history. It no doubt owed something to Egypt, if, indeed, it was not established on the island by Egyptian traders. "Of the jewelry worn by the Pharaoh and his nobles, in the Old Kingdom," writes Professor Breasted, "almost nothing has survived, but the reliefs in the tomb chapels often depict the goldsmith at his work, and his descendants in the Middle Kingdom have left works which show that the taste and cunning of the first dynasty had developed without cessation in the Old Kingdom."[1] The Cretan ornaments have distinct local characteristics. Like the painters and potters, the goldsmiths showed a distinct feeling for nature, as in their leaf and flower designs; one notable ornament is the Cretan equal-limbed cross. Of special interest, too, is a clover-leaf ornament—an anticipation of the Irish devotion to the shamrock.

At the time the articles in the Mochlos hoard were manufactured, there must have been many wealthy men in Crete. Those whose ships visited Troy and Spain

[1] *A History of Egypt*, p. 94.

were probably the possessors of articles of silver as well
as gold. But none of these have been discovered. Perhaps some of the Early Minoan silver artifacts were so
highly prized that they were kept as heirlooms. Dr.
Xanthondides found two silver daggers in a tomb at
Kumasa, near Gortyna, while excavating tombs of the
Early Minoan III Period. They were ribbed and of triangular shape, like other daggers of bronze. Associated
with these metal objects were steatite "libation vases", a
rough marble figure of the mother-goddess, three miniature vases with lids on a reel-shaped stand, and an earthenware vessel of teapot shape with geometric ornamentation.
Sir Arthur Evans discovered several silver bowls of the
Middle Minoan Age at Knossos. Among the finds of
the American archæologists at Gournia is a shapely silver
cup with handles, from a house tomb, which recalls
Homer's reference to "a silver cup, the work of the
Sidonians".[1] It is, however, of much greater antiquity
than anything which can be credited to the Phœnicians.
Perhaps it was won by the individual in whose grave it lay
for displaying skill as a boxer. A double silver cup was
awarded to the Homeric athlete Epeius, who "knocked
out" Euryalus at the funeral games that followed the
burning of Patroclos.[2] Joseph,[3] who was so greatly
honoured by the Pharaoh, was the possessor of a silver
cup, and must therefore have been wealthy as well as
influential.

The Cretans may have received their supplies of silver
from Troy, where, as is shown by the articles made from
that metal in "Priam's treasure", it was abundant enough.

Some hold that this silver came from Spain, and their
theory will be dealt with later in this chapter. Others
favour the view that the Trojans and Cretans imported it

[1] *Odyssey*, IV, 618.   [2] *Iliad*, XXIII, 741 *et seq.*   [3] *Genesis*, xliv, 2.

from Lydia or Cilicia. It is possible that silver was
obtainable by the island mariners at primitive commercial
centres at or near Miletus, Ephesus, or Pitane. But of
this there is no direct proof. The remarkable fact has
to be given recognition in this connection that no traces
of early Ægean trade have been found at any of these
points.[1] Even the islands of Samos, Chios, and Mitylene
have failed to yield any indications of commercial connections with Crete and the Cyclades during the Early
Bronze Age. "Except for their north-western corner",
writes Mr. Hogarth, "the Asiatic coasts of the Ægean
lay, until very late, outside the culture-area associated
with the name of that sea. But if 'tis true, 'tis strange!
Why did the Cretan and other Ægean sea-rovers, whether
pirates or merchants, or both, fail to settle on these particular coasts and isles? They had pushed their wares
into Hissarlik, and had filled all the opposite shores of
Europe with a culture much higher and more vigorous
than any which has left a contemporary trace in Anatolia." Mr. Hogarth believes that "there must have
been some strong continental power dominating all the
west-central coast of Asia Minor from an inland capital.
It must have been a non-maritime power, careless about
developing its coast lands, but careful to keep others away
from them." This power was the Hittite—the confedera-
tion of peoples controlled by the Hatti, the "white Syrians"
of Greek tradition, whose ancient capital was situated at
Boghaz'köi. It is possible that the early Ægean influ-

---

[1] Mrs. Hawes suggests that "the objects given in exchange by the Cretans for European products were of as inferior and ephemeral character as those with which modern
traders dupe the native; hence the phenomenon noted by Burrows (*The Discoveries in
Crete*, p. 190) that genuine Ægean articles are absent from districts where Ægean influence is undeniable" (*Gournia*, p. 10). Asia Minor may have received chiefly supplies of
wine and food-stuffs. Pharaoh Meneptah of the XIX Dynasty sent shiploads of grain
to the Hittites in time of famine (*A History of Egypt*, Professor Breasted, p. 465).

ences which permeated Anatolia were introduced through the medium of Troy.

Troy appears to have existed during the Late Stone and Early Bronze Ages as the capital of an independent state. Its earliest settlers were probably of the Mediterranean race, and congeners of the Neolithic folk of Thrace and the Danube area, who had pressed northward through Syria and round the southern Anatolian coast, or by way of the "Cilician gates", to the western shores of the Ægean Sea, afterwards crossing into Europe. This racial movement, which radiated also throughout the agricultural valleys of Anatolia, appears to have taken place before the broad-headed Hatti, who were a pastoral people, became the dominant race. It may be also that there survived among the mountains descendants of the ancient Palæolithic races. The Etruscans, for instance, whose racial affinities are obscure, are believed to have come from Anatolia.

The Danubian cultural area was of wide extent. It included part of southern Russia and part of southwestern Austria, the whole of Thrace and Macedonia, and a portion of Thessaly. At several centres a high form of Neolithic culture was developed. "There is reason to believe", writes Mr. Hogarth in this connection, " that some population, racially kin to that which developed the Ægean culture, was present on the Anatolian coasts from early times, and also that there had been very early passage of influences, and perhaps of peoples, from Balkanic Europe to Asia Minor. Not only has the earliest sub-Neolithic stratum at Hissarlik produced pottery and weapons closely resembling those of Neolithic Danubian graves, but at two other places where sub-Neolithic settlements have been explored in north-west Asia Minor, Danubian analogies are even more certainly to be remarked.   Those places are Boz Eyuk in Central Phrygia, and Yortan in Mysia.   The vases of the latter site, where there is a cemetery of the earliest Bronze Age, show close analogies with Cypriote forms, and suggest that the earliest migrants from Europe spread sporadically far down through the peninsula to the Levant."[1]

Like Anatolia, the Danubian area was a melting-pot of races.   In addition to the Armenoids of Hatti type who invariably clung to an upland habitat, but also fused in localities with the Mediterranean peoples, the fair northern peoples pressed southward to absorb the local culture and fuse with the earliest settlers.   The ethnic friction which resulted caused periodic migrations of displaced peoples.   There was, therefore, much crossing and re-crossing of the Hellespont and the Bosphorus in the Late Neolithic and Early Bronze Age Periods.

Troy, by reason of its situation, must have been ever a meeting ground of various ethnic elements.   Many desperate conflicts, no doubt, were waged on its windy plain long ages before the Homeric era.   There were rich spoils besides in its citadel to attract the invader.   It lies at the end of the northern trade route which runs through Anatolia towards Mesopotamia, and must ever have been a "market-place" for traders, who could exchange there their far-carried commodities for the products of Thrace and the Ægean.

Various axes of green and white jade, which Schliemann found in the stratum of the first city, may be relics of an ancient trading connection with the east, as the knives and arrow-heads of obsidian appear to be of a connection with the Cyclades.

When the jade objects were first found they caused a flutter in archæological circles.   It was pointed out that

[1] *Ionia and the East,* p. 58.

scrapers and other articles made of jade had been found associated with the Swiss lake-dwellings, and at Neolithic sites in Brittany and in Ireland, as well as elsewhere throughout Europe. The belief obtained generally that these jade artifacts were imported into Europe from the borders of China, and Professor Fischer expressed the wish "that before the end of his life the fortune might be allotted to him of finding out what people brought them to Europe".[1] Professor Max Müller believed that the jade-carrying immigrants were the Aryans. "If", he wrote, "the Aryan settlers could carry with them into Europe so ponderous a tool as their language, without chipping or clipping a single facet, there is nothing so very surprising in their having carried along, and carefully preserved from generation to generation, so handy and so valuable an instrument as a scraper or a knife, made of a substance which is *aere perennius*."[2]

It is not now believed, however, that all the jade objects found in Europe came from "a common far-distant home in the Kuen Luen Mountains". Since Müller connected his Aryans with jade, the two species of it, nephrite (jade proper) and jadeite, have been found in different parts of Europe. Nephrite has been discovered in Silesia, Austria, and North Germany, and it is believed to exist in Sweden, while jadeite, or a similar rock, was found not long since among the Alps. It is probable, therefore, that the Swiss and other scrapers were chipped from pebbles of jade picked up by the European Neolithic people. The quantity and quality of the Hissarlik axes, however, suggest an eastern source of supply, and it may be that these and the Maltese polished axe pendants of jade are genuine relics of primitive commerce. As the latter were charms, it would appear that the magical qual-

---

[1] Schliemann's *Ilios*, p. 242.   [2] Letter to *Times*, Dec. 18th, 1879.

ities of jade were given recognition at a remote period. Among the Greeks it was the "kidney stone", and among the Spaniards, who imported it from Mexico, the "colic stone". Various rare stones were believed by the ancient peoples to have curative qualities. Instances could be cited of the possession, by representatives of ancient families at the present day, of stone charms of this kind that have long been treasured as heirlooms.

Although archæologists are less inclined nowadays than they were a generation ago to believe in the existence of Neolithic trade-routes which extended from the borders of China to Brittany, or to connect certain races with relics of similar character found in widely separated districts, there can be little doubt regarding the existence of commercial relations between different cultural areas. The introduction of metal appears to have done much to stimulate international trade. In the Early Bronze Age the influence of the Ægean, which may have "inspired every stage of culture" at Hissarlik, as Mr. Hogarth suggests, appears to have penetrated Thrace. Evidence has been forthcoming that two main trade-routes crossed Germany, one from the head of the Adriatic, and the other from the lower Danube valley. It has been suggested that some of the amber found in Crete came down these trade routes from the Baltic.[1] France was similarly crossed by the Rhone valley trade-route, down which, in time, tin from Cornwall was carried. That the Cretans were the earliest seafarers to come into direct touch with these routes is suggested by various interesting links of evidence. The most remarkable are the Egyptian glass beads found in South Germany, and the Egyptian blue-glaze beads taken from ancient graves on Salisbury Plain, which will be dealt

[1] Much of the Cretan amber is evidently from the Adriatic.

with in a later chapter, as they are connected with the Late Minoan Period.

Certain Continental archæologists incline to the belief that not only Crete but even Egypt was in direct touch with Western Europe at an extremely remote period. Summarizing their views, Angelo Mosso writes: "The vases found at Amerejo in Spain have the characteristic form of the Egyptian vases of the close of the Neolithic Age. The resemblance of the Egyptian idols with those of Crete and the Continent is an established fact; the burial sites are similar; the flat copper axes of Egypt cannot be distinguished from those of the Continent; the evolution of art in Southern France and in Spain went on during the Neolithic Age, and we know that navigation was general on the Mediterranean in the times preceding the introduction of copper—all these data give good reason to suppose that the pre-Dynastic Egyptians had relations with the west which enabled them to procure cassiterite, which when mixed with copper rendered it harder. . . . We hope", he adds, "that new discoveries may throw light on the relations of Egypt with England."[1]

There can be little doubt that the Cretan mariners sailed westward as far as the coast of Spain, although the precise period at which they first undertook voyages in this direction may remain uncertain. Spain could supply silver, copper, and other metals. The brothers Siret[2] are of opinion that this country was the source of the earliest supplies of silver, the metal having been taken from the silver-bearing veins before the discovery was made how to extract it from lead as described by Pliny.[3]

---

[1] *The Dawn of Mediterranean Civilization*, p. 62.
[2] *Les premiers ages du metal*, H. & L. Siret, p. 227.
[3] *Nat. History*, XXXIII, 31.

Mosso favours the view that the silver articles found in Crete were made from silver carried from Spain by the early mariners who sailed westward to fetch tin from the Cassiterides Islands. He makes no reference to the Cilician mines.[1]

It is difficult to fix the movements of the early traders in chronological order. We cannot therefore ascertain from the archæological evidence available when the Cretans came into touch with the western Iberians, with whom they apparently shared a culture of common origin. Prior to the Bronze Age a comparatively high civilization was developing in southern Spain. The votive figures found in this region resemble those of Cyprus, Hissarlik, Crete, and the Cyclades; even the sacral horns were given recognition. Spanish Early Bronze Age artifacts also show close resemblances to Ægean forms, and the brothers Siret found in several places in Spain goblets similar to those taken from Early Minoan strata in Crete, and others from the tombs of Abydos in Egypt. These vessels were associated with flat copper axes and copper knives with silver rivets, as well as stone and bone implements. Tin appears to have been less plentiful at the period to which these finds belong than silver. It may have come from the Balearic Islands, Brittany, or England—the first named being the most probable source.

At Marseilles, where Greek merchants established themselves in later times, the visits of the Cretans must have stimulated trade along the Rhone valley route, which became gradually suffused with Ægean influences. The trade-route from the head of the Adriatic, leading towards the Brenner Pass, was similarly affected. Sicily and Italy have yielded suggestive evidence of early contact with Crete. Daggers and flat axes of Cretan shape

[1] *Dawn of Mediterranean Civilization*, pp. 372-3.

have been found in Italian tombs of the early metal age. Sardinia appears to have been visited also; it has yielded, among other things, specimens of characteristic Ægean axe adzes, which have also been found at Troy.

One of the most interesting links between Ægean, Trojan, Danubian, and Western European cultures is the spiral decoration, which appears to have been introduced along the trade-routes.

"The developed spiral", writes Mr. Hall, "appears suddenly in Egyptian art on seals and (rarely) in painting, at the beginning of the Twelfth Dynasty,[1] or shortly before," that is, "at the end of the Third Early Minoan, or beginning of the First Middle Minoan Period in Crete."[2] It appears to have been introduced into Egypt from Crete, for it occurs on objects of Early Minoan II and III date. There are spirals on the Trojan gold pins of "Priam's treasure". Mr. Hall favours the view of Much, the German archæologist, that "the spiral originated in metal wirework". He thinks it may have been "an invention of early gold workers in Lydia that reached Troy, was in the Cyclades translated into stone carving, in Crete transferred to pottery and to the designs of button seals, and as a seal design came to Egypt, where it was promptly adopted as the characteristic decoration of the new form of seal that had as suddenly become popular in the Nile land, the scarab".[3]

The spiral ornament travelled along the trade-routes through Europe. Rings made of silver wire twisted in a spiral have been found by the brothers Siret in Spanish tombs which have yielded the goblets of Cretan form, already referred to. In the Danubian cultural area the spiral occurs on pottery of the early metal age. Follow-

---

[1] C. 2000 B.C.   [2] Or Middle Minoan II, according to Hawes.
[3] *The Journal of Egyptian Archæology*, Part II, pp. 115, 116.

DECORATIVE MOTIFS AND SYMBOLS

Figs. 1 to 8. Minoan and Celtic patterns compared. The treatment in different areas of motifs, which were probably of common origin, is of special interest. Numbers 7 and 8 are identical. Fig. 9. The equal-limbed Cretan cross. Fig. 10. The swashtika symbol—cross with arms bent. Figs. 11 and 12. Celtic knot developed from swashtika by connecting points of bent arms by curves—single treatment (point to point) in 11 and double treatment with swashtika reversed (inner curves corner to elbow and outer curves point to point) in 12. Figs. 13 to 17. Religious Symbols, perhaps connected with belief in weapon spirits; 13, Shield and crossed arrows of Egypto-Libyan goddess Neith; 14, Mycenean 8-form shield as symbol; 15, Cretan deity on seal; 16, Scoto-Celtic "spectacle" symbol shown upright as on standing stone; 17, Scoto-Celtic "crescent and arrow" symbol.

ing the road along the Moldau and the Elbe, it reached the shores of Jutland, and ultimately passed into Scandinavia. It reached England either along the Rhone or Danube valley routes. Reference has been made to the Yorkshire chalk drums on which it was inscribed. The New Grange stones are decorated with it, and early Scottish sculptured stones show local adaptations of the design. Eastward from the Danubian area it penetrated as far as Koban in Russian Armenia, between the Caspian and Black Seas, where it occurs on objects taken from a prehistoric cemetery in which Babylonian influence is also in evidence.

The earliest connection between Crete and northern Europe is indicated by the finds of Baltic amber in Early Minoan strata. It probably had a religious significance. Amber was carried down the Elbe and Moldau route as well as through the Rhone valley to the shores of the Mediterranean, and across to England, Scotland, and Ireland. It is believed that this trade was flourishing along the Elbe route before 2000 B.C.

The manner in which early commerce was conducted between the peoples of northern and southern Europe is indicated by Herodotus, who refers to offerings sent to Delos by the Hyperboreans. "They" (the Delians), he wrote, "declare that certain offerings, packed in wheaten straw, were brought from the country of the Hyperboreans into Scythia, and that the Scythians received them and passed them on to their neighbours upon the west, who continued to pass them on until they reached the Adriatic. From hence they were sent southward, and when they came to Greece, were received first of all by the Dodonæans. Thence they descended to the Maliac Gulf, from which they were carried from city to city, till they came at length to Carystus. The Carystians took them over to Tenos, without stopping at Andros; and the Tenians brought them finally to Delos."[1]

Reference has been made to the engraving of a ship on a ring from the Mochlos hoard. It is shown sailing from the shrine of the mother-goddess, who evidently protected seamen as well as landsmen. A similar ship, carrying two sails as well as oars, was depicted on a seal stone of steatite, which also belongs to the Early Minoan Period. Two crescent moons above the mast seem to indicate that the voyage was to extend over a couple of months.

Other seal engravings show vessels with one, two, or even three masts. Some have complex riggings and well-braced yards. A seal from Mirabello shows a one-masted vessel with a square sail.[2] An ivory model of a ship found by Sir Arthur Evans in a tomb at Knossos has a hatch over its hold to protect the cargo. Terra-cotta and alabaster models were discovered at Aghia Triadha, near Phæstos, by the Italian archæologists. A terra-cotta model from Palaikastro belongs to the Early Minoan Age.

"The modern vessels of the Cretan fishermen, and especially those of the fishers for sponges from the Isle of Kalimnos, differ little", writes Angelo Mosso, "from the ships of antiquity."[3] Occasionally Maltese boats are found to have the Horus eye on the prow, like the ancient Egyptian boats of the dead found in tombs. Beside the eye a flag is sometimes painted. There were ensigns on the prows of pre-Dynastic Nilotic vessels. Neolithic ships carved on rocks in Upper Egypt had sails and oars like the Cretan vessels, which they resemble in shape. Maltese boats retain the high prows of the prehistoric ships, and

---

[1] *Herodotus*, IV, 33.
[2] Probably "white sails and twisted ropes of ox-hide" (*Odyssey*, II, 425–6).
[3] *Dawn of Mediterranean Civilization*, p. 280.

Italian cargo boats have oar helms similar to those of the Egyptian river vessels. Seafarers have ever been intensely conservative. Some of the curious superstitions that still prevail among them may be as old as the pre-Dynastic pottery of Egypt and the maritime seal stones of Crete. Early Minoan sailors may have whistled to conjure the wind spirit, like our own fisherfolks, as they steered between the rocky isles of the Ægean Sea, or struck out boldly now westward to Sicily, and anon eastward towards Cyprus and the Syrian coast.

CHAPTER XI

Life in the Little Towns

Local Cultures—Power of Rulers limited—The Town of Gournia: its West-end Palace and Villas and East-end Workmen's Houses—Glimpses of Industrial and Domestic Life—The Public Shrine for Goddess Worship—Vasiliki Remains—A Strategic Key—Pottery Links with Turkestan and Spain—The Country of the Eteocretans—Port Sitia and Petras—The Seaport Town of Palaikastro—The "Fair Havens" of Paul—An Important Sanctuary—Fire Offerings—Costumes of Human Figurines—Ladies' Fashions—Their Big Hats and Elaborate Gowns—Theories regarding Fire Ceremonials—Fire Customs in Britain—Zakro's Port of Safety—Citadel and Merchants' Houses—Præsos and the "True Cretans"—Mingling of Races in Crete.

ALL portions of Crete were not affected similarly during the Early Minoan Period by the progress achieved by its pioneers of civilization and the cultural influences that swept to and from the island shores northward and southward like the seasonal air currents. Indeed, the rural communities of the high plateaux and deep mountain gorges, especially in the west, were hardly touched at all, and followed as primitive ways of life as do their descendants at the present day. "It is still possible on the mountain sides, where the crop is scanty, to see", write Mr. and Mrs. Hawes, "men and women plucking the corn."[1] This simple method of harvesting obtains also on the isolated Hebridean island of St. Kilda.

Nor did the shoreland seats of Cretan progress advance on precisely the same lines. Each had its local culture, its groups of artisans and traders, and, perhaps, its indepen-

---

[1] *Crete the Forerunner of Greece*, p. 37.

dent chief or king. Like early Egypt and Babylonia, the island appears to have been divided into a number of petty states. These may have occasionally waged war one against another before an early Minos established a central government at Knossos and codified the laws, as did Hammurabi the Great. Indeed, it is generally believed among archæologists that some of the disasters, like the burning of towns and palaces, which are still traceable on the island, were due to local wars.

It is of interest to find in this connection that in Plato's story of the "Lost Atlantis" references are made to island chiefs. These dignitaries owed allegiance to the king, whose powers, however, were limited by the constitution. When the people celebrated their annual festival, at which a bull was captured and sacrificed, "they poured libations down on the fire, and swore to do justice according to the laws on the column, to punish anyone who had previously transgressed them, and, besides that, never afterwards willingly to transgress the inscribed laws, nor ever to rule, or obey any ruler governing otherwise than according to his father's laws". There were ten chiefs at this ceremonial. "They did not allow the king authority to put to death any of his kinsmen, unless approved of by more than half of the ten."[1] Here we have, in contrast to Oriental autocracies, a system of government which is of distinctly European character. The king, like his subjects, had to act in accordance with the laws of the state. Apparently the stone benches in the "throne room" of the palace of Knossos were occupied by men whose status was defined in the constitution. We should perhaps, therefore, recognize this interesting apartment as the meeting-place of Europe's first Parliament.

One or two industrial and trading towns sprang up in

[1] *The Critias*, Section XV.

Crete which appear to have been, if not entirely independent of Knossos, at anyrate sufficiently so to ensure their development. A group of these were situated on the "tail" of Crete formed by the Gulf of Mirabello, and embraced by the modern provinces of Hierapetra and Sitia. This part of the island is approached from Knossos and Phæstos through twisting valleys among the Lasithi mountains, where there are many passes which could be held by small forces against large armies. The isthmus narrows to only 8 miles between the Gulf of Mirabello and the modern town of Hierapetra, and several small river valleys penetrate to the central uplands from either shore. The mountain spine of Crete is divided by the longest of these valleys, which is followed by the modern road between Hierapetra and Kavasi. To the east a rugged mountain range protects the frontier of Sitia, dominated by the peak of Aphendis Kavusi, which rises to a height of 4829 feet above the sea-level. Sitia is the ancient country of Eteocretans, who were believed by the Greeks to be the earliest settlers on the island.

In a little valley called Gournia, because of its trough-like shape, which opens on the Gulf of Mirabello, discovery was made by Mrs. Hawes, then Miss Harriet Boyd, the distinguished American archæologist, of the ruins of a compact little town. It is picturesquely situated on a limestone ridge, about a quarter of a mile from the sea beach. A little river flows past through cultivatable land, and wild carob trees surround it. The shoreland is rugged and rocky, with many murmurous creeks, and across the gulf, which narrows here like a Highland loch, are long rolling hills with here a hollowing curve and there an aspiring peak.

Gournia, like other Cretan towns, was unfortified. It had very narrow streets which were paved, and some were

"cursed streets of stairs", as Byron sang of Malta. The
two longest central thoroughfares ran north and south,
and these were approached from west and east by ascending streets, those on the east side being the steepest. A
spacious oblong public court—the public "park"—opened
from the south, and above it on the western slope was the
little palace with doors opening on the streets, and elbowed
by private houses like a noble cathedral in a modern town.
The "west end" was evidently the fashionable part of
ancient Gournia. A little beyond the palace, a narrow
street leading eastward from the western main thoroughfare, slopes upward towards the public shrine of the
mother-goddess. The large eastern wing of the town
was the most populous and thickly built.

An excellent idea of what the houses were like is
obtained from a series of enamelled plaques discovered by
Sir Arthur Evans in a basement chamber of the palace of
Knossos. These apparently were once part of an elaborate
mosaic. The artists took pride in depicting a variety of
houses, and happily paid sufficient attention to minute
details, so as to convey to us across a gap over thirty
centuries an excellent idea of the methods of construction,
and to a certain degree the habits of life of the occupants.
All the roofs were flat, but some were surmounted by
small attics erected in the centre, which gave the square
buildings an ink-bottle shape. The houses vary from
two to four stories in height. Their aspect is somewhat
modern. Single windows had four panes, and double
windows from two to six. "The red pigment in the
windows of the mosaic", writes Sir Arthur Evans,[1] "suggests that some substitute for window glass was in use—
perhaps oiled and scarlet-tinted parchment." But all
windows were not thus covered. Some were quite open,

[1] *Annual of the British School at Athens*, Vol. VIII, p. 14 *et seq.*

and in certain instances the windows of a second story had scarlet filling, while those of the third had none. "The upper door-like windows," Sir Arthur says, "recall a feature repeated in some of the miniature wall paintings. In these, groups of ladies are seen standing in similar openings, as upon a balcony. In other cases the women seem to be seated at open windows of a more usual type, and in one instance there is visible a part of a curtain, apparently of light material, perhaps drawn at night as a protection against mosquitoes."

One type of house has a single door; another has two doors like a modern semi-detached villa. In cases where no doors are shown, the gables or backs of houses may be represented. Tenements are suggested by plain erections, with what appear to be outside stairs ascending from basement to roof. Towers, perhaps watch-towers, are also represented. Some buildings appear to have been constructed of stone in the rectangular method, others with rubble strengthened by horizontal beams; in many cases, too, the ends are shown on a villa front of round beams, which supported the roof and the floors.

In Gournia the earlier and poorer houses had loose walls of small stones set thinly in clay. Improved methods of construction can be traced stage by stage until the masonry resembles the "Cyclopean" style, which apparently was of northern origin. Lime, plaster, and clay were used for facing walls. Upper stories, as a rule, were of brick, supported by timber.

This interesting town was entirely destroyed by fire about 1500 B.C. "The conflagration", writes Mrs. Hawes, "left proof of its strength in many parts of the excavations. Wooden steps and posts were entirely burned away, leaving deposits of charcoal and marks of smoke grime; bricks were baked bright red. In a ground-floor

room of the palace lay a large tree-trunk, which had supported an upper floor or roof, completely charred through,
but retaining its original shape; the central hall of the
palace was choked with such timbers.   Limestone was
calcined, steatite was reduced to crumbling fragments; in
a doorway of the palace lay a shapeless lump of bronze,
once the trimmings for the door.   Strangest of all was the
effect on plaster. . . . The intense heat reconverted it
into unslaked lime, and this, under the first rain, again
formed plaster, encasing vases, or anything else on which
it fell, in an air-tight, almost petrified mass.   Sometimes
at the core such a mass was still moist.   In time, we
looked to rooms where the destruction had been most
complete, and where the pick struck such solid opposition,
to yield us the best returns; for in them the possessions
of the ancient burghers remained undisturbed, awaiting
the patience of our workmen to knife them out."[1]   Articles
of pottery which were thus hermetically sealed for over
3000 years have retained much of their ancient beauty of
colour as well as of form.

Small portions of the town at the north-western and
south-western ends were reoccupied after the conflagration
took place.   But if an attempt was made to revive the
prosperity of Gournia, it did not meet with success.   The
site was completely abandoned before, or during, the
Homeric Age, and has since offered no attractions to
settlers.

Built as it was on a limestone foundation, where every
inch of space was valuable and no levelling was possible,
Gournia retains few traces of its original structures.   A
refuse heap in its vicinity has yielded pottery fragments
of the Early Minoan III Period (*c.* 2600–2400 B.C.), and
burials on the neighbouring slopes are of even remoter

[1] *Gournia*, p. 21.

date. Apparently the valley was inhabited from the beginning of the Bronze Age (*c.* 2800 B.C.), first by agriculturists, then by traders and artisans, for whose wares the mariners found a ready market. Finds of obsidian suggest that the site was first chosen by a community of the "crofter-fishermen" class, which produced daring seamen and enterprising traders.

The oldest buildings in the town belong to the Middle Minoan III Period (*c.* 1900–1700 B.C.). These are situated at the extreme north-eastern and south-western ends, and it seems possible that other dwellings intervened. The town as a whole dates from the Late Minoan I Period (*c.* 1700–1500 B.C.). Possibly many of the houses of which traces survive occupy the sites of others of greater antiquity and slighter construction. A town of growing prosperity was likely to be entirely rebuilt in the process of time. Besides, political changes may have occurred and caused disasters, like those which overtook the earliest palaces of Knossos and Phæstos in the Middle Minoan II Period, although no traces of these survive among the Gournia ruins, and the town as we find it may date from a first reoccupation period. Thus there may have been a Gournia I which was succeeded by Gournia II, the town with which we are dealing, and there might have been a Gournia III had the social revival, which is indicated by the few later buildings of the reoccupation period, been allowed to develop.

For some 200 years, that is, from about the late period of the Hyksos occupation of Egypt till about the beginning of the reign of Thothmes III, the great conquering Pharaoh, Gournia was a flourishing and important industrial and trading centre. The stones which pave its little streets were worn down by the booted feet of its busy citizens. In an age when traders had to barter wares

THE RUINS OF THE LITTLE TOWN OF GOURNIA

23

which were worthy to compete with the products of Egypt, art was stimulated by commerce. The best pottery was of as exquisitely graceful design as the finest ceramic products of any country in any age, and the decorative designs were often as elaborate as the soft colour effects were worthy of the high degree of technical skill attained. The artists sometimes developed the spiral and geometric motives, and sometimes used with fine effect familiar seashore subjects, like the octopods, sea-urchins, sea-snails, sea-anemones, corals and shells, as well as riverside reeds and flowers waving in soft winds. Mottled designs with shading effects were also in favour, and the resulting colour effects were no doubt as pleasing to contemporary purchasers as they are to us at the present day. Some of the vessels were evidently copies of the products of metal workers, for the decorators painted on imitation rivets. One of the models was the silver cup found in the house tomb, and already referred to. It is of graceful shape, with two handles and a finely fluted rim.

The special charm of Gournia is the light it throws on the everyday life of its citizens. Bronze hooks of modern shape and a pierced leaden sinker indicate that they fished from the rocks, and visited in boats those feeding-places in the little bay where shoals were to be found at certain states of the tide. It may be because they used shell-fish for bait that they decorated their shrines and pictures with shells, thus associating them with the mother-goddess who provided the food supply. That there was a fishing community in the small towns is suggested by a fresco at Phylakopi, Melos, which depicts fishermen carrying fish, which they grasp by the tails, from the sea beach. No doubt they were sold in the market-place as, we gather from tomb pictures, was the case in Egypt.

One of the most interesting finds was a carpenter's kit which had escaped the attention of the plunderers and the ravages of fire. It lay under a floor, where it may have been concealed by a workman who, poor fellow, probably hoped to find it again. It contained, among other things, several bronze chisels, a saw, a double axe, and a pair of tweezers. In a room of the same house were storage jars, clay weights which had probably hung from a weaving-frame, a three-legged cooking-pot, cups and bowls, a jug, a whetstone, and so on. Another room yielded a bronze sword, as well as a variety of household vessels. In the storeroom stood an oil vat made by a potter. But a more complete specimen was discovered in another and older house. It rested on a stone slab, its spout projecting outward on a level with the base. "There can be little doubt as to its use", writes Mr. Bosanquet, describing a similar vat found in another Cretan town. "In the modern process the olive kernels before being pressed are drenched with hot water, and the product after pressing contains more water than oil. The oil in due course separates itself and rises to the surface, and it is necessary either to bail it out from the top or to drain away the water from the bottom. . . . The latter method is in general use, large and complicated tanks being constructed on this principle; the Præsos jar illustrates the simplest form of it, in which, after the contents have been allowed to stand some time, the tap is set running and the water escapes, a watcher being ready to stop the flow and change the recipient as soon as the oil appears."[1] Spouts which were utilized to run off water and oil from the vats have also been found. Various household articles discovered in different parts of Gournia include "Ali Baba" storage jars, a shallow dairy basin in

[1] *Annual of the British School at Athens*, Vol. VIII, p. 268.

which milk was set for cream, fillers, ewer-like jugs, clay
bottles, cooking-pots, hand-lamps resembling little flower
vases, cream jugs, and small saucepans. A "flaring-
bowl" on three legs no doubt provided sufficient light
for a well-sized room. Of special interest was the discovery in the basement of the palace ruins of seven
stone and earthenware lamps, three of which were broken.
Probably they were used to illuminate a large room on
an upper floor, as Mrs. Hawes suggests. They are of
more elaborate design than those found in the houses
of burghers, being shallow shapely bowls with socketed
pedestals for fixing on a stone or metal standard. Three
round projections like billiard-table pockets held the floating wicks, and were connected with gutters. Apparently
this lamp was made in a variety of forms.

There were no fireplaces in the Cretan houses, but on
chilly evenings apartments could be warmed with portable
fire-boxes, the lids and sides of which were perforated.
House drain-pipes found here and there indicate that
sanitary appliances were not confined to palaces.

The little town shrine, situated high on the limestone
ridge, is one of the most fascinating attractions of ruined
Gournia. It was approached by a narrow and ascending
paved road, "a much-worn way", says Mrs. Hawes.
Much worn also are the three stone steps leading into
the little enclosure with low protecting walls. It was but
10 feet square, and could not therefore have accommodated
more than three or four persons at a time. Here grew a
sacred tree, and below it stood a round clay table, or altar,
which was found entire with a fragment of a cultus vase
standing upon it. There appears to have been three
figures of the mother-goddess. One of crude and formal
shape is almost entire. A snake curls round the waist and
round one of the shoulders, and the arms are upraised

in the Egyptian attitude of adoration, forming the "Ka" sign. The eyes are hollow, and the mouth is not shown. Other two heads are similarly mouthless, and one resembles the face vase designs of Troy. Two clay doves were probably associated with one of the idols. Portions of arms entwined by snakes may have belonged to the third. A double axe with a disk in relief on a fragment of clay had evidently a symbolic significance. Three tube-shaped cultus vases have the horn symbols surmounting the handles, as well as six to eight loop handles formed by conventionalized snakes. These are usually referred to as "trumpets".

In the palace and elsewhere other sacred objects were found. One is a bronze figure of a man or god standing on a pedestal with a nail-like projection, like the Babylonian votive figures. His hair is pleated in three long tails, one of which wriggles like a snake down his back, while two fall in front and, following the shoulder lines, meet across his breasts. A loin-cloth is attached to the usual waist girdle. The figure stoops forward slightly, with head tilted sideways; the left arm hangs by his side, and the right is raised and doubled in, so that the hand points towards the heart across the body. Probably this was a religious pose. Small figurines of a seated goddess, a miniature 8-form shield, a bronze cockle-shell, and an earthenware imitation of a triton shell were probably charms.

The little palace of Gournia was being gradually remodelled when the destroyers swept through it, robbing its treasures and slaying the occupants. Like the greater palace at Knossos it was erected in labyrinthine style, with narrow corridors and groups of apartments leading one from the other. There was also a central court, and an outer court which may have been a market-place. It appears to have been in some parts two, and in others three stories high, the roof of the central court being flat to form a terrace, to which access could be obtained from the windows of the second story.   On the basement were storerooms, bathrooms, public rooms, and probably bedrooms.   So thoroughly was the palace rifled before being set on fire, that few finds of any value have been discovered in its rubbish-heaped apartments.

A goodly number of seal stones were found in Gournia, of Middle and Late Minoan design.   These were used to impress the trade-marks of merchants and others, and were attached to a belt worn round the wrist.   Some of the signs look like hieroglyphs: others have a religious character.   One of the most interesting of the latter class is a female figure wearing a bell-mouth skirt, standing on the back of a deer.   This may be a form of the early Artemis.   Hittite deities usually stand on animals' backs. Another seal shows two females, who appear to be dancing like the women in one of the Palæolithic cave pictures. A third has a prancing bull, a fourth three goats dancing round in a circle with legs opposed, suggesting the Babylonian dancing he-goats, which have a stellar significance; a fifth the double axe, a sixth the familiar octopus, while a seventh is a lion crouching below a palm-tree, perhaps an Egyptian design.   One of the most beautiful seals is of green onyx, on which two dragon-flies with heads opposed and wings outspread are exquisitely carved.   It is worthy of the best Cretan gem-engraving artisans.

If there was a Gournia I, it must have been of much less account than Gournia II.   The strongest settlement on the isthmus during Early Minoan times was at Vasiliki, which lies about 2 miles inland on the road to Hierapetra. Its oldest ceramic remains (Early Minoan II) make it contemporary with the Mochlos settlement, and antedate the pottery fragments (Early Minoan III) of the Gournia refuse-heap.

The Vasiliki remains are situated on a limestone knoll in a narrow valley, which was anciently the strategic "key" of the isthmus. The highway runs past it, and it commands a wide prospect north and south. Rough limestone ridges rise on either side. Brigands from the hills would have found it difficult to capture, and merchants could not carry their wares along the trade route if its chief were hostile.

The knoll is protected on the northern and western sides by a bare cliff about 15 feet high: its southern and eastern sides slope down to the banks of a mountain torrent. Buildings were erected on the summit, which is comparatively level.

The little citadel, or fortress town, was first built about 2500 B.C., or earlier. It was not a place of any importance during Middle and Late Minoan times, when Gournia was flourishing.

Mr. Seager, the American archæologist, who undertook the excavations at this important site, has divided the history of Vasiliki into four periods.[1]

Of the buildings of Period I no traces survive. Obsidian artifacts found in this early strata are of superior type to those from Gournia. They indicate a commercial connection with Melos, perhaps through Mochlos, then a promontory. The pottery, with the exception of a few fragments, is hand-made, and had been developed from Neolithic varieties. "The goblets", says Mr. Seager, "show an advance upon a Knossian form of the First Early Minoan Period, which in turn has been compared with pottery found by Dr. Petrie in First Dynasty deposits at Abydos."

[1] *Gournia*, pp. 49, 50.

The Period II buildings can be traced. Trading relations with the Cyclades had evidently become more intimate. One of the popular wares was a buff clay hand-made variety, painted in Cycladic style. It resembles fragments found at Phylakopi in Melos, and other fragments from sites in eastern Crete. Here we have a departure from the Bronze Age ceramic sequence at Knossos, indicating local development on independent lines. Obsidian was still used, bronze being evidently scarce.

Period III was the most flourishing period at Vasiliki. The houses of Period II were levelled, and the whole settlement was rebuilt. It is uncertain whether or not this change was due to a fresh ethnic infusion into the district or to intertribal strife which affected the "balance of power". Vasiliki had now apparently trading connections with Egypt, Cyprus, and Troy. A distinctive pottery, the mottled variety, displaced all others in popularity. It was wheel-made, and the Egyptian potter's wheel had therefore come into use. The wheel-made fragments of Periods I and II may have been imported, but this, of course, is uncertain. The possibility remains that there were early trading relations, direct or indirect, with the Delta region or Libya. "Some of the Vasiliki shapes", writes Mr. Seager, "occur in Cyprus, and the hard red surface of certain pieces resembles both the early incised ware of Cyprus and the black-topped pottery of Dr. Petrie's Dynastic Egyptians." The "black top" was probably the result of baking pots upside down over an open fire. Certain Vasiliki forms—the "spout vase", the "bulged bowl", the "egg-cup" and "tea-cup"— have been found in the second city of Troy, but the Trojan variety is less finely wrought than the Cretan. This mottled pottery has been discovered also on the

Cycladic island of Amorgos and in Spain. Reference has already been made to its resemblance to Turkestan specimens which Mrs. Hawes has examined. It may, as has been suggested, have been distributed along the tin trade and copper trade routes which were "tapped" by Cretan mariners. At the close of Period III Vasiliki was destroyed by fire. So thoroughly was the settlement plundered that, as Mr. Seager writes, "only three pieces of bronze were found on the site: two half axe-heads . . . and a dagger of the Early Minoan triangular shape". The pottery was preserved as at Gournia among the heaps of fallen plaster from the upper stories. Lower stories were constructed of stone.

In Period IV, which was disturbed and decadent, hutlike houses were erected. The mottled pottery went out of use and was substituted by a coarse variety, with white geometric designs painted on a dark surface, similar to the Early Minoan fragments found in the Gournia refuseheap. After a period of uncertain duration, represented by a deposit of $1\frac{1}{2}$ metres, the knoll was abandoned. The builders of Gournia II may have established their sway over the isthmus. It seems probable that a political upheaval took place. The Gournia crania of the Early and Middle Minoan Periods indicate that the population was mainly long-headed. Broad-headed skulls were represented by only 8.5 per cent among those found. The proportion of broad-heads increased greatly in Late Minoan times.[1]

Stepping eastward from Gournia we pass the little island of Mochlos and the larger one of Psyra. Mochlos, as indicated, has yielded important relics of the Early Minoan Period. On Psyra there have been excavated the ruins of houses of Late Minoan date, which were con-

[1] *Gournia*, p. 59.

THE ISLAND OF MOCHLOS, OFF THE NORTH COAST OF CRETE

On which was discovered the hoard of jewellery described on page 238.

24

temporary with those of Gournia. In one a portion of painted relief has survived. Characteristic pottery and finely executed stone vases have also been brought to light.

Our faces are turned towards the land of the Eteo-cretans, the "true Cretans" of classic tradition, whose archæological records go back to the Neolithic Period. At the village of Kavasi, our road, which is little better than a mule-track, begins to ascend, and we cross the high frontier of Sitia through a steep, rocky pass. Then we descend into a stretch of country lying between the central mountain spine of Crete and its northern shore, from which many torrent-shaped gorges and narrow valleys run inland. Several villages are passed ere we reach Sitia Bay. At Mouliana, Dr. Xanthoudides has excavated beehive tombs which contained, among other things, long bronze swords. These belong to the much-disturbed Late Minoan Period. Farther on is the village of Khamezi, where the same archæologist has assigned a house ruin to Middle Minoan times. We pass through the valley of Skopi, which leads us towards Sitia Bay. The valley of Sitia, which is embraced by the looping River Stomio, is exceedingly fertile. The olive and the vine flourish exceedingly, as do also the grain crops. Villagers elect to dwell on elevated sites on account of the malarious conditions of the low grounds.

About a mile distant from Port Sitia, along the sandy shore, is a low headland jutting out from the hills that fringe the eastern side of the valley. Round it the rough highway twists sharply, and on the summit is the little hamlet of Petras. Here the deep bay is sheltered from northerly gales, and affords a safe anchorage close to the shore. We recognize at once that Petras must have been an important place in ancient days. Like Vasiliki, it was

(O 808)

a strategic "key" of a trade route; the highway which it
dominates is the easiest approach to the Eteocretan Highlands; the natural harbour was the "nursery" of a sea
trade, and the valley provided a surplus of food to promote it.

Mr. Bosanquet conducted excavations on this site in
1901.[1] The results, although not too encouraging, were
not without importance. The hillock had been reclaimed
fifteen years previously by a couple of Moslem brothers,
who employed "a large force of labourers to demolish the
ancient masonry, and to form the hill-side into cultivation
terraces". The destruction wrought was "systematic and
complete". Large blocks of limestone and ashlar had
been built into the field walls. Traces were obtained on
the west side of the village of a building nearly 19 yards
long, but it was impossible to determine its breadth. In
one apartment was found a Kamares jar which is probably
of Middle Minoan date. A round tower once stood on
a plateau above the headland, which was approached by a
road cut for a few yards through the rock, and another
was situated below the highway. A rubbish heap on the
north-east slope of the settlement yielded "masses of
Kamares pottery in all degrees of coarseness and delicacy".
Mixed with the heap were stone chippings, suggesting the
process of rebuilding, probably in Late Minoan times.
Obsidian flakes taken from trial pits indicate that Petras
was inhabited from the Early Minoan Period, if not from
Neolithic days.

From Petras we follow the serpentine track along the
rugged shore for a few miles, and then turn southward
round the hill range surmounted by Mount Modi towards
Grandes Bay. It is a lonely journey. There is an abundance of game on foot and wing, but the chief stalkers

[1] *Annual of the British School at Athens*, Vol. VIII, pp. 282-5.

are the ground vermin. The hills are intersected by a maze of tortuous valleys, with patches of faded grass and clumps of murmuring trees, broken by bald brown ridges and bluff grey crags. Seaward we have glimpses through winding glens and over basin-shaped valleys of beetling cliffs and streaks of sandy beach fretted by foaming waves, and of blue islands girdled by the dazzling waters in bright sunshine.

At length we descend towards Palaikastro, which lies about 3 miles across a beautiful valley. Olive groves stretch from the foot-hills towards fields of waving grain that form a belt along the shoreland of gravelly ridges and yellow sand.

The bay is flanked on either side by promontories that jut seaward like the great toes of a crab. Towards the south-east its graceful inland curve is broken by a little headland with steep sides, resembling an overturned boat, but with a flat summit. Between this bluff acropolis and the southern range of hills stood the ancient town of Palaikastro. Its site is known as Roussolakkos, which signifies "the red hollow", the redness being due mainly to the crumbling bricks of ancient buildings embedded in the accumulated debris of long centuries. Part of the plain is marshy on the north side of the acropolis.

Perhaps this sheltered bay is the natural harbour referred to in the Biblical narrative of Paul's voyage in "a ship of Alexandria sailing into Italy. . . . We sailed under Crete over against Salmone; and, hardly passing it, came into a place which is called The Fair Havens, nigh whereunto was the city of Lasea."[1]

Although larger and more important as a trading-centre than Gournia, Palaikastro was less compactly built. Excavations have revealed a long straggling town re-

[1] *Acts*, xxvii, 6–8.

sembling an overgrown village. It was traversed from one end to another by a paved thoroughfare, appropriately named "Main Street" by the representatives of the British School at Athens. Towards the western end another street crossed at right angles, and a second, branching to the right in the south-east quarter, ran round a block and joined another side street. Plunderers, ancient and modern, have wrought much havoc among the buildings; some of its hewn boulders appear in the field walls of the little farms in the vicinity.

The house ruins which have been unearthed are of a Late Minoan town contemporary with Gournia. Traces have been also obtained of an earlier town of the Middle Minoan II Period, which was probably destroyed.

Outlying sites indicate that the valley was inhabited from the earliest times. One of these has been located at Magassa, the mountain village already referred to, where the coarse archaic pottery, stone houses, and obsidian flakes belong to a period long anterior to the introduction of metal. Rock shelters indicate even more primitive conditions of life.

The houses were larger than those at Gournia, and were more massively built. No doubt they resembled the villas of the Knossian mosaic with two or three stories, elaborate windows, and attics, resembling "deck houses", on the flat roofs. One or two had spacious apartments, and it is possible that they were occupied by several families closely related.

The pottery ranged from Middle Minoan times to the Late Minoan Period of decline. In a single room of a house in Main Street were found seventeen shapely "fillers". Some are of the type carried by the "cup-bearer" of the Knossian fresco, while others are of pear form with narrow necks, jutting lips, and small handles.

DECORATED POTTERY FROM PALAIKASTRO

The central vase shows an interesting treatment of an octopus motif.

In addition to these and other highly-decorated vases, special interest attaches to the many domestic utensils, including cooking-vessels, pans for baking bread, candle-sticks, lamps, and portable fire-boxes.

An important sanctuary site has been excavated by Professor Myres near Palaikastro. It is situated on the ridge of hills that fringe the southern side of the valley, and rises abruptly behind the town, and on the slope of its highest eminence, called Petsofà. Here were unearthed a large number of clay votive figurines of human beings, animals, &c., in strata enclosed by walls. Evidently there had been a sacred building here, but it cannot be described as a temple, for its ruins resemble those of the ordinary dwelling-houses at Palaikastro. Three distinct layers were cut through. The lowest is of clay, red on the surface, but containing no relics. "It doubtless represents", writes Professor Myres,[1] "the original packing of earth to level the enclosure; and in that case its red colour is due to prolonged baking by the bonfire on its surface." The next layer, which is of dark earth, was full of ashes and charcoal fragments, and "crowded with figurines". Broken pottery and figurines were also found in the surface layer.

The male figurines have either painted or modelled upon them the characteristic Cretan loin-cloths and kilts, with waist-girdles and boots or slippers. In one instance there is a body "wrapper" in relief, which is drawn over either shoulder, and crosses at the back and over the breast. This garment presents "very close analogies", says Professor Myres, "with the Scottish plaid, which is first wound round the waist and then has the ends crossed in front, brought over the shoulders, crossed again on the back, and secured by being tucked through the waist folds, so that the ends hang down like a tail".

[1] *Annual of the British School at Athens,* Vol. IX, pp. 356 *et seq.*

Most of the female figurines have the usual pinched waists, tight bodices, and bell-shaped gowns. The head-dress varies, and in some cases looks startlingly modern. In one case we have a Dolly Varden hat with crimped brim and a trimming of rosettes; in another a low crown with the brim curving in front like an inverted horseshoe, and one of the expanding sides set off with a frill or plume; a third is high and conical, looking somewhat like a lamp. Sometimes the head-dress is an elaborate hair-dressing, probably on a frame, resembling a high peaked nightcap bending forward, and crossed by a couple of broad white bands. The bodice has always a low neck, the breasts being covered by a thin under-garment, or, as the frescoes suggest, a stiff model of the bust. Usually a wide standing collar rises to a point behind the back, jutting outward.

Traces of paint indicate that the costumes of the Cretan ladies were not awanting in tasteful colour-effects. Some of the hats appear to have been white, while brown, green, and black gowns were decorated with triple horizontal bands between which triple bands crossed at a slope. Like the bodices, these might also be elaborately embroidered in various colours with striking designs.

These male and female votive figurines appear to have been representations of worshippers who deposited them perhaps as charms to protect themselves against the influences of evil. Most of them are standing, but a proportion are seated on four-legged chairs or low stools with or without backs.

That cures were also supposed to be effected by placing models in the purging bonfire, is suggested by the large number of votive arms, legs, heads, and bodies. The single limbs vary in length: in one case a protruding thumb suggests that it is the affected part. There are several forearms with or without hands, and in one case the whole arm is attached to part of a female body. Detached feet and heads, the upper part of a female showing protruding breasts, and a male body with leg stumps may indicate the locations of disease. On the other hand, it is possible that those who deposited these models may have desired to increase the skill of the hand, the strength of arms and legs, the supply of human milk, and so on. A man setting out on a journey might have cast into the sacred fire the model of his legs, so as to ensure his safe return.

The Petsofa fire ceremonies may have been of similar significance to those which were anciently held in our own country. Our ancestors believed that all the forces of evil were let loose at times of seasonal change, and human beings and their domesticated animals required to be specially protected against them. At the beginning of each quarter they lit great bonfires to thwart the demons and fairies, and also to secure luck and increase. The quarter-day was the "settling-day" between mankind and the supernatural beings: those which were the source of good things were propitiated, and those which were the source of evil were baffled by the performance of ceremonies of riddance. In parts of the Scottish Highlands boys still light Beltane (May Day) fires and drive cattle over the ashes to charm them against the influence of the evil eye, the spells of witches, and the attacks of fairies. The New Year's Day bonfire is even more common. It is uncertain whether it has been called a bonfire because bones used to be burned in it or because it was the source of "boons". In England the Midsummer fires were called "Blessing Fires".[1] As in Scotland and Ireland, the folks danced round them and leapt through the flames

---

[1] *Brand's Popular Antiquities*, Vol. I, p. 306.

when they burned low.   Brand quotes an interesting old translation, which runs:

Then doth the joyful feast of John the Baptist take his turne,
When bonfires great, with lofty flame, in everie towne doe burne;
And yong men round about with maides doe daunce in everie
  streete,
With garlands wrought of motherwort, or else with vervain sweete,
And many other flowres faire, with violets in their handes,
Whereas they all do fondly thinke, that whosoever standes,
And thorow the flowres beholdes the flame, his eyes shall feel
  no paine.
When thus till night they daunced have, they through the fire
  amaine
With striving mindes doe runne, and all their hearbes they cast
  therein.
And then with wordes devout and prayers they solemnly begin,
Desiring God that all their illes may there consuméd be;
Whereby they thinke through all that yeare from agues to be free.

Others made a wheel of fire, which they cast down at night from a mountain-top.

They suppose their mischiefes are all likewise throwne to hell,
And that from harmes and daungers now in safetie here they
  dwell.

Sometimes the folks are also represented at these festivals,

> Supping mylk with cakes
> And casting mylk to the bonefire.[1]

The beliefs enshrined in these old customs, which have survived after so many centuries of Christian influence, afford us a clue to the motives of the Cretans who cast images into their fires.   In addition to the male and female figurines found at Petsofa there is also a large number of models of tame and wild animals.   The com-

---

[1] *Brand's Popular Antiquities*, Vol. I, pp. 300 *et seq.*

monest of them is the ox, which suggests that the charm-
ing of cattle was of great antiquity. Calves, dogs, goats,
and rams were probably represented for a similar purpose.
It cannot be held, however, that the models of unclean
animals and ground vermin were cast in the fire because
men desired that they should be increased in number or
protected against attack. These included the fox and
weasel, the hedgehog, which was supposed to steal the
milk of cows, and the pig, which was abhorred as in
Egypt, Palestine, Wales, and Scotland. Apparently the
offerings were made for a variety of reasons, like those
made at "wishing wells" and "wishing trees" in our own
country at the present day by the folks who perpetuate old
customs in a playful spirit. The Cretans probably pronounced blessings over the models of domesticated animals,
and curses over the bestial enemies of mankind, believing
that spells were confirmed by the magical action of fire.
In ancient Egypt images of the Apep devil-serpent were
cursed and spat upon before being committed to the
flames, so that its power of working evil might suffer
decline.

Other clay models found at Petsofa include miniature
cups, vases, bowls, and jugs, as well as little plaques with
lumps of clay representing bread. In such cases the desire
was apparently to ensure the food-supply. Tree-like
objects suggest a belief that fruit-crops could be increased
by the influence of the fire spell. Several symbolic objects
were, no doubt, protective offerings. These included
articles with four C spiral terminations and balls of clay,
which may have been charms against the "evil eye", like
the "luck balls" which were manufactured and sold in
these islands in comparatively recent times.

Another Eteocretan seaport which drove a busy trade
in the Late Minoan I Period was Zakro. It is situated

about 8 miles from Palaikastro. Rather than follow the rough mule-path over the plateau and through twisting vales and narrow gorges, we prefer to sail round the rugged coast with its beetling cliffs and shingly slopes. On our way we pass the boats of the sponge divers. The famous sponges which grow along the eastern shores of Crete are still in as great demand as in the days when Hellenic warriors utilized them as comfortable pads—which also absorbed perspiration—in their helmets and boots. We wonder at the power of endurance displayed by the divers. One has been submerged for ninety seconds; here another has waited on the floor of the ocean thirty seconds longer, but we are informed that he is not a record-breaker.

We tack round a rugged headland and enter the little natural harbour of Zakro, which affords excellent anchorage near the shore. It is sheltered from every wind except the east, which, however, is of rare occurrence. The gusty north winds are deflected by the mountains, and when they rage on the open sea and toss high billows round Cape Plaka, Zakro Bay is comparatively peaceful. Many a Minoan ship must have run in here to escape a sudden *meltem* which was strewing the Mediterranean with ribbons of snowy foam.

The little saucer-shaped plain, fronted by a beach of sand and shingle, is marshy in part, and consequently malarious. It has, however, its vineyards, patches of cornfield, and clumps of olive-trees, and a small population. High and frowning ridges of bluish limestone enclose it on every side, and the River Zakro, which flows southward from a gorge on the western side, and turns abruptly eastward towards the sea, has a resemblance here to the letter L. The valley behind the plain stretches for about 6 miles, and varies from 1 mile to 2 miles in breadth. It is approached through narrow rocky passes, one of which leads to Upper Zakro.

On two mountain spurs on the northern side of the plain, which are separated by a dell, are ruins of houses. Their builders selected these elevated sites to escape malaria. The acropolis was on the highest part of the western spur, and could be approached from the southern side only. Here, within the area enclosed by massive walls, are the Zakro pits of archæology. The largest was visited by Italian archæologists in the early days of Cretan research, but was not thoroughly explored until Mr. Hogarth conducted his systematic excavations in 1901.[1] The deposit was about 8 feet in depth. It yielded three obsidian flakes and fragments of implements of bone and of bronze pins and blades. There were also bits of stone vessels. " The mass of the find", Mr. Hogarth writes, " was in earthenware, and included about eighty unbroken vases among thousands of fragments." Four-fifths of the pottery was Late Minoan I, and the remainder of the Kamares variety (Middle Minoan), with Eteocretan characteristics. The Vasiliki mottled ware was represented, but there was no trace of Neolithic ceramic products. Some pottery was obtained in a second pit and among the foundations of houses.

On the opposite spur are the ruins of well-built houses of a prosperous community. The foundations of these were of stone, and the upper stories of brick supported by timber. Brick was also used for the inner walls, which were faced with plaster. Floors were covered by concrete. Evidence was forthcoming that the little town had been destroyed by fire. The buildings varied in size and design. One had fifteen apartments on the ground floor, and was probably a small palace; another had six, and a third eight.

[1] *Annual of the British School at Athens*, Vol. VII, pp. 122 *et seq.*

These houses yielded some bronze relics and a good deal of pottery, including a characteristic Cretan shell-shaped crucible for smelting copper, perforated by a number of holes at one end. But the most remarkable relics were the clay seal impressions. Of these Mr. Hogarth found about five hundred, a sure evidence that Zakro was the home of rich and prosperous merchants. Trade was conducted with Anatolia, and perhaps also with Mesopotamia, along the routes terminating on its coast, as well as with Egypt. Zakro's position suggests that its trade with Egypt was direct, and not by way of Cyprus. At the present day it is the last port of call for Ægean craft bound for the Libyan coast, where sponges are also obtained.

The pottery from the pits indicates that there was an earlier Zakro in the Middle Minoan II Period, when Palaikastro I was founded. Apparently Zakro II was destroyed, like Gournia II and Palaikastro II, in Late Minoan II times (c. 1500–1450 B.C.).

Zakro's dead were buried in caves in the adjoining gorge. In the vicinity of Upper Zakro the scanty sur-viving remains of buildings, and the tombs which have been located, suggest that the valley had settlers from the Early Minoan Period until early Hellenic times. There are still a few poor villages.

In our survey of Eastern Crete we come last of all to Præsos, the ancient capital of the "true Cretans". It does not lie many miles from Upper Zakro as the crow flies, but is separated from it by a ridge of rugged hills that runs north and south. The most convenient way of approach is from Sitia. This inland site is perched on a small plateau enclosed by two streams. These unite below in front of it, and form the River Sitia, which runs through a 7-miles-long valley towards Sitia Bay. Southward the road shrinks to a narrow pass, which could easily be closed against an enemy. It makes a long detour by way of Klandra and Zyro towards Zakro valley.

The Præsians informed Herodotus that Crete was twice stripped of its inhabitants, only a remnant being left on each occasion. The first disaster resulted from the expedition which Minos led against Sicily, and the second after the Trojan war, when the greater part of the population was stricken by famine and pestilence. Men of various nations flocked to Crete, "but none came in such numbers as the Grecians".[1]

Evidently classical writers believed that the "true Cretans" were representative of the aboriginal inhabitants —the ancient seafarers who suppressed the island pirates and colonized the mainland of Greece, the Cycladic islands, and Lycia and Caria in western Anatolia. But excavations at Præsos have failed to support this hypothesis. Before the Early Hellenic Period the little town was not a place of any importance. It was certainly not a centre of Minoan civilization. The people who erected the inland stronghold were evidently invaders who came before the Greeks—perhaps they were the destroyers of Zakro and Palaikastro. It may be that, like the Hellenes, they were of Indo-European speech, and represented an early wave of mingled Achæan and Pelasgian stock from the continent.[2] As there are traces that they perpetuated Minoan religion in early classical times, it may well be that they fused with the people they conquered, and were influenced by their modes of thought, and that in consequence the Greeks did not realize that they were intruders like them-

---

[1] *Herodotus*, VII, 170, 171.

[2] In classical times the Eteo Cretans did not speak Greek. They used Greek characters, however, in their inscriptions which have not yet been read. The oldest inscription belongs to the sixth century B.C. It may be that this language was not Indo-European. Professor Conway, however, thinks it was.

selves. The conquered people may have been early settlers from Anatolia, and not of the same racial stock as the settlers of North African origin.

The Præsian invasion probably occurred in the Late Minoan III Period. All the buildings which can be credited to the so-called "true Cretans" are of a later age. The earlier inhabitants, the real "true Cretans", are represented by the relics found in the cave of Skalais above the river gorge at the north side of the plateau. Here, in what may have been either a dwelling or burial-place, were found fragments of pottery of the Neolithic and Early Minoan Periods, and also some sherds of the Kamares (Middle Minoan) variety. Prior to the coming of the founders of Præsos, who erected beehive tombs and worshipped a mother-goddess closely resembling the Trojan deity, the plateau was probably a grazing-place for the inhabitants of the fertile valley stretching towards Sitia Bay. In Homeric times the island had many ethnic elements. The following reference in the *Odyssey* is significant:—

> There is a land amid the sable flood
> Call'd Crete; fair, fruitful, circled by the sea.
> Num'rous are her inhabitants, a race
> Not to be summ'd, and ninety towns she boasts.
> Diverse their language is; Achaians some,
> And some indigenous are; Cydonians there,
> Crest-shaking Dorians, and Pelasgians dwell.[1]

In the next chapter we will visit the important sites of Southern Crete.

[1] *Odyssey*, XIX.

CHAPTER XII

The Palace of Phæstos

The Great Messara Plain—Site of Phæstos—The Trial Pits—Neolithic
Remains—The Whale's Backbone—Religious Significance of Sea-shells—
Ancient Musical Instruments—The Iron Charm—Beliefs regarding Iron—
Obsidian Razors—First and Second Palaces of Phæstos—Grand Stairway and
"Hall of State"—Villa of Aghia Triadha—Famous Cat Fresco and Egyptian
Prototypes—Sculptured Stone Vases—The King and his Warriors—Boxers
and Bull-baiters—Procession on "Harvester Vase"—A Painted Sarcophagus—
Bull Sacrifice—Charioteers of Hades—Burial Ceremony—Priests and Priestesses
—The Double-axe Symbol—Beliefs about Ravens and Doves—The Other-
world.

HAVING surveyed eastern Crete we return to Candia with
some knowledge of the character of the ancient civilization
which culminated in the palace glories of Knossos. It
remains with us next to visit the southern part of the
island, which is fragrant with the memories of Minoan
Phæstos, and the city of Gortyna, established by the invading Greeks and rebuilt by the Romans.

We strike southward by the road which crosses and
ascends the river valleys until we reach Daphnes, and find
a break in the mountain spine of the island which leads us
to the great Messara plain. The sea is shut off by rugged
Kophino mountains that fringe the coast and divert the
flow of the River Hieropotamos towards the west.

Phæstos had a strategic situation. Its palace stood
upon a low mountain spur commanding the western
approach to the Messara Plain. When the site was located
by Professor Halbherr, the Italian archæologist, slight

traces only remained of its ruins in a field of rustling barley. A noble panorama of mountain scenery is here unfolded before us. To the north-east is Mount Dicte, and to the north-west the greater Mount Ida, the monarchs of sublime and massive mountain ridges. "The outline of the mountains", writes Mosso, "differs little from that of the Apennines, but the blue colour is more intense. . . . Between the ridges the slopes fade in the distance till the blue blends with the grey of the sky. The villages look like eagles' nests perched on the cliffs, each girt round with a garland of olives, they too shading into blue. . . . Before the sun sets the shadows in the ravines of Ida deepen into indigo, and the rocks of the whole chain become violet—an optical phenomenon rarely seen in the Alps. The poets of classical Greece allude to this violet colour in the mountains round Athens. In Italy only the shadows become violet, but here in Crete the rocks are violet."[1]

When the palace of Phæstos was excavated, it was found to be of smaller extent than that of Knossos. Beneath its ruins were found traces of an earlier building resting on a Neolithic deposit.

An interesting account is given by Mosso of trial pits he sunk below the latest palace floor to the virgin soil, with purpose to ascertain the character of the earliest strata. The deepest of these was $5\frac{1}{2}$ metres on a slope of the hill, while the shallowest was only $\frac{1}{2}$ metre. Evidently the ground had been levelled for the foundations of the palace.

As at Knossos, it was found that the earliest settlers were in a more advanced stage of civilization than those in eastern Crete, who built stone houses and hollowed out rock shelters. This is of special interest in view of the

---

[1] *Palaces of Crete and their Builders*, pp. 57, 59.

theory, tentatively urged in some quarters, that there were settlements of peoples from North Africa and Anatolia in Neolithic times.

The deep pit at the western side of the palace yielded important finds. About 6 feet down, the foundations of a primitive dwelling were laid bare. On the floor was lying a portion of a whale's backbone, which, like similar relics from the Ligurian caves, may have been regarded as a charm. Lower down in the remains of a still older dwelling were sea-shells which had evidently a religious significance, as the Knossian shrine objects have indicated. Two varieties of well-baked pottery came to light—a dark and a red. Animal bones included those of the oxen, sheep, boars, hares, and birds. Certain pointed bone implements may have been potter's tools. The carved femora of great birds are believed by Mosso to have been mouthpieces of musical instruments—the pipes of Pan or a primitive bagpipe.[1] At a depth of 4 metres there was a roughly-shaped headless figurine of the mother-goddess. It has the characteristics of Cycladic and Trojan relics of like character. Near the figure lay a piece of magnetite. "According to the analysis", Mosso writes, "it consisted of oxydized iron. We may be certain that it was a sacred stone from the fact that the Neolithic folk had not made a weapon or a hammer of it. Possibly they believed it to be a meteoric stone: it was known at that period that these stones came from heaven, for they appear with a luminous track and fall to earth with a sound."[2]

In Egypt iron was anciently known as "the metal of heaven". One theory of heaven was that it was formed of a rectangular plate of iron which rested either on the mountains that surrounded the earth or on pillars. This

[1] *Dawn of Modern Civilization*, pp. 69, 70.
[2] *Palaces of Crete and their Builders*, p. 29.

divine metal was used as a charm.   In the Scottish Highlands it is supposed to prevent fairies and other demons
from attacking mankind, and it serves a similar purpose
in India and West Africa.   The fact that Copts are forbidden to use it to exorcise demons indicates that it was
of magical potency in ancient Egypt.   Perhaps it was on
account of its association with pagan religious beliefs, like
the ear-rings worn by Jacob's wives, that it was not used
in the construction of the Jewish altar.

> Then Joshua built an altar unto the Lord God of Israel in
> Mount Ebal, as Moses the servant of the Lord commanded the
> children of Israel, as it is written in the book of the law of Moses,
> an altar of whole stones, over which no man hath lift up any iron.[1]

A piece of magnetic iron was found in the Neolithic
stratum of Troy, which also yielded small ritual dishes
like those of Phæstos.   It has already been stated that the
Phæstian ceramic sequence accords with that of Knossos.
Obsidian knives gave indication, as elsewhere on the island,
of trading relations with Melos before the age of metal.
"These knives", writes Mosso, "cut so well that during
the excavation I always kept one in my pocket to cut my
pencil point."[2]   They continued in use long after the
introduction of bronze.   An excavator informed the writer
that he found a worker with an obsidian razor.   Asked
why he used it, he remarked that his father had done so
before him.   In Egypt the earliest razors were of flint.
A small flint razor recently found in northern Scotland
had a comparatively good shaving edge, as was proved
when put to the test.

The ruins of the early palace of Phæstos were levelled,
and formed in many parts a foundation for the later
palace.   Owing to this fortunate circumstance, pottery

---

[1] *Joshua*, viii, 30, 31.   [2] *Dawn of Mediterranean Civilization*, p. 89.

THE GRAND STAIRCASE, PALACE OF PHÆSTOS

and other relics were preserved. The early palace was erected in the Middle Minoan I Period (c. 2200 B.C.), and the work of constructing the second begun in the Late Minoan I Period (c. 1700 B.C.). Excellent specimens were obtained from the first buildings of the fine Middle Minoan Kamares pottery. But other finds were of scanty character. A little gold lay beside charred wood. It probably "ornamented a small piece of furniture", as Mosso suggests. Remains were also discovered "of a cabinet with quadrangular tablets of very hard terracotta which fitted together, and some cornices in repoussé work with undulating designs, resembling the cornices which were in fashion at the beginning of last century". Evidently the Cretans, like the Egyptians, had excellent furniture.

The later palace was of less extent than its rival at Knossos, which, however, it resembled in many details. Nor has it yielded so many relics. The destroyers appear to have plundered it thoroughly before setting it on fire.

The most imposing feature is the "grand staircase", between 40 and 50 feet wide, which led up to the Hall of State, or Reception Hall. There is nothing to compare with this noble entrance at Knossos. It has been conjectured that state ceremonials were observed in the hall, the walls of which were probably decorated with frescoes. A small room leading off the hall is surrounded by stone benches, and may have been a "waiting-room" for guests and ambassadors. In the interior of the palace is a spacious central court, 150 feet long and 70 feet broad, surrounded by a maze of apartments, as is the one at Knossos. The theatral area was at the south-east corner.

About 2 miles towards the north-west of Phæstos, at the hamlet of Aghia Triadha, there was a smaller palace picturesquely situated on a sloping mountain ridge, and overlooking the sea. It is usually referred to as a "royal villa". The ceramic remains on the site indicate that it was occupied as far back as the First Middle Minoan Period. When the villa was erected in First Late Minoan times, portions of an earlier building were utilized. It was an imposing building, and was entered by a flight of steps. Around it stood in the first period a number of substantial houses, which may have been occupied by rich traders or Cretan aristocrats. In the second period the villa appears to have been a communal dwelling.

Like the Knossian palace, the villa was, when the destroyers had wreaked their vengeance upon it, not entirely plundered of its archæological treasures. Frescoes have been happily preserved. The most famous of these depicts a cat hunting birds in a marsh. It was evidently painted by one who had seen similar studies in Egyptian tombs at Beni Hassan and Thebes. The Cretan artists were inferior draughtsmen to their Nilotic contemporaries, but they were finer impressionists. In Egypt the cat is statuesque and cold; at Aghia Triadha the ferocity and murderous instincts of the callous animal are conveyed with impressive vivacity; the artist undoubtedly conveys the mood, although his technique is faulty. The Egyptian was essentially a stylist, and rarely produced the nervous art which was so characteristic of Crete.

Three stone vases, with figures sculptured in relief, which were found in the villa, are triumphs of Minoan art. On one is a group of warriors with shields, and two outstanding figures, one posed stiffly with outstretched right arm, and grasping a long staff or lance as if issuing a military order, and the other with a drawn sword resting on his right shoulder, standing at attention. The second vase is divided into four zones, in which appear the figures of boxers, bulls, and toreadors. Some of the boxers wear helmets, and others are bare-headed; they all appear to have something equivalent to the boxing-glove on each of their hands. The bull-baiter is seen leaping between the horns of the rearing bull. In Crete, as in Plato's "Lost Atlantis", the sport or religious ceremony of bull-baiting was conducted without weapons. The gymnast seized the approaching animal by the horns and turned a somersault over its back, coming down behind the animal. Various representations of this feat are shown on seals found on Cretan sites and at Mycenæ. Sir Arthur Evans found at Knossos ivory figures of leaping gymnasts who were probably bull-baiters. On a gold cup from Vaphio, which is preserved in the museum at Athens, are two figures of bulls. One is charging furiously, while a female gymnast grips the left horn under one arm and the right horn between her legs. A male gymnast is falling off its back. The other bull is caught in a net. A Knossian fresco depicts two women and a man attacking a bull.

The third vase from Aghia Triadha is called by some archæologists the "Harvester Vase" and by others the "Warrior Vase". Round it marches a carved procession of animated human figures who are evidently taking part in a ceremony. That this ceremony was of religious character seems certain, because one of the men is holding up before him the Egyptian metal rattle called the sistrum, which was used to summon the god and charm away demons in Egyptian temples, and is referred to in the chants. "Do we not behold the excellent sistrum-bearer approaching to thy temple and drawing nigh," called the Isis priestess, invoking Osiris. . . . "Behold the excellent sistrum-bearer and come to thy temple. Come to thy temple immediately! Behold thou my heart, which

grieveth for thee.   Behold me seeking for thee. . . .
Lo! I invoke thee with wailing that reacheth high as
heaven." [1]

This sistrum-bearer on the vase has not a pinched
Cretan waist, and may represent an Egyptian.   He is
singing or wailing, as are also three of his immediate
followers who may be women with upper garments of
leather.   Perhaps they are invoking the spirit of the
slain corn-god.

The procession appears to be led by a long-haired
elderly man, wearing a bulging robe decorated with a
scale pattern and heavily fringed.   He carries a long
round-handled staff over his right shoulder.   Is he a
priest, or a victim in a wicker-work cage who is about
to be sacrificed?   All the figures are marching in step—
performing, in fact, a sort of Germanic "goose step",
and most of them carry three-pronged forks, the prongs
being attached by cords to the long handles.   These resemble the harvesting-forks still in use in Crete.   Some
of them, however, are fitted with short scythe-like blades,
which may have been used either for cutting corn or
pruning trees.   A single figure—evidently a youth, is
stooping low and grasping the thighs of a man who turns
round with open mouth as if shouting defiantly a ceremonial utterance of special significance.

Those who see in the procession the celebration of
a naval victory hold that the three-pronged implements
are really weapons.   But no such weapons have been
found in Crete.   If the ceremony was not a harvest one,
it may have been connected with the spring-time invocation of the deity of fertility.   Mr. Hall, who regards the
vase as one of "the finest pieces of small sculpture in the
world", sees upon it "a procession of drunken roistering

---

[1] *The Burden of Isis*, by J. T. Dennis, pp. 21 *et seq* and 29 *et seq*.

27

THREE VASES, SCULPTURED IN STONE, FOUND AT AGHIA TRIADHA

The largest of the three is known as the "Boxer Vase", and measures 18 inches high. The "Harvester Vase", on the left hand of the centre subject, is shown on a larger scale in plate facing page 212. The other small vase (actual size, 4 inches high) is described on page 286.

peasants with agricultural implements."[1] "Extraordinary technique was required", write Mr. and Mrs. Hawes, "to represent four abreast, each seen distinctly, one beyond another. The Parthenon frieze presents no more difficult problem in low relief."[2]

Another decorated object found at Aghia Triadha is a sarcophagus of limestone shaped like a chest, which has been assigned to a period prior to 1400 B.C. It is 52 inches long, 18 inches broad, and 32 inches in depth. The body which it enclosed must have lain in a crouched position, like the bodies placed in the pre-Dynastic Egyptian graves and in those of the Late Stone and Bronze Ages in Western Europe. The sarcophagus had been covered with plaster on which were painted scenes of undoubted religious significance. At either end are chariots. In one, which is drawn by two griffins, a woman is escorting a swathed pale figure, apparently the deceased, on the way to the Otherworld; in the other, which is drawn instead by horses, are two female figures. A long panel on one of the sides is unfortunately badly damaged. It appears to represent a sacrificial scene. A bull is being slain, and a man plays on a double flute while its blood pours into a vessel. The panel on the other side is in a good state of preservation, and affords an interesting and suggestive glimpse of Cretan funerary services. At one end the swathed figure of a youth stands before a tomb or shrine beside a conventionalized representation of the sacred fig tree. In front, and facing the deceased, a priest approaches carrying the model of a boat — perhaps the "ferry boat" of Hades in which the soul is to reach the "Isle of the Blest", after crossing the valleys and mountains like the Indian Yama

---

[1] *The Ancient History of the Near East*, p. 54.
[2] *Crete, the Forerunner of Greece*, p. 129.

and Babylonian Gilgamesh. Two priests follow behind, carrying offerings. Turned in the opposite direction are three priestesses, or, as some think, two priestesses and a priest. The first pours a red liquid, either wine or the blood of the sacrificed bull, into a large vessel placed between two erect posts on pedestals. These posts are surmounted by double axes on each of which a raven is perched. The second priestess carries a couple of vases suspended from a pole, one in front and one behind, which is carried on her right shoulder. The third figure —either a priestess or a priest—plays a seven-stringed lyre held high in front.

The costumes are of special interest. Facing the deceased the three priests wear robes suspended from their waists which terminate with tail-like appendages. These are evidently the skins of animals. Egyptian priests wore panthers' skins. The first priestess, who bends down beneath the double axes, likewise wears an animal's skin, but she has also an upper garment with half sleeves and a broad blue sash which comes down under her left arm to the waist. Probably this sash formed a St. Andrew's Cross on the back like the plaid on the Petsofa figure, which Professor Myres has compared to the Scottish plaid. The second priestess wears a long blue gown suspended from her shoulders and reaching her ankles. The bodice has a floral edging and the gown is decorated. She wears a flat round cap, and appears to have a sash like that of the first priestess. The lyre player is similarly attired, but has no sash, and the head is bare.

In the next chapter the significance of the tree-pillars and double axes will be dealt with. Here it may be noted that the ravens take the place of the doves as the birds of the Mother Goddess. The reason is obvious.

Doves symbolized fertility and immortality, while ravens were associated with destruction and death. In the Scottish legends regarding Michael Scott, ravens and doves, flying from opposite directions, approach his corpse after death. The fact that the doves are the first to alight is taken as an indication that Michael's soul will go to heaven. The ravens are the messengers of Satan. Throughout Europe and Asia the ravens are birds of ill omen, who foretell death and disaster. They were associated in Greece and Italy with Apollo, the great patron of augurs. Crows were similarly of ill repute. According to some writers, a number of them fluttered over Cicero's head on the day he was murdered. Dark and melancholy birds were evidently regarded as forms of the spirits of darksome Hades. They were, it would seem, associated from an early period with a sepulchral cult. So were doves. Perhaps the raven cult believed in a gloomy after-life in a Hades as dismal as that of Babylonia, while the dove cult had hopes of ultimate happiness. In Egypt both the cults of Osiris and Ra believed in Heavens and Hells. The Ra cult associated their Paradise with the sun: it was a place of everlasting light; while their Hell was a place of darkness, lit for but a single hour in the twenty-four by the sun's rays. In it lost souls were tortured in pools of fire, or they remained in the place of outer darkness, where they suffered from extreme cold.

In this religious scene on the Cretan sarcophagus, the raven spirits of Hades, perched above the double axes, appear to be receiving a propitiatory offering of blood or wine. It may be inferred, therefore, that they could be prevailed upon to show favour to the dead. The kings and heroes of the Greek epics were transported to the "Island of the Blest", while others had to sojourn

in gloomy Hades.   Perhaps the Cretan who was interred
in the sarcophagus was regarded as being worthy of a
happy fate in the after-life.   He was, no doubt, a youth
of high birth.   In Egypt the paradise of Ra was reserved
in early times for kings and queens and their families.

CHAPTER XIII

Cave Deities and their Symbols

Demeter and the Nameless Fates—Forms of Mother-goddess—The "Eagle
Lady" with Snake Girdle—Prototype of Hittite and Assyrian "Winged Disk"
—How Composite Monsters became Symbols—The Caves of Zeus—Lasithi
Plateau—The Dictæan Votive Offerings—The Chariot of a Deity—Cave of
Kamares—The Plain of Nida—Sacred Cave of Mount Ida—Mountain Religion
—Well Worship—The "Seven Sleepers" Belief—Cretan Tammuz a Cave God
—Pillar Symbols in Crete, Egypt, and Babylonia—Pillars as Mountains and
"World Spines"—The Osirian Spine Amulet—Tree and Pillar Worship—
"Horns of Consecration" as Sky Pillars—Double-axe Symbol—Spirits in
Weapons—The God of the Axe.

"THE Cretans say", Diodorus Siculus wrote, "that the
honours rendered to the gods, the sacrifices and mysteries,
are of Cretan origin, and other nations took them from
them. Demeter passed from the Isle of Crete into Attica,
then into Sicily, and thence into Egypt, carrying with her
the cultivation of corn."[1]

On the other hand Herodotus, writing of the Pelasgi,
says: "In early times the Pelasgi, as I know by information I got at Dodona, offered sacrifices of all kinds and
prayed to the gods, but had no distinct names or appella-
tions for them, since they had never heard of any. They
called them gods (θεοὶ, disposers) because they had
arranged all things in such a beautiful order. After a
long lapse of time, the names of the gods came to Greece
from Egypt, and the Pelasgi learnt them, only as yet they
knew nothing of Bacchus, of whom they first heard at a
much later date."[2]

[1] *Diodorus Siculus*, V, 77.   [2] *Herodotus*, II, 52.

There is, no doubt, a kernel of real historical truth in these traditions. The Demeter to whom Diodorus refers is not, of course, the beautiful goddess whom the Grecian sculptors conceived of, but rather the Phigalian cave monster, the black horse-headed fury with snakes hissing from amidst her tangled locks. In early times she had many forms—terrible and mystical forms. Some idea of these is obtained from the study of the seal impressions discovered by Mr. Hogarth at Zakro. In one phase she is the "eagle lady"—a woman with prominent breasts, widespread wings, and an eagle's head, wearing the snake waist girdle and the bell-shaped gown, or simply an eagle with a fan tail, and nothing human but her breasts. Several seal specimens show that this primitive form developed into a symbol which may have been a prototype of the Hittite winged disk and the Assyrian disk of Ashur. One is a column with fan tail and surmounted by winged human breasts, above which is a round bee-hive-shaped cap; others are variants, and then comes a fully developed symbolic object, with breasts represented by double spiral coils resting on a double bee-hive-shaped body with double outspread wings.

In another phase the goddess has a goat's head, wings, a short columnar body, and spreading skirt. A god is similarly depicted with pants and waist girdle. A ram's head appears on another seal impression of like character, and in a variant the head of a "sea horse". Winged sphinxes recall Egyptian forms. Of special interest is a bull-head deity with female breasts, wings, crouched-up legs and fan tail, which may have been bisexual. This form tends also to grow into a decorative symbol. The Minotaur was a bull-headed god.

Composite monsters include deities with human bodies and lions' heads resembling those of Egypt, two dogs' heads divided by a wing and united by a fan tail, a female sphinx with human breasts, butterfly wings and lion's legs, a human head with wings and lion's legs, and so on. The form of the Hittite and later Russian double-headed eagle is suggested by a conventionalized lion's head with birds' heads protruding from the ears, curving inward in opposition. In almost all cases the animal and composite animal forms tend to become decorative symbols.

The "Black Demeter" of Phigalia was, as has been indicated, associated with cave worship. In Crete there were many sacred caves. Of these the two most famous were those reputed in classical traditions to be the birthplace of Zeus. One is on Mount Ida and the other on Mount Dicte.

It is possible that these rival caves were sacred to rival cults. Beneath Mount Dicte was situated the city of Lyttos, which was, according to legend, hostile to Knossos and an ally of Gortyna. In references of this character there may be memories of ancient inter-state rivalries in Minoan Crete which survived into the Hellenic Period.

Hesiod,[1] dealing with the Zeus birth-legend, relates that the goddess Rhea carried her babe to Lyttos. Other writers were familiar with the legend that Zeus was nursed in the Dictæan cave. Diodorus[2] apparently endeavoured to reconcile the conflicting claims on behalf of the Dictæan and Idæan sanctuaries by stating that the god was first concealed in the one and then transferred to the other to be educated.

According to Dionysius of Halicarnassus[3] it was the Dictæan cave which Minos entered to receive from Zeus the code of Cretan laws. Lucian states that Europa, the mother of Minos, was carried thither by Zeus, his father, who had abducted her.[4]

[1] *Theog.*, V, 477.   [2] V, 170.   [3] *Ant. Rom.*, II, 61.   [4] *Dial. Mar.*, XV, 3.

To visit the Dictæan cave we must first reach the
upland plain of Lasithi, to the south-east of Knossos,
which is about 5 miles long, and roughly half that in
breadth, and has an elevation above the sea-level of some
3000 feet. Mountains surround it on every side, the
highest peaks being Aphendis Sarakinos (Mount Dicte),
which rises to 5223 feet, and Selena to the north-east,
which is almost as lofty. A river traverses the plain from
end to end, and is fed by many hill torrents. It finds no
valley outlet, but pours into a great cavern towards the
north-west. According to local belief, it appears again
lower down as the river Aposelemis, which enters the sea
a few miles east of Candia.

This upland is approached from the west across the
Pediadhan Plain, situated at an elevation of about 200 feet;
the mule track then winds its way sheer up the mountain
face. From the east the traveller leaves the western shore
of the Gulf of Mirabello, and following the valley of the
river Kalopotamos, makes a similarly difficult ascent by a
zigzag path.

The Lasithi plain, embosomed among sublime mountains, is exceedingly fertile and comparatively populous.
The climate resembles that of the more favoured parts of
Switzerland. Neither olive trees nor carob trees grow
upon it, but the vine flourishes and the grain crops are
excellent. The nightingale which pipes so sweetly in
lower valleys is here unheard. At morn and sweet even-
tide, however, the thrush and the blackbird carol amidst
the pear and apple trees. On yonder grassy slopes are
the familiar wild flowers of temperate climes, including
the homely yellow buttercup. The winter is somewhat
severe, and it is customary when it approaches to drive
flocks and herds to the lower valleys, where they are
sheltered and fed until the advent of Spring.

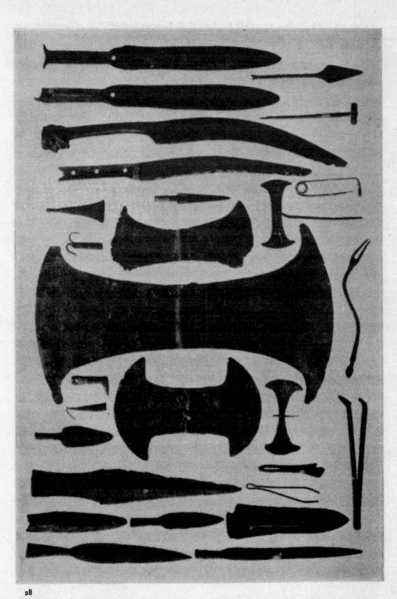

WEAPONS AND IMPLEMENTS, IN BRONZE, FROM THE DICTEAN CAVE

Including double axes, spear-heads, knives, daggers, fish-hooks, fibula, tweezers, gimlet, &c.

On one of the ridges of Mount Dicte are the ruins of the city of Lyttos, and on another, right opposite, the modern village of Psychro. Five hundred feet above Psychro is the double cavern associated with the legends of Zeus—the famous Dictæan cave. As far back as the "'eighties" it was known to contain archæological relics. The earliest finds were made by goatherds who were accustomed to shelter in it, and after these passed into the hands of dealers, various archæologists paid visits to Psychro and the cave. It was not, however, until 1900 that thorough and systematic exploration of it was conducted by Mr. D. G. Hogarth.

This accomplished archæologist did not achieve success without overcoming considerable difficulties. Rock-falls had occurred in the cave, and he had to have recourse to blasting operations. Besides, part of it is ever flooded. "Water flowing in from the east has", writes Mr. Hogarth, "penetrated in two directions right and left. The main flow to southward has excavated an abyss, which falls at first sheer and then slopes steeply for some 200 feet in all to an icy pool, out of which rises a forest of stalactites."[1]

Inside the cave were found portions of walls, a paved way, and bits of sawn marble an inch thick which may have covered it, an altar-like edifice beside which lay a small stone "table of offerings" and fragments of about thirty other "tables", lamps, cups, broken vases and ashes. Professor Myres found one of the cave "tables" in 1896, and another was purchased from dealers by Sir Arthur Evans in the same year.

The deposit, which was deepest and least disturbed in the north-west part of the upper cave, was divided by strata of pottery fragments and animal bones, between which lay ash and carbonized matter. The oldest pottery

[1] *Annual of the British School at Athens*, VI, 96.

was of the Kamares (Middle Minoan) variety. In the surface layer were lamps of the Roman period and a silver Byzantine cross, indicating that long after the cave ceased to attract crowds of votaries, the memory of its sacred character survived among the people. Terra-cotta figurines were also found.

When the upper cave was thoroughly explored, Mr. Hogarth prepared to take his departure. Before leaving, however, he sent some of the workers down the steep slope to conduct a search in the lower cave. Here, to the astonishment of everyone, a great archæological harvest awaited the gleaners. Hundreds of metal offerings were lying in the mud around and below the water, and among the niches formed by stalagmite, some being almost enclosed like flies in amber. In two days the lower cave was cleared. "Four days later", Mr. Hogarth relates, "I took all the bronze pieces, amounting to nearly 500, the objects in gold, hard stone, ivory, bone and terra-cotta, a selection of the stone tables of offerings and of the pottery and specimens of skulls, horns and bones found in the upper Grot, to Candia. What I left under the care of the village (Psychro) officials included no fewer than 550 unbroken specimens of the common type of little wheel-made plain cup, all obviously new at the time they were deposited in the cave, and a great store of bones." [1]

The bronze figurines of human shape are of both sexes. They are usually posed in devotional attitudes, and may represent votaries or deities, or include both. One figurine is clearly Egyptian. It wears the high double plumes of the god Ra, and seems to have been deposited about 900 B.C. by some pious wanderer who believed, perhaps, that the Theban deity and the Cretan

[1] *Annual of the British School at Athens*, VI, p. 101.

Zeus were identical. Animal figurines include rams, bulls, and oxen. An ox and a ram with projections from their shoulders fit into a miniature chariot which may have been a god's vehicle. On a gem in Sir Arthur Evans's collection a chariot is drawn by goats, as was the car of Thor, the Germanic Zeus. Models of weapons are comparatively numerous. These include the double axe, lance-heads, darts, and knives. A knife with a slightly curved blade has a human head finely carved at the end of the handle. Among the ivory and bone ornaments special interest attaches to "three volute-like objects" which, as Mr. Hogarth remarks, "are closely paralleled by Bosnian fibula plates". They also suggest the well-known "spectacle" symbols on Scottish sculptured stones. Hairpins, needles, and brooches figure among the finds.

There are two conspicuous caves on the slopes of Mount Ida, in which votive offerings were deposited. The first, on the southern side, is situated above the village of Kamares, and is faintly visible from Phæstos. Professor Myres explored it in the "nineties" and found, among other relics, the first specimens of the now famous "Kamares pottery". The other cave, towards the northeast, has been identified as the rival of the one on Mount Dicte. In front of it a colossal altar was carved out of the rock, but at what period there can be no certainty. Professor Halbherr, who conducted excavations here, was less successful than Mr. Hogarth. He obtained, however, a number of votive offerings in terra-cotta and bronze. The latter, which include shields, come down to the ninth and perhaps even the eighth centuries B.C., and show strong traces of Dorian influence.

This Zeus cave on Mount Ida can be approached from the romantic plain of Nida or Nitha, which lies about 5 miles east of the central peak of Ida at an elevation of over 3000 feet. It is about 2 miles long and $\frac{1}{2}$ mile broad. The snow vanishes in the month of May. The secluded upland is then covered with fresh green pasture, to which shepherds drive their flocks, as did their ancestors in ancient days, when the grass in the lower valleys withers in the great summer heat. Yellow wild flowers of the buttercup variety are as thick in the grass as are poppies in some fields of corn. This fact may have given rise to the classic legend that the sheep which graze on Nida plain acquire golden teeth. Modern shepherds say that the pollen of the wild flowers does leave on the teeth of their sheep a perceptible yellow stain. Travellers who have climbed up to the plain speak with enthusiasm of its cool, bracing atmosphere, and the clear starry nights of wonderful listening silence amidst the serenity and grandeur of the mountains. Ancient Cretans who worshipped their deities in such places must have experienced the feelings of awe and devotion that so profoundly impress the mind in lofty solitudes " far from the madding crowd's ignoble strife ".

The practice of performing religious and magical ceremonies in caves goes back, as we have seen (Chapters I and II), to remote Palæolithic times, when the huntsmen dwelt in them, buried their dead in them, and in some drew figures of animals and demons or gods on roofs and walls. In Crete, caves were sanctuaries in the Neolithic Age. The cave of Skalais at Præsos, for instance, has yielded Neolithic as well as Kamares pottery. No votive offerings earlier than Middle Minoan have been found in the Dictæan cave. The lowest stratum begins with that period. Outside in the terrace deposit the Neolithic fragments were apparently deposited by water. What seems probable is that the Lasithi plain was a mountain lake in Neolithic times, and that it gradually subsided as its river found a

BRONZE IMPLEMENTS FROM GOURNIA

The group shown above was taken from a carpenter's kit which had been concealed in a house in
Gournia.   The implements include saws, axes, chisels, adzes, nails, &c.

subterranean outlet. For a considerable interval afterwards the cave may have been completely filled with water. If so, it was probably regarded as sacred on that account. Elsewhere sacred caves have invariably wells, and some of these are supposed to be possessed of curative properties. Drops of water falling from roofs are said to cure deafness, restore fading eyesight, and heal wounds. In these islands "wishing wells" receive offerings of pins and other objects, especially on May Day. Rags of clothing are attached also to trees or bushes overhanging wells anciently sacred. This practice obtains in Crete as well as in the British Isles and throughout Western Europe. Writing at Aghia Triadha, Angelo Mosso has recorded: "Every day . . . I passed a curious tree covered with fetishes. . . . Near a ruined church stands an olive-tree hung with bits of rag which the peasants tie on the branches, hundreds of shreds of every colour, worn by rain and wind. . . . I asked what the curious decoration of the tree was, and was told that anyone who suffered from malarial fever binds it to the tree with a shred of his clothing, a handkerchief, or a ribbon, and says a prayer, hoping to be cured thereby. . . . Witchcraft is common in Crete. Rags and dirty bits of stuff, into which the witches profess to have banished diseases, are constantly found in the walls of churches."[1] Here we have one reason why offerings were deposited in caves and thrown into the fire at Petsofa, near Palaikastro. The "wishers" affected a ceremonial connection with a sacred place to "switch on" the good influence and "switch off" the evil influence, which was negatived by being bound.

The "seven sleepers" of various countries lie in sacred caves. They appear to be identical with the spirits of vegetation, which slumber during the winter and return

[1] *The Palaces of Crete and their Builders*, pp. 200–1.

in spring. At the beginning of each year the Greeks held a festival which was called "the awakening of Hercules". The god returned, like Tammuz, from the underworld to bring fertility to the earth. Deities of this class were supposed to be born anew every spring. Mr. Bosanquet found at Palaikastro, in the Hellenic temple of Jupiter Dicteon, a grey marble tablet with the following inscription:—

"Hail, O great child, son of Kronos, omnipotent, who cometh yearly to Dicta seated on the hyena, escorted by demons. Accept the song which we raise to thee accompanied by the lyre and flute, standing round thy altar, O benefactor.

In this place the Cureti received thee, O immortal child, from the hands of thy mother Rhea."[1]

Evidently the cave-god of Crete, whom the Hellenes identified with their Zeus, was supposed to awake from his underworld sleep each year. In other words, the Earth Mother gave birth to him in the mountain sanctuary. This young god is found associated with the goddess on Cretan seals. It has been shown in a previous chapter that there also existed a variant myth about a young goddess which survived in the Demeter-Persephone legend. At what period the myth of Rhea and her son was introduced we have no knowledge. It was possibly of Anatolian origin. The Phrygian Kybele-Attis myth is of similar character.

It would appear that we have traces in Crete of more than one religious cult. But behind all the developed conceptions and imported beliefs lay, apparently, the background of primitive religion which the earliest settlers had brought with them and adapted to local needs. The oldest religious practices survived, no doubt, among the

[1] *Palaces of Crete and their Builders*, A. Mosso, pp. 201, 202.

masses of the people, just as the practice of tying rags on the olive-tree at some spot anciently sacred survives at the present day.

The comparative study of Cretan religious symbols tends to show that, like the Pelasgians, the Minoans worshipped deities of the underworld—the "hidden deities" of Egyptian religion—who were "Fates" or "Disposers", and were originally nameless. That is, they worshipped the spirits of nature and the spirits of ancestors. These symbols include pillars, the "horns of consecration", and the double axe. Withal there were sacred wells and mountains and sacred animals associated with the "Great Mother" which were represented in symbols, as is shown by the evidence of the seal impressions.

The worship of pillars seems to have been connected with the worship of trees and mountains. In Egypt it was believed by certain cults that the iron vault of heaven was supported by two mountains. "Out of one mountain came the sun every morning, and into the other he entered every evening. The mountain of sunrise was called Bakhau, and the mountain of sunset Manu."[1] Another theory was that the sky rested on two pillars, and a later one, which obtained, however, before the pyramid texts were inscribed, set forth that there were four pillars—"the pillars of Shu"—one at each cardinal point. The pillars in time were regarded as the sceptres of the gods of the four quarters. According to the teachings of the Ra sun cult, the cave-like openings which the sun entered at evening and emerged from at morning were guarded by lions, or the deities with lions' bodies and human heads which the Greeks called "sphinxes". The northern Egyptian lion-god was Aker.

In Babylonia it was believed that the sky was sup-

[1] *The Gods of the Egyptians*, E. Wallis Budge, Vol. I, pp. 156, 157.

ported by the world-surrounding chain of hills. Reference is made in the Gilgamesh epic to the mountain of Mashu or Mashi; that is, "the mountain of the Sunset". Its cave-like entrance is guarded by scorpion-men, or a scorpion-man and a scorpion-woman.

> Their backs mount up to the rampart of heaven,
> And their foreparts reach down beneath Arallu (the Under-
>   world) . . .
> From sunrise to sunset they guard the sun.[1]

There was a door on the cave, and Gilgamesh was allowed to pass through it to penetrate the dark tunnel leading to the Sea of Death, which only Shamash (the Sun) could cross.[2]   Gilgamesh was the first "opener of the way".   Like the Indian Yama and the Egyptian Apuatu (Osiris) he discovered the path leading to Paradise, and discovered how mortals could be ferried over the dreaded sea.

The symbols of the Babylonian gods Ea, Anu, and Enlil were tiarras, or mountain-like cones, resembling somewhat the bee-hive-shaped caps on the Zakro sealings. Temples were erected like pillars or peaks.   Ea's temple at Eridu, like that of Merodach at Babylon, was called E-sagila, which signifies "temple of the high head", or "the lofty house".   Enlil's temple was E-kur, "mountain house".   Various deities were symbolized as pillars surmounted by heads.   Nergal's symbol was a lion's head on a pillar, Zamama's a vulture's head on a pillar, Merodach's a lance-head on a pillar, and so on.   Anshar, "the most high", was, in astronomical lore, the polar star, which was figured as a he-goat, or satyr, on the summit of the peak of heaven.   The Assyrian Ashur was sometimes symbolized by a disk enclosing a feather-robed archer,

---

[1] King's *Babylonian Religion*, p. 166.   [2] *Babylonian Myth and Legend*, p. 177.

resting on a bull's head, with spreading horns, on the summit of a standard.

Ea, in one of the myths, built the world "as an architect builds a house".[1] According to the *Rigveda* the Aryo-Indian god Indra similarly constructed the house of the universe, which appears to have been supported by the "world tree".[2] The world-supporting tree, Ygdrasil, figures in Teutonic mythology. Mount Meru, the Indian Olympus, which supports the Paradise of Indra, is "the world spine". In Egypt the *ded* (*dad*, or *tet*) amulet is the spine of Osiris in his character as the world-god.

According to Wiedemann *ded* means "firm", "established". This amulet was laid on the neck of the mummy to ensure resurrection. In Chapter CLV in the Book of the Dead the picture of the symbol is given, and the deceased, addressing Osiris, says: "Thy back (backbone) is thine, thou who art of the still heart (Osiris) . . . I bring unto thee the *ded*, whereupon thou rejoicest. These are the words to speak over a gilded *ded* made from the heart of the sycamore and placed on the neck of the glorified one."[3]

The *ded* symbol is a pillar surmounted by four crossbars. Budge says that these bars "are intended to indicate the four branches of a roof-tree of a house which were turned to the four cardinal points". In the story of the search made by Isis for the slain Osiris it is related that a tree grew round his body and completely enclosed it. The King of Byblus had this tree cut down and made it a pillar for the roof of his house. Isis flew round the pillar in the form of a swallow, and was permitted subsequently to carry it away.

---

[1] *Jastrow's Religious Belief in Babylonia and Assyria*, p. 88.
[2] *Indian Myth and Legend*, p. 10.
[3] *Religion of the Ancient Egyptians*, A. Wiedemann, p. 290.

The body of Osiris was afterwards dismembered by
Set, but Isis collected the portions. The backbone was
found at the Nilotic city of Daddu or Tettu. At this cult
centre Osiris was "lord of the pillars", and the hiero-
glyphic signs of the city include two Osirian pillars with
cross-bars. Here a great festival, which the Pharaoh
attended, was held once a year, and observance was made
of the solemn ceremony of setting up "the pillar symbol
of the backbone of Osiris".[1]   Like the amulet, the pillar
may have been made from "the heart" of the sycamore
tree.

In his fusion with the world-god Ptah, Osiris was
invariably represented as a mummy grasping in his hands
in front of him a staff surmounted by the *ded* cross-bars,
and the *ankh* or life symbol.

Bata, the hero of a well-known Egyptian folk-tale,
who is evidently an early form of Osiris, exists for a time
as a blossom on a tree-top, then as a bull, and then as two
trees which grew up on either side of the entrance to the
King's palace.[2]

It will thus be seen that the sacred pillar, tree, or
mountain was the god, or the spine of the god, which
supported the universe. As the world-god Ptah sits on
a mountain, his head supports the sky, and his feet reach
to the underworld.

The idea that a spine was a charm for stability in life
and death is probably of great antiquity. Spines of fish
were laid on the bodies of the dead in Palæolithic times.
In Crete the necklaces made from the vertebræ, of an ox,
or sheep, had, no doubt, a magical significance. The
Ligurian and Cretan Neolithic people who carried home
portions of the backbones of whales may have believed

[1] Budge's *Gods of the Egyptians*, Vol. II, p. 122.
[2] *Egyptian Myth and Legend*, pp. 53 *et seq.*

that by doing so they prolonged their lives and charmed their dwellings against attack and disaster.

The dolmens and the single standing-stones—the archæological "Bethels"—which were set up in the Neolithic and Bronze Ages throughout Europe, may have been symbols of the god of the pillars, as well as "spirit-houses" of the dead. In India standing-stones are usually erected below trees. The tree spirit may have been believed to sleep for part of the year in the stone.

A mass of evidence has accumulated to indicate that pillars, mountains, and trees were worshipped in Crete, pre-Hellenic Greece, and Anatolia. The "Lion's Gate" of Mycenæ shows two lions supporting the sacred pillar. They are evidently, like the Egyptian lions, the guardians of the world deity. Cretan seals depict the mother goddess on a mountain-top supported similarly by a couple of lions, and also standing or seated between a lion and a lioness. The Cretan pillar is seen similarly guarded by lions, griffins, bulls, sphinxes, or wild goats. When the sacred tree is shown like the pillar, animals guard it also. An intaglio seal shows water-demons on either side of a sacred tree, heraldically opposed, and holding jugs above the branches. These demons have been compared to the Egyptian hippopotamus goddess Taurt. The Babylonian lion-headed eagle, a form of Nin Girsu (Tammuz), which figures on the silver vase of a Sumerian King of Lagash, is supported by two lions, on the backs of which its claws rest. The Anatolian goddess Kedesh, who was imported into Egypt in the Empire Period, stands nude on the back of a lion. The lion was evidently the symbol of the earth, and the various figures of lions devouring animals, found in various countries, probably symbolized the earth receiving its propitiatory sacrifice. Myths about the mother-serpent (the earth-serpent) attacking and disabling the eagle may have been connected with a similar belief.

Sir Arthur Evans, who first threw light on the significance of the pillar and other symbols of Crete,[1] believes that tree and pillar worship in Palestine and Anatolia was "taken over from the older stock" by Semites and Hittites. A later infusion of Minoan ideas into Anatolia and Palestine was caused by the colonizing Philistines, Carians, and Lycians who were of Ægean origin.

"The undoubted parallelism observable between the tree and pillar cult of the Mycenæan (Ægean) and that of the Semitic world", writes Sir Arthur Evans, "should be always regarded from this broad aspect. . . . The coincidences that we find, so far as they are to be explained by the general resemblance presented by a parallel stage of religious evolution, may be regarded as parallel survivals due to ethnic elements with European affinities which on the east Mediterranean shores largely underlay the Semitic. . . . The worship of the sacred stone or pillar known as Masseba or nosb is very characteristic of Semitic religion." There were also Semitic sacred hills and sacred trees. The two pillars, supporting the Philistine temple of Dagon, which were pulled down by Samson, no doubt had a sacred character. In Scandinavian legends the sacred tree supports the chief's dwelling. Sigmund, Volsung's son, draws from the house tree, called "Branstock", the magic sword which Odin thrust into it, saying: "He who draws the sword from the stock shall have it as a gift from me, and it will stand him in good stead".[2]

In Crete altars and tables of offerings were supported on pillars. On seals a columnar form was sometimes

---

[1] "Mycenæan Tree and Pillar Cult and its Mediterranean Relations", in *The Journal of Hellenic Studies*, Vol. XXI, pp. 99 *et seq.*

[2] *Teutonic Myth and Legend*, pp. 289 *et seq.*

given, as has been indicated, to animal-headed deities. Pillars were actually worshipped, being the abodes ·of spirits. On a cylinder from Mycenæ, for instance, a male figure is posed in an attitude of adoration before "five columns of architectural character with vertical and spiral flutings". No doubt the pillars of Egyptian and Grecian temples had originally a religious significance. In Christian churches ancient Pagan symbols have been perpetuated as architectural conventions. The cock, which was supposed to be a charm against demons, and consequently perched as a sentinel on the "world tree" of Teutonic Mythology, still appears on spires, where it indicates how the wind blows. In Scottish Mythology the north wind brings the evil spirits and the south wind the good spirits. "Shut the windows towards the north, and open the windows towards the south, and do not let the fire go out", is an instruction given in a folk-tale by a man who desires his house to be guarded against the visits of demons. The Teutonic Jotuns were in the east. Thor always went eastward to wage war against them.

The "horns of consecration" were originally the horns of the sacred bull or sacred cow. In Egypt the cow-goddess Hathor was a world-deity. Heaven rested on her back, and the under part of her body, which is usually shown covered with stars, formed the firmament. Her four legs were thus the sky pillars. Another belief was that the sky rested on the horns of the sacred animals. Thus we find a reference in the "Book of That which is in the Underworld" to the "Horn of the West",[1] apparently the same as the "pillar of the west" and "Sunset-Hill". The sun-god Ra, who absorbed the attributes of all other deities, is referred to in the "Pyramid Texts" as the deity with "four horns, one toward each of the car-

---

[1] *The Gods of the Egyptians*, Vol. I, p. 205.

dinal points".[1] In Crete the horns were of great ritual
importance. "At times", Sir Arthur Evans writes,[2]
"these have the appearance of being actually horns of
oxen, but more generally they seem to be a conventional
imitation of what must be regarded as unquestionably the
original type—that is, a kind of impost or base terminating at the two ends in two horn-like excrescences. Sometimes this cult object appears on the altar. At other times
it rises above the entablature of an archway connected
with a sacred tree or on the roof of a shrine. It is fre-
quently set at the foot of sacred trees." Occasionally the
double axe is surmounted on a staff between the horns.
A horned cult object in terra-cotta, with the eye symbol of
Anatolian pottery painted on the base, was found in one
of the Cretan votive caves. The horned symbol has been
found associated with early Bronze Age relics in Sardinia,
Italy, Switzerland, Spain, and the Balearic Islands, which
were probably the Cassiterides Islands in which tin was
found. It may be that the Cretan symbol was distributed
by early sea-traders. In Syria the altar of Astarte had
horns. The "horns of the altar" are referred to in the
Bible.

The double-axe symbol was evidently of remote origin.
Weapons were in the animistic stage of primitive culture
believed to be possessed of spirits, and were given individual names. "Every weapon has its demon" is an
ancient Gaelic axiom. The sword of the Scoto-Irish folk-
hero Finn-mac-Coul was called "Mac-an-Luin". In the
Indian epic, the *Mahábhárata*, the warrior Arjuna receives
a celestial weapon from the god Shiva. "And that weapon
then began to wait upon Arjuna", the narrative proceeds.
"And the gods and the Danavas (Titans) beheld that

---

[1] *Development of Religion and Thought in Ancient Egypt*, J. H. Breasted, p. 116.
[2] *Journal of Hellenic Studies*, Vol. XXI, p. 135 *et seq.*

PILLAR AT KNOSSOS, INCISED WITH DOUBLE-AXE SYMBOLS

terrible weapon in its embodied form stay by the side of Arjuna of immeasurable energy."[1] Rama of the *Râmâyana* is adored by the spirits of his celestial weapons.[2] The Indian weapons were all named.

That this belief goes back to Palæolithic times is suggested by the evidence of Egypt. "The common word given by the Egyptians to God, and god, and spirits of every kind, and beings of all sorts, and kinds, and forms, which were supposed to possess any superhuman or supernatural power, was", says Professor Budge, "'Neter'. The hieroglyph used as the determinative of this word, and also as an ideograph, is the axe with a handle. The common word for goddess is Netert." Professor Budge shows that "from the texts wherein the hieroglyphics are coloured it is tolerably clear that the axe head was fastened to its handle by means of thongs of leather".[3] As holes were bored in axes at an early period, Mr. Legge considers that the fastenings indicate that the symbolic use of the axe "goes back to the Neolithic and perhaps the Palæolithic Age". He adds: "It is now, I think, generally accepted that the use of the stone axe precedes that of the flint arrow-head or flint knife; and it thoroughly agrees with the little we know of the workings of the mind of primitive man that this, the first weapon that came into his hands, should have been the first material object to which he offered worship". An axe is worshipped by a priest in Chaldæan garb on an Assyrian agate cylinder. The axe also appears as a symbol "in the prehistoric remains of the funereal caves of the Marne, of Scandinavia and America".[4] We have already alluded to its appearance on the standing-stones of Brittany, and to

[1] "Vana Parva" section (Roy's translation), p. 127.
[2] *Indian Myth and Legend*, pp. 256 and 381.
[3] *The Gods of the Egyptians*, E. Wallis Budge, Vol. I, pp. 63 *et seq.*
[4] *Proceedings of the Society of Biblical Archæology*, Vol. XXI, pp. 310, 311.

the theory that Labyrinth is derived from *Labrys*, "the axe". Professor Maspero shows that in Egyptian "a town *neterit* is 'a divine town'; an arm *neteri* is 'a divine arm'". He adds that "*neteri* is employed metaphorically in Egyptian as is 'divine' in French".[1]

Votive axes, too small for use, have been found in Cretan graves and sanctuaries. The earliest form was the single flat axe: the double-headed axe was first made after copper came into use. Mosso gives interesting particulars regarding votive axes found on the Continent. Some of these are of a friable sandstone, and could have served no practical purpose.[2] Small axes, which were pierced for suspension, were used as charms in Malta and elsewhere. The sacred axe survives to the present day in the Congo.

[1] *Etudes de Mythologie et d'Archéologie Egyptiennes*, Tome II, p. 215.
[2] *The Dawn of Mediterranean Civilization*, pp. 132 *et seq.*

CHAPTER XIV
Decline of Crete and Rise of Greece

Contemporary Rulers of Crete, Egypt, and Babylon—Crete in the Age of Abraham—Political Changes in Western Asia—Inter-state Struggles in Crete —Relations of Palace Kings with Small Towns—Egyptian Labyrinth and Cretan Palaces—The Rise of the Hittites—Their Raid on Babylon—Fall of Knossos—Lycian Tradition of Royal Rivals—Hyksos in Egypt—Hyksos Relic in Crete—Introduction of the Horse—Cretan Culture in the Cyclades and on Greek Mainland—The Golden Age of Minos—Eighteenth Dynasty Wars of Egypt—The Cause of Racial Movements—Overthrow of Minoan Power—Crete's Trade with Egypt and Western Europe—Egyptian Beads in English Bronze-age Grave—The Tin Trade of Cornwall—Pelasgian and Achæan Conquerors—Last Period of Cretan Civilization—Prehistoric Dynasties of Greece—The Northern Conquerors—Sea-raid on Egypt—The Homeric Siege of Troy—Dorian Anarchy—Ionia the Culture Cradle of Historic Greece.

CRETE's Early Minoan Age embraces roughly about six hundred years, from 2800 B.C. till 2200 B.C. During its third period Troy II was destroyed by fire. In Egypt the Sixth Dynasty Kings, which included Pepi I and Pepi II, reigned over a powerful kingdom for a century and a half, and then followed an obscure period of three centuries, during which rival States struggled for supremacy. In the end the princely family of Thebes rose into prominence and established the Eleventh Dynasty. Babylonia was similarly divided into petty kingdoms. About 2650 B.C. the northern Semitic State of Akkad became powerful under Sargon I, who was reputed to be of miraculous birth and to have been rescued as a babe from an ark which was set adrift on the River Euphrates.[1]   His son, Naram Sin, erected the famous stele which depicts him winning a victory over a pigtailed people in a wooded and mountainous country.   He flourished about the beginning of Crete's Early Minoan II Period, and, like his father, proclaimed himself "King of the Four Quarters". It is possible that both these monarchs penetrated Syria and Palestine.   They appear to have held sway over part of Elam and Sumeria.   Towards the close of the Early Minoan II Period, Gudea was patesi of the Sumerian city of Lagash and traded with Syria.   The power of Akkad appears to have been shattered by an invasion of the Gutium from the north.   After these invaders were expelled, dynasties flourished in the Sumerian cities of Erech, Ur, and Isin.   Thereafter the Amorite migration culminated in the rise of the Hammurabi Dynasty at Babylon.

Some authorities believe that the Herakleopolite Kings of Egypt of the Ninth and Tenth Dynasties were descendants of foreign conquerors who entered through the eastern Delta and destroyed the mummies of the great Pyramid Kings of the Fourth and Fifth Dynasties.   This is possible, but the evidence is of so slight a character that any conclusions drawn from it cannot be regarded as definite.

When we reach Crete's Middle Minoan Period (2200–2100 B.C.) a new Age begins to dawn over the ancient world.   The Theban Kings of the Eleventh Dynasty establish their sway over the whole of Egypt.   In Babylonia the Sumerian power suffers decline, and two sets of invaders, the Amorites in the north and the Elamites in the south, wage a determined struggle for

---

[1] In this tradition two Semitic rulers, Sharrukin and the later Shargan-Sharri, were confused.

supremacy. This is roughly the Age of Abraham, whose migration from Sumeria northward through Mesopotamia into Palestine appears to have been one of the results of the ethnic disturbances waged in his native land.

Troy has fallen, and invaders from Thrace have penetrated eastward through Anatolia to constitute an element in the Muski-Phrygian blend. The Hittites are powerful in Cappadocia, and are extending their sway into northern Syria.

Of special interest is the Biblical reference to the battle of four kings against five.

"And it came to pass in the days of Amraphel King of Shinar, Arioch King of Ellasar, Chedorlaomer King of Elam, and Tidal King of Nations; that these made war with Bera King of Sodom, and with Birsha King of Gomorrah, Shinab King of Admah, and Shemeber King of Zeboiim, and the King of Bela, which is Zoar."[1]

Amraphel is believed to be Hammurabi of Sumer (Shinar), Arioch of Larsa (Ellasar) a Sumerian city king who was a son of the Elamite monarch, and Tidal a Hittite ruler. This confederacy may have been formed against common enemies in the Western Land (Syria and Palestine) in the interests of trade. It could not have been of long endurance. After twelve years of subjection the western tribes rebelled,[2] and the four allies again "smote them". Thereafter Hammurabi threw off his allegiance to Elam and extended his sway over the greater part of Babylonia and Assyria, while he also included the Western Land in his sphere of influence. About the same period (2000 B.C.) the Twelfth Dynasty was established in Egypt, its first great king being Amenemhet I.

During the Middle Minoan I Period, which is roughly contemporary with the Eleventh Dynasty of Egypt, the

---

[1] *Genesis*, xiv, 1–2. [2] *Ibid.*, xiv, 4 *et seq.*

earlier palaces of Knossos and Phæstos were erected.   It is probable that they were occupied by independent rulers who occasionally came into conflict like the Babylonian city kings.   Each may have had his sphere of influence on the island.   At any rate it seems certain that such great buildings represented centralized power which drew into the service of the monarchs large masses of the population.

Both palaces were destroyed at a later period, but as they did not fall simultaneously they do not seem to have been attacked by a common enemy from across the sea. The fact that the first Phæstos palace endured longest suggests that its monarch was the conqueror of Knossos and the destroyer of the first palace there.

The fall of Knossos occurred in the Middle Minoan II Period (c. 2100–1900 B.C.).   Evidences have been forthcoming both at Knossos and Phæstos of disturbances in the early part of this period.   At its close the first Knossian palace was destroyed.   The later palace must have been rebuilt soon afterwards, for portions of the earlier walls were utilized.   Probably the stricken State made a speedy recovery.   It may have, indeed, overthrown its rival in turn.   When the first palace of Phæstos fell, its destruction was so complete that it lay in ruins for about a century.   The second palace was not erected until the Late Minoan I Period, which began about 1700 B.C.   No portion of the earlier buildings were then made use of.   The whole site was completely levelled and covered with cement over the Middle Minoan remains, which were happily preserved in this way among its ruins. It is possible that this second Phæstian palace was erected by the ruler of Knossos.   According to Strabo, Phæstos was a colony of the northern State.

Before the first palaces were erected at Knossos and Phæstos, small towns flourished in eastern Crete.   One

MINOAN POTTERY FROM ZAKRO

Including examples of " Kamares " ware.   The central vessel in the lower row shows the use of
the double-axe symbol.

of these, as has been indicated, was situated near the island of Mochlos, where the tomb treasures give indications of commercial and industrial prosperity during the Early Minoan Age. Vasiliki was also, without doubt, an important trading and governing centre. Petras, on the shore of Sitia Bay, may have been the stronghold of one of the petty States then in existence.

When the first palaces of Knossos and Phæstos were erected the Cretans were trading with the Twelfth Dynasty merchants of Egypt. The spiral design had become popular among Nilotic seal engravers, who combined it with the lily flower, and the Cretan potters imitated them. Middle Minoan vases from Phæstos are decorated with the Egyptian lily spiral, which in one case is utilized in quite a new way. The papyrus designs were also taken over by the Cretan artists, and used with characteristic freedom. So greatly admired were the Kamares vases of Crete's Middle Minoan Period that they were freely purchased in Egypt. Professor Flinders Petrie found fragments of them in a tomb at Kahun of the Twelfth Dynasty, while a Cretan vessel was found by Professor Garstang in a grave of similar date at Abydos.

It was during the Twelfth Dynasty that the great Egyptian Labyrinth was erected. Its builder was Pharaoh Amenemhet III. According to Herodotus it had twelve covered courts and three thousand apartments, half of which were underground. "No stranger", says Strabo, "could find his way in or out of this building without a guide". It is possible that the Egyptian Labyrinth was an imitation of the mazy palaces of Crete.

Probably it was owing to its close commercial connections with Crete that Egypt received during the Twelfth Dynasty such liberal supplies of tin that bronze was freely manufactured.

Towards the close of Crete's Middle Minoan II Period
the Twelfth Egyptian Dynasty came to an end, and the
Sebek-Ra rulers of the Thirteenth Dynasty established
their sway, which became centralized in Upper Egypt.
Foreign settlers were increasing in number in the Delta
region.   In Asia great ethnic disturbances, due to widespread migrations, were in progress.   The Hittites had
grown powerful and were known both in Egypt and Babylonia.   Assyria was overrun by a non-Semitic people who
ultimately established a military aristocracy in northern
Mesopotamia and brought into existence the Kingdom of
Mitanni.   In time the Hammurabi Dynasty of Babylon
was overthrown by Hittite raiders, who were followed by
the Kassites.

It is possible that the fall of Knossos may have not
been unconnected with the social and racial changes due
to the settlement on the island of roving bands of pastoral
fighting-folks.   These may have been employed as mercenaries by rival Cretan kings.   A memory of the ancient
island conflicts appears to survive in the following reference by Herodotus to the Lycians: "The Lycians", he
wrote, "are in good truth anciently from Crete, which
island, in former days, was wholly peopled by barbarians.[1]
A quarrel arising there between the two sons of Europa,
Sarpedon and Minos, as to which of them should be king,
Minos, whose party prevailed, drove Sarpedon and his
followers into banishment.   The exiles sailed to Asia, and
landed on the Milyan territory.   Milyas was the ancient
name of the country now inhabited by the Lycians; the
Milyæ of the present day were, in those times, called
Solymi.   So long as Sarpedon reigned, his followers kept
the name which they brought with them from Crete, and
were called Termilæ, as the Lycians still are by those who

[1] That is, non-Greeks.

live in their neighbourhood. . . . Their customs are partly Cretan, partly Carian."[1] Herodotus also noted that the Lycians took " the mother's and not the father's name"— an interesting and perhaps significant fact when we consider the prominent part taken in social life by the Cretan women.

That the destruction of Knossos was due to internal revolt, which may or may not have received outside aid, is highly probable. It was rebuilt at the beginning of the Middle Minoan III Period, but before its rulers had attained to the full height of their power a long era of prosperity was in store for the smaller towns. Gournia, Zakro, Psyra, and Palaikastro began to be important trading centres before 1700 B.C., and ere the second palace of Phæstos was erected. It was after the Knossian palace was remodelled that these towns were destroyed.

Ere the Middle Minoan III Period had drawn to a close the Hyksos invaders had overrun Egypt, and the Hittites, Mitannians, and Kassites were in ascendancy in Mesopotamia and Anatolia. Commercial relations between Crete and Egypt were no doubt hampered for a time, but they appear to have been resumed again. Perhaps the island kingdom received refugees from the Delta region. These may have introduced the art of writing on papyrus with a pen, which came into practice before the beginning of the Late Minoan I Period.

The Late Minoan I Period endured for about two centuries (c. 1700–1500 B.C.). Trade became exceedingly brisk, and Gournia, Palaikastro, and eastern towns reached their highest development. The fact that Zakro became important suggests intimate relations with Egypt. Sir Arthur Evans has discovered at Knossos an alabastron lid bearing the personal name of one of the late Hyksos

[1] *Herodotus,* I, 173.

Pharaohs, Khian, whose throne name, Seuserenra, appears on a figure of a lion found at Baghdad. A seal impression found by the same excavator in the royal villa near the palace belongs to the early part of Late Minoan I. It is of special interest because the subject is a horse which has been carried overseas in a one-masted vessel. This animal was introduced into Babylonia by the Kassites, and was called "the ass of the east". The Mitannians, who were probably allies of the Kassites, had horses and chariots, and the horse appeared in Egypt during the Hyksos era. Perhaps the successful invasion of the Hyksos was due to the use of cavalry.

Sir Arthur Evans is of opinion that his Knossian seal impression is a record of the introduction into Crete of the thoroughbred horse. Mr. and Mrs. Hawes state, however, that they possess an Early Minoan seal stone on which a horse figures. This fact is interesting. It may not indicate that the horse was a domesticated animal, although it may have been a sacred one. The Demeter of Phigalia, as has been stated, was horse-headed. In the Palæolithic Age there were wild horses in Europe, and in one of the cave-pictures of the Aurignacian Period a man is shown beside small horses with a stave on his shoulder, suggesting that he is herding them. At this remote period the animal was freely eaten. There is no evidence that the horse was used in warfare much earlier than the Kassite Period in Babylonia, and it was certainly quite unknown in Egypt before the Hyksos Age.

Cretan culture extended during the Late Minoan I times through the Cycladic islands. At Phylakopi, in Melos, a second city came into existence round its obsidian "factory". Cretan products were freely imported and Cretan script was in use. In one of its buildings, which may have been the palace, was found a well-preserved fresco showing flying fish skimming over transparent waters in which lie shells, sponges, and rocks. It was undoubtedly the work of a Cretan artist. In all probability there was a Minoan colony at Phylakopi.

But Cretan influence was not confined to the islands. Both Mycenæ and Tiryns on the Grecian mainland were stimulated by it as early as the Middle Minoan III Period. The contents of the shaft graves of Mycenæ, which Schliemann assigned to the Homeric Age, are of Late Minoan I antiquity (c. 1500 B.C.), as are also boar-hunt frescoes recently found at Tiryns, which are distinctively Cretan, and the famous Vaphio cups with the bull-snaring scenes. The Peloponnesian colonies of Crete appear to have been established in the Middle Minoan III Period (c. 1800–1700 B.C.). In Bœotia there were settlements in Late Minoan I times, if not earlier, and tombs have yielded Cretan, and imitations of Cretan products, which confirm the traditions of the source of early Grecian culture, the religious mysteries, and so forth. With Cretan modes of life came Cretan modes of thought to a people who were not much advanced from the Neolithic stage of culture. It is probable that the islanders formed a military aristocracy from which sprung the kings who ruled the various important city States in pre-Homeric times.

Pausanias[1] tell us that the lion gate of Mycenæ and the walls of Tiryns were the work of the Cyclopes who laboured for Proctus. He writes, too, with conviction of the men in ancient days who "were guests at the tables of the gods in consequence of their righteousness and piety", and adds that "those who were good clearly met with honour from the gods, and similarly those who were wicked, with wrath. The gods in those days were sometimes mortals who are still worshipped, like Aristæus, and

[1] II, 46.

Britomartis of Crete, and Hercules, the son of Alcmena, and Amphiarus, the son of Œcles, and beside them Castor and Pollux." [1] So were the ancients who believed in giants and gods identified with them.

During the last century of the Late Minoan I Period the Hyksos were overthrown in Egypt, and the Theban Eighteenth Dynasty was established. The Cretans were known then in the Nile valley as the Keftiu, and characteristic wasp-waisted figures carrying Minoan vases were depicted in the tombs. It was during this period that the later Phæstian palace was erected.

The Late Minoan II Period, also known as the "Palace" Period, began towards the close of the reign of Pharaoh Thothmes I, the father of Queen Hatshepsut. It lasted for about half a century, from c. 1500 till 1450 B.C. One by one the coast towns perished, the latest to survive being Palaikastro, which some identify as the ancient city port of Heleia. Some think that Palaikastro existed as late as the Late Minoan III Period, and was ruled by an independent prince.

It is uncertain whether the towns were plundered by piratical bands from the Cyclades and the Greek mainland, or were wiped out by the central Cretan power which was established at Knossos. The later Knossian palace was remodelled during Late Minoan II times, and did not therefore suffer from the depredations of invaders. It would seem that we now reach the age of the legendary Minos who struck down all rivals and became supreme ruler in Crete. "The first person known to us in history as having established a navy", writes Thucydides, "is Minos. He made himself master of what is now called the Hellenic Sea, and ruled over the Cyclades, into most of which he sent his first colonies, expelling the Carians

[1] VIII, 2.

and appointing his own sons governors; and thus did his best to put down piracy in those waters, a necessary step to secure the revenues for his own use. For in early times the Hellenes and the barbarians of the coast and islands, as communication by sea became more common, were tempted to turn pirates, under the conduct of their most powerful men; the motives being to serve their own cupidity and to support the needy. They would fall upon a town unprotected by walls, and consisting of a mere collection of villages, and would plunder it; indeed, this came to be the main source of their livelihood, no disgrace being yet attached to such an achievement, but even some glory. An illustration of this is furnished by the honour with which some of the inhabitants of the continent still regard a successful marauder, and by the question we find the old poets everywhere representing the people as asking the voyagers—'Are they pirates?'—as if those who are asked the question would have no idea of disclaiming the imputation, or their interrogators of reproaching them for it. The same rapine prevailed also by land." [1]

The Empire of Minos appears to have embraced part of the Greek mainland. Athens was compelled to send its annual tribute of youths and maidens to Knossos, and Tiryns, Mycenæ, Lakonia, Pylos, and Orchœmenos became important centres of Ægean culture. The tradition that the Cyclopes who erected the walls of Tiryns came from Lycia may be due to the tendency to foreshorten historical events. It is possible, however, that Minoan traders had already settled on the Anatolian coast and maintained commercial relations with the Peloponnese and Crete.

Thothmes III of Egypt, the great conqueror, flourished

[1] *History of the Peloponnesian War*, I, 4, 5 (Richard Crawley's translation).

during the later part of the Late Minoan II Period.   In the hymn addressed to him as from the god Amon, the priestly poet declares:

> I have come giving thee to smite the western land,
> Keftyew (Crete) and Cyprus are in terror.[1]

The activities of Thothmes did not extend to Crete, but there can be little doubt that his operations exercised a marked influence on the trade of the island kingdom. Probably it prospered greatly under the settled conditions which he brought about, as it had evidently prospered after the expulsion of the Hyksos from Egypt.   A brisk demand for Cretan imports in the Nile valley may well have been one of the causes of the commercial " boom " which is suggested by the increasing wealth of Knossos during the Late Minoan II Period.

The great Egyptian wars, however, were bound in time to affect Crete in another direction.   The expulsion of the Hyksos brought about a pressure of peoples in Syria, Anatolia, and south-eastern Europe, which was to test the stability of existing States.   Semitic hordes poured towards Babylonia and hampered trade; at the same time they reinforced the growing power of Assyria.   The Mitannian area of control was being circumscribed and Hittite prestige seriously affected in Cappadocia.   Ere the Hittites were able to profit by the weakening of the Syrians and Mitannians, against whom Thothmes III was battling constantly, they must have been forced to direct their expansion westward.   The plain of Troy was probably at this period the scene of many conflicts.   In the Danubian area there appears to have been much ethnic friction. Invasions from Anatolia and the constant pressure exercised by northern tribes directed a steady stream of pas-

---

[1] Breasted's *History of Egypt*, p. 319.

toral fighting-folks southward through the Balkans and into the northern States of Greece. The mainland capitals, including Mycenæ and Tiryns, which had become centres of Ægean culture and trade, must have offered strong temptations to the hardy mountaineers of Thessaly, whence the Achæans are supposed to have come. Probably the migrations of the pastoralists were propelled by migrations from the north. The ultimate result of these migratory "folk-waves", which increased in volume as time went on, was the destruction not only of the Minoan Empire, but the complete overthrow of Knossian power in Crete itself. The Palace Period was the Golden Age of Cretan culture, which suffered steady decline after 1450 B.C.

It was probably during this half-century of Minoan ascendancy that Crete's overseas commerce assumed its greatest dimensions. The organized navy ensured the safe passage in the Ægean Sea of ships which tapped the Danube valley trade, and penetrating the Dardanelles got into touch with caravans from the east. It also helped to foster trade with western ports. The Rhone valley route running to Marseilles appears to have been, as has been indicated, one of the sources from which British tin was received.

At what period this traffic had origin is at present wrapped in obscurity. It seems probable, however, that it was carried on as early as 1500 B.C. One of the reasons for this belief is the discovery of Egyptian relics in southern England. Among the relics taken from Bronze Age graves are numerous Egyptian beads of blue-glazed faience. "They are beads, moreover, which", writes Professor Sayce, "belong to one particular period in Egyptian history, the latter part of the age of the Eighteenth Dynasty and the earlier of that of the Nineteenth Dynasty.... There is a large number of them in the Devizes Museum, as they are met with plentifully in the Early Bronze Age tumuli of Wiltshire in association with amber beads and barrel-shaped beads of jet and lignite. Three of them come from Stonehenge itself. Similar beads of 'ivory' have been found in a Bronze Age cist near Warminster: if the material is really ivory it must have been derived from the East. The cylindrical faience beads, it may be added, have been discovered in Dorsetshire as well as Wiltshire." Mr. H. R. Hall, dealing with the same Egyptian relics, says: "My own interest in the matter is due to the fact that in the course of the excavations of the [Egyptian] Fund at Deir el Bahari, we discovered thousands of blue glaze beads of the exact particular type (already well known from other Egyptian diggings) of these found in Britain. Ours are, in all probability, mostly of the time of Hatshepsut, and so date to about 1500 B.C."[1] Similar beads have also been discovered in Crete and Western Europe. The British finds help to fix the age of Stonehenge, the inner circle of which, according to Professor Boyd Dawkins, is formed of stones taken from Brittany.

By whom were these Egyptian beads carried to Britain between 1500 B.C. and 1400 B.C.? Certainly not the Phœnicians. The sea-traders of the Mediterranean were at the time the Cretans. Whether or not their merchants visited England we have no means of knowing. It is possible that they did. It is also possible, and even highly probable, that during the early Bronze Age in England, which may have been of greater antiquity than has hitherto been supposed, there existed a comparatively high degree of civilization, and communities of traders.

According to Diodorus Siculus, tin was carried in wagons by the people of Belerium (Land's End) to the

[1] *The Journal of Egyptian Archæology* (January, 1914), pp. 18–19.

Island of Ictis,[1] which could be reached at low tide. The tin was purchased on Ictis by traders and then shipped to Gaul, being afterwards conveyed overland to the mouth of the Rhone on pack-horses. Ships crossed the English Channel as early as Neolithic times, when the earliest settlers of the Mediterranean race migrated from Gaul. The Veneti of Brittany in Cæsar's time had a navy, as well as trading-vessels, like the ancient Cretans. In the early Bronze Age amber was imported into England from the mouth of the Elbe, so that a connection was established between our shores and the Danubian trade route. Gold was carried from Ireland and Wales and Scotland to Scandinavia. It may have been due to the racial migrations which followed the expulsion of the Hyksos from Egypt that "the men of the round barrows" invaded these islands in the early British Bronze Age. Probably they followed in the tracks of the traders up the valleys of the Danube and the Elbe as well as from the Alpine districts towards Brittany. It need arouse no surprise that the effects of the distant Egyptian wars should have been felt in Europe. The building of the Chinese wall, which directed westward the drift of Asiatic nomads, was the indirect cause of the fall of Rome.

Crete's Late Minoan II Period of splendour and commercial prosperity was brought to an abrupt close by the sack of Knossos. This disaster must have fallen like "a bolt from the blue". It was evidently as unexpected as it was complete. Workmen were engaged in renovating the stately dwelling, new frescoes were being painted, and builders were erecting a new wing, when the invaders

---

[1] One theory is that Ictis is the Isle of Wight. Some geologists contend that at this period the island was not entirely cut off from the mainland. The Isle of Thanet has also been identified as Ictis. Another theory is that the reference is to St. Michael's Mount on the south coast of Cornwall, which is connected with the mainland at low water by a causeway.

swept inland from the seashore, put to the sword soldier and artisan, and probably women and children, then plundered the palace and set it on fire. Phæstos palace and the villa of Aghia Triadha shared similar fates.

It may be that the invaders attacked Crete when its army and navy were engaged elsewhere. The tradition recorded by Herodotus, which is of special interest in this connection, sets forth that Minos went to Sicily in search of Dædalus, the great architect, and there was murdered. An expedition followed to avenge his death, and besieged Camicus for five years. Their efforts were, however, unsuccessful. On their way home their vessels were wrecked on the south coast of Italy, where they founded the town of Hyria. Thereafter, the Præsians informed Herodotus, "men of various nations flocked to Crete, which was stripped of its inhabitants".[1] Memories of Minoan colonies may have mingled with this tradition. One of the several cities called Minoa was situated in Sicily.

It is generally believed that the destroyers of Knossos were not Achæans alone, but the mixed peoples on the Greek coast who had come under the influence of Minoan civilization. Thucydides says that after Minos had formed his navy, and communication by sea became easier, "the coast populations began to apply themselves more closely to the acquisition of wealth, and their life became more settled; some even began to build themselves walls on the strength of their newly acquired riches". These Cretanized mainlanders were subjected to the constant pressure of the northern tribes. "The country called Hellas", wrote Thucydides, "had in ancient times no settled population; on the contrary, migrations were of frequent occurrence, the several tribes readily abandoning their

[1] *Herodotus*, VII, 170, 171.

RUINS OF THE "ROYAL VILLA", AGHIA TRIADHA.   (See page 286)

32

homes under pressure of superior numbers. . . . The. goodness of the land favoured the aggrandizement of particular individuals, and thus created faction, which proved a fertile source of ruin. It also invited invasion."[1] It is possible, as some have urged, that Minos himself was a conqueror of Crete, and was supported by Pelasgians and Achæans who had acquired the elements of Minoan culture on the mainland.

The Late Minoan III Period begins with a partial revival of Minoan civilization. A portion of the Knossian palace was reoccupied, and new houses were erected at Gournia and Palaikastro beside the ruins of those which were destroyed in the early Palace Period. Trading relations with Egypt were resumed, and hundreds of Cretan vases of *Bügelkannen* type were imported into the Nile valley. These and others were imitated in faience and alabaster by Egyptian artisans. But Cretan culture was on the down grade. The island artisans of the Late Minoan III Period were imitators of their predecessors, and sometimes slovenly imitators; they invented nothing new. It was an age of decadence and transition. Ultimately Knossos and the small towns were entirely deserted, and the people retreated to the inner mountain valleys and plateaux. The Cretans ceased to be known in Egypt as the Keftiu during the reign of Amenhotep III, the father of Akhenaton.[2] The founders of Præsos, who claimed to be the "true Cretans", were no doubt descendants of the old Minoan peoples and the Achæo-Pelasgian elements from the Continent.

But although Late Minoan III culture perished by slow degrees in Crete, it flourished in Cyprus. Apparently large numbers of Cretans and Cretan colonists from the mainland settled on that island and achieved a political

---

[1] *The Peloponnesian War*, I, 2–8.   [2] Before 1375 B.C.

ascendancy over the natives.   Others settled on Rhodes.
About the same time the Minoan colonies in Lycia and
Caria were strongly reinforced, and for a period, if Greek
tradition is to be relied upon, the Carians monopolized
the sea trade of the Ægean.   It is believed that large
numbers of Cretans also fled to Phœnicia and stimulated
maritime enterprise in that quarter.   " In the Homeric
poems ", says Professor Myres, " more visits are paid by
western seafarers to Phœnicia and Sidon than 'Phœnician'
merchants pay to the west. . . . The wide Phœnician trade
of historic times had clearly begun to grow as the Minoan
sea-power failed."[1]

About a century after the fall of Knossos, Mycenæ,
Tiryns, and other mainland towns had reached the height
of their prosperity.   It is possible that they owed their
supremacy to Hittite influence.   At any rate, persistent
Greek legends associate their rulers with Anatolia.   The
walls of Tiryns were reputed to have been built by Cyclopes from Lycia, and Pelops, who gave his name to the
Peloponnesus, was reputed to have come from Asia Minor.
" The account given by those Peloponnesians ", says Thucydides, " who have been the recipients of the most creditable
traditions is this.   First of all Pelops, arriving among a
needy population from Asia with vast wealth, acquired
such power that, stranger though he was, the country was
called after him; and this power fortune saw fit materially
to increase in the hands of his descendants."[2]   The complicated family history of Pelopidæ and Atridæ is of special
interest in this connection.   Atreus, son of Pelops, married
his son Plisthenes to Aerope, granddaughter of King Minos
of Crete.   Her father had given her and her sister to the
King of Eubœa, because it had been foretold he would die
by the hand of one of his children.   The sons of Aerope

---

[1] *The Dawn of History*, p. 215.   [2] *The Peloponnesian War*, I, 6–9.

were Agamemnon and Menelaus. Afterwards Atreus married Aerope, his daughter-in-law, and brought up her sons, who were consequently called the Atridæ. But this fickle lady deserted Atreus and became the wife of his brother Thyestes. Then Atreus took to wife Pelopea, whose descendants were called the Pelopidæ. He was not aware that this lady was his brother's daughter. Many crimes and calamities are associated with the traditions of these princes and princesses. The chief interest they have for us here is the wonderful relation the traditions regarding them bear to the history of the period. A Minoan king of Crete is to be slain by his own kin from the mainland, and invaders from Anatolia intermarry with Cretan stock in the Peloponnesus. This appears to be as good history as the reference in Ezekiel to the ethnics of Jerusalem: "Thy birth and thy nativity is of the land of Canaan; thy father was an Amorite, and thy mother an Hittite".[1] Mycenæ's mother was a Cretan and his father an Anatolian, perhaps of Indo-European speech like the military aristocracy of the Mitannian State, which appears to have for a period achieved political ascendancy over the Hittites.

In this connection special interest attaches to our own legends about the invading giants who gave their names to Alban (Albion) and Erin. It seems probable that these giants symbolized the folks who overran Great Britain and Ireland in the early Bronze Age. "Alban" (genitive of "Alba") or "Albion" and "Alps" are derived from a common root, signifying "white". Were the invaders of ancient Britain "Whitelanders", i.e. an Alpine folk?

The Mycenæan period of Greek civilization was remembered as that of the third or Bronze Race of Hesiod.

---

[1] *Ezekiel*, xvi, 3.

"Their gear was of bronze, they had bronze houses; they tilled the soil with bronze; black iron there was none." Nestor, in the *Iliad*, refers to the Bronze Age folk as the heroes of an earlier generation who were greater than Agamemnon and his host.

> I lived with men, and they despised me not,
> Abler in counsel, greater than yourselves.
> Such men I never saw, and ne'er shall see,
> As Pirithous and Dryas, wise and brave,
> Cœneus, Exadius, god-like Polypheme,
> And Theseus, Ægeus' more than mortal son.
> The mightiest they among the sons of men. . . .[1]

Another element which entered into the ethnic fusion in Mycenæan Greece was the Danubian. The influence of Danubian culture extended as far south as Thessaly, where the Achæans were predominant. These Achæan pastoralists were drifting southward into the Peloponnesus as early as the Late Minoan I Period, and some of them may have reached Crete. But their greatest migration appears to have occurred at the close of the Pelopid Dynasty, and it is probable that they were the late conquerors of Mycenæ and Tiryns. After holding sway in the Peloponnesus for a period of uncertain duration, they were overthrown in turn by the Dorians.

About the time that the legendary Pelops secured the ascendancy of his stock on the Greek mainland, Crete was in a state of decay. In Egypt the brilliant reign of Amenhotep III marked the zenith of Egyptian power in the Nile valley and Syria. Mitanni, in northern Mesopotamia, which was ruled by kings with Indo-European names, was being threatened on one side by the growing power of Assyria, and on the other by that of the Hittites.

[1] *Iliad*, Book I, 309–15 (Derby's translation).

After Akhenaton, the dreamer king, ascended the Egyptian throne and inaugurated his religious revolution, the kingdom of Mitanni was overthrown, and the Egyptian Empire in northern Syria went to pieces. The Hittites had leagued themselves with the Amorites, and were pressing southward, gaining control of the trade routes from Babylonia and Egypt.

The eastward expansion of the Hittites was accompanied by a shrinkage of their power in the west. Reinforced by folk-waves from Thrace, the people of the Phrygian area then began to gather strength, and asserted themselves later as the Muski,[1] the forerunners of the historic Phrygians. The sixth city of Troy also came into prominence. It was contemporary with Mycenæ and Tiryns, and like these cities owed its rise to the fusion of Danubian and Ægean cultures, the latter predominating.

This was Homer's Troy, and so powerful did it become that when the Achæans entered into possession of the Peloponnesian centres of Mycenæan culture they found that it constituted a serious menace to their ascendancy.

As in Egypt, descent in Crete and its colonial settlements was by the female line. The Achæan chiefs therefore followed the example of Atreus by marrying a royal princess, so as to secure the succession of their descendants to the thrones of the various States which they overpowered. Menelaus had married Helen, Queen of Sparta, and departed overseas on an expedition. During his absence, Priam, King of Troy, abducted Helen, who became the wife of his son Paris. The Trojans were thus enabled to claim Sparta as part of their dominions. On his return, the Achæan monarch found it necessary to fit out a great

[1] Pronounced *Moosh'ke*. In the Old Testament they are referred to as "the Meshech." (*Ezekiel*, xxxii).

expedition and inaugurate the famous siege of Troy, so as to recover the queen by whose right he held the Spartan throne. Such appears to be the historical germ of the Homeric narrative.

The Greeks dated the period of the Trojan war as from 1194 till 1184 B.C. This appears to be an accurate calculation. A few years previously, in 1200 B.C., the second great sea raid on Egypt took place during the reign of Rameses III of the Twentieth Dynasty. Perhaps the absence of Menelaus was not unconnected with this adventure.

The first sea raid occurred about a quarter of a century earlier, during the reign of Merne-ptah, son of Rameses II. It was conducted in conjunction with the Hittites, and taken part in by the Shardana, who may have given their name to Sardinia; the Akhaivasha, usually identified with the Achæans; the Shakalsha, who may have been Cretanized Sicilians; and the Tursha, perhaps the Turseni, who were represented in Etruria. The piratical peoples were probably remnants of the Cretans and their conquerors. They were defeated by Merne-ptah, but some settled in Libya and became mercenaries in the Egyptian army.

The second raid was of great dimensions. It included the Danauna, the Danaans, the Shakalsha, the Tursha, the Tikkarai, who may have come from Zakro in Crete, and the Pulesti, the Philistines. The sea force which sailed south by Cyprus was supported by land raiders from North Syria and Anatolia. Among the latter were the Philistines, who gave their name to Palestine. Rameses III won victories on sea and land, being assisted by the raiders' kinsmen, the Shardana mercenaries.

It is suggestive to find that the siege of Homer's Troy occurred a few years afterwards. The conquerors of pre-Mycenæan Greece, having been foiled in their attempt to overrun Egypt, sought expansion eastward, and had first to strike down the Phrygian city which threatened their supremacy.

Troy VI had been built about 1500 B.C., that is, about the beginning of Crete's Late Minoan II or Palace Period. It was surrounded by great stone walls 16 feet thick and 20 feet high, which were surmounted by first a brick and then a stone parapet, which added another 6 feet to them. The walls were flanked by three great towers about 30 feet in height. As the stone-work has Egyptian characteristics, it is possible that the builders were imported from Egypt during the Eighteenth Dynasty. There were at least three city gates, and these were all on the southern side. Wells were sunk to the water-bearing strata of the hill.

When Troy VI was set on fire it did not suffer so greatly, being largely built of stone, as did the second city. The houses were, however, overthrown, and the upper portions of the walls demolished. Scarcely an object of any value survived the sack of the wealthy city. The ceramic remains are partly Mycenæan, or Late Minoan III, and partly Trojan.

After the fall of Troy the European elements in Anatolia were strengthened. Carian and Lycian pirates infested the seas. There were also settlements of Ægean stock in Cilicia. The Muski-Phrygians, pressing eastward from central Anatolia, appear to have contributed to the overthrow of the tottering empire of the Hittites. In Palestine the Philistines gradually extended their area of control, moving steadily southward, as the Empire of Egypt shrank by slow degrees.

The Achæans of Greece met in time the same fate as their predecessors of the Late Mycenæan Period, the Pelopid Dynasty. About two generations after the Trojan war the Dorians, who had been gradually filtering southward through Thessaly, gradually achieved ascendancy. In time, assisted by Illyrian allies, they overran the Peloponnese. The dispossessed Achæan aristocracy and followers were forced into the land of the Ionians, which afterwards became known as Achaia. Dorians also found their way to Crete, which, like Rhodes, was eventually conquered.

For generations Greece was devastated by inter-tribal wars, and lapsed into a condition of decline. Periodic migrations took place of its merchants and traders and artisans, and these settled in Crete, Sicily, Sardinia, and Italy. Many found refuge in Anatolia, where grew up Ionian Greece along the coastland of Lycia and Caria.

"It was in Ægean Ionia", writes Mr. Hall, "that the torch of Greek civilization was kept alight, while the homeland was in a mediæval condition of comparative barbarism; Cyprus, too, helped though she was too far off for her purer Minoan culture to affect the Ægean peoples very greatly. It was in Ionia that the new Greek civilization arose: Ionia, in whom the old Ægean blood and spirit most survived, taught the new Greece, gave her coined money and letters, art and poesy, and her shipmen, forcing the Phœnicians from before them, carried her new culture to what were then deemed the ends of the earth."[1]

---

[1] *The Ancient History of the Near East*, p. 79.

INDEX

Achæans, in Crete, 279, 280, 328.
— bronze and iron used by, liii.
— burial rites of, xxxviii.
— Dorian conquest of, 335.
— Hammer god of, xlvii.
— Ridgeway's theory regarding, xlviii.
— Germanic claims regarding, xlviii, xlix, li, lii.
— southward movement of, 325, 332.
— the, in Homeric period, 333, 334.
Acheulian man, intellectual life of, 27.
— period, 15, 23.
— stage, in Palestine, 53.
— stage, lost Atlantis theory and, 103.
Achilles, shield of, Cretan references and, 128.
Adonis, 180.
— as a bi-sexual deity, 170.
— as son and lover of Aphrodite, 157.
— Cretan god and, 156.
Ægean civilization, how term is applied, 191 et seq.
Agamemnon, Thucydides on, 80.
Ages of the world, the geological, xix, 9, 23, 24, 25.
— of the world, the mythical, 5, 6, 7, 8.
— of the world, the mythical, history of Heroic Age, 76 et seq.; in Greece, 331, 332.
— the Archæological, 26 et seq.
— the Archæological, Palæolithic and Neolithic links in Egypt, 52.
— the Archæological, Palæolithic stages in Palestine, 53.

Ages (cont.)
— the Archæological, in Palæolithic period, 23, 24.
— the Geological, duration of, 24, 25.
Aghia Triadha, sarcophagus of, 289, 290.
— — small palace of, 285 et seq.
Agni, the Indian god, Cretan Zeus and, 156.
Agricultural religion in Crete, 163.
— — Isis-Osiris and Demeter-Triptolemus myths, 180.
— — culture gods and, 156, 157.
— — Egypt as source of, 156.
— — Mediterranean race and, 164.
— — seasonal forms of goddess, 183, 184.
— — stone worship and, 184.
Agriculture, drought and flood demons, xxiv.
— in pre-dynastic Egypt and Crete, 149.
— Neolithic implements, 217.
— origin of, 196, 197.
— Other World beliefs associated with, xl.
— primitive harvesting in Crete and Scotland, 252.
— problem of source of, 156, 164, 222.
— religion associated with, xxvi.
— how knowledge of, spread, xxvi, xxvii.
Aker, Egyptian lion god, 303.
Albion, tribal giant of, 331.
Alcinous, the Phæacian king, as a Cretan, 131, 132 et seq.

337